D1383138

Structure and mobility

This book is published as part of the joint publishing agreement established in 1977 between the Fondation de la Maison des Sciences de l'Homme and the Press Syndicate of the University of Cambridge. Titles published under this arrangement may appear in any European language or, in the case of volumes of collected essays, in several languages.

New books will appear either as individual titles or in one of the series which the Maison des Sciences de l'Homme and the Cambridge University Press have jointly agreed to publish. All books published jointly by the Maison des Sciences de l'Homme and the Cambridge University Press willl be distributed by the Press throughout the world.

Cet ouvrage est publié dans le cadre de l'accord de co-édition passé en 1977 entra la Fondation de la Maison des Sciences de l'Homme et le Press Syndicate de l'Université de Cambridge. Toutes les langues européennes sont admises pour les titres couverts par cet accord, et les ouvrages collectifs peuvent paraître en plusieurs langues.

Les ouvrages paraissent soit isolément, soit dans l'une des séries que la Maison des Sciences de l'Homme et Cambridge University Press ont convenu de publier ensemble. La distribution dans le monde entier des titres ainsi publiés conjointement par les deux établissements est assurée par Cambridge University Press.

Structure and mobility

The men and women of Marseille, 1820–1870

William H. Sewell, Jr.
University of Arizona

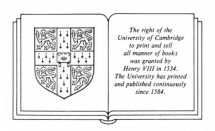

The right of the
University of Cambridge
to print and sell
all manner of books
was granted by
Henry VIII in 1534.
The University has printed
and published continuously
since 1584.

Cambridge University Press

Cambridge
London   New York   New Rochelle
Melbourne   Sydney

& Editions de la Maison des Sciences de l'Homme
Paris

Published by the Press Syndicate of the University of Cambridge
The Pitt Building, Trumpington Street, Cambridge CB2 1RP
32 East 57th Street, New York, NY 10022, USA
10 Stamford Road, Oakleigh, Melbourne 3166, Australia
and Editions de la Maison des Sciences de l'Homme
54 Boulevard Raspail, 75270 Paris Cedex 06, France

First published 1985

Printed in the United States of America

Library of Congress Cataloging in Publication Data
Sewell, William Hamilton, 1940–
Structure and mobility.
Bibliography: p.
Includes index.
1. Marseille (France) – Social conditions.   2. Social
indicators – France – Marseille.   3. Social mobility –
France – Marseille – History – 19th century.   4. Social
structure – France – Marseille – History – 19th century.
5. Labor and laboring classes – France – Marseille –
History – 19th century.   I. Title.
HNH38.M35S48   1984   305'.0944'912   84-5860
ISBN 0 521 26237 2
ISBN 2 7351 0085 3 (France only)

To my father, who taught me to count

Contents

Figures and Tables

x   List of figures and tables

Tables

xii   List of figures and tables

Preface

The origins of this book go back to the autumn of 1967, when I was doing research in Marseille for a doctoral dissertation on the history of the city's working class in the nineteenth century. At the time, I was trying to make sense of workers' involvement in the Revolution of 1848. I had determined that some of Marseille's skilled trades had very high rates of participation in the revolutionary movement of 1848, whereas other skilled trades – which did not differ systematically in wages or working conditions – remained conservative or passive. The reasons for this difference were elusive. However, I knew that the nineteenth-century population of Marseille had grown very rapidly and that this rapid growth had been fed by prodigious levels of migration. I wondered whether different groups of skilled workers were differently affected by migration, but I had found no way of determining the proportion of immigrants in different trades. The late Edouard Baratier, then head archivist of the Archives Départementale des Bouches-du-Rhône, was the first to suggest that I look at marriage registers. When a couple was married, he pointed out, their occupations and birthplaces were recorded on a register; using these documents, it would be possible to estimate the proportion of natives and immigrants in each of the city's major occupational groups.

When the first bound volume of the *actes de mariage* of 1846 was brought to my table, I discovered unsuspected treasures. These documents gave not only the occupations and birthplaces of both spouses, but their names, ages, and addresses, their fathers' occupations, the current residence or place of death of their parents, and the names, ages, occupations, and addresses of four witnesses. Finally, the bride and groom and the witnesses all signed their names at the bottom of the marriage act – if they were capable of doing so. I soon realized that these documents could be used to determine not only the proportion of immigrants in different trades, but patterns of residence, occupational recruitment, literacy, intermarriage, friendship, and occupational mobility for every category of the population. The range of evidence provided by this document was staggering; it far surpassed what was available in contemporary censuses or other quantifiable sources.

From that moment forward, analysis of the marriage registers gradually took on a life of its own. I did use them to calculate the proportion of immigrants in different working-class trades; in fact, it turned out that every

xiii

one of the skilled trades that remained passive or conservative in 1848 had a sizable majority of natives of the city, whereas the radical trades had recruited their members primarily outside of Marseille. The marriage registers made it possible to distinguish between a group of conservative, inward-looking, exclusive trades and a group of radical, outward-looking, open trades, and therefore to explain patterns of political participation in 1848 with unusual precision. But this use of the marriage registers, however satisfying, was only a beginning. Preliminary work on social mobility, literacy, and the social and geographical backgrounds of immigrants opened up the possibility of a systematic quantitative description of some of the most important social structures and social processes of nineteenth-century Marseille.[1]

For some time I conceived of my analysis of the marriage registers as a kind of descriptive statistical prologue to the history of working-class radicalization. But as time went by and the analysis progressed, the would-be prologue grew into a separate book, with a style, a problematic, a narrative rhythm, and themes of its own. Historians may find it austere – highly quantitative, occasionally technical, and lacking in personalities and color. But the issues confronted by the book are crucial for understanding nineteenth-century cities and nineteenth-century social change. How did capitalist economic development affect the size and composition of urban occupational groups? How did massive urban population growth change the structure and character of city neighborhoods? Did economic changes transform the status hierarchy of urban society? What were the social origins of the thousands of men and women who migrated to nineteenth-century cities? Did massive rural–urban migration have deleterious effects on the immigrants and on urban society? Were the migration experiences of women significantly different from those of men? Did massive migration breed urban crime? Did changes in the economic and social structure result in rising or declining levels of social mobility? Did natives of the city monopolize the available opportunities for upward mobility, or did immigrants find their share of the more prestigious and better-paying jobs? Did the processes and the results of women's social mobility differ from men's? These and related questions can be answered with considerable precision using quantitative data from the marriage registers, supplemented, of course, by data from many other sources. By posing and answering these questions, I have tried to put together a closely argued analytic description – a kind of closeup sociological portrait – of an entire urban society during the epochal changes of the nineteenth century.

The book has been deeply influenced by the methods, theories, and outlook of sociology – of American quantitative sociology, to be more precise. Many of the chapters begin with an invocation of sociological theories or findings, and the analysis of quantitative data is largely structured by sociological questions and methods. To historians, the book may seem more sociology than history. Although I hope it will be accepted as a contribution to sociology,

I believe that it deviates in important ways from sociological styles and problematics. First, sociologists – with exceptions – tend to use an extensive specialized vocabulary. What seems to them a legitimate scientific language most historians would condemn as pseudoscientific jargon. I have eschewed the use of specialized vocabulary in this book whenever possible and have tried to define such terms when their use could not be avoided. I have done so not because I disdain sociological terminology as jargon, but because I wish to be able to communicate with an audience of historians and "lay" readers not initiated into the language of professional sociology. Second, although this book is highly quantitative, I have avoided using mathematically complex quantitative techniques (for example, multiple-regression, path analysis, or log-linear modeling) even where these might have been appropriate for the data and the questions being asked. With the exception of Chapter 4, where simple correlation coefficients are calculated, the analysis is carried out strictly by means of simple counts and cross-tabulations. I am acutely aware that this occasionally makes the analysis somewhat cumbersome and inexact. But I believe it also allows the statistically uninitiated to follow my argument. I have consciously sacrificed precision and elegance for readability.

There is also another reason for my choice of simple over sophisticated quantitative methods – one that derives from a far deeper difference between historical and sociological outlooks. Sociologists, again with exceptions, generally have had as their object the establishment and verification of social laws, or, less grandiloquently, causal generalizations. Historians, by contrast, have seen their task as the description of unique events, situations, or sequences. Although all historians necessarily generalize and all sociologists necessarily describe, there remains a distinctive difference in orientation. This difference has a bearing on the choice of quantitative techniques. More statistically sophisticated techniques tend to yield coefficients assessing the relative strengths of hypothesized causal factors – indicating that, say, the occupation of a man's father has a greater influence on the probability of his finding a nonmanual job than does his country of origin. Such coefficients have the advantages of precision and of comparability across contexts, but they also are highly abstract. Cross-tabulations, for all their cumbersomeness, are much more concrete and closer to lived experience. They make it hard to formulate, say, precise statements about the relative influence of occupational background and national origin on social mobility, but they will indicate clearly that nearly all Italian immigrants in Marseille, whatever their occupational backgrounds, were consigned to manual work, whereas even workers' or peasants' sons who immigrated from Switzerland or the French countryside frequently found their way into the bourgeoisie. I would rather convey to my reader these lived details of social experience than make a precise test of competing causal hypotheses. This study is informed by causal hypotheses drawn from sociology, but it uses them more to order the description of social life and social change in Marseille than to subject them to systematic statistical tests.

This book has been long in the making, and it has benefited from many persons and institutions along the way. During my dissertation research in Marseille I was generously assisted by Professor Pierre Guiral of the University of Aix-en-Provence and by two of his students, E. Chinard, and Victor Nguyen. The head archivists of the Archives de la Ville de Marseille – M. Ramière de Fortanier – and of the Archives Départementales des Bouches-du-Rhône – first M. Edouard Baratier and then Mme. M. Villard – have been consistently helpful both during my lengthy first visit and during my briefer subsequent ones. The efficiency of these archives, the wealth of their collections, and the unfailing kindness of their staffs have made it a pleasure to do research in Marseille. I wish also to thank the Archives de la Chambre de Commerce de Marseille, the Bibliothèque de la Ville de Marseille, and the Musée du Vieux Marseille, whose curator, Mlle. Jullian, gave me photographs of dozens of prints illustrating various facets of life in nineteenth-century Marseille.

Quantitative research of the kind undertaken in this study is expensive. It has been supported over the years by several institutions. The most important source of funding was a grant (SOC 72-05249-A01) from the National Science Foundation. A Research Training Grant from the Social Science Research Council financed my initial dissertation research in Marseille in 1967 and 1968. The University of Chicago, the Institute for Advanced Study, and the University of Arizona also have provided me with various types of support.

Much of the research reported in this book was carried out by a long series of research assistants: Kenneth East, Susan Anderson, Ann Lesch, Ronnie Dane, Allon Fischer, Cynthia Truant, and Sherry Sinclair. Ronald Pateman's mastery of the computer saved me many headaches and made possible analyses I could never have performed on my own. Nikki Matz typed the bulk of the final manuscript with admirable zeal and skill. I have received helpful comments on various portions and stages of this manuscript from Stephan Thernstrom, Joan Scott, James Jackson, Ronald Aminzade, James Lehning, Robert Bezucha, and Ellen Sewell. Hans Rosenberg, the director of my dissertation, gave me penetrating criticisms of my dissertation chapters and unstinting personal and intellectual support. The late Allan Sharlin was associated with this book from 1969, when he worked as my research assistant while still an undergraduate at the University of Chicago, until his untimely death in March of 1983. His continuing support, friendship, criticism, and ideas have helped to shape the book in many ways. To its detriment, it will never receive the close critical reading he had promised once the manuscript was completed.

The influence of my sociologist father pervades this study. Being raised by a ''dust-bowl empiricist'' imparts a special bent to the mind. I trust he will accept the book as the homage of a loyal and grateful son.

1 Introduction: Marseille and urban history

The nineteenth century was the heroic age of urban growth. There had, of course, been some great cities for millennia. But it was only with the spread of the industrial revolution over the continents of Europe and North America – and subsequently over South America, Australia, Asia, and Africa – that urbanization on a modern scale became possible. At the beginning of the nineteenth century, there were only four cities in Europe with a population of more than a quarter million – London, Paris, Naples, and Moscow. By the end of the century there were forty-nine.[1] This spectacular urban growth was part of a vast transformation of nineteenth-century European society – a transformation of cities and countryside alike, and of relatively backward as well as industrially advanced nations.

This book is a study of one city that experienced the prodigious urban transformation of the nineteenth century – Marseille, a great port on the Mediterranean coast of France. With a population of some 100,000 at the beginning of the nineteenth century, Marseille was already a very large city by contemporary standards, second only to Paris among French cities, and one of the twenty or so largest cities in the world. Yet its growth in the nineteenth century was on an entirely different scale from anything it had experienced in the two and one half millennia since it was founded by Greek colonists in the sixth century B.C. Figure 1.1 shows how the explosive growth that began in Marseille after 1820 contrasts with the slow rise of the prior century and a half. Only the two or three decades of repopulation that followed the terrible plague of 1720 showed anything like the growth rate of the period following 1820. Taking the period from 1660 to 1821 as a whole, the population of Marseille rose at a rate of about 0.4 percent per year; from 1821 to 1872, the period covered by this study, the annual rate of increase was nine times as high, or about 3.7 percent. Otherwise put, the population of Marseille grew nearly five times as much in the five decades from 1821 to 1872 as in the entire century and a half that preceded them. The statistics leave no doubt; in matters of elementary demography, Marseille in the middle of the nineteenth century was a very different city from Marseille under the Old Regime.

As a glance at Table 1.1 will demonstrate, Marseille's population growth was by no means exceptional for a European city in the nineteenth century. Marseille's population increased by 182 percent from 1801 to 1872, and by

1

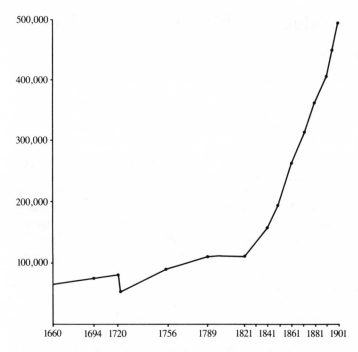

Figure 1.1. Population of Marseille, 1660–1901.

342 percent from 1801 to 1901. Some nineteenth-century cities grew considerably faster than this, and others considerably slower. Although Liverpool and Odessa were the only major European port cities to grow significantly faster than Marseille in the first seven decades of the century, the North European ports of Rotterdam and Hamburg also grew faster over the century as a whole. On the other hand, major industrial cities generally grew considerably faster than Marseille, and so did many capital cities – not only Paris, London, Berlin, and Vienna, but Brussels, Budapest, Saint Petersburg, and Warsaw. Among cities with mixed functions, some grew faster than Marseille, some slower. All the most important British cities, whatever their function, grew more rapidly than Marseille, and German cities also grew more rapidly over the century as a whole – although this was mainly due to their very rapid post-1870 growth rates. By contrast, cities in Spain, Italy, the Low Countries, and Scandinavia generally grew somewhat more slowly than Marseille. All in all, Marseille's nineteenth-century population growth was not far from the norm for large European cities.

Marseille's growth was quite exceptional, however, for a French city. It is a well-known fact of demographic history that urbanization proceeded more slowly in France than in most other countries that industrialized in the nine-

Table 1.1. *Nineteenth-century population of major European cities, in thousands*

	Population, 1800	Population, 1870	Population, 1900	Increase, 1800–70 (%)	Increase, 1800–1900 (%)
Capital cities					
Berlin	172	826	1,889	380	998
Brussels	66	314	599	376	808
Budapest	54	202	732	274	1,255
Copenhagen	101	181	401	79	297
Dublin	165	246	373	49	126
Lisbon	180	242[a]	356	34	97
London	1,117	3,890	6,586	248	490
Madrid	160	332	540	108	238
Moscow	250	612	989	145	296
Paris	547	1,852	2,714	239	396
Rome	163	244	463	50	184
St. Petersburg	220	667	1,267	203	476
Stockholm	76	136	301	79	296
Vienna	247	834	1,675	238	578
Warsaw	100	252	638	152	538
Port cities					
Barcelona	115	346[b]	533	201	363
Bristol	64	183	339	186	430
Hamburg	130	240	706	85	443
Liverpool	80	493	704	516	780
Marseille	**111**	**313**	**491**	**182**	**342**
Naples	427	449	564	5	32
Odessa	6	121	405	1,900	6,750
Palermo	139	219	310	58	123
Rotterdam	53	116	319	119	502
Industrial cities					
Belfast	37	174	349	370	843
Birmingham	74	344	523	365	607
Glasgow	77	522	776	578	908
Leeds	53	259	429	387	709
Lodz	0.2	34	315	17,000	157,500
Manchester	90	351	645	250	617
Sheffield	31	240	409	674	1,219
Mixed cities					
Amsterdam	201	264	511	31	154
Breslau	60	208	423	247	605
Cologne	50	107	456	114	812
Dresden	60	177	396	195	560
Edinburgh	83	244	394	194	374
Leipzig	30	107	456	257	1,520
Lyon	110	323	459	194	317
Milan	135	262	493	94	265
Munich	40	169	500	322	1,250
Turin	78	208	336	167	331

[a]Figure is for 1878.   [b]Figure is for 1880.
Source: Brian R. Mitchell, *European Historical Statistics, 1750–1975*, 2d ed. (London, 1981), pp. 86–9.

Table 1.2. *Growth of French cities with populations of 25,000 or more in 1801*

	1801	1872	Increase (%)
Marseille	111,130	312,864	182
Paris	547,736	1,851,792	238
Lyon	109,500	323,417	196
Bordeaux	90,992	194,055	114
Rouen	87,000	102,470	18
Nantes	73,879	118,517	60
Lille	54,756	158,117	189
Toulouse	50,171	124,852	149
Amiens	40,289	63,747	49
Nimes	38,800	62,394	61
Orleans	36,165	48,976	36
Montpellier	33,913	57,727	70
Angers	33,000	58,464	77
Caen	30,900	41,210	33
Besançon	30,000	49,401	65
Nancy	29,740	52,978	78
Brest	27,000	66,272	145
Rennes	25,904	52,044	101
Versailles	25,000	61,686	147

Sources: The figures for 1801 are from Charles H. Pouthas, *La Population française pendant la première moitié du XIX* *siècle* (Paris, 1956), p. 98. The figures for 1872 are from Statistique de la France, *Résultats généraux du dénombrement de 1872* (Nancy, 1874), pp. 112–121.

teenth century. Over the seven decades from 1801 to 1872, only three of the nineteen French cities that began the period with a population of 25,000 or more grew by more than Marseille's 182 percent: Paris (238 percent), Lyon (196 percent), and Lille (189 percent) (see Table 1.2). This time span is actually unfavorable to Marseille, for its population was constant for the first two decades of the century – the era of the Napoleonic wars. Over the half-century from 1821 to 1872, Marseille's rate of increase was greater than that of either Paris or Lyon. Indeed, among the nine cities that had attained 100,000 or more by 1872, only Saint-Etienne, which had been a small industrial town of only 19,103 in 1821, had grown more rapidly than Marseille (see Table 1.3). If most French cities were spared some of the problems usually associated with explosive urbanization in the nineteenth century – impersonality and demoralization, overcrowding, bad housing, inadequate sanitation, and the like – this clearly must not have been the case for Marseille.

Faster growing than most French cities, near the average for European cities – from the strictly demographic point of view, Marseille was reasonably representative of the wider experience of nineteenth-century urban growth. But this

Table 1.3. *Growth of French cities with populations of 100,000 or more in 1872*

	1821	1872	Increase (%)
Marseille	109,482	312,868	186
Paris	663,846	1,851,792	179
Lyon	118,265	323,417	173
Bordeaux	89,202	194,055	118
Lille	63,373	158,117	150
Toulouse	52,310	124,852	140
Nantes	68,327	118,517	73
Saint-Etienne	19,103	110,814	479
Rouen	86,736	102,470	18

Sources: The figures for 1821 are from Charles H. Pouthas, *La Population française pendant la première moitié du XIXe siècle* (Paris, 1956), pp. 101–19. The 1872 figures are from the Statistique de la France, *Résultats généraux du dénombrement de 1872* (Nancy, 1874), pp. 112–121.

is not a strictly demographic study, even though demographic data play an important role in the research. It is, rather, a study of urban social structures and social processes and of how these changed or, in some cases, remained stable during a period of massive demographic expansion. On these matters, the whole question of representativeness becomes far more problematic. Data on nineteenth-century population growth are readily available for cities in all European nations; the data for Marseille can easily be compared with those for other cities. But on such complex questions as economic and occupational structures, neighborhood patterns, migration, and social mobility, very little of a comparative nature is known. There are studies that deal with some of these matters for nineteenth-century French cities, and others that do so for English, German, and North American cities, but none ask quite the same set of questions asked here or use the same range of data.[2] Even after some twenty years of pathbreaking work in the so-called new urban history, much research is still at an exploratory stage. Whether Marseille's experiences of urban social transformation are representative or not can only be answered by future research. For the present, the important thing is to identify, delineate, and analyze the various transformations that occurred and to trace the interrelations between them. Given constraints of time and money, this is only possible at the level of a local study, where detailed information allows an examination of the fine structures of urban social life.

This book is a detailed description and analysis of the changing patterns of Marseille's social life in the half-century of rapid growth from 1820 to 1870. Like many other works in the now thriving genre of urban social history, it attempts to reconstruct the experiences of ordinary urban dwellers, rather than chronicling the affairs of the city's most prominent citizens. The problems of documentation posed by this approach are by now quite familiar to professional historians. Prominent people – this is true by definition – left their mark in the documents traditionally utilized by historians: memoirs, government records, newspapers, and the like. But the information such documents provide about other groups or classes of the urban population is normally scattered, biased, and unsystematic, clearly insufficient for a serious history of the general citizenry. However, even the most obscure citizens – at least in the modern world – come into contact with the apparatus of the state at some points in their lives, and the state keeps records of the contacts. They are counted by the census taker; they are born, married, and buried, and these events are certified and recorded by state officials; they pay taxes, and the state assesses their property and notes the amount of the payment; occasionally they get into trouble with the law, and the state records the nature of their offense and the court's judgment. Of course, these sources give only a very limited description of the individuals who compose the population; but what they lack in detail they more than make up in the comprehensiveness of their coverage. By subjecting these "bureaucratic" sources to quantitative analysis, it is possible to reconstruct important life experiences of a representative cross-section of the urban population.

To date, the quantifiable sources exploited most intensively by historians have been tax records, censuses, and vital records. Examinations of the social structures of rural, preindustrial populations have been based above all on tax records. In part this is simply a matter of availability – national censuses were established in the major Western countries only around 1800, so studies of seventeenth- or eighteenth-century populations must do without systematic census enumerations. In France, where property ownership was very widespread before the rise of modern industry, tax records are particularly valuable for documenting the structure of preindustrial populations. In rural France, even people whose main source of income was labor on the fields of others were likely to cultivate a tiny morsel of land on their own account. An analysis of the tax rolls therefore yields information on virtually all strata of the rural population. In preindustrial cities, however, tax records yield a much less comprehensive profile of the social structure. The nobility, magistrates, the bourgeoisie, and shopkeepers are well represented, but the sizable population of journeymen, laborers, and urban poor slips through the historian's net.[3]

The establishment of regular census enumerations around 1800 created a new and valuable source for the history of social structure, a source that has been exploited most thoroughly in North America. The census recorded information about the entire population – or at least about everyone the census takers managed to reach. Because the summary tables constructed by census officials are not detailed enough to answer the most interesting historical questions, historians have generally utilized the original registers kept by the census takers – called the "manuscript census" in the United States, "enumerators' books" in Britain, and "listes nominatives" in France. These registers contain the name, age, sex, place of residence, and relationship to head of household for the entire population, and often include occupation, birthplace, property ownership, and perhaps other information as well. They can therefore be used to establish the age, sex, neighborhood, and occupational distribution of the city and to chart the relationships between, for example, occupation and age, occupation and sex, neighborhood and occupation, and so on.[4] In addition, historians have developed methods to answer more complicated questions with census data. One line of research has been the analysis and classification of family and household structures, which are then related to such other factors as occupation, age, migration, and residential patterns.[5] A second has been to trace individuals from one census to the next. This enables historians to determine how many and what sorts of people stayed in the community from decade to decade rather than moving elsewhere – a quantity historians have dubbed the "persistence rate." It also enables them to trace the experiences of those who remained: their changes in family status, acquisition of property, intracity moves, and occupational mobility.[6] Studies based on one or another of these methodologies have become very common in recent years, especially in North America. As a consequence, our knowledge of household structures, persistence rates, and experiences of intragenerational occupational mobility has grown vastly since the pioneering work of Stephan Thernstrom two decades ago.[7]

Vital records – records of marriages, births, and deaths – have also been widely exploited by historians, but usually to answer strictly demographic questions. Historical demography has been transformed by the methods of "family reconstitution" pioneered by Louis Henry in the 1950s, methods that rely entirely on vital records.[8] But in many areas of nineteenth-century Europe, vital records can also be exploited in a very different fashion to yield detailed information on questions of social structure and social mobility. The richest of the vital records, at least in France, are marriage registers.[9] When a couple married, both spouses were required to provide the state with their names, ages, places of birth, addresses, occupations, and fathers' names and occupations. All this information was duly recorded on the official *acte de mariage* (marriage act), which was then signed by both spouses (if they could sign their names) and by four adult male witnesses, each of whom also gave his age, occupation, and address. (For a sample *acte de mariage*, see Figure 1.2). Although the marriage registers do not include the entire population, they constitute a very extensive sample of the young-adult population, and they allow the historian to describe this population in fascinating detail. They yield figures not only for a city's occupational distribution, but also for patterns of intermarriage, residence, migration, intergenerational occupational mobility, and literacy. They also contain the same information for women as for men, which means that women's social experiences – often slighted in urban histories – can be treated as fully as men's. Very few nineteenth-century

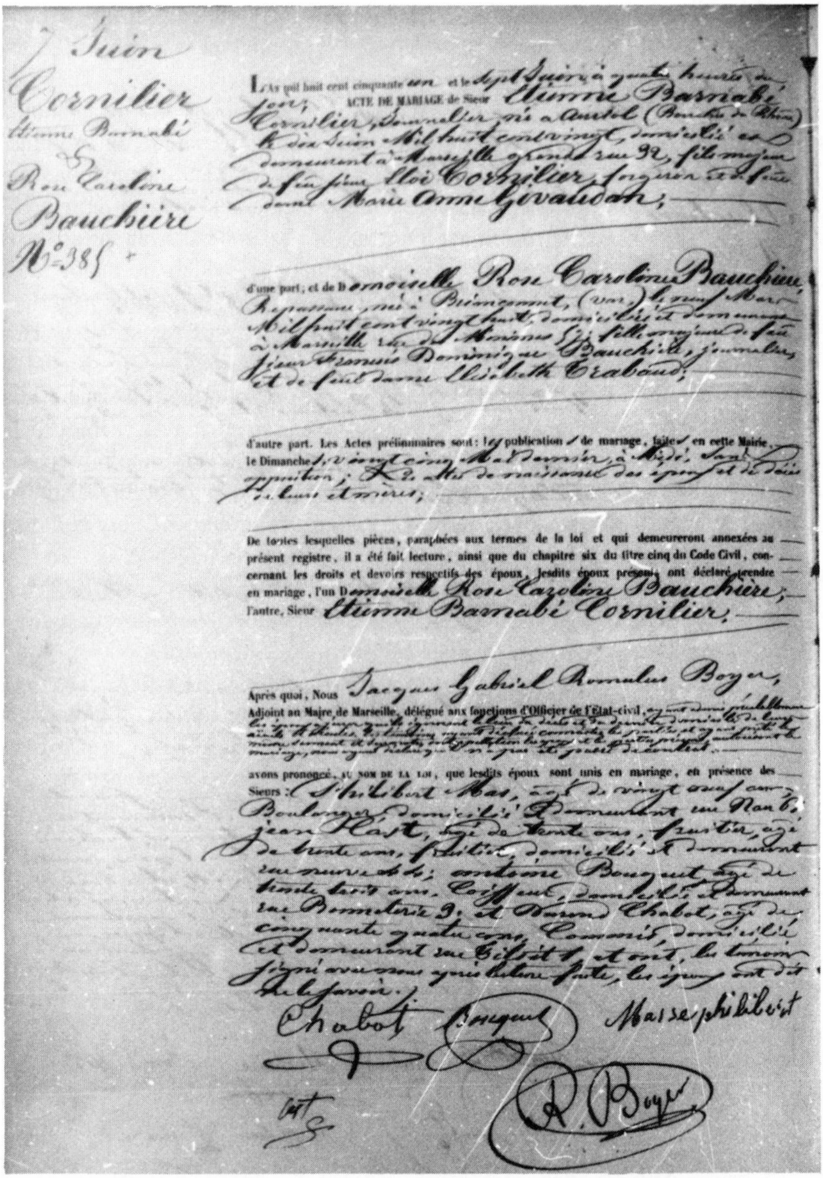

Figure 1.2. An *acte de mariage*. Courtesy Archives Départmentales des Bouches-du-Rhône.

censuses contain as much information about the individuals who compose the population, and none reveal as much about relations with people outside the immediate household. Marriage registers are a uniquely valuable historical source because they place persons in a larger nexus of relations – with their parents, with a native community, with their spouses and the spouses' families, and with witnesses.

This study is based on a wide range of quantitative sources, including the *listes nominatives* of the 1851 census, records of prosecutions for theft and other crimes, and assorted nineteenth-century statistical inquiries. But Marseille's marriage registers form the core of the documentation. Data from the marriage registers of 1821, 1822, 1846, 1851, and 1869 have been recorded, put into machine-readable form, and analyzed by computer. These data provide detailed pictures of urban society at three distinct periods spanning a half-century. The years 1821 and 1822 were chosen to fall after the disruptive effects of the Napoleonic wars but before the beginnings of rapid population growth. Because the French *état civil* is closed to researchers for 100 years, 1869 was the latest year available at the time recording and coding began. The years 1846 and 1851 were originally chosen to fall just before and after the great economic crisis that touched off, and then was intensified by, the Revolution of 1848. In the end, however, the two years were combined and analyzed as a single unit; the patterns they revealed differed only slightly. The marriage registers, supplemented by other sources of data, make possible an examination both of the changing *structure* of urban society and of *mobility* – movement of individuals into and within the social structure of Marseille.

This book is divided into two parts, the first on structure, the second on mobility. Part I describes five analytically distinct but empirically intertwined aspects of Marseille's social structure: a booming economy, a changing occupational structure, a surprisingly constant status ordering of occupations, a rapidly expanding framework of urban neighborhoods, and a demographic structure marked by a massive influx of migration. Part II analyzes two types of mobility: the migration of people into Marseille and the recruitment of people into various positions in the occupational structure.

It is in the analysis of mobility that the unique qualities of the marriage-register data can be exploited most fully. Because the marriage registers indicate the spouses' birthplaces, they can be used to estimate the volume of migration into Marseille and to determine where the immigrants came from. Moreover, because the marriage registers also indicate the occupations of the spouses' fathers, they can be used to determine the socio-occupational backgrounds of immigrants and to compare the backgrounds of men and women who migrated to Marseille from different areas. The marriage registers make possible a much more fine-grained analysis of migration than is usual in histories of nineteenth-century cities. The picture of migration that emerges from this analysis differs sharply from the lugubrious portrait Louis Chevalier has painted of migration into Paris in the first half of the nineteenth century.[10] Chevalier's account, which depicts migration to Paris as an onslaught of impoverished and disoriented hordes that sank the city into the depths of social pathology, is a mid-twentieth-century variant of a very old conservative lament that glorified rural life and was hostile to cities. The evidence indicates that most migration to Marseille, like most of the twentieth-century migration studied by anthropologists and sociologists, was actually a rather orderly affair. Many of the immigrants came from relatively comfortable backgrounds, with skills, capital, and connections that gave them a good start in the city. And even when the proportion of peasants' sons and daughters among the immigrants swelled later in the century, the peasants who came were generally well qualified for the urban labor market. The levels of literacy of immigrant peasants' sons were surprisingly high, far above those of their village compatriots. There is also evidence that young immigrants maintained ties with their families and often formed community bonds with their immigrant countrymen and countrywomen once they arrived in the city. Although migration was a disorienting and painful experience for some, it was not – at least in Marseille – the potent source of misery, crime, and disorder that Chevalier would have us believe.

The marriage registers also make possible an unusually close look at social mobility. Historians have usually regarded social mobility from the angle of social justice or class formation. The absence of a strongly class-conscious workers' movement in the United States has long been attributed to American workers' unusually good opportunities for upward social mobility – which are said to induce individualism and competitive social attitudes and to inhibit the development of class solidarities.[11] This issue understandably has been particularly important in work on American social mobility, but it has had an influence on European mobility research as well.[12] This book approaches social mobility from a very different angle. It attempts to demonstrate that, at least in Marseille, variations in social-mobility patterns over time are largely determined by changes in the composition of, demand for, and supply of labor. In Marseille, the amount of upward mobility from peasant or working-class birth to nonmanual or bourgeois status at the time of marriage rose substantially between the early 1820s and the late 1860s. But most of this rise in upward mobility can be explained by two macrostructural changes: first, a massive increase in migration of rural and small-town men and women, which biased the occupational origins of the labor force downward, and, second, a change in the economy that increased opportunities for nonmanual jobs more rapidly than opportunities for manual jobs. The increase in upward mobility was not the result of any dramatic "opening" or "democratization" of the basic structure of society; it arose mainly from shifts in patterns of demand and supply in the labor market. Moreover, Marseille's workers do not seem to have experienced the rise in upward mobility as a sign of the increasing justice of the social order: They became more radical rather than less as their opportunities for upward mobility improved.

The case of Marseille suggests that patterns of social mobility may have very little to do with class consciousness. The real explanations for variations in working-class politics should probably be sought in other realms, for example, in patterns of class alliances and cleavages, in cultural and ideological differences, and in the courses of specific social and political struggles.[13] The historical study of both social mobility and class formation would be improved if mobility were considered as at best contingently and indirectly related to the development of working-class consciousness. Social mobility is best understood not from the perspective of political consciousness or social justice, but from the perspective of large-scale changes in the structure of economy and society. Mobility, this book argues, depends on structure.

But if increases in the overall level of social mobility were largely the consequence of changes in the social structure, different groups in the population responded differently to the available opportunities. Using the marriage-register data, it is possible to trace out in detail the different behavior of men from different geographical and occupational backgrounds, ranging from an enthusiastic influx into respectable white-collar work by immigrant peasants' sons to a cautious preference for traditional working-class jobs on the part of native-born workers. The men's occupational-mobility data confirms the conclusions drawn from the migration data: Throughout the nineteenth century, male immigrants had higher rates of upward occupational mobility than did natives of the city.

Previous historical studies of social mobility have rarely considered women's social-mobility patterns – partly because of technical problems in tracing women from census to census, and partly because it has not occurred to them to do so. Because the marriage registers indicate the bride's occupation, as well as that of her father and her husband, women's social mobility is as easy to study in nineteenth-century Marseille as men's. Nineteenth-century employment patterns, which afforded very restricted opportunities to women, meant that little significant social mobility could take place through women's occupational achievements. The most important form of social mobility for women was experienced through marriage. A comparison of the occupations of brides' fathers with those of their husbands reveals the marriage-based patterns of upward or downward social mobility – or of social stability – of the various categories of women who got married in Marseille. Much as among men, it was immigrant women who took the most conspicuous advantage of the opportunities for upward mobility that were available in Marseille's marriage market. Within the constraints and opportunities generated by large-scale structural changes, immigrant men and women dominated the quest for upward mobility. More ambitious and venturesome than natives, they were the leaven of society in nineteenth-century Marseille.

Part I
Structure

In the half-century from 1820 to 1870, Marseille's society underwent multiple and interrelated structural changes. Underlying all the other changes was a prodigious growth and transformation of the city's economy – an industrial revolution, a burgeoning of maritime trade, and a restructuring of commercial institutions. These are the subject of Chapter 2. The economic changes had important effects on the city's occupational structure, increasing the proportion of the labor force engaged in unskilled labor, clerical work, and service occupations while decreasing the proportion in skilled trades, maritime occupations, and agriculture. The nature and pace of these changes in the occupational structure are the subject of Chapter 3. Chapter 4 investigates the status rankings of various occupations, finding changes in ranking surprisingly slight despite major transformations in the structure of the labor force and economy. The burgeoning population and economy of Marseille also spawned a rapid physical expansion of the city – an increase in the housing stock, the development of new neighborhoods, and a change in the spatial layout of the city. This is the subject of Chapter 5. Chapter 6, finally, investigates the demographic structures that resulted in the rapid growth of Marseille's population and demonstrates the fundamental importance of migration as the source of population growth. These structural changes, taken together, form the foundation of the changes in mobility that are investigated in Part II of the book.

2 The economic structure

The growth of Marseille's population in the nineteenth century was based upon a sustained boom in its economy. Although Marseille had long been an important maritime city, it was the nineteenth century that established it as France's preeminent port. In the nineteenth century Marseille also became a major industrial center and an increasingly important seat of regional administration. Although the port continued to give the city a special flavor, nineteenth-century Marseille had a fully diversified economy: It was the economic capital of Mediterranean France and a center of commerce, finance, administration, and industry. This chapter recounts the growth and transformation of Marseille's economic structure, from the long depression of the Revolutionary and Napoleonic wars to the end of the Second Empire in 1870.

The economy before 1815

Ever since Marseille was founded by Greek colonists in the sixth century B.C., its economic life has been dominated by its port. But this domination has meant different things over the centuries, as patterns of world trade have changed. From the Middle Ages through the sixteenth century, Marseille was part of a great Mediterranean commonwealth of mercantile cities. Long after its subjection to the French crown in 1481, Marseille had more commercial contacts with distant Mediterranean ports such as Constantinople and Alexandria than with cities of the French mainland, which were effectively cut off by the difficulties of land transportation.[1] During this period Marseille was as much an entrepôt in the complex redistribution of goods among Mediterranean ports as a place of entry of foreign goods into the French domestic market. In the late seventeenth and eighteenth centuries, the absolute monarchy's imposition of increasing administrative centralization and the gradual improvement of the road system facilitated communication with the north of France, but the entrepôt trade remained an extremely important part of Marseille's commerce. In fact, the centralizing monarchy consecrated the separation of Marseille from the mainland by chartering it as a free port in 1669.[2] Under the regime of the free port, goods could be imported and reexported without payment of customs duties, and the industries of Marseille could use imported raw materials duty-free. Duties had to be paid, however, when goods were transported inland, making reexportation more profitable than

15

Table 2.1. *Marseille's trading partners in international commerce, 1789*

Trading partner	Percent of total trade, in value
Italy	24
Spain	7
North Africa	7
Eastern Mediterranean	27
Total, Mediterranean	65
Northern Europe	7
West Indies	24
Other Atlantic Ocean	3
Indian Ocean and Far East	1
Total, extra-Mediterranean	35

Source: Charles Carrière, *Négociants marseillais au XVIIIe siècle: Contribution à l'étude des économies maritimes* (Marseille, 1973), vol. 1, p. 72.

trade with the rest of France and discouraging the sale of Marseille's manufactures on the domestic market. At the same time, Marseille's merchant marine was given a virtual monopoly on the Levant trade (that is, trade with the eastern Mediterranean), and foreign ships were prohibited from trading with French colonies in the West Indies.

These new regulations gave important advantages to the shipowners and merchants of the city and contributed to a rapid expansion of commerce in the late seventeenth and eighteenth centuries. But the most important factor in the growth of Marseille's maritime commerce in the eighteenth century was the booming Atlantic trade – above all, trade with the West Indies. According to the calculations of Charles Carrière, trade with the West Indies grew four times as fast as Mediterranean trade during the eighteenth century.[3] Although Mediterranean trade still constituted 65 percent of Marseille's international commerce at the end of the old regime, extra-Mediterranean trade had reached 35 percent, led by the West Indies with 24 percent (see Table 2.1). The rise of commerce beyond the Mediterranean did not necessarily diminish the importance of entrepôt trade; in fact, nearly half Marseille's imports from the West Indies were reexported.[4] Moreover, all the principal industries of Marseille – soap manufacture, sugar refining, tanning, the manufacture of hats and woolen hosiery – used imported raw materials and exported most of their products. All of them flourished during the eighteenth century.

The overall rise of Marseille's commerce in the eighteenth century can be seen in Figure 2.1, which plots the number of ships entering the port from 1710 to 1814. Until 1793, the trend was relentlessly upward, in spite of occasional dramatic crises. With the exception of the sharp decline of 1721–2,

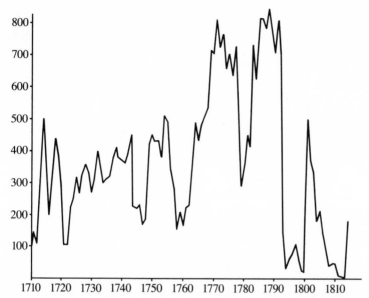

Figure 2.1. Number of ships entering the port of Marseille, 1710-1814.
From Charles Carrière, *Négociants marseillais au XVIIIe siècle: Contribution
à l'étude des économies maritimes*, 2 vols. (Marseille, 1973), vol. 1, p.
114.

which resulted from a major outbreak of plague in Marseille, all these crises
were results of naval warfare: the War of the Spanish Succession, the War
of Austrian Succession, the Seven Years' War, the War of American Independence, and, most drastically, the wars of the French Revolution. But
between the 1710s, the first decade for which figures are available, and the
1780s, the last decade before the French Revolution, the number of ships
entering the port per year more than doubled. These figures actually underestimate the overall rise in commerce because the average size of ships also
increased over this period. This impressive increase in Marseille's maritime
commerce gave rise to a concomitant rise in industry and to a significant
growth of population. The number of inhabitants of the city increased from
65,000 in 1660 to 75,000 in 1694, and, despite the death of some 30,000 in
the plague of 1720–1, the total had reached 88,000 by 1756. Population
continued to grow in the last years of the Old Regime and attained 110,000
by the outbreak of the French Revolution.[5]

The years of the Revolution and the Empire were a time of deep economic
depression in Marseille. The city's dependence on maritime trade made
its economy extremely vulnerable to the long political and military crisis.
The loss of colonies, the emigration of merchants and capitalists, the long
naval blockades, the destruction of much of the French navy and merchant

marine, and finally the self-imposed commercial strangulation of the Continental System virtually paralyzed the port of Marseille. The number of ships entering the port dropped abruptly with the beginning of war in 1793, and it remained depressed until the fall of Napoleon, except for a brief respite after the peace of Amiens in 1801. The English and Greeks took over much of the Levant trade, the longtime staple of Marseille's commerce, and the English and Americans came to dominate trade with the West Indies.[6] Because maritime commerce was the prime mover of Marseille's economy, the depression was felt in all sectors. One result was a fall in population from 110,000 on the eve of the Revolution to 95,000 in 1811.[7]

Nevertheless, industry suffered much less than maritime commerce. The interruption of maritime commerce had disastrous effects on some industries, for example hat manufacture, which had produced almost exclusively for Saint-Domingue, and sugar refining, which depended on cane from the West Indies. But Marseille's status as a free port was suppressed in 1794, and for some industries the gain of domestic markets made up for the loss of foreign markets. Tanning expanded slightly during the wars,[8] and soap manufacture, by far the most important single industry in Marseille, was not much affected by the crisis.[9] The continuing prosperity of the soap industry also spawned an immediately successful new industry – the manufacture of synthetic lye. This industry, using the newly invented Le Blanc process, was established in the environs of Marseille in 1808 and 1809 and grew to employ between one and two hundred workers by 1814.[10] This growth continued during the Restoration, with production doubling between 1814 and 1818 and once again between 1818 and 1828.[11]

The industrial sector of the economy weathered the crisis better than the maritime sector, largely because of the opening of the internal French market. Although maritime commerce continued to be the most important element in the economy of Marseille in the nineteenth century, the relationship between the maritime and industrial sectors had been permanently changed during the Revolution and Empire. During the nineteenth century most of Marseille's manufactures continued to use imported raw materials, but their main market was now on the French mainland. Although Marseille remained an important commercial entrepôt, its chief role in the nineteenth century was as a Mediterranean port of entry into the steadily growing French national economy.

Maritime commerce

The period from the Restoration of the Bourbons in 1814 to the fall of the Second Empire in 1870 was one of unprecedented economic growth in Marseille. One measure of this growth was the increase in population. Having dropped to 95,000 in 1811, the population rose to 132,000 in 1831, 195,000 in 1851, and 313,000 in 1872 – more than tripling in sixty years.[12] Both industry and commerce played their parts in the expansion of the economy. Marseille's industries, now producing primarily for the expanding French domestic market, grew steadily from 1814 to 1848, with plant size and mechanization increasing to the point that one can speak of a genuine "industrial revolution" in Marseille in the 1830s and 1840s. But for all the dynamism of Marseille's industries, the dominant force in the economy's expansion continued to be maritime commerce. By the late 1830s Marseille was the fifth largest port in the world, trailing only New York, London, Liverpool, and Hamburg in the quantity of cargoes unloaded onto its docks.[13] This prominence of Marseille in the world's economy, together with the absence of general European wars, the expansion of world trade, the advance of industry in Marseille, in France, and in the rest of Europe, and the improvement in communications from Marseille inland, resulted in a huge expansion in the traffic of the port.

Two statistical series for the activity of Marseille's port exist for these years: the total carrying capacity of the ships entering the port per year (available from 1825 on) and the amount of customs duties collected each year (available from 1814 to 1855).[14] The former – carrying capacity of ships – is probably more reliable, but is misleading to the extent that it measures only the physical volume and not the value of commercial transactions. The figures for customs duties, on the other hand, are a measure of the value of goods entering the port, but they are probably less reliable than the capacity figures because of variations in the rates at which customs duties were charged. Thus an increase in importation of goods paying high duties would have more effect on the total of duties collected than an equivalent rise in importation of goods with low duties. In any case, the correspondence between the two series is reasonably close, which should increase our confidence in both of them (see Figure 2.2). As measured by these two series, the growth of Marseille's maritime commerce was prodigious. From the five-year period 1825–9 to the five-year period 1866–70, the total carrying capacity of the ships arriving in Marseille per year quintupled. Given that the amount of customs duties collected per year had already increased substantially from 1815–19 to 1825–9, the overall increase in the traffic of the port from the late teens to the late sixties must have been at least sixfold.

The curves described by these two statistical series reveal three distinct periods in the economic history of Marseille. The first was a long period of consistently rising commercial activity stretching from the Restoration of the Bourbons in 1814 to the outbreak of the Revolution of 1848. During these years maritime commerce increased so steadily that a downturn rarely lasted for more than a year. On only one occasion, from 1833 to 1835, did yearly figures for carrying capacity of ships entering the port remain below a previous

Customs duties
in 1,000 francs

Carrying capacity
in 1,000 tons

Figure 2.2. Activity of the port of Marseille, 1815–70. From Jules Julliany, *Essai sur le commerce de Marseille*, 2d ed., 3 vols. (Marseille, 1842), vol. 1, pp. 145, 162, and vol. 3, p. 462; Casimir Bosquet and Tony Sapet, *Etude sur la navigation, le commerce et l'industrie de Marseille, pendant la période quinquennale de 1850 à 1854* (Marseille, 1857), pp. 23–9; Octave Teissier, *Histoire du commerce de Marseille pendant vingt ans (1855–74)* (Paris, 1878); and *Travaux de la Société de Statistique de Marseille*, 36 vols. (Marseille, 1837–73), vol. 1, p. 70, vol. 11, pp. 48–9, and vol. 19, p. 92.

peak for more than one year, and the crisis of these years was attributable not to economic causes, but to a severe cholera epidemic in 1834–5, which caused ships to avoid Marseille and practically halted normal economic life during the months of the epidemic. The figures for customs duties show more fluctuation, but here too only the crisis caused by the cholera epidemic of the mid-1830s was serious enough to cause the curve to fall for two years in a row.

The second period was a deep depression lasting from 1848 to 1852. The crisis of these years was mainly a product of the political troubles touched off by the Revolution of 1848. The Revolution threw the possessing classes into panic, with the result that investment fell off sharply and unemployment

Table 2.2. *Number and average carrying capacity (in nautical tons) of ships docking in Marseille, 1820–70*

	Sail-powered		Steam-powered		Total	
Year	No.	Average capacity	No.	Average capacity	No.	Average capacity
1820	4,402	68			4,402	68
1830	5,522	89			5,522	89
1840	6,458	96	232	300	6,690	103
1850	6,802	103	474	249	7,276	112
1860	7,195	131	1,260	347	8,455	163
1870	6,898	178	2,178	438	9,076	241

Source: Paul Masson, gen. ed., *Les Bouches-du-Rhône: Encyclopédie départementale*, vol. 9, *Le Mouvement économique: Le Commerce* (Marseille, 1926), pp. 36, 54, 72, 75.

rose. It was not until Louis Napoleon's coup d'état at the end of 1851, and the establishment of the authoritarian Second Empire in 1852, that investors regained their confidence and economic expansion began again.[15] The Second Empire, which lasted from 1852 to 1870, saw a return to the growth of the pre-1848 years, but with a far less steady rhythm. There was a very rapid expansion from 1852 to 1856, followed by a period of stagnation until 1866, when another extremely vigorous boom developed. Rather than rising by moderate and regular increments as it had between 1815 and 1848, maritime commerce advanced by spurts in the 1850s and 1860s.

As the volume of Marseille's maritime commerce increased, so did the size of the ships entering the port. In 1820 the average carrying capacity of ships docking in Marseille was 68 tons. By 1850 it was 112 tons, and by 1870 it had reached 241 tons.[16] The number of ships trading in Marseille consequently expanded much less rapidly than the total cargoes. In the late 1820s the number of ships entering the port each year varied from 5,000 to 6,000. By the late 1860s, when the volume of commerce was five times as great, the number of ships had less than doubled, to between 9,000 and 11,000 a year.[17] Part of the increase in the average size of ships resulted from the growing proportion of steam-powered vessels. Steam navigation in the Mediterranean began in the 1830s; 232 steamers entered the port of Marseille in 1840, and thereafter the number roughly doubled each decade, reaching 2,178 in 1870 (see Table 2.2). In 1840, steamers accounted for only 3 percent of all ships entering the port, and for only 10 percent of all cargoes; in 1870, 24 percent of the ships were steamers, and they carried 44 percent of all cargoes.[18] From the beginning, steamships were very large vessels. In 1840, when the average sailing ship docking in Marseille had a carrying capacity

Table 2.3. *Marseille's trading partners in international commerce, 1833 and 1860*

	Percent of total carrying capacity	
Trading partners	1833	1860
Italy	34	26
Spain	11	10
North Africa	12	13
Eastern Mediterranean	14	23
Total, Mediterranean	71	72
Northern Europe	9	12
West Indies	5	2
Other Atlantic Ocean	13	11
Indian Ocean and Far East	2	3
Total, extra-Mediterranean	29	28

Source: Paul Masson, gen. ed., *Les Bouches-du-Rhône: Encyclopédie départementale,* vol. 9, *Le Mouvement économique: Le Commerce* (Marseille, 1926), pp. 174–5, 183–5.

of 96 tons, the average steamship had a capacity of 300. By 1870 the average steamer had a capacity of 438 tons, and the average sailing ship 178 tons.

As these figures indicate, the average size of sailing ships docking in the port of Marseille also increased substantially, especially after 1850. Part of the reason was probably the need to build bigger ships to compete with steamers. But the larger average size of vessels was also due to a change in the composition of trade. In the period 1827–36, nearly half the total volume of Marseille's commerce (47 percent) was accounted for by coastal trade – *cabotage* – carried in small vessels calling in nearby Mediterranean ports, either in France or on the adjacent coasts of Spain or Italy. This trade, which was carried mainly in small vessels, grew only slowly, rising by less than 60 percent over the following four decades, whereas longer-distance international trade, generally carried in much larger ships, grew sixfold. By 1857–66, the coastal trade had fallen to less than a quarter of the total, and by 1867–76 to less than a fifth of all trade.[19]

Although international trade as a whole grew much more rapidly than coastal trade, it was less wide ranging in the nineteenth century than it had been in the eighteenth. Figures on the total carrying capacity of the ships engaging in trade with different countries indicate that a little over 70 percent of Marseille's foreign commerce was with Mediterranean ports, both in 1833 and in 1860 (see Table 2.3). This is appreciably above the figure for 1789, which was 64 percent. Although the 1789 figures are not directly comparable, because they measure the value of cargoes rather than carrying capacity, it seems likely that extra-Mediterranean commerce played a less important role in the nineteenth century than in the eighteenth. The sharpest drop from the eighteenth to the nineteenth century was in trade with the West Indies, which fell from around a quarter of the total in 1789 to a twentieth or less in the nineteenth century. There also seems to have been a restriction in the range of the Mediterranean trade. In 1830, Italy had clearly replaced the Eastern Mediterranean as Marseille's leading trading partner. By 1860, however, there was a reversal of this trend, and the Eastern Mediterranean had almost attained parity with Italy. If the growth of Marseille's maritime commerce in the eighteenth century was built on trade with distant ports, and especially with the West Indies, the still more impressive growth of the nineteenth century rested on a fuller exploitation of the economic potential of the Mediterranean basin.

There was a certain stability in the cargoes carried by ships trading in Marseille in the nineteenth century (see Table 2.4). This stability is particularly clear in the import figures, which are available for 1828 and 1860. Industrial raw materials were especially prominent: lumber, lead, sugar cane for Marseille's refineries, and sulfur for its chemical industry were among the top ten imports in both years – as was olive oil, intended more as a raw material for Marseille's soap industry than as a foodstuff. Wheat was the only foodstuff other than olive oil that was among the top ten imports in both years, but salted cod, rice, and fruits made the list in 1828, and coffee did so in 1860. On the whole, the list of imports was more dominated by industrial goods in 1860 than in 1828. Especially impressive was the rise of oil grains, the raw material for Marseille's oil-pressing industry, to the second largest import in 1860. The rising importance of industry is even more apparent in the export figures. In 1828, wines and spirits were by far the leading export, and such reexported goods as madder (a dyestuff), wheat, and coffee all figured prominently. In 1860, coal from the mines of southern France was by far the leading export, wines and spirits had fallen to fourth, and the products of Marseille's industries were now much more prominent – refined sugar, flour, tiles and bricks, metal products (many produced by Marseille's booming machine-construction industry) and linseed cakes (a by-product of Marseille's oil-pressing industry) were all among the top seven exports.

Industrial revolution

The growing importance of industrial raw materials and of products of Marseille's manufacturers in the city's imports and exports points to a significant growth of industry. Particularly in the 1830s and 1840s, Marseille experienced a genuine "industrial revolution," with all the characteristics implied by that term: increasing mechanization of production, increasing use of steam power, the concentration of labor into factories, and the destruction or absorption of

Table 2.4. *The ten leading imports and exports of Marseille, 1828, 1860 (in thousands of tons)*

Imports, 1828		Imports, 1860	
Commodity	Weight	Commodity	Weight
Olive oil	36.6	Wheat	112.0
Wheat	24.7	Oil grains	102.1
Lumber	15.5	Lumber	92.1
Sugar cane	14.8	Sugar cane	55.2
Sulfur	10.6	Coal	44.7
Salted cod	6.3	Olive oil	23.8
Madder	4.5	Sulfur	21.5
Lead	4.4	Lead	20.2
Rice	3.5	Coffee	19.4
Fruits	3.4	Lead ore	18.8

Exports, 1828		Exports, 1860	
Commodity	Weight	Commodity	Weight
Wines and spirits	18.6	Coal	106.7
Refined sugar	6.4	Refined sugar	35.7
Madder	5.5	Flour	28.8
Soap	3.6	Wines and spirits	25.2
Wheat	3.2	Bricks and tiles	21.8
Lead	2.8	Metal products	16.3
Coffee	2.3	Linseed cakes	15.7
Salt	2.3	Wheat	15.2
Glass bottles	2.1	Lumber	14.5
Bricks and tiles	1.9	Lead	12.7

Source: Paul Masson, gen. ed., *Les Bouches-du-Rhône: Encyclopédie départementale,* vol. 9, *Le Mouvement économique: Le Commerce* (Marseille, 1926), pp. 239–42, 245–8, 288–91, 296–7.

smaller, technologically backward firms by larger, more modern competitors. Between 1828–30 and 1866–9, the number of workers employed in factories in Marseille grew nearly fivefold, from about 2,400 to nearly 11,700. Meanwhile the average number of workers per plant within the factory sector grew from 19 to 45 (see Table 2.5). Assuming that increasing scale of plant also meant rising productivity, the overall increase in the output of factory industry must have been considerably greater than fivefold – as high, in other words, as the prodigious increase in the traffic of Marseille's port during these same years. Already in the 1840s, Jules Julliany, a leading local merchant who also wrote extensively on the economy of Marseille, could boast that ''Marseille and its environs are now bristling with chimneys whose black smoke announces from afar that our city joins an industrial genius to its commercial

Table 2.5. *Factory industry in Marseille*

Industries	1828–30			1848			1866–9		
	No. of firms	No. of workers	Workers per firm	No. of firms	No. of workers	Workers per firm	No. of firms	No. of workers	Workers per firm
Cotton spinning	10	200	20	3	42	14	—	—	—
Wool washing	10	290	29	7	300	43	—	—	—
Tanning	37	400	11	52	650	12	34	1,114	33
Sugar refining	20	600	30	6	1,000	167	3	1,600	533
Soap	43	700	16	40	600	15	60	950	16
Chemicals	6	250	42	6	500	83	12	575	48
Oil pressing	—	—	—	13	500	38	30	950	32
Tobacco	—	—	—	2	1,095	548	1	1,650	1,650
Machines	—	—	—	6	1,064	177	14	1,560	111
Other iron and steel	—	—	—	7	224	32	9	530	59
Lead	—	—	—	1	200	200	4	325	81
Pianos	—	—	—	2	120	60	1	120	120
Gas	—	—	—	1	100	100	2	305	152
Glass	—	—	—	3	150	50	3	221	77
Flour milling	—	—	—	33	317	10	76	1,450	19
Saw mills	—	—	—	—	—	—	5	106	21
Copper	—	—	—	—	—	—	7	221	32
Total	126	2,440	19	182	6,862	38	261	11,677	45

Sources: The figures for 1828–30 are from Christophe de Villeneuve-Bargemont, *Statistique du département des Bouches-du-Rhône*, 4 vols. (Marseille, 1821–34), vol. 4, pp. 672, 674, 697; and Jules Julliany, *Essai sur le commerce de Marseille*, 2d ed., 3 vols. (Marseille, 1842), vol. 3, pp. 218, 392–3. The figures for 1848 are from the National Assembly's "Enquête sur le travail agricole et industriel," *Archives Nationales*, C 947. The figures for 1866–9 are from Paul Masson, gen. ed., *Les Bouches-du-Rhône: Encyclopédie départementale*, vol. 8, *Le Mouvement économique: L'Industrie* (Marseille, 1926), pp. 160–2; and the results of the census of 1866, *Archives de la Ville de Marseille*, 2F 162c.

genius, and that it can hold in its powerful hands the sceptre of Manchester and that of Liverpool."[20]

Not all Marseille's industries prospered in this period. The nineteenth century actually saw the disappearance of textile production. In the early nineteenth century there were two textile industries of some importance in Marseille – cotton spinning and the washing and combing of raw wool, which was subsequently spun into yarn in more important woolen centers elsewhere in France. In 1828–9 there were ten cotton-spinning firms employing 200 workers and ten wool-washing firms employing 290. By 1848 there were only three cotton-spinning firms with 42 workers, and by 1869 the cotton industry had completely disappeared – eclipsed by the larger and more technologically advanced cotton manufactures of Northern France and of England, Switzerland, and Germany. The wool-washing industry declined a little later. It still employed 300 workers (250 of them women) in seven firms in 1848. By 1869, however, the wool-preparation industry had also disappeared.[21] Marseille found its nineteenth-century industrial vocation in other fields than textiles.

There were also some industries that experienced only minor technological progress between 1815 and 1870. Soap manufacture, Marseille's most important industry under the Old Regime, was one of these. From 1830 to 1848 the numbers of firms and of workers in the soap industry were virtually constant. There were 43 firms with 700 workers in 1830 and 40 firms with 600 in 1848. Between 1848 and 1869, the number of firms increased to 60 and the number of workers to 950, but the average number of workers per factory remained essentially unchanged. Although the number of workers per factory remained small, between 15 and 16, and although most operations were carried out by hand even in 1869, soap manufacture was very much a factory industry in one sense: The investment in plant was substantial. The average soap factory was a sizable building containing cutting equipment, molds, and several vats heated by coal-burning furnaces. The workers were under the supervision of a foreman, and division of labor was fairly advanced.[22] In spite of technological stagnation, soap manufacture continued to hold the top rank among Marseille's industries in the nineteenth century, both because its annual product was worth more than that of any other industry[23] and because it stimulated the growth of two other important industries, the manufacture of synthetic lye and oil pressing.

The synthetic lye industry, which was founded with government assistance during the Napoleonic era, was Marseille's only important industrial innovation during the first quarter of the nineteenth century and was the first truly large-scale industry in Marseille. From the beginning, nearly all its product was consumed by the soap industry, displacing the soap industry's use of natural lye.[24] By 1830 there were six lye firms with 250 workers, and by 1848 the same number of firms employed 500 workers. Growth slowed considerably during the next two decades, however. By 1869, the number of workers in the industry had expanded a little, to 575, but the number of firms had grown to 12. The average number of workers per plant actually declined from 83 to 48.

The oil-pressing industry was one of the most spectacular industrial creations of the first half of the century. Until 1830 nearly all the soap produced in Marseille used olive oil as its raw material, but the success of competitors in using less expensive grain-produced oils convinced Marseille's soap manufacturers to do the same. This opened the way for establishment of a modern oil-pressing industry. The first plants were built around 1830, and by 1833 there were four factories in Marseille producing 200 tons of oil. From 1833 to 1842 there was a rash of construction of oil-pressing factories, and by this latter date some 26 factories, employing some 700 workers, were producing oil, mostly from sesame seeds, and another ten factories were under construction. Of the 36 total factories in activity or under construction, 20 were powered by steam engines; the remainder used water power, except for 2 small plants driven by animal power.[25] By the mid-1840s the boom had ceased, and increasing competition soon drove most of the firms into bankruptcy, with the largest and most mechanized firms prevailing over the small and backward. As a result, the number of oil-pressing firms dropped from 36 in 1842 to only 13 in 1848; but the number of workers employed in the industry dropped only slightly, from 700 to 500, with the result that the average number of workers per plant rose from 19 to 38. During the same interval the total product of the industry actually rose from 12.3 million to 15.6 million francs. By 1848 the oil-pressing industry, which had been nonexistent before 1830, was the third industry of Marseille in the value of its product, accounting for almost 10 percent of Marseille's industrial production.[26] During the next two decades, growth was far more gradual. By 1869 there were 30 oil-pressing firms with 950 workers; as with the chemical industry, the average number of workers per factory actually dropped during the Second Empire.

At midcentury the second rank among Marseille's industries was held by sugar refining, with a product worth 20 million francs per year.[27] Sugar refining was profoundly transformed during the 1830s and 1840s. Like the soap industry, sugar refining had been one of Marseille's principal industries under the Old Regime, employing 450 workers in 17 factories on the eve of the Revolution,[28] but, unlike the soap industry, it was decimated by the depression of the revolutionary years, when it was almost totally deprived of sugar cane. The industry rebounded with astonishing rapidity during the Restoration, and by 1829 there were 20 plants employing 600 workers. The sugar-refining industry was unusually susceptible to economic crises: Consumption of sugar fell drastically in times of economic hardship, when consumers were forced to restrict expenditures. This vulnerability in times of crisis was one reason for the extraordinary degree of concentration that developed in the sugar industry. Between 1830 and 1838, half the sugar refineries in Marseille were forced to close down, bringing the number of firms to 10, but the number of workers employed in the industry as a whole rose from 600 to nearly a thousand. In 1841 the industry entered another crisis, which cut the number of firms to 7 and the number of workers to under 500.[29] Then, during the boom of the mid-1840s, the industry rose back to its level of 1838, and by the onset of the crisis of 1848–52 the 6 firms still in business employed 1,000 workers. By 1869, the number of firms had fallen to only 3, whereas the number of workers had risen to 1,600. The net result of the intermittent booms and crises from 1830 to 1869 was that the number of firms fell from 20 to 3 and the average number of workers per plant skyrocketed from 30 to 533. By midcentury the sugar-refining industry of Marseille had emerged as a truly modern large-scale factory industry. As early as 1842, Julliany could assert without exaggeration that some of Marseille's refineries, "in the scale of the buildings, the force of the machines and the perfection of the apparatus, may be compared to the most remarkable manufactures of France and of foreign lands."[30]

The only possible challenger to sugar refining as Marseille's most technologically advanced industry was another creation of the 1830s and 1840s – mechanical construction. This industry, which had not existed in Marseille before 1830, began as a response to the growing use of steam engines in both navigation and industry. From the beginning, most of the firms were large in scale and had heavy investments in fixed capital. The 8 firms existing in 1842 had a total of 700 workers, for an average of 88 workers per plant – above that of sugar refining, which was then only 68 per plant. There was further concentration in the next six years, and by 1848 the 6 remaining firms employed 1,050 workers, or an average of 177 per plant, slightly above sugar refining's average of 167. During the 1850s and 1860s, however, this movement of concentration was reversed. Although the number of workers in the mechanical industry rose by some 500 between 1848 and 1866, the number of firms more than doubled, from 6 to 14. As a result, the average number of workers per plant fell from 177 to 111. Most of Marseille's mechanical-construction firms produced and repaired steam engines, usually for steamships, but sometimes for use in mines or factories. A second type of firm specialized in building and equipping factories. One built most of the oil-pressing factories in the Marseille area; another specialized in the construction of flour mills, which it erected in Barcelona, Tunis, Palermo, and Naples, as well as in the environs of Marseille.[31] In addition to the mechanical industry proper, there were also iron foundries and metal-refining factories that were essentially annexes of the mechanical industry. In 1848 there were 7 such factories with 224 workers; by the late 1860s there were 9 with 530 workers.

Tanning was already an important industry in Marseille under the Old Regime. In many respects its history parallels that of the soap industry – until the 1860s. It was not much affected by the economic crisis of the Revolution and Empire, and until the 1860s it grew only slowly without important technological changes. Tanning required a sizable investment in fixed capital (building, vats, and equipment), but the number of workers per plant was small and did not increase over time. There were 37 tanneries with 400 workers in 1830 and 52 with 650 in 1860.[32] There was, however, a consolidation in ownership; during the 1850s, a certain Jullien acquired 13 tanneries employing about 250 workers. When it turned out that most of these tanneries were in a quarter of the city slated for demolition during the great public-works projects of the 1860s, Jullien decided to build a large modern tanning factory in the northern suburbs of Marseille. This factory, which soon became the largest tannery in France, occupied 400 workers in 1867.[33] Although no other tanning establishment rivaled Jullien's, the late 1860s saw a general movement of concentration in the tanning industry. The number of plants fell to 34 in 1869, whereas the number of workers rose to 1,114. The average number of workers per plant, which had been 11 in 1830 and 12 in 1848, rose to 33 in 1869. Even if Jullien's tannery is left out of account, there were 22 workers per plant in 1869, representing a considerable increase since 1848. The industrial revolution arrived late in the tanning industry, but it was well under way by 1869.

Another industry that underwent growth and concentration during the 1860s was flour milling. There had always been flour mills in Marseille and the surrounding countryside, but it was not until the liberal commercial treaties of the early 1860s that Marseille's flour millers could use imported grain in years of good and bad harvest alike without paying excessive duties. Only then did flour milling become a genuine factory industry. From 33 mills employing 317 workers in 1848, the number rose to 64 with 1,050 in 1869. The scale of plant also increased, although only moderately, from 10 workers per plant in 1848 to 16 in 1869. Many of the flour mills used steam engines; the remainder were powered by water. Most of the grain used by the flour-milling industry was imported, and 80 percent of the flour produced was then exported.[34]

Of the remaining factory industries of Marseille, by far the largest was the tobacco industry. It was unusual in several respects: It was run as a concession of the state tobacco monopoly; it employed almost exclusively female labor; and it was technologically entirely a handicraft industry. The large number of women employed in the industry were concentrated in a single building and were kept under strict surveillance by a staff of male overseers, but cigars were rolled by hand. In 1848 there were 2 cigar factories employing 1,014 women and 81 men; in 1869 the single remaining factory had a total of 1,650 employees. Finally, several other kinds of factories were established in Marseille between 1830 and the 1860s: piano, gas, lead pipe, and glass works already existed in 1848, and sawmills and copper foundries had joined the list by 1869. Moreover, other industries were approaching the factory stage by 1869; the asphalt, candle, and brewing industries all employed between 100 and 300 workers and had exceeded an average of 10 workers per plant. Marseille's industrial revolution was a diverse and complicated affair. In some cases old and well-established industries, such as sugar refining, tanning, and flour milling, were transformed by new techniques and processes. In other cases major new industries were created, such as chemical manufacture, oil pressing, and machine construction. In some industries concentration and increasing scale were irreversible, but in others – for example the chemical, oil, and machine industries – an initial burst of concentration in the 1830s and 1840s was reversed in the 1850s and 1860s. Whether measured by the total number of workers in the factory sector or by the average size of plant, industrialization proceeded most rapidly in the 1830s and 1840s. The total number of workers nearly tripled from 1828–30 to 1848 but less than doubled from 1848 to 1866–9; the average number of workers per plant, having doubled from 19 to 38 during the 1830s and 1840s, rose only modestly, to 45, by the end of the 1860s. Yet the continuing advance of factory industry was undeniable. Factory production maintained its hold in all the new industries established in the 1830s and 1840s and spread to others in the following decades.

Even by 1870, Marseille had not become a factory town. Factory workers were still outnumbered by handicraft workers, and all the most important factory industries were dependent on maritime commerce for raw materials, for markets, or for both. The soap industry sold most of its product in France, but its chief raw material was either imported olive oil or oil made from imported oil grains by Marseille's oil-pressing industry. These it processed with lye produced in Marseille from imported raw materials. The tanning and sugar-refining industries both used imported raw materials and then sold their products on the domestic market. The machine-construction industry not only used significant amounts of imported iron and steel, but exported many of its products, or produced steam engines for locally based ships that helped to swell the volume of Marseille's maritime trade. The flour-milling industry imported the bulk of its wheat and exported the bulk of its flour; the wool, cotton, tobacco, lead, and sawmilling industries all used imported raw materials. Marseille's industrial revolution was different in scale and in character from the types of industrialization made familiar by the economic-history textbooks – for example, the iron- and coal-based industrialization of the Ruhr Valley or the cotton-textile-based industrialization of Lancashire. It was a form of industrialization specific to port cities and tied to the growth of maritime commerce.

Handicraft industry

Factory industry, together with maritime commerce, made up the dynamic, risk-taking, capitalistic sector of the economy. This sector accounted for most of the capital accumulation that took place, and its growth and fluctuations governed the growth and fluctuations of the economy as a whole. Nonfactory industry was characterized by small firms, low capital investment, and minor technological change. With a few exceptions, it produced essentially for the local market, either servicing the capitalistic sector (for example, crate and barrel making, rope and sail making, ship repairing) or servicing the population at large (for example, building, manufacture of garments and household objects, food processing, the luxury trades). The spectacular changes wrought by the rise of factory industry drew a great deal of attention from government officials and private observers, but documentation is scarce on handicraft industry, where the changes were far less dramatic.

It is clear, however, that the handicraft sector continued to employ a very large portion of the population, even as late as the 1860s. In 1851 some 18,300 men were employed in handicrafts, as against 5,500 in factories; in 1866 there were 28,800 as against 10,000 factory workers.[35] Although factory industry grew much more rapidly, artisans still outnumbered factory workers by nearly three to one in the late 1860s. Marseille's experience, which was by no means unusual, suggests that the rise of factory industry did not necessarily result in a decline of handicrafts – at least not immediately. We are all familiar with the case of the British hand-loom weavers, reduced to poverty and finally extinguished altogether by the adoption of the power loom.[36] But the case of weaving was quite exceptional; most early factories were not in direct competition with handicraft production. This certainly was the case in Marseille, where the industrial revolution of the 1830s to the 1860s took place in industries that either had not existed before (machine construction, oil pressing, chemicals) or had been large in scale and heavily capitalized even under the Old Regime (soap making, sugar refining, and, to a lesser extent, tanning). In no case did new, large-scale mechanical technology invade a flourishing handicraft trade and bring hardship or precipitous decline in numbers to the work force. If anything, the effect of factory industry on Marseille's handicraft trades was quite the opposite. New factories brought new workers and greater overall wealth to the community, and this rise in wealth and population increased demand for the consumer goods (food, housing, clothing, furniture, vehicles, household utensils, and the like) that were produced by Marseille's handicraft industries. The spread of the factory, far from being a threat to handicraft industry, was a source of increased demand for its products.

There also seems to have been relatively little change in the scale of artisan firms. In this period three statistical inquiries, one dating from 1829, the second from 1848, and the third from 1866, attempted to determine both the number of workers and the number of firms in Marseille's various industries.[37] The figures they yield cannot be considered more than rough approximations, but they show very little change over time. The ratio of workers to firms in handicraft industry was 5.7 to 1 in 1829, and 5.2 to 1 in both 1848 and 1866.

Although the imprecision of the figures does not rule out the possibility of a small increase in scale, it seems reasonably certain that handicraft firms were not, on the average, much larger in 1866 than in 1829.

This does not mean that nothing changed in the handicraft sector. There are, in fact, good reasons to assume that significant changes took place. Marseille was increasingly integrated into the national market, first primarily by water transportation up the Rhône River and later by railroad, and the same boats and railroad cars that carried an ever-increasing volume of international cargo and factory products from Marseille to the rest of the country also made available to Marseille's consumers an increased volume of furniture, pots and pans, clothing, books, barrels, carpets, tools, and a wide array of other handicraft goods that competed with locally made products. The intensified competition that arose from this integration into the national market could have different effects on different industries. Crate and barrel making, for example, seems to have declined between the 1820s and the 1860s, even though the demand for crates and barrels rose with the increase in Marseille's maritime commerce. In this case lower-cost producers outside Marseille must have taken an increasing share of the market. Candy making, on the other hand, grew very rapidly over the same years – producing, one assumes, for a market stretching far beyond Marseille.[38] But candy making was an exception. Marseille did not become a major center of handicraft industries producing for markets outside the immediate region – as was the case, for example, of Paris and Lyon. Marseille's comparative advantage was in maritime commerce and in industries linked to maritime commerce; its handicraft trades continued to serve the local population.

Intensified competition could, however, lead to important changes in the organization of production, even in trades that showed neither unusual expansion nor unusual contraction. Perhaps the most important change of this kind was the substitution of ready-made goods for made-to-order goods. Traditionally, each customer would pick out the materials and consult with the producer about the design of an item he wished to purchase; his workers would then make the item to the specifications of the customer. The production of ready-made goods – *confection* in French – was quite different: Workers would make a large number of identical items (tables, shoes, trousers, crockery), which were then offered up for sale to consumers at a lower price than comparable made-to-order goods. The lower prices were possible because costs, especially labor costs, were lower. When items being produced were identical, the entrepreneur could assign each worker to one step in the process of production. One shoemaker would cut leather for the uppers to a predetermined pattern, another would sew them up, a third would cut the soles, a fourth would sew soles to uppers, and so on. As a result, each worker became extremely adept at his or her particular task, and the product was made faster and therefore more cheaply than comparable made-to-order goods. The system of *confection* also enabled the entrepreneur to employ less-skilled and lower-paid workers. Sometimes production of ready-made goods was combined with a putting-out system, in which workers, especially ill-paid women, carried out their tasks at home rather than in the master's workshop.

E. P. Thompson has chronicled the advance of ready-made production – and the consequent depression of wages and skills – in London handicrafts in the 1820s and 1830s; recent research shows that it was common in certain Parisian crafts, particularly shoemaking and tailoring, as early as the 1830s, and that such changes were taking place in several industries in mid-nineteenth-century Toulouse.[39] Similar changes were certainly under way in Marseille's shoemaking industry in the 1840s. Testimony at a trial of shoemakers arrested for leading a strike in 1845 referred at one point to "workshops where up to eighty workers were employed," but also stated that during the strike certain workers "without danger to themselves, could not, except in hiding, receive and fabricate the work that was given to them by their masters." The trial record also refers to both "directors of workshops" and *entrepreneurs d'ouvrage* – a term that implies work on a putting-out basis.[40] It appears, then, that some shoes were made in small workshops, others in very large shops where division of labor was probably advanced, and still others in the workers' own rooms or garrets. Although we have no direct evidence for tailors, the widespread underemployment and the large number of female workers revealed by the parliamentary inquiry of 1848 suggests that a similar process was under way in Marseille's tailoring trade as well.[41] We can only guess how far such changes may have spread beyond the shoemaking and tailoring trades.

Handicraft industry was by no means the most dynamic sector of nineteenth-century Marseille's economy. Yet it continued to account for a significant proportion of the city's industrial production – about 45 percent of the total industrial product, according to the estimate of the parliamentary inquiry of 1848[42] – and a much larger proportion of the industrial labor force. Economically it was secondary to factory industry and maritime commerce, but socially it was of enormous importance. Workers in the handicraft sector set the tone of life in the popular quarters of the city, and they dominated the radical movements that played a crucial role in Marseille's politics from the Revolution of 1848 to the Commune of 1871.[43] Economically, Marseille was a capitalist city, but socially it was still a city of artisans.

Social-overhead capital

The continuing growth of Marseille's population and economy put serious strains on some of the city's basic facilities. As early as the late 1830s, it became clear that important public-works projects would have to be undertaken if the city were to continue its expansion during the following decades.

New sources of water had to be tapped, a better transportation link to the interior of France had to be forged, and the port had to be expanded. The middle years of the nineteenth century were years of heavy investment in what economists call social-overhead capital. To the commercial expansion and industrial revolution of these years were joined three huge construction projects destined to change the basic conditions of Marseille's economic life.

The Canal de Marseille

The city of Marseille had always been short of water. The basin surrounding Marseille is served only by two paltry and irregular streams called the Huveaune and the Jarret. Their waters had been carefully husbanded ever since the Middle Ages – in pictorial representations of medieval Marseille an aqueduct leading from the Jarret to the walled city is one of the most prominent features. The city was always liable to serious water shortages in years of drought, and these came all too often in Marseille, where rainfall is extremely irregular. A project for tapping the Alp-fed waters of the Durance River had been suggested as early as 1701, and as the city began its rapid growth in the years after 1815, the need became ever more apparent. The project was finally settled upon in 1838. Although the distance from Marseille to the Durance was not excessive, the mountainous terrain to be crossed required numerous switchbacks and meanderings, thereby increasing the length and the cost. The canal was financed by the municipality of Marseille, which floated a loan at 4.5 percent, the interest charges to be paid by a surtax on flour, that is, by taxing the poor. The total cost of the project, which was not completed until 1851, was over 11.5 million francs.[44]

The more forward-looking members of Marseille's business community were inspired by the grandeur of this immense undertaking, and some of them cherished exaggerated notions about the benefits that would flow from the canal. The canal would not only provide plentiful water for drinking, housekeeping, irrigation, sewers, and street cleaning, but would also be a major source of power for industry. By the middle of the century, when the waters of the Durance finally began to flow in the pipes and fountains of Marseille, the steam engine had already made water power obsolete as a means of propelling industrial machinery. But if the completion of the canal did not cause a spurt of industrial growth, its benefits to the city were nevertheless of fundamental importance. When the canal was completed, the amount of water available to the city jumped eighteenfold, from 108 to 2,000 liters per second, thereby removing one of the most serious barriers to further expansion of the city.[45]

The Marseille–Avignon Railway

The second great public-works project of this era was the construction of a railroad line from Marseille to Avignon. During the Restoration and July Monarchy the flow of commerce between Marseille and the Rhône Valley had increased greatly. From 88,704 tons in 1817, it rose to 131,027 in 1824, and to 373,528 per year in 1840–6.[46] Nearly all this traffic was by boat, through the shifting and treacherous delta of the Rhône River to Arles, where the cargoes were reloaded onto river boats – most of them steam powered after 1830 – and transported up the Rhône, usually to Lyon. The huge volume of this commerce made a rail line linking Marseille directly with Rhône, and eventually with Lyon and Paris, a matter of pressing importance to the economy of Marseille and a potentially lucrative venture for entrepreneurs.

In 1843 the government conceded the line from Marseille to Avignon to Paulin Talabot, who was destined to play a central role in the economic development of Marseille during the next two decades. Talabot, at once an engineer and financier, was a former disciple of Saint-Simon and one of that colorful and audacious breed of entrepreneurial adventurers so prominent in the economic life of mid-nineteenth-century France. He had already built the successful rail line from Alais to Beaucaire, and by adding the adjacent line from Marseille to Avignon he hoped to lay the foundation of a vast industrial and financial empire dominating the entire Rhône Valley.[47] Work on the line began later in 1843 and continued until 1852, when the bridge across the Rhône linking Beaucaire and Tarascon was completed. It was a difficult and expensive undertaking, eventually costing some 86 million francs, of which 41 million were paid by the state and the remainder by Talabot's company. Included in the line was the longest railway tunnel yet to be dug in France, stretching a distance of over 4.5 kilometers through the mountains guarding the northern approach to Marseille.[48] Construction was nearing completion when the Revolution of 1848 and the ensuing economic crisis placed Talabot's company in financial distress and forced it partially to suspend work. It was not until March 1849 that the line was open all the way from Marseille to Avignon, and not until 1857 that a rail link all the way from Avignon to Paris was completed.[49]

The port

The steady growth in Marseille's maritime traffic made the construction of a new port basin imperative. The port was already overcrowded in the last years of the Old Regime, and by the middle 1830s the situation became critical. Several stopgap measures were undertaken, such as razing buildings along the northern edge of the port from 1837 to 1840 to expand the surface of the docks, and dredging the port's southeastern corner to make room for another twenty to thirty ships. Finally a new ship-repairing basin was dug near the southwestern extremity of the port, and when it was put into service in 1840 the entire port proper was free for loading and unloading of commercial vessels.[50] But even after these improvements, the docks measured only 3,200 meters for an annual traffic of seven to eight thousand ships. By contrast, Le Havre, Marseille's chief French competitor, had 5,920 meters of docks for fewer than five thousand ships. The minor improvements were thus insufficient to alleviate the problem; in spite of the additions made to the area of usable docks, the traffic of the port grew far faster than the available space. The problem was exacerbated by the appearance of steamships, which were much larger than sailing vessels and difficult to accommodate in the confines of the old port.

It was clear that a new basin comparable in size to the old port would be needed. Given the geography of Marseille, this meant a gigantic program of construction (see Figures 5.1–5.4). The old port of Marseille is nestled between two steep and rocky hills and is the only part of the coastline that naturally has at once shelter against storms, good access to the shore, and sufficient depth of water, all of which are required for a good port. The immediately adjacent coastline to the north and south of the old port was so jagged, steep, and rocky as to make the difficulty and cost of construction almost prohibitive. Only farther to the south, beyond the jagged mountainous outcropping of Endoume, was the coastline less accidented, and the great distance of this area from the old port meant that the advantage of lower construction costs would have been more than outweighed by the difficulty of communication with the old port and the center of the city.

For eight years, from 1835 to 1843, engineers, entrepreneurs, the chamber of commerce, and representatives of the local and national governments haggled over dozens of rival plans for new port basins, finally deciding on the area immediately to the north of the old port.[51] The job was immense and expensive. It required extensive filling of the jagged coastline and the construction of a long breakwater. Work on the project began in 1844 and advanced rapidly, considering the difficulty of the job. The new basin was already usable in 1847, when it was crowded by vessels carrying wheat to provision France's exhausted granaries, and was finally completed in 1853. By 1848 the local director of the Ponts et Chausées (the government civil-engineering corps) had decided that a further northward extension was necessary.[52] But the Revolution of 1848, and the financial insolvency and reduction in port traffic which it brought in its wake, interrupted plans for extension. It was not until 1856 that work began on a series of three new port basins stretching northward along the coast. This new extension of the port differed from the extension begun in 1844 in that it not only increased the quantity of available space, but also qualitatively changed methods of handling maritime commerce. The new port basins included a *dock à l'Anglais*, which at once reorganized and mechanized the port facilities of the city. The new dock had hydraulic cranes and lifting equipment, which reduced the part of manual labor in loading and unloading ships, and it also included new facilities for delivery, storage, and customs, and centralized the entrepôt, which had previously been scattered throughout the city.[53]

Construction of the new port was undertaken by two large capitalist companies, the Société des Ports de Marseille, headed by the banker Mirès, and the Compagnie des Docks et Entrepôts de Marseille, headed by none other than Paulin Talabot, the director of the Marseille–Avignon Railway. The capital for both companies was drawn primarily from Paris. The Compagnie des Docks was charged with building, equipping, and running the docks themselves, whereas the Société des Ports acquired the land adjacent to the new port basins and was responsible for the extensive leveling and filling operations that were necessary to make this land economically usable.[54] The first of these tasks – the building and running of the docks – was a highly successful operation, but the second proved unprofitable. The terrain belonging to the Société des Ports proved very difficult to sell – in part because it was cut off from the center of Marseille by the old city, a teeming and almost impassable mass of buildings perched on the hill between the old port and the new. Mirès, not the sort of man to be deterred by such obstacles, proposed to the municipality that the entire old city be demolished to improve access to the new port basins. The municipality, understandably reluctant to undertake a project that would have turned a quarter of its people out of their homes, turned the proposal down, and shortly afterward, in 1861, Mirès failed, dragged down by his huge, unprofitable, and immobile investments in Marseille.[55]

Mirès was followed by an equally hardy entrepreneur, Emile Pereire, the cofounder of the famous and powerful Crédit Mobilier who took over the Société des Ports and fused it with the Paris-based Crédit Immobilier. Pereire soon convinced the city to undertake a less ambitious version of Mirès's plan of demolishing the old city, with Pereire's company doing the work and acquiring the land and buildings that would be constructed. The project consisted of building a broad street, the rue Impériale, through the old city to the new port. This required cutting a deep gash through the hill and the demolition of a large part of the old city. The work was undertaken in 1862 and accomplished with astonishing speed, considering the scale of the project: By 1864 the rue Impériale was open to normal traffic, and it was soon lined with large and elegant buildings.[56] The rue Impériale cut the transportation distance from the new ports to the city center in half and was for many years the commercial axis of the city.[57] Yet Pereire's investments proved no more profitable than Mirès's – the buildings along the street proved difficult to rent, and the land adjacent to the new port, although increased in value by the construction of the rue Impériale, continued to move slowly. In fact, the weight, the unprofitability, and the immobility of Pereire's investments in Marseille were one of the principal causes of the failure of the Pereire brothers' financial empire in 1867.[58]

The development of the quarter adjacent to the new port was thus instrumental in the demise of two of the most important French banking empires of the era – a fact that must have given a certain spiteful satisfaction to the merchants of Marseille, many of whom had opposed such grandiose development schemes and resented the dominance of outsiders over the city's economy. But these very merchants – and the city as a whole – were also beneficiaries of the financiers' excesses and misjudgments. The construction of the new port, together with the development of the adjacent quarter and the building of the rue Impériale, provided the foundation for nearly a century of future expansion of Marseille's commerce.

Commercial revolution

The construction of new port basins not only reshaped the northern quarters of the city and made room for a new generation of steamships, but fundamentally restructured the handling of the cargoes that passed through Marseille. The key to the old system of cargo handling was the Société des Portefaix – the society of longshoremen. This society was a continuation of the privileged guild of longshoremen that had existed under the Old Regime. Although all guilds were officially abolished in 1791, the longshoremen were allowed by municipal authorities to reestablish theirs in fact in 1815. The society maintained a monopoly over all loading and unloading operations, banning nonmembers from the docks and keeping all dock work under strict surveillance. This monopoly, of course, meant high wages for the longshoremen. But in spite of the high labor costs, Marseille's merchants accepted the society's power on the docks.[59]

The practices of the longshoremen's society had grown up with the traditional organization of commerce in Marseille. Under the Old Regime, and right down to the 1850s, it was typical for each voyage of a ship to be financed by a different group of businessmen. The ship's captain, merchants whose goods would be carried, and perhaps a banker or a wealthy retired capitalist would become partners for a single voyage. When the ship returned, the profits or losses would be divided and the partnership dissolved, and a new partnership, normally including a different set of partners, would be established. A given merchant would be involved in several different ventures at once. He might have three ships coming in during a two-week period and then have none the next month.[60] A merchant's demand for labor was therefore sporadic: He wanted to be able to hire a team of men to load or unload a ship when he needed them, and he wanted to be sure that they would do the work efficiently and honestly with a minimum of supervision. The long-shoremen's society, by maintaining a pool of strictly disciplined workers who could be trusted to carry out the merchant's orders, provided the merchants exactly what they needed. The strict discipline maintained by the society was made especially important by the layout of the old port, which was surrounded by crowded, labyrinthine, working-class neighborhoods where a dishonest longshoreman could disappear in an instant with valuable cargoes – a danger enhanced by the fact that goods in entrepôt had to be carried to entrepôt warehouses scattered throughout the city. The longshoremen's society main-tained close surveillance over loading and unloading operations and auto-matically expelled any member convicted of theft.[61] In effect, it provided both policing and management of work on the docks as well as the labor power to load and unload ships.

The construction of new port basins in the 1850s and 1860s utterly reor-ganized the handling of cargo, and in doing so it destroyed the privileges of the longshoremen. The new docks were novel in four respects. First, they were located at some distance from the crowded working-class quarters of the old city. Second, they centralized the entrepôt in one location. Third, they had hydraulic cranes and lifting equipment, which reduced the part of manual labor in the loading and unloading of ships. Fourth, the loading and unloading operations were to be organized and supervised by subaltern em-ployees of the Compagnie des Docks.

The dock, with all its equipment and buildings, was not completed until 1864, but it began operation on a limited scale as early as 1859. From the beginning it was locked in conflict with the longshoremen's society, which rightly feared that the dock would destroy its monopoly. Beginning in 1859 all steamships entering the port were required to unload at the new dock, and the management would not allow longshoremen to work unless they became employees of the company and submitted to its discipline. The longshoremen countered by refusing to work at the dock under these conditions, and the company was forced to compromise, allowing longshoremen to do some kinds of work without becoming employees of the dock.[62] But the compromise solution was tenuous, and the conflict came to a head again when the dock began full-scale operation in 1864. Once again the company insisted that anyone engaged in loading and unloading ships be an employee of the dock, and once again the longshoremen's society responded by refusing to work under the dock's conditions. This time the company was prepared; it simply manned the docks with unskilled laborers, especially Italian immigrants, and offered merchants lower rates than the longshoremen could match. The long-shoremen countered by garnering the support of many local merchants, who were hostile to the growing power of the company. Although the longshore-men had broad support in the community, the dock had economic and technical superiority, and the end result of the conflict was a total victory for the dock.

The longshoremen's society was destroyed, and the privileged longshoremen became proletarianized employees of the company.[63]

The restructuring of Marseille's port facilities was paralleled by a dramatic transformation of its merchant marine. The growing role of steam navigation in Marseille's maritime commerce during the Second Empire was described earlier in this chapter. Ships based in Marseille accounted for much of the overall rise in steamship tonnage. Thanks to a massive infusion of outside capital, several huge steamship lines were formed in Marseille in the 1850s and 1860s. Marseille's steamer fleet grew from 30 vessels with a carrying capacity of 4,247 nautical tons in 1850 to 201 vessels with a carrying capacity of 93,760 tons in 1869. In 1850 Marseille had 31 percent of the nation's steamer tonnage, the same percentage as Le Havre. In 1869, Marseille had 64 percent and Le Havre only 11 percent.[64]

The first and most important of the new joint-stock steamship lines was the Messageries Maritimes, founded in 1852 and soon renamed the Messageries Impériales. The Messageries, which had headquarters in Paris, quickly became the giant of the French merchant marine; by 1869 the Messageries's fleet of 67 ships represented three-fifths of Marseille's steamer tonnage, and nearly 37 percent of the nation's.[65] The role of outside capital was by no means limited to the Messageries Impériales. In fact, of the four largest shipping companies in Marseille at the end of the Second Empire, only one, the Compagnie Marseillaise de Navigation à Vapeur, founded in 1853 by the Fraissinet family, was controlled by Marseillais. It was the third-largest shipping company in Marseille at the end of the Second Empire. Of the remaining large shipping firms, one, the Société Générale de Transports Maritimes à Vapeur, founded in 1865, was controlled exclusively by outsiders, among them the Société Générale (an important Parisian joint-stock bank), the Banque de Genève, and the ubiquitous Paulin Talabot. The last of the large firms, the Compagnie de Navigation Mixte, founded in 1852, was controlled by a group of capitalists from Marseille and Lyon, with its headquarters and a majority of it stockholders in Lyon. In addition to these four large companies, there were a number of smaller shipping concerns, the largest of which had as many as ten ships. These smaller companies were all owned by Marseillais, but taken together they had only a little more than 10 percent of the city's steamer tonnage.[66]

The period of the Second Empire also saw a transformation of Marseille's financial structure. Although a center of international trade, Marseille had never been an important center of international finance. Until 1835, when the Banque de Marseille was opened, credit was available only from private bankers known as *disposeurs*. The *disposeurs* were commonly either former merchants or merchants who carried on banking as a sideline. According to Jules Julliany, *disposeurs* considered the discount rate "as a sort of thermometer which showed a sign of security and prosperity in its diminution and a sign of trouble and disrepute in its rise."[67] Hence they closed their doors whenever the discount rate began to rise, that is, exactly when credit was getting scarcer. They would refuse to discount papers or grant loans until the discount rate began to fall once again, at which time they would extend credit on good terms, thus tending to exacerbate the already present inflationary tendencies. The credit structure therefore had a disequilibrating effect on the economy. Whatever cyclical tendencies were present were exaggerated by the action of the *disposeurs*, thereby encouraging unwise speculation in good times and bringing about the bankruptcy of essentially sound ventures in bad.

The need for a more dependable source of credit soon became apparent to the city's more forward-looking capitalists. As early as 1830, a proposal was made for the establishment of a state-chartered *banque départementale*, which would issue bank notes and discount commercial paper, but the project died when Marseille's businessmen failed to buy enough shares to amass the needed starting capital.[68] The project was revived, however, and near the end of 1835 the Banque de Marseille was chartered by the state as a joint-stock company. It opened its doors in 1836, with capital of 4 million francs. Its stated policy of continuing to discount commercial paper even in the most trying times was tested in the bank's first year of operation, for a financial crisis was in progress when it opened its doors. In spite of these unpropitious circumstances, the bank made good on its promises and discounted over 72 million francs worth of commercial paper in its first year. The level of discounts dropped to 39 million the following year, but rose to 75 million in 1838 and rose steadily thereafter to a high of 285 million in 1846. The amount of deposits, the number of bank notes in circulation, and the dividends paid to stockholders likewise rose steadily.[69] The bank was, thus, an important aid to the commerce of Marseille. But its sphere of operations remained too small for it to solve singlehandedly the problem of insufficiency and irregularity of credit.

Several small banks, none having a capital of over a million francs, were established in Marseille between 1849 and 1853, and although they improved the availability of credit, they were not large enough to have any massive effect on the credit structure. Meanwhile, the Banque de Marseille was transformed into a branch office of the Banque de France, continuing to function as a supplier of notes and as a clearinghouse for other banks. The most important creation of the 1850s was the Crédit Foncier de Marseille, a bank specializing in financing real property. Founded in 1852, it continued to operate independently until 1856, when it was absorbed by the larger Crédit Foncier of Paris and reduced to the status of a branch office. The most important series of financial creations took place in the middle 1860s. In 1865 the Société Marseillaise de Crédit Industriel et Commercial was founded, with capital of 20 million francs. The Crédit Lyonnais created a branch in Marseille in the same year and was followed by the Société Générale in 1866 and the

Comptoir National d'Escompte in 1869.[70] By the end of the Second Empire Marseille no longer suffered from inadequate financial institutions and was thoroughly integrated into the national credit structure. Not only was outside capital available for large projects, such as the new port and the formation of steamship lines; the facilities of large, national, joint-stock banks were also available for financing day-to-day mercantile activities.

These three transformations of Marseille's commercial life during the 1850s and 1860s – the new docks, the new steamship lines, and the new banking structure – amounted to a commercial revolution as far-reaching as the industrial revolution of the 1830s and 1840s. A merchant who had left the city in 1820 to return in the 1840s might well have been astonished by the increased volume of maritime commerce, but he would have found little changed in the ways of doing business. A merchant who left in the 1840s and returned at the end of the 1860s would have been totally disoriented by the changes that had taken place. Besides the obvious visible signs – the railway, the new port basins crowded with steamships, the rue Impériale cut through the old city – he would quickly have found that the organization of commerce was now vastly different. Although small groups of merchants, ship captains, and capitalists still pooled their resources to finance single voyages of sail-powered ships, cargoes were increasingly carried in steamships owned and financed by large shipping lines. When cargoes arrived in Marseille, whether in sail-powered or steam-powered vessels, they were unloaded by workers supervised by the Compagnie des Docks, not workers hired by the merchants and supervised by the longshoremen's society. And when a merchant needed credit to see a commercial transaction through to its completion, he would now be more likely to turn to a large joint-stock bank than to a *disposeur* – a fellow-merchant turned banker.

All these changes had three common features. First, they indisputably increased the efficiency of commercial operations. Second, they all entailed the creation of large-scale, specialized, bureaucratic organizations. The new banks, the new shipping companies, and the Compagnie des Docks all employed swarms of managers, office workers, and supervisors to do work previously performed much more informally by merchants and their employees – or by longshoremen. The merchant, whose occupational identity previously had shaded indistinctly into that of banker or shipowner, and who previously had hired and paid his own dock workers, now found his sphere narrowed to specifically commercial operations as these auxiliary functions were taken over by specialized bureaucratic institutions. Third, these changes all resulted from the intervention of outside capital. Parisian capitalists had a broader vision of Marseille's potential than its native mercantile community, and they had the resources and the ruthlessness to undertake grandiose projects. The commercial revolution of the Second Empire meant a growing ''foreign'' domination of Marseille's commercial life. ''Marseille,'' as the scion of one old Marseillais mercantile family put it, "no longer seems to belong to herself."[71] In the burgeoning national and international capitalist economy of the mid-nineteenth century, Marseille's commerce was too important to be left to the Marseillais.

3   The occupational structure

The occupational structure of Marseille reflected the city's economic structure, and it changed as the economy changed. Most of the changes were of the sort generally associated with industrialization: The proportion engaged in artisan industry and agriculture declined, while the proportion engaged in unskilled and semiskilled factory trades, service trades, and clerical occupations rose. This much can be said at the outset. But these unexceptional statements are not very informative unless the size and content of occupational categories, and the extent and rhythms of change, can be specified more precisely. Such specifications are the task of this chapter.

Describing Marseille's occupational structure requires systematic quantitative evidence about the number and characteristics of the men and women engaged in the city's various occupations. The descriptions in this chapter will be based primarily on two sources of quantifiable data: the marriage registers from 1821, 1822, 1846, 1851, and 1869, and a 10 percent sample of the *listes nominatives* of the census of 1851. For reasons discussed more fully in Appendix A, neither of these sources yields an entirely accurate estimate of Marseille's occupational distribution. The basic problem with the marriage registers is clear: They systematically overrepresent younger, marriage-age men and women, and they underrepresent recent migrants to the city. The *listes nominatives* are, in principle, a complete count of the population and therefore should be the best source of information on the occupational structure. But before 1851 the census takers did not indicate occupations, so it was impossible to construct a census-based estimate of the occupational structure at or near the beginning of the period covered by this study. In addition, only a fraction of the *listes nominatives* of the censuses falling at the end of the period – those of 1866 and 1872 – have been preserved. In the end only the *listes nominatives* of the census of 1851 proved to be worth using. They almost certainly yield the most accurate available estimate of Marseille's nineteenth-century occupational distribution. But, as explained in Appendix A, even these figures leave out a significant number of young, single, adult males, and therefore have to be augmented by further calculations. Truly reliable occupational figures, in short, cannot be obtained. But with the figures at hand it is possible to provide acceptable and very useful approximations.

To make sense of the data derived from the *actes de marriage* and the

44

listes nominatives, the hundreds of different occupations practiced in Marseille must be placed into a limited number of more or less homogeneous categories. There are many different schemes available for categorizing occupations, all of them more or less plausible and all of them somewhat arbitrary. The criteria on which these schemes are based vary, but most attempt either to arrange occupations in a hierarchy of wealth, status, or prestige, or to arrange them according to their economic functions.[1] These two analytically distinct criteria of categorization are very closely intertwined in real life; certain types of work regularly bring higher rewards than others. In this study, however, the problems of hierarchy and function will be kept as distinct as possible. The occupational categories described in this chapter are based chiefly on economic function rather than on differences of wealth or status. The problem of hierarchy will be taken up in Chapter 4.

Functional classifications of occupations can be of varying degrees of elegance and elaboration, from a simple dichotomy of white-collar and blue-collar workers to the detailed and complicated schemes used by modern sociologists or census bureaus. Here again, two different principles of classification can be distinguished. The first is to divide occupations by industrial sector – whether into very broad categories like agriculture, manufacturing, and services, or into smaller and more refined industrial classifications like building, textiles, metallurgy, transportation, public service, and so on. The second commonly used principle divides occupations by the type of work performed, whatever the industrial sector. Thus, in a classification of this sort, proprietors, clerical employees, and skilled workers employed in a single firm or a single industry would be ranged into three different occupational categories. Generally speaking, the classification by industrial sector is more useful if the main concern is description of the economy and economic growth. But for description of social structure and social change, classification by type of work performed is generally preferable, because the economic interests, lifestyles, educational levels, and other social experiences of an individual or group are likely to have more in common with those who perform similar kinds of work in other industries than with those who perform very different kinds of work in the same industry. For this reason, the scheme of classification adopted in this study is based on the type of work performed.

Men's occupations

The occupations of Marseille's men have been divided into ten categories of unequal size and importance: (1) businessmen and professionals, (2) rentiers, (3) sales and clerical employees, (4) small businessmen, (5) artisans, (6) service workers, (7) unskilled workers, (8) maritime workers, (9) agriculturalists, and (10) a small residual miscellaneous category. Categories 1 through 4 make up what are conventionally called the nonmanual or white-collar occupations; here they will also be denominated by the French terms bourgeois or bourgeoisie. Categories 5 through 8 are the manual, or blue-collar, or working-class occupations. The contents, characteristics, and defining features of these ten categories are discussed in the paragraphs that follow. A complete list of the occupational titles included in each category is given in Appendix B.

1. *Businessmen and professionals.* This is a compound category that includes two quite different economic functions. Businessmen are entrepreneurs who invest their capital in industry or commerce and make their living from profits. Most of these denominated themselves by the omnibus term *négociant*, which is probably most accurately rendered in English as "merchants," but there were also bankers, ship captains, ship owners, and industrialists of various sorts. Also included are salaried business executives and agents – rare before the 1860s, but increasingly common thereafter. Professionals are learned or highly trained persons who perform a variety of specialized services for others and generally make their living from fees or salaries. In nineteenth-century France the professions were generally designated as *professions libres*. These included doctors, lawyers of various sorts, professors, journalists, pharmacists, engineers, and the like. Into them can be assimilated the former privileged occupations of the Old Regime, occupations that continued to confer an elite status in the nineteenth century: military officers, the clergy, and high-ranking government officials. There were also certain professions that serviced the business community, such as accountants and brokers.

Taken as a whole, businessmen and professionals formed the small and wealthy elite of Marseille – together with the *propriétaires* and rentiers of category 2. Although they performed two different types of economic functions, together these occupations formed a socially distinct community that stood at the pinnacle of society, both in nineteenth-century Marseille and in nineteenth-century French urban society in general.

2. *Rentiers.* This category includes men who lived on their investments and did not work for a living at all. In French they were denominated either as rentiers or as *propriétaires* (proprietors). In a sense, these were not occupations at all, but a lack of occupation made possible by wealth; hence in the occupational classifications of the French census, *propriétaires* and rentiers were generally excluded from the active population. In most contemporary Western societies, the rentier is a rare social type, but not so in nineteenth-century France. Under the Old Regime it was considered degrading to be gainfully employed in any but the privileged professions of the clergy, the military, and public service; to live nobly – *vivre noblement* – was to live on one's revenues without working. Thus the nobility had been essentially a rentier class, and those nonnobles who wished to rise in the esteem of their fellows copied the nobility, investing in land or in government bonds the profits they accumulated through commerce and manufacture and living as

lavishly and tastefully as they could afford on their revenues. Although the nobility as a privileged order had disappeared in the French Revolution of 1789, the prestige associated with its lifestyle lingered on through the nineteenth century. A significant proportion of the richest men in Marseille and in other French cities lived as rentiers and *propriétaires*. However, not all the rentiers and *propriétaires* who appear in the census and marriage-register samples can be assumed to have been men of great wealth. They included some of modest fortune who preferred leisure to work and a sizable number of older men who had retired on pensions or savings. The rentiers are a somewhat mixed category that ranged from the rich and powerful at the top to the mediocre at the bottom.

3. *Sales and clerical employees.* This category is composed of salaried subordinate employees working at nonmanual tasks. Both the kinds of tasks and the levels of skill and responsibility exercised varied widely. This category included trusted assistants of wealthy lawyers or businessmen whose responsibilities, skills, and incomes could be very substantial, together with bookkeepers, secretaries, menial office workers, shop assistants, and subordinate employees of the state. The largest number of sales and clerical employees were designated by the omnibus term *commis*, which is probably best rendered in English as "clerk." Men called *commis* ranged from the top to the bottom of the sales and clerical category: from sons of opulent merchants who would one day become partners or inherit their fathers' firms and fortunes to the most menial shop assistants. Many others were called by the equally vague term *employé*. Others had a bewildering variety of more specific occupational titles: traveling salesmen, cashiers, bailiffs, policemen, customs inspectors, employees of the *octroi* (a municipal tax levied on food and other consumption goods), school teachers, and many others.

But in spite of their wide variety, sales and clerical employees had certain characteristics in common. On the one hand, as subordinate salaried employees they were distinct from the professionals, merchants, and small businessmen who were their employers. On the other hand, their jobs required them to read, write, and calculate fluently, at a time when these skills were still relatively scarce in the population at large. Their command and everyday exercise of these symbolic arts gave even the poorest-paid sales and clerical employees a presumptive claim to bourgeois status, and they typically marked this status by their dress, their manners, and their language – proper French, rather than the local dialect of Provençal, which was still the everyday language of most workers as late as the 1840s. All of this is summed up in an ironic portrait of the bourgeois youth of the 1820s, drawn by Victor Gelu, a local writer of Provençal songs.

From the age of 18, he wore spectacles, for style as much as for need. He was stiff, false, pretentious and sugared. His gaity was never expansive. He laughed only as one laughs in the sacristy. He never smoked, but he began to take snuff early . . . .

He was proud of his calligraphy and his orthography.... He had a narrow chest, a stooped back, fleshless arms, a thin voice, sunken cheeks, a pale complexion.... Because even at home he spoke only in French, which in his estimate was better than perfect, he believed himself a distinguished gentleman. Thus he never set foot in the old quarters of Marseille for fear of rubbing up against the populace. And thus he measured with superb disdain all those robust toilers of our old quarters, whose strong necks, vigorous arms, solid backs, brilliant health, confident regards, masculine voices, and joyous faces excited his envious pity. At the age of sixteen, he entered as a supernumary in one or another sales counter or office. There he vegetated on his leaden tail for his entire adulthood, until finally he was perhaps, promoted to the high dignity of bookkeeper.[2]

4. *Small businessmen.* This category is composed of working proprietors of small firms. The occupational title of most proprietors engaged in retail trade was *marchand*, usually qualified by a suffix indicating the kind of wares sold: *marchand de meubles* (furniture), *de papier* (paper), *de volailles* (poultry), etc. *Marchand* is probably best rendered in English not by its cognate "merchant," which usually implies large-scale wholesale trade of the sort carried on by a *négociant*, but by "shopkeeper." Included in the same category are owners of barber shops, of cafés and restaurants, of wine shops and taverns, and of hotels and lodging houses. Finally, the small-business category also includes working proprietors of small manufacturing establishments, commonly designated *fabricants* or *maîtres* with a suffix indicating the particular trade: for example, *fabricant de chaises* (manufacturer of chairs), or *maître menuisier* (master joiner). Most of these men were at once skilled workers engaged personally in the manufacture of commodities and shopkeepers who sold the commodities to their customers. The more prosperous *fabricants* might employ as many as ten or fifteen workers, whereas others might employ no one but themselves.

At the top of the small-business category, some of the men who called themselves *marchands* or *fabricants* may have been wealthier than some of the city's *négociants*, but most of them were rather small operators. The lifestyles of Marseille's small businessmen also doubtless covered a wide range, but were probably closer to artisan lifestyles than were those of clerical employees.[3] This was particularly true for those keepers of barbershops, wine shops, inns, cafés, and restaurants who catered to working-class clienteles, and for small manufacturers, who had usually passed through apprenticeships in their trades and commonly still labored in their workshops side by side with their employees.

5. *Artisans.* This category is composed of manual workers in various industries. The word artisan is ambiguous in its present usage and is sometimes taken to imply an independent or self-employed craftsman. In the nineteenth century, in both English and French, "artisan" meant any skilled craftsman – one who "exercised a mechanical art"[4] – whether as a self-employed proprietor or as a wage earner. The artisan category described here, however,

is meant to include only wage earners; proprietors belong in the small-business category. But this is easier said than done. On the marriage registers or *listes nominatives*, most proprietors in the artisan trades simply designated themselves by the name of the trade, leaving off the prefix indicating proprietorship. They called themselves *menuisier* (joiner) or *cordonnier* (shoemaker) rather than *maître menuisier* (master joiner) or *fabricant de chaussures* (shoe manufacturer). This poses a serious statistical problem in the attempt to distinguish wage earners from proprietors. Whenever possible, this problem will be approached by more or less plausible calculations. But at the same time, the lack of any clear linguistic marker dividing proprietors from wage earners was itself an important indication of how nineteenth-century Marseillais thought about the differences between masters and workers in the artisan trades. It implies that many masters and workers still identified themselves with a trade community that included both workers and masters rather than with opposing classes of proprietors and proletarians. This sense of common membership in a trade community is one aspect of the very strong cultural heritage from the corporate or guild system of the Old Regime that retained a powerful hold on French artisan trades in the nineteenth century.[5]

The majority of men in the artisan category were employed in the small-scale, highly skilled trades that produced most of Marseille's consumer goods. The variety of these trades is bewildering. There were food-processing trades: butchers, candy makers, brewers, and bakers. There were clothing trades such as shoemakers, stockingers, hatters, and tailors. There were metalworking trades (blacksmiths, locksmiths, cutlers, cooking-pot makers) and woodworking trades (coopers, cratemakers, turners, wheelrights, cabinet makers). There were the building trades (masons, carpenters, stonecutters, sawyers, painters, plasterers, joiners, paperhangers, glaziers, marblecutters) and the luxury trades (jewelers, watchmakers, gilders, tapestry weavers, goldsmiths, perfume makers, book binders). Nor are these conventional categories exhaustive; there were also rope makers, sail makers, printers, basket weavers, potters, brushmakers, and dozens of other more or less obscure specialties. The detailed occupational code used in this study, which recognized over one hundred sixty small-scale handicraft trades, was not sufficient to encompass the full variety of Marseille's skilled crafts, and scores of additional trades wound up in a miscellaneous artisan category.

In spite of their diversity, these handicraft trades had certain elements in common. Production was generally carried out in small workshops, where the master worked side by side with his employees. There was rarely any intermediary between the worker and the master – the scale was too small and the work too various to require foremen. With some exceptions, such as the tailoring and shoemaking trades discussed in Chapter 2, division of labor was rather rudimentary – a worker generally made his product from beginning to end, rather than carrying out a single routinized task. Under these relatively autonomous working conditions, each worker was expected to know his trade well and had to pass through two to four years of apprenticeship before becoming a full-fledged craftsman. Because it took time and training to acquire the requisite skills, wage levels in the handicraft trades were generally well above the wages of unskilled laborers. Most of these trades also had labor organizations of some sort, which helped to oversee apprenticeship, to protect workers from unscrupulous masters, and to maintain and occasionally improve the conditions of work and remuneration. These trades were, in short, structured communities, bound by a body of custom that was enforced, at least in part, by the collective organization of the workers.[6]

It is this combination of characteristics (skill, high wages, on-the-job autonomy, labor organizations) that defines artisans for the purpose of this study. By these criteria, certain occupations outside the small-scale handicraft trades belong in the artisan category. This was true of some occupations carried out in factories. The outstanding cases were the various metal trades practiced in the machine-construction factories that came to Marseille in the 1830s and 1840s. Most workers in the mechanical industry – mechanics, forge workers, foundry workers, iron casters, fitters, coppersmiths – labored in large factories that had an advanced division of labor and a sizable staff of foremen to coordinate the complex processes of fabrication. But in the days before assembly lines and interchangeable parts, the construction of machines required a very high level of skill, and the quality of the product depended above all on the finesse and dexterity of the workers. Although they were employed in factories, workers in the mechanical industry maintained typically artisan characteristics – personal responsibility for the quality of their product, high levels of skill, high wages, and strong labor organization. The same was true of workers in three other factory industries: tanning, bottle making, and ship building.

The artisan category also includes two trades practiced on the docks: packers and longshoremen. The longshoremen were not highly skilled, but they were the best-organized, best-paid, and all in all the most privileged and autonomous working-class occupation in the city. With the tacit cooperation of the municipal authorities, the longshoremen managed to keep their guild intact from the Old Regime right down to the 1860s, monopolizing all loading and unloading of ships and virtually excluding all but sons and relatives of longshoremen from their association. Furthermore, it was the longshoremen's society, not the shipowners or the merchants, that maintained discipline on the docks. The longshoremen were true aristocrats of labor. The packers, though less privileged than the longshoremen, were also among the best-paid and best-organized workers in Marseille. All these groups – the skilled factory workers and the less skilled but highly privileged dock workers – had far more in common with craftsmen working in small industry than with the unskilled laborers who worked in other factory and transportation trades.

6. *Service workers*. These were manual employees who were engaged not in the manufacture or transportation of goods, but in furnishing services of various kinds. The services purveyed varied widely – from shoeshining and haircutting, to cooking and serving food and drinks, to personal domestic service, to protective service. Service workers differed from both artisans and unskilled workers not only in the nature of the work they performed, but also in their social relations. Although both artisans and unskilled workers spent their days in contact with members of their own class and trade, service workers were in constant contact with the men and women they served, often men and women from higher strata of the population.

7. *Unskilled workers*. These were workers in industry and transportation who possessed few skills, made low wages, and lacked the collective organization of the artisans. Most unskilled workers simply called themselves *journaliers* (day laborers) rather than identifying the particular job they performed. This vague nomenclature brings out one of the most prominent characteristics of unskilled labor: its instability. Lacking specialized skills, unskilled laborers moved frequently from job to job without developing commitment to any particular occupation. In addition to *journaliers*, there were a number of more specific occupations that belong in the unskilled category. These include four factory trades (soap makers, sugar refiners, oil-pressing workers, and chemical workers), transportation workers (carters, wagon drivers, and loaders), ditch diggers, and an assortment of other occupations – well diggers, street sweepers, woodcutters, quarrymen, and the like. These trades varied appreciably in both skill and wages, but on the whole they were distinctly inferior to the highly skilled and well-organized trades in the artisan category.

8. *Maritime workers*. This category includes sailors, fishermen, small boatsmen of various sorts, and other miscellaneous seagoing occupations. All were manual workers, but because their working hours were spent at sea, they had relatively little contact with the rest of the working-class world.

9. *Agriculturalists*. This category includes both working proprietors and wage laborers, both of which are usually designated in the sources by the single title of cultivator *(cultivateur)*, although occasionally there are titles indicating land ownership *(cultivateur-propriétaire)* or wage-earning status *(journalier-cultivateur, valet de ferme)*. The agricultural category also includes some more specialized occupations, such as gardeners, wine growers, and shepherds.

10. *Miscellaneous workers*. This small residual category contains occupations that are either extremely obscure or simply fail to fit into any other category – such as peddlers, soldiers, rag pickers, and the like.

Women's occupations

The labor force of nineteenth-century Marseille had a sizable feminine component. However, the social significance of women's work was very different from that of men's work.[7] The social status of a household was determined essentially by the occupation of its male head, whereas the work of its female members was seen above all as supplementary income. This difference was marked clearly by women's wage rates. At midcentury, women's wages rarely rose above 1.25 francs a day even for skilled work, at a time when unskilled males usually made at least 2 francs and skilled males at least 3 francs a day.[8] Women's occupations were also heavily concentrated in a few traditionally feminine industries: above all, domestic service and the needle trades in Marseille, but also textiles in cities that had more important textile industries. Furthermore, women's commitment to the labor force was characteristically much less permanent than men's. Except in relatively opulent families, where women generally did not work at all, women moved in and out of the labor force according to need and circumstance. They generally worked before marriage and were employed after marriage when necessity compelled it, although work after marriage was usually of a sort that could be done at home and therefore could be combined with housekeeping tasks.

Because of the subordinate cultural and social significance of women's work, statistics for women's occupations are generally much rarer and poorer than for men's occupations. Women's occupations were collected only partially in the census of 1851 and were entirely omitted from the marriage registers of 1821–2. However, both the census of 1851 and the marriage registers of 1846–51 and 1869 contain enough information to describe this significant portion of Marseille's labor force and to divide female occupations into several distinct categories. The following paragraphs define and sketch in the contents of the occupational categories of Marseille's female work force.

1. *Rentières.* It was quite common for women from wealthy families to have property or *rentes* of their own, often bestowed on them either by their fathers or, in the case of widows, by their late husbands. These women are designated in the marriage registers and *listes nominatives* as rentières or *propriétaires*, or occasionally as *pensionaires*. Even more than among their male counterparts, the fortunes and social statuses of these women varied widely, from the proud and opulent matron to the poor widow eking out her existence on a pension.

2. *Businesswomen and professionals.* Few prosperous women, whether married or single, actually worked for a living. There were, however, a small number of women who exercised occupations of a distinctly bourgeois character. Most common were professionals: teachers, actresses, nurses, and mid-

wives. There were also a number of female *négociantes* and a few clerks. But these respectable career women were a rarity in nineteenth-century France.

3. *Small businesswomen.* Some of the women in this category were simply the female counterparts of the male shopkeepers; indeed, some probably inherited their businesses from their husbands. But although Marseille's small businesswomen included proprietors of all sorts of commercial establishments, they were especially concentrated in retailing food and cloth, and in keeping cafés, restaurants, inns, and lodging houses – specialties that fitted with conventional feminine role definitions. The female small-business category also differs from the male small-business category in another respect: It includes both proprietors and hired saleswomen. The reason for this is that the distinction was extremely unclear among women working in retail trade. Some women were specifically designated as *revendeuses* (sellers), but some of them may have been self-employed hawkers rather than employees of some larger establishment. Likewise, many of the *marchandes*, particularly in food retailing, were also probably hawkers with essentially no capital and with very low incomes. There were also a large number of women whose occupational titles clearly indicate ambulatory hawking rather than ownership of a small shop – *partisannes, colporteurs, marchandes ambulantes.* In short, the feminine small-business category includes a number of very small operators and some employees of larger operators, as well as a few relatively comfortable, more heavily capitalized shopowners who differed from males in the small-business category only in their sex.

4. *Needle-trade workers.* These were everywhere among the largest employers of female labor in nineteenth-century Europe.[9] The omnibus occupational title was *couturière*, probably best translated as seamstress, but there were also tailors, waistcoat makers, lingerie makers, milliners, and embroiderers. Many, perhaps most, of these women worked at home, either on their own account or under contract with a putter out, but some carried on their trades in small workshops.

5. *Other craft workers.* Besides the needle trades, Marseille's women were also employed in a number of other handicraft occupations. Some were employed at subordinate tasks – at lower salaries – in trades dominated by men. Others were employed in distinctly feminine trades, for example, cigar makers, straw plaiters, and lace makers.

6. *Laundresses.* A large number of women worked in this traditionally feminine specialty, often in their own homes, both as washerwomen and as pressers.

7. *Domestic servants.* These were women who performed various domestic chores, normally living in the household where they served. Besides room and board they usually received a very small money wage. The largest number were simply called domestics, but there were also cooks, maids, housekeepers, and caretakers.[10]

8. *Unskilled workers.* These were women whose occupational titles indicated no skilled specialty. Most were simply called *journalières* (day laborers), but there were also *femmes de peine* (literally, women of pain), *ouvrière*, (workers), and *porteuses* (carriers).

9. *Agriculturalists.* Most of these were called cultivators *(cultivatrices)*, but there were also peasants, gardeners, shepherdesses, etc.

10. *Miscellaneous workers.* This small residual category includes a variety of trades that fit into none of the other categories. Of these the largest and most important were prostitutes, generally denominated *filles soumises.*

Marseille's occupational distribution: men

How were these various occupations distributed in the population of Marseille, and how did the distribution change over time? Information on occupations is fullest for the middle of the nineteenth century, where data exist from both marriage registers and the census.[11] It therefore seems best to begin with the midcentury and then work back and forward. The distributions of male occupations derived from the census of 1851 and from the marriage registers of 1846–51 are given in Table 3.1. The figures presented in this table include two statistical adjustments that require some discussion. First, as was mentioned earlier in this chapter, relatively few of the proprietors of small-scale handicraft firms indicated that they were proprietors when giving their occupations to the officers of the *état civil* and the census. These proprietors belong in the small-business category, but because their occupational designations do not distinguish them from workers, they fall into the artisan category instead. It is possible, however, to estimate the number of men who are thus miscategorized. The "Enquête sur le travail industriel et agricole" (Inquiry on industrial and agricultural labor), a detailed survey made by Marseille's Chamber of Commerce under the auspices of the National Assembly in 1848, gives figures indicating a ratio of workers to masters of 5.2 to 1 in the handicraft trades of Marseille in this year.[12] By applying this ratio to the *listes nominatives* and marriage-register samples, we can generate an estimate of the number of self-designated artisans who were actually employers rather than workers. (The logic of this estimation procedure and the resulting calculations are provided in Appendix C.) The figures given in Table 3.1 for small businessmen and for artisans therefore include both the original unadjusted figures and adjusted figures that reclassify a certain number of men from the artisan to the small-business category. The adjusted figures are given in italics.

Table 3.1 also includes another correction. As explained in Appendix A, there is good reason to believe that about 3,000 inhabitants of rooming houses or hotels were missing from the *listes nominatives* preserved in the municipal archives. Table 3.1 takes into account the probable occupational distribution

Table 3.1. *Male occupational structure, census of 1851 and marriage registers of 1846–51 (corrected figures in italics)*

Occupational category	Census					Marriage Registers	
	1. No. cases in sample	2. Percentage of adult male population	3. Missing cases estimated	4. No. of cases suggested	5. Percentage of augmented adult male population	6. No. cases	7. Percentage of cases
1. Business and professional	327	5.5	16	343	5.5	151	5.1
2. Rentier	261	4.4	9	270	4.3	77	2.6
3. Sales and clerical	558	9.4	26	584	9.4	289	9.7
4. Small business	466	7.9	13	499	7.7	218	7.3
4a. Small business, corrected	*696*	*11.8*	*23*	*719*	*11.6*	*368*	*12.3*
5. Artisan	2,170	36.6	107	2,277	36.6	1,361	45.5
5a. Artisan, corrected	*1,940*	*32.7*	*97*	*2,038*	*32.7*	*1,211*	*40.3*
6. Service	205	3.5	11	216	3.5	86	2.9
7. Unskilled	1,051	17.7	73	1,114	18.0	416	13.9
8. Maritime	319	5.4	21	340	5.5	145	4.9
9. Agriculture	446	7.5	7	453	7.2	201	6.7
10. Miscellaneous	125	2.1	17	142	2.3	42	1.4
Total	5,928	100.0	300	6,228	100.0	2,986	100.0

Table 3.2. *Itinerancy by occupation, men*

Occupational category	Percentage itinerant, unadjusted	Percentage itinerant, adjusted
1. Business and professional	12.9	17.0
2. Rentier	8.5	11.6
3. Sales and clerical	13.1	17.0
4. Small business	7.7	10.2
5. Artisan	13.6	17.8
6. Service	14.6	19.1
7. Unskilled	19.6	25.0
8. Maritime	18.6	23.8
9. Agriculture	4.2	5.8
10. Miscellaneous	8.8	11.8
All categories	13.1	17.1

of these itinerant males who are presumed to be missing from the *listes nominatives*. This adjustment is made by assuming that 300 itinerant males are missing from the 10 percent *listes nominatives* sample (corresponding to 3,000 missing from the entire *listes*). The further assumption is made that the 800 men in the *listes nominatives* sample who were living alone in rooming houses or hotels had the same occupational distribution as the 300 who were missing. This is a speculative assumption, but it seems more plausible than any alternative. On the basis of this assumption, the 300 missing cases (column 3) are apportioned among the ten occupational categories, and the resulting adjusted totals (column 4) are expressed as percentages (column 5). As can readily be seen from an examination of Table 3.1, this correction does not change the figures drastically. The main differences are a slight rise in the percentage of unskilled workers and a slight fall in the percentages of small businessmen and agriculturalists.

These adjusted totals can also be used to make an estimate of the proportion of itinerants in each occupational category. Table 3.2 gives estimates of these proportions, using both unadjusted and adjusted figures. The unadjusted figures show an itinerancy rate of 13.1 percent for the adult male population as a whole, and the adjusted figures yield a rate of 17.1 percent. Not surprisingly, itinerancy seems to have been particularly common among unskilled workers and maritime workers, and was particularly rare among agriculturalists, small businessmen, and rentiers. The remaining occupational categories were very close to the overall average.

The marriage registers of 1846–51 and the 10 percent sample of the *listes nominatives* constitute samples of different populations. The marriage registers certainly do not faithfully represent the population at large, and the unadjusted census figures, although far more comprehensive, are incomplete.

The adjusted census figures are probably the best estimate of the actual occupational structure of Marseille at midcentury. The occupational distribution yielded by the census of 1851 and the marriage registers of 1846–51 are different in several respects, as an examination of columns 2, 5, and 7 in Table 3.1 will show. The most striking difference is in the artisan category, which accounts for 40.3 percent of the men on the marriage registers, as against 32.7 percent in the augmented census estimate. On the other hand, the census estimate yields notably higher percentages for unskilled workers and rentiers, and marginally higher figures for most other categories.

One can think of plausible explanations for some of these differences. Occupational groups whose members tended to be relatively old should be underrepresented in the marriage-register sample. Because the mean age for all employed males in the census sample was 37.6, it is not surprising that rentiers (mean age 54.8), businessmen and professionals (mean age 43.2), agriculturalists (mean age 41.7), and small businessmen (mean age 41.4) appear more commonly on the *listes nominatives* than on the marriage registers. It might also be argued that the high rates of itinerancy among unskilled workers caused many of them to escape the marriage-register sample. Similarly, maritime workers, who also had high rates of itinerancy, were more common on the *listes nominatives* than on the marriage registers. These two factors might also help to account for some of the surplus of artisans in the marriage registers. Artisans were relatively young (mean age 34.9) and their rate of itinerancy was relatively low, so it follows that they should be somewhat more common on the marriage registers than on the *listes nominatives*. But in the case of artisans it is hard to see how these factors could account for all the large difference that actually occurs, and one must consequently maintain a healthy skepticism about both estimates. This simply points up again that neither the marriage registers nor the census can give more than an approximate estimate of Marseille's occupational distribution.

In spite of the differences between the figures drawn from the two sources of data, the general outlines of the occupational structure of mid-nineteenth-century Marseille are clear. In the first place, Marseille was a predominantly working-class city. According to the marriage-register estimates, 62.2 percent of the adult male population were manual workers, and the augmented census estimates give a very similar figure of 59.7 percent. Of these workers, a clear majority were artisans, although the two estimates disagree on the extent to which artisans outnumbered other workers. There were about half as many bourgeois as workers: Nonmanual occupations accounted for 29.7 percent in the marriage-register estimates and 30.8 percent in the adjusted census estimates.[13] Of these, the vast majority were shopkeepers and sales and clerical employees, whereas the elite of businessmen, professionals, and rentiers accounted for fewer than 10 percent of all adult males and fewer than a third of the bourgeois. Finally, about 7 percent of Marseille's men were engaged

Table 3.3. *Male occupational structure, marriage registers (corrected figures in italics)*

Occupational category	1821–2		1846–51		1869	
	No. cases	Percentage	No. cases	Percentage	No. cases	Percentage
1. Business and professional	95	5.7	151	5.1	131	6.1
2. Rentier	37	2.2	77	2.6	35	1.6
3. Sales and clerical	141	8.4	289	9.7	329	15.2
4. Small business	105	6.3	218	7.3	162	7.5
4a. Small business, corrected	*189*	*11.3*	*368*	*12.3*	*245*	*11.4*
5. Artisan	755	45.1	1,361	45.5	841	39.0
5a. Artisan corrected	*671*	*40.1*	*1,211*	*40.5*	*758*	*35.1*
6. Service	23	1.4	86	2.9	118	5.5
7. Unskilled	152	9.1	416	13.9	302	14.0
8. Maritime	122	7.3	145	4.9	116	5.4
9. Agriculture	220	13.1	201	6.7	111	5.1
10. Miscellaneous	24	1.4	42	1.4	13	0.6
Total	1,674	100.0	2,986	100.0	2,158	100.0

in agriculture, and another 2 percent or so were engaged in miscellaneous, unclassifiable occupations.

How did the occupational distribution change in the half-century covered by this study? This question can be approached by comparing figures derived from the marriage registers of 1821–2 and 1869 with the figures from 1846–51. The occupational distributions from all three sample periods are given in Table 3.3. As was the case for the 1846–51 marriage registers, the 1821–2 and 1869 small-businessmen and artisan categories have been adjusted to compensate for errors of classification, with adjusted figures given in italics. (For a discussion of the calculations by which these figures were derived, see Appendix C.) Table 3.3 reveals several important changes in the distribution of occupations: rises in the proportions of sales and clerical employees, unskilled workers, and service workers; and declines in rentiers, artisans, maritime workers, and agriculturalists. All these changes, as was remarked at the outset of this chapter, were precisely what should be expected in an industrializing economy and society.

One of the most striking changes in these figures was the decline in agriculturalists, who accounted for 13.1 percent of the grooms in 1821–2, but

Table 3.4. *Male occupational structure, marriage registers; agriculture excluded (in percent; corrected figures in italics)*

Occupational category	1821–2	1846–51	1869
1. Business and professional	6.5	5.4	6.4
2. Rentier	2.5	2.8	1.7
3. Sales and clerical	9.7	10.4	16.1
4. Small business	7.2	7.8	7.9
4a. Small business, corrected	*13.0*	*13.2*	*12.0*
5. Artisan	51.9	48.9	41.1
5a. Artisan, corrected	*46.1*	*43.5*	*37.0*
6. Service	1.6	3.1	5.7
7. Unskilled	10.5	14.9	14.8
8. Maritime	8.4	5.2	5.7
9. Miscellaneous	1.7	1.5	0.6
Total	100.0	100.0	100.0
Number of cases	1,454	2,785	2,047

only 6.7 percent in 1846–51 and only 5.1 percent in 1869. This change, however, does not reveal much about the transformations taking place in urban society. The commune of Marseille included not only the city proper, but a significant area of agricultural land as well, so that occupational figures given in Table 3.3 include both an urban and a rural component. As the city grew in the course of the nineteenth century, the rural component of the commune of Marseille shrank and the urban component expanded. Thus, the declining proportion of agriculturalists was due less to changes in the nature of the urban economy and social structure than to the urban population progressively crowding the rural population out of the commune.

To discern changes taking place within the urban sector, it is preferable to exclude the shrinking rural sector altogether and examine the occupational distribution of the nonagricultural population. This is done in Table 3.4. Here the trends in the occupational structure stand out clearly. Between 1821–2 and 1846–51, the main changes were a slight decline in the proportion of artisans, a sharper decline in the proportion of maritime workers, and a rise in the proportion of unskilled workers and service workers. From midcentury to 1869, there was an accelerated decline in the proportion of artisans, a drop in the proportion of rentiers, a continued rise in the proportion of service workers, and a sharp rise in the proportion of sales and clerical employees. The period before the great economic and political crisis of 1848–51 was marked principally by the industrial revolution of the 1830s and 1840s, which reduced the relative weight of the maritime sector and greatly increased the number of unskilled laborers working in factories. The years of the Second Empire were marked above all by the changes in the nature of business organization, which we have dubbed a "commercial revolution." These

Table 3.5. *Occupational distribution, subcategories, marriage registers; agriculture excluded (in percent)*

Occupation	1821–2	1846–51	1869
Merchant	2.3	2.0	2.5
Ship captain	1.0	0.9	0.7
Other business	0.3	0.4	1.3
Military officer	1.6	0.6	0.1
Professional	1.4	1.5	1.7
Rentier	2.5	2.8	1.7
Total elite	*9.0*	*8.2*	*8.1*
State employee	3.8	4.5	4.5
Private employee	5.9	5.9	11.5
Total sales and clerical	*9.7*	*10.4*	*16.1*
Industry	7.0	6.8	5.2
Commerce	2.9	3.1	3.1
Service	3.1	3.4	3.6
Total small business	*13.0*	*13.2*	*12.0*
Dock workers	6.4	3.7	2.9
Factory workers	4.4	6.2	8.1
Building-trades workers	8.4	10.7	7.8
Small craft workers	27.0	22.9	18.3
Total artisan	*46.1*	*43.5*	*37.0*
Coachmen	0.6	1.3	2.5
Cooks and waiters	0.5	0.6	1.7
Miscellaneous service workers	0.6	1.1	1.5
Total service	*1.6*	*3.1*	*5.7*
Journaliers	3.4	7.1	9.3
Factory workers	3.5	2.3	0.2
Transportation workers	2.0	3.8	3.8
Miscellaneous unskilled workers	1.5	1.7	1.5
Total unskilled	*10.5*	*14.9*	*14.8*
Seamen	6.5	4.1	4.3
Fishermen	1.7	0.7	0.7
Miscellaneous maritime workers	0.3	0.4	0.6
Total maritime	*8.4*	*5.2*	*5.7*

changes greatly inflated the number of clerical employees. Finally, the entire five decades were marked by a rapid increase in the proportion of service workers – a familiar feature of traditional societies undergoing substantial increases in wealth – and by a slow decline in the relative importance of the artisan sector.

The nature and timing of these changes in Marseille's occupational structure can be discerned more clearly when these larger occupational categories are divided into their component parts. This is done in Table 3.5.

A *changing elite*

Between 1821–2 and 1846–51, there was only one notable change in the composition of Marseille's elite: a sharp decline in the proportion of military officers, which accounted for all the elite's overall decline from 9.0 percent to 8.2 percent of the male work force. The abundance of military officers in 1821–2 was probably an aftermath of the Napoleonic wars, during which a huge number of officers had been commissioned. One also suspects that many of the officers living in Marseille were actually on military pensions rather than on active duty and that by 1821–2 their military titles were more honorific than real. In any case, the proportion of officers had declined precipitously by 1846–51 and was destined to sink even lower by 1869. Except for military officers, however, the composition of Marseille's elite was remarkably stable during this period. Merchants and rentiers were the dominant groups, with professionals and ship captains of intermediate importance; other business occupations were relatively rare.

During the Second Empire, the composition of the elite changed far more dramatically and a more "modern" elite emerged. The traditional elite occupations of rentiers and military officers declined sharply, whereas the proportion of ship captains declined slightly. On the other hand, the proportion of merchants rose substantially and the proportion of men in other business occupations, especially brokers, agents, and executives of the great new shipping firms, rose dramatically. In 1821–2, business occupations (merchants, ship captains, and other businessmen) accounted for 39 percent of the elite category, and in 1846–51 they accounted for 40 percent; by 1869, they accounted for well over half (57 percent). At the same time, the composition of the business community was changed by the emergence of new forms of commercial organization. Maritime commerce continued to be the dominant activity of Marseille's businessmen, but it was carried on in a very different fashion in the era of joint-stock shipping companies. In the era of the sailing ship and ad-hoc partnerships, merchants and ship captains arranged their ventures with a minimum of intermediaries. During the Second Empire, the numerical importance of ship captains declined as ships became bigger and faster, and a host of intermediaries – both the bureaucracies of the joint-stock shipping companies and a swarm of brokers – inserted themselves between captain and merchant. The business community therefore became both larger and more differentiated as the scale of enterprise increased. Figures on the composition of Marseille's elite therefore underline the importance of the commercial revolution that took place during the Second Empire.

Sales and clerical *employees*

Figures on the proportion of sales and clerical employees also bear out the importance of the commercial revolution of the 1850s and 1860s. Between

1821–2 and 1846–51, sales and clerical employees working in the private sector were a constant proportion of the active male population at 5.9 percent. What increase took place in the category as a whole was confined to the public sector, where an increasingly bureaucratic state multiplied its legions of postmen, customs clerks, policemen, tax collectors, and office workers. But between 1846–51 and 1869, bureaucracy multiplied above all in the private sector. Sales and clerical employees in the private sector nearly doubled their proportion from 5.9 percent to 11.5 percent of the active male population, and sales and clerical employees as a whole rose to 16.1 percent of the work force, becoming the city's largest occupational category after the artisans. It is a commonplace of sociology that the middle classes of fully industrialized societies are numerically dominated by sales and clerical employees. Once again it was only during the 1850s and 1860s, with the proliferation of large-scale enterprises in shipping, in banking, and throughout the economy, that the bourgeoisie of Marseille began to take on a typically modern shape.

Small businessmen

The small-business category as a whole made up a virtually constant proportion of the population between 1821–2 and 1869, passing from 13.0 percent to 12.0 percent of the male work force. But there were significant changes in the components of the small-business category. The proportion of small-scale entrepreneurs in the manufacturing sector fell slowly from 7.0 percent of the work force in 1821–2 to 5.0 percent in 1869.[14] This is, of course, the other side of the declining numerical weight of the artisans. The proportion of retail shopkeepers remained essentially constant between 1821–2 and 1869. Partially compensating for the relative decline of small manufacturers was a rise of proprietors of service establishments. As the population became both wealthier and more mobile, demand for the services of hotels, restaurants, cafés, barber shops, wine shops, inns, and the like increased, and so did the number of their proprietors.

Artisans

Overall figures for artisans show a relatively slow decline from 1821–2 to 1846–51 and a much more rapid decline thereafter. However, these figures conceal some interesting variations within the category. It will be recalled that the artisan category includes not only workers in small-scale handicraft industries, but skilled factory workers and dock workers as well. The patterns of change in the latter groups differed substantially from the patterns in small-scale handicraft industry. Not surprisingly, factory artisans constituted a steadily increasing proportion of the work force, rising from 4.4 percent in 1821–2 to 6.2 percent in 1846–51 and 8.1 percent in 1869.[15] By contrast, the proportion of longshoremen and packers declined sharply between 1821–2 and 1846–51 and fell again by 1869, to less than half its initial level. The decline in the second period is not hard to explain, for the massive reorganization of work on the docks that took place in the 1860s made loading and unloading ships vastly more efficient. But the sharp decline between the 1820s and midcentury is initially puzzling, given the rapid increase in the port's traffic and the unrelenting and successful opposition of the powerful longshoremen's society to all labor-saving innovations on the docks. The picture is clarified when we take into account figures for carters, wagon drivers, and loaders, who are part of the unskilled-worker category. Unskilled transportation workers rose sharply from 2.0 percent of the male work force in 1821–2 to 3.8 percent in both 1846–51 and 1869. When unskilled transportation workers are combined with transportation workers in the artisan category, the result is a slow and regular decline, from 8.4 percent of the male work force in 1821–2 to 7.5 percent in 1846–51 and 6.7 percent in 1869. The sudden rise in the proportion of unskilled transportation workers between the 1820s and the midcentury seems to be accounted for mainly by a change in the division of labor between well-paid and highly organized longshoremen and ill-paid and unorganized carters, loaders, and wagon drivers. As the traffic of the port grew between the 1820s and 1840s, it appears that the longshoremen abandoned all auxiliary tasks to unskilled laborers and concentrated exclusively on the loading and unloading of ships – rather than increasing their numbers and threatening the solidity of their organization. The result was a sharp decline in the proportion of longshoremen in the population, a decline that was largely offset by a sharp rise in the proportion of unskilled transportation workers.

Of the remaining artisans, the building trades[16] also had a pattern of their own. The proportion of builders in the work force rose markedly from 1821–2 to 1846–51 and then declined to below the initial level by 1869.[17] In 1821–2 the city was just beginning its period of nineteenth-century growth, and the building industry was just emerging from the long slump of the revolutionary and Napoleonic era. But from the mid-1820s to the late 1840s, population grew at an unprecedented rate, and the building industry was therefore extraordinarily active. This presumably accounts for the large proportion of builders in 1846–51. The fall in the relative proportion of builders from midcentury to 1869 is harder to explain. Rapid population growth continued, and demand for housing therefore must have remained high. However, there were some changes in the organization and technology of the building industry – evident in the construction of large apartment buildings that lined the newly created thoroughfares of this period – and this larger scale of enterprise may have resulted in greater labor efficiency.

The rest of the artisan trades, which produced a vast array of consumer goods in hundreds of small workshops, had a far more regular pattern of change. The proportion of the work force in these trades declined steadily throughout this period, from 27.0 percent in 1821–2 to 22.9 percent in 1846–51 and 18.3 percent in 1869.[18] It is this sector, which comprised the largest portion of the artisan labor force from the beginning to the end of the period covered by this study, that one sees clearly the decline of handicrafts that is so familiar a feature of the economic and social history of nineteenth-century Europe. The slow and steady decline of the small-scale handicraft sector dominated the more fluctuating fortunes of other types of artisans, to bring the artisan category as a whole down from 46.1 percent of the work force in 1821–2 to 43.5 percent in 1846–51 and 37.0 percent in 1869. But important as this decline was, it is equally important to note that artisans remained the dominant element of the working-class population and by far the largest single occupational group in the city. Thus, in spite of all the economic changes that had occurred in the intervening half-century, Marseille's typical worker on the eve of the Commune was still an artisan.

Unskilled workers

Figures on the composition of the unskilled category are not very satisfactory; indeed, they are in some respects quite misleading. Most misleading are the figures for unskilled factory workers,[19] which show a decline from 3.5 to 2.3 percent between 1821–2 and 1846–51 and a virtual disappearance – down to 0.2 percent – by 1869. In fact, as is known from other sources, the number of unskilled factory workers was rising throughout this period. Apparently the proportion of factory workers who simply listed their occupation as *journalier* – rather than identifying the industry in which they worked – rose over time, until virtually all called themselves *journaliers* in 1869. This interpretation is consistent with the figures for *journaliers*, which rose from 3.4 percent of the male work force in 1821–2 to 7.1 percent in 1846–51 and 9.3 percent in 1869. It would seem to imply that workers in the soap, woolen, and sugar industries, who generally identified their specific occupations in the 1820s, had lost any sense of commitment to their particular jobs by the 1860s and come to think of themselves as general laborers. One might speculate that this apparent change in self-definition corresponded to greater job instability in these industries, but evidence to test this hypothesis is lacking.

Figures on unskilled transportation workers (carters, wagon drivers, loaders) are rather better. These figures, which have already been discussed above in connection with the longshoremen, show a rise from 2.0 percent of the male work force in 1821–2 to 3.8 percent in both 1846–51 and 1869. The proportion engaged in other miscellaneous but specifically identified unskilled jobs – quarrymen, road workers, masons' laborers, etc. – showed little tendency to change between the 1820s and the 1860s. The sum of the changes in all these subcategories was a sharp rise in the proportion of unskilled workers from 1821–2 to 1846–51 and essentially no change from then until 1869. At the same time, it is certain that the composition of the unskilled labor force changed over time, although these changes are not always reflected in the figures. The proportion of transportation workers certainly rose between the 1820s and midcentury, and the proportion of unskilled factory workers rose throughout the entire period. But what happened to other types of unskilled labor is far from certain. Did the proportion of semiemployed casual laborers rise or fall over time? If so, according to what rhythm? These questions cannot be answered with the data at hand. For that matter, neither the figures for the overall proportion of unskilled workers nor the pattern of change over time that they seem to reveal can be accepted uncritically. After all, the figures are based on marriage registers, and, to judge from the comparison of midcentury marriage registers with the census, they seem to underrepresent unskilled workers significantly. Unskilled workers were probably the least stable segment of the occupational structure, so measures based on the settled population can give only very tentative and uncertain estimates of their numbers and their evolution.

Service workers

In no category of the labor force was growth so steady or so spectacular as in the service trades. From only 1.6 percent of the male labor force in 1821–2, they increased to 3.1 percent in 1846–51 and 5.7 percent in 1869. Although the proportion in all types of service trades rose impressively, the rise was particularly steep for coachmen and stable boys, who increased fivefold from .5 to 2.5 percent of the labor force between 1821–2 and 1869. Nothing could attest more graphically to the growing wealth of Marseille's elite than these figures. But rises in other service trades were almost as impressive. Both the proportion of food-service workers and the proportion in other service trades, mainly guards, night watchmen and the like, nearly tripled. The increasing wealth of Marseille's population brought about a truly remarkable rise in all types of service occupations.

Maritime workers

The proportion of maritime workers in the labor force fell sharply from 1821–2 to 1846–51 and remained essentially stable from then until 1869. The drop took place among both seamen and fishermen, although it was particularly pronounced among fishermen. The decline of seamen took place in spite of extremely vigorous growth in maritime commerce. The decline was presumably due in part to the increasing role of foreign ships and sailors in Marseille's trade between the 1820s and 1850s, although it may also reflect some increase in labor efficiency in the shipping industry as the average size of ships grew. There was an increase, however, in the miscellaneous-maritime category, which included small-boatmen, pilots, maritime mechanics, etc. This would seem to indicate an increasing specialization and division of labor within the shipping industry. But, taken as a whole, the proportion of maritime workers in Marseille declined as the city's economy became less dominated by maritime commerce.

Marseille's occupational distribution: women

As has already been remarked, data for women's occupations are harder to find and poorer in quality than comparable data for men. Brides' occupations are recorded faithfully on the marriage registers of 1846–51 and 1869, but were omitted entirely in 1821 and 1822; this means that the discussion of changes in women's occupations is limited to the last two decades of the period covered in this study. In addition, the collection of information on women's occupations in the census of 1851 was somewhat irregular. Some of the census takers carefully transcribed the occupations of all women, whereas others took down occupations of fathers and sons but often left mothers' and daughters' occupations blank.[20] As a result, it is impossible to know with any exactitude what proportion of women worked for remuneration. The census figures indicate 42.6 percent of women over 17 as employed and 55.4 percent as not employed, but this clearly understates the proportion employed. By how much, it is impossible to know.

But, in spite of all their shortcomings, the census data tell a good deal about patterns of work in Marseille's female population. The first question they can help to answer is: Who worked and who did not? Employment varied sharply by marital status. According to the census figures, no less than 63 percent of unmarried women were employed, as against only 27.6 percent of married women.[21] Among widows, the proportion employed was intermediate, at 45 percent. Indeed, unmarried women made up a majority of all employed adult women, although only a third of the women over 17 were unmarried. For many women, marriage and childbearing brought an end to employment, and whereas the death of a husband often sent a woman back to work, an inheritance or the earnings of an adult son often spared them this burden. Employment also varied by age. Very few females are indicated as being employed before their middle teens, although many probably assisted mothers in their work. The highest rate of employment was for the 18-to-22-year-old group, of whom 53.1 percent were employed. Thereafter, the proportion employed fell gradually to under 20 percent for women over 73 (see Figure 3.1).

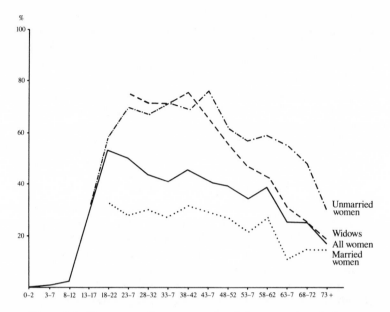

Figure 3.1. Percentage of women employed, by age and marital status.

The relationship between age and employment is complicated, however, by marital status. Because employment rates were much higher among unmarried than married women, much of the reason that the proportion of women employed fell after 18 to 22 was that higher proportions were married in the older age groups. If the relationship of age and employment is examined separately for married women, unmarried women, and widows, the picture is rather different (see Figure 3.1). Among married women, the proportion working was highest between 18 and 22 – probably because such a high percentage of these young wives had no children yet – but remained very near this peak level through the middle forties. For unmarried women, the percentage employed rose to around 70 percent in the 23-to-27 age group and remained at about that level until the middle forties, thereafter falling gradually to about 55 percent in the middle sixties and then plunging to just under 30 percent for the over-73 age group. Rates of employment were higher for young widows than for unmarried women; most of them had children to support, and their husbands, having died young, probably left them little by way of inheritance. But from the middle forties on, the proportion of widows who were employed plummeted, approaching the rates for married women in the over-73 age group. The most important factor in this dramatic fall was probably the age of the widows' sons – or sons-in-law – who by the time a woman had reached her fifties were usually old enough to support her.

These three curves seem to imply certain well-defined attitudes toward women's work, attitudes that applied to women of all marital statuses. First, they imply that employment generally was not very positively valued for women. Whereas most women were employed until they were married, most stopped once they had a husband to support them. Furthermore, not all of the unmarried women worked. The figures show that no fewer than a quarter of the unmarried women in their twenties, thirties, and forties chose idleness – or housework in their parents' or a relative's home – over remunerative employment. The employment patterns of widows are consistent with the same conclusion: Young widows worked, if necessary, to support their children, but once their children reached adulthood, the widows generally ceased to be employed and were supported by their sons. This is, of course, in the starkest contrast to work patterns and attitudes toward work for men. Labor was considered to be an inescapable duty for men among all but the very wealthiest classes of the population, and few men were rentiers or lived off someone else's earnings even among the aged.

These curves also imply a consistent set of attitudes about age and employment. Although employment was not really desirable for women of any age, it was far more acceptable at some ages than at others. This seems to be implied by two features of the employment-by-age curves of all three marital-status groups. First, for all marital-status groups, the percentage employed was stable at a high level from the twenties through the forties. Second, employment was something of a rarity for aged women, even in the unmarried group. The uniformity of the curves in this respect implies a commonly accepted age of adult vigor – the twenties, thirties, and forties – during which remunerative employment was acceptable if a woman or her family needed her income. But it appears that as old age approached, say between 50 and 65, women were supposed to be spared the burden of labor even if this imposed financial hardship. By contrast, a man of comparable age, in spite of the well-known fact that women of this age are generally far healthier than men, would be expected to continue to work full time to support his family.

What were the occupations of the women who did work for a living? As a glance at Table 3.6 will show, the census and the marriage registers give rather different answers. Both the census and marriage-register figures show the needle trades, domestic service, and unskilled labor as the largest categories at midcentury, but they do not agree on the relative importance of these occupational groups. Of course, the marriage-register figures give the occupations women had been exercising before marriage and therefore are in no way comparable to the overall census figures, which include married, unmarried, and widowed women. The closest fit to the marriage registers of 1846–51 should be the unmarried category in the census. A comparison of

Table 3.6. Occupations of women over 17, census and marriage registers (in percent)

Occupational category	Census, 1851					Marriage registers	
	1. Unmarried	2. Married	3. Widowed	4. Total	5. Mean age in years	6. 1846–51	7. 1869
Not employed	33.5	71.4	40.1	53.8	39.7	25.1	22.8
Rentière	2.8	1.0	15.0	3.6	54.6	2.2	0.7
Business and professional	1.3	0.4	3.0	1.1	44.6	0.6	0.8
Small business	4.0	5.9	10.6	5.9	41.7	6.0	5.8
Needle trades	15.5	6.9	7.3	9.9	32.6	28.7	31.8
Other crafts	3.2	2.3	3.1	2.7	34.6	5.6	3.4
Laundry	4.9	2.6	3.7	3.8	36.2	8.0	6.0
Domestic service	26.4	2.1	7.1	11.2	33.2	10.6	22.3
Unskilled	5.4	6.3	8.5	6.3	39.3	9.5	5.0
Agriculture	0.4	1.0	0.5	0.7	38.5	3.4	1.0
Miscellaneous	2.5	0.1	1.0	1.1	34.3	0.3	0.2
Total	99.9	100.0	99.9	100.1	38.6	100	99.8
Number of cases	2,250	3,348	926	6,524		3,107	2,230

these two sets of figures (columns 1 and 6 in Table 3.6) should therefore help to define the peculiarities of the census and marriage-register samples.

The proportion of women with no occupation listed was higher among unmarried women in the census than on the marriage registers of 1846–51. This difference presumably results from the omission of women's occupations by some of the census takers. The proportions of *rentières*, bourgeoises, domestic servants, and persons in miscellaneous occupations were appreciably higher in the census than in the marriage registers, and the proportion in the remaining occupations were appreciably higher in the marriage registers. The higher proportion of *rentières* in the census is probably due to never-married older women, and the higher proportion in miscellaneous occupations is accounted for primarily by nuns and prostitutes, who, like wealthy old maids, escaped the marriage registers altogether. The case of domestic servants is less obvious, because domestic servants could and did marry, although most of them ceased to work as domestics once they did. The difference between the census and marriage-register figures is large: Domestic servants made up 26.4 percent of the unmarried adult women in the census of 1851 but only 10.6 percent of the brides in the 1846–51 marriage registers. Conversely, the remaining occupational categories – small businesswomen, needle-trade workers, other craft workers, unskilled workers, and agriculturalists – made up a much higher proportion of the brides than of the unmarried women in the population. The question therefore becomes: Why did so few domestics find their way into Marseille's marriage registers?

The answer probably lies in the peculiar recruitment patterns of domestic service. Domestic servants came almost exclusively from outside the city.[22] A young woman from the countryside or a small town would contract to enter the service of a city family, which would in turn provide room and board and a small cash payment. Some young women used domestic service as an entry into urban life, eventually marrying city youths or moving on to better-paying and less restricting work in the needle trades or other urban industries. But many domestics stayed in the city only temporarily, saving up money for a dowry and returning to their natal towns or villages to marry and settle down.[23] Comparison of census and marriage registers seems to show that, at midcentury, somewhat more than half the city's domestics conformed to this latter pattern. As a result, they were counted by the census but did not appear in the marriage registers.

If the underrepresentation of domestics in the marriage-registers can be attributed to this factor, the comparison of unmarried women from the census with recent brides from the marriage registers shows no inexplicable differences between the two sets of figures. This seems to imply that neither is wildly inaccurate. The main error is probably a general underreporting of nonemployed women in the census. But because the working patterns of unmarried and married women were so different, and because so few of the

Table 3.7. *Occupations of employed women over 17,*
census of 1851

Occupational category	Percent of female work force
Rentière	7.8
Business and professional	2.4
Small business	12.7
Needle trades	21.5
Other crafts	5.9
Laundry	7.7
Domestic service	24.3
Unskilled	13.7
Agriculture	1.6
Miscellaneous	2.4

city's domestic servants ever found their way into the marriage registers, even flawed census data are preferable to data derived from marriage registers. Hence, the census totals reported in column 4 of Table 3.6 are surely the most accurate available description of the female occupational structure.

The shape of the women's occupational structure can be made clearer, however, by eliminating the nonemployed women and looking only at women whose occupations were listed. When this is done (see Table 3.7), domestic servants accounted for nearly a quarter of the employed women, and the needle-trade workers accounted for another fifth. Most of the remainder were manual workers, either unskilled laborers or laundresses, or workers in a wide variety of handicraft trades. There were also a significant number of women in small commerce, but, as mentioned above, many of these were employed hawking food in the markets and were hardly substantial businesswomen. The proportion of women working in occupations of a distinctly bourgeois character was thus extremely small – at most half of the small-business category together with those classified as bourgeoises, or fewer than 10 percent of all employed women and fewer than 5 percent of all adult women in the city. Their numbers were about equaled by *rentières*, some of whom certainly were relatively prosperous, but many of whom were probably living in straightened circumstances on small pensions. In short, women's employment in nineteenth-century Marseille was overwhelmingly plebian in character. Work was nearly always manual and was nearly always in distinctly feminine trades, where wages were generally half or less than half the prevailing level for men's occupations. And in the few occupations where women worked beside men – principally handicrafts – they were usually assigned to distinct and subordinate tasks and paid much less than their male counterparts. Women's work, although essential both to society and to the family economy, was thus separate from and inferior to men's work in nineteenth-century Marseille.

Changes in the women's occupational structure can be estimated only by comparing columns 6 and 7 of Table 3.6, which are drawn from the marriage registers of 1846–51 and 1869. The most striking change is in domestic servants, who rose from 10.6 to 22.3 percent of the brides. This may represent a real change in the proportion of domestic servants in the population – perfectly likely, given the rising figures for male service workers in this period. But it is also possible that some of the increase resulted from a change in the marriage patterns of domestic servants, with more staying on and marrying in Marseille rather than returning to their natal villages to settle down. Most of the other changes also ran parallel to changes in men's occupations. *Rentières* became an increasingly rare type among women, just as rentiers became increasingly rare among men. And the decline in agriculturalists was part of the progressive elimination of agriculture from the commune. Only the decline in female unskilled workers runs counter to the trend of male occupations.

Men and women combined

The male and female census totals from 1851 can be combined to arrive at an estimate of the occupational structure of the entire work force (see Table 3.8). According to this estimate, some 95,390 of a total population of 177,880 – or 53.6 percent of the entire population – were engaged in remunerated employment. Of these, fewer than one-third were women. Given the underreporting of women's occupations, the real figure was probably over a third, perhaps between 35 and 40 percent. The male and female work forces were differently distributed. Males made up a far higher proportion of the work force in the most lucrative and highest-status occupations – businesspersons and professionals and clerical and sales employees – and all the city's maritime workers were men. Women outnumbered men only in the service trades, although there were nearly as many *rentières* as rentiers. Men also made up a particularly high percentage of the persons reported as employed in agriculture, but from what is known about the division of labor in nineteenth-century French farming families, it seems certain that this is simply an error in reporting: Peasants' wives and daughters doubtless shared in the labor of their farms in rural Marseille just as they did elsewhere in the country. In the remaining categories – small businesspersons, artisans, and unskilled workers – women made up between 25 and 35 percent of the work force, or about the same as in the work force as a whole.

The occupational structure of the entire employed population differed from the male occupational structure in two important respects. First, the proportion of persons in positions of high status and authority was considerably smaller: The addition of women increases the relative importance of badly remunerated

Table 3.8. *Occupational structure of Marseille's work force, men and women over 17 combined; census of 1851*

Occupational category	Number of male workers[a]	Number of female workers	Total workers	Percentage of all workers
Rentier	278	235	513	5.3
Business, professional, sales, and clerical[b]	970	72	1,042	10.9
Small business	745	385	1,130	11.8
Artisan[c]	2,130	825	2,955	31.0
Service[d]	227	962	1,189	12.5
Unskilled	1,197	412	1,605	16.8
Maritime	362	—	362	3.8
Agriculture	460	49	509	5.3
Miscellaneous	159	71	230	2.4
Total	6,528	3,011	9,539	99.8

[a]Taken from Table 3.1, column 4, in this chapter.
[b]This includes male occupational categories 1 (business and professional) and 3 (sales and clerical) and female category 2 (business and professional).
[c]Includes female categories 4 (needle-trades) and 5 (other craft).
[d]Includes female categories 6 (laundry) and 8 (domestic service).

and subordinate positions. Second, the proportion of service workers was much higher, surpassing all but artisans and unskilled laborers in numbers. This makes clearer than ever the highly labor-intensive and hierarchical character of the world of work in nineteenth-century Marseille. It was a society where most of the population had to labor hard and obscurely to win their meager portion of bread, and where the prosperous were few and amply attended by a large population of servants. In this respect, Marseille in the nineteenth century, in spite of all the changes wrought by industrialization, rapid urban growth, and political revolution, remained very much in the traditional mold.

4 Occupational status

The relative status of occupations was occasionally mentioned in Chapter 3, but these discussions were never taken up systematically. The aim of this chapter is to determine as precisely as possible the relative standings of Marseille's male occupations and occupational categories and to see whether the standings changed significantly with changes in the occupational structure. The argument will be slightly more technical in this chapter than in the rest of the book, because construction of occupational-status scales involves the use of some elementary statistics. However, the statistical techniques will be explained as they are used, and even the totally uninitiated should be able to follow the argument.

The problem of occupational status has been a major preoccupation of recent sociology, and particularly of recent American sociology. There are many ways of measuring occupational status. Perhaps the most obvious method is to arrange occupations in order of the average wealth or income of their members. But in recent decades sociologists have generally preferred to use linear scales of occupational prestige, which are based on the rankings assigned to different occupations by respondents in nationwide surveys. Rankings done by different individuals or groups tend to be very similar, indicating that the prestige of occupations is highly stable and determinate in contemporary American society. Furthermore, prestige rankings of occupations correlate closely with rankings based on other criteria, such as average levels of wealth or education.[1]

As studies of social stratification in the American mode have proliferated in other countries, sociologists have also attempted to make cross-national comparisons of occupational rankings and to construct standard prestige scales that could be applied in all areas of the world. To historians, who tend to emphasize the peculiarities of different societies rather than their similarities, these efforts have met with surprising success. In the contemporary world, in both highly industrialized and relatively underdeveloped countries, the prestige attached to various occupations tends to be highly uniform.[2]

Historical research on occupational stratification has generally used somewhat cruder methods of ranking. Most commonly, occupations are simply arrayed arbitrarily into common-sense categories of varying complexity and plausibility, from a simple dichotomy between "white-collar" and "blue-collar" occupations to schemes that designate seven or eight separate strata.

74

The main alternative to common-sense schemes has been to rank occupations by average wealth, or income, or tax assessments. Work of this sort has been done successfully for a number of different societies and historical eras.[3] There have been few, if any, attempts to construct scales of occupational rank based on other criteria than material prosperity. The obvious reason for this is technical. Governments have long been diligent about assessing wealth in order to apportion taxes, and this has made it relatively easy to estimate wealth or income in past societies. But the survey techniques devised by contemporary sociologists cannot be applied to the dead, and other means of measuring such phenomena as occupational prestige or level of education have not been devised.

Construction of status scales

In fact, the marriage registers discussed and used in Chapter 3 contain three kinds of information that can be used to measure the status of occupations. First, when a couple married they were required to sign their names at the bottom of the marriage act if they were capable of doing so. By checking for the presence or absence of a signature, it is possible to determine whether the spouses were literate. In an age when illiteracy was not uncommon, being able to read and write was a significant resource, one that marked off its possessor from his or her illiterate fellows.[4] Literacy was an important qualification in the labor market; the most secure and lucrative careers usually required literacy, and literacy probably enhanced chances for advancement in any line of work. Literacy also enhanced a person's general social and political efficacy, for those who could read and write had access to a world that transcended face-to-face oral communities. In nineteenth-century Marseille this was a factor of particularly decisive importance. Marseille was a part of France, and the language of national politics and national culture was French. But at least until the middle of the century, the spoken language of the city's popular classes was a dialect of Provençal. Literacy, by definition, was in French; it alone was taught in the schools, and Provençal had essentially ceased to be a written language until it was reinvented by the literary movement known as the Provençal renaissance around the middle of the nineteenth century.[5] To be literate, therefore, meant to have command of the national language; to be illiterate often meant to have only a limited knowledge of French. At a time when Marseille was being drawn increasingly into the political and social life of the French nation, those who did not know French were significantly limited in their ability to understand and cope with their rapidly changing urban society. Linguistic dualism made literacy especially salient in Marseille. For this reason a ranking of occupations by the proportion of their members who could sign their marriage acts should be a particularly sensitive indicator of the occupation's social standing.

A second method of ranking occupations is a more direct measure of prestige. When a couple married, their marriage act had to be signed by four adult male witnesses. A marriage was an important social occasion, and witnesses were normally chosen with care. About one-tenth of the witnesses were relatives of one of the spouses (most commonly an uncle or a brother), the rest presumably being friends of the bride or groom or both. Because a wedding ceremony was, among other things, an occasion for displaying the social standing of the spouses and their families, the criterion for choosing witnesses was not merely closeness of friendship. In the first place, witnesses were usually considerably older than the spouses. In 1821–2, the median age of witnesses was 41, as against 27 for grooms and 24 for brides. In 1846–51 and 1869, the gap was less pronounced: 37 for witnesses, 30 for grooms, and 25 for brides in 1846–51; and 38 for witnesses, 30 for grooms, and 25 for brides in 1869. Witnesses not only tended to be older than the bride and groom, they also tended to be of higher social standing. Businessmen, professionals, and rentiers made up only 9 percent of the grooms in 1821–2, 1846–51, and 1869, but they made up 19 percent of the witnesses in each of these years. Men from these occupational categories, which were generally the richest in the city, were overrepresented among the witnesses by a margin of more than two to one in each of the periods for which data were collected. Conversely, unskilled workers, who were the most universally destitute occupational group in the population, made up 8 percent of the grooms in 1821–2, 13 percent in 1846–51, and 14 percent in 1869; but they made up only 3, 4, and 6 percent of the witnesses. In short, the bride and groom and their families tended to call upon friends or acquaintances of higher social status than themselves to act as witnesses at their weddings; furthermore, it seems reasonable to assume that they did so to enhance their own standing in the eyes of the community. If this assumption is true, then the ability of men in a given occupation to obtain businessmen, professionals, and rentiers as witnesses at their weddings should be a reliable measure of that occupation's own level of prestige. The second occupational ranking is based on this assumption.

The final method of ranking occupations makes use of data on the occupations of brides. In nineteenth-century France, it was a sign of status for a man's wife or daughter not to work. It was, in the first place, part of a respectable bourgeois life style. The bourgeois woman was not to be soiled by contact with the tawdry world of work; she was to manage the household and make her home a haven against the storms of the outside world.[6] Such, at least, was the ideal, and it seems fair to assume that nonemployed wives were a sign of at least pretensions to bourgeois respectability. It also indicated a certain level of financial success. A man's income had to be quite substantial for the family to forgo the earnings a wife or daughter could bring in; most families could not afford to keep their women out of the labor market, however much they might have desired the respectable life style it symbolized. On the whole, one can assume that men whose brides did not work for a living were of higher status than those whose brides had occupations. Whether or not a bride worked was, of course, primarily a measure of the status and life style of her father and his family, not of her husband. But it seems safe to assume that the status of the father and husband were generally similar, and even safer to assume that few young women who had been spared from work before marriage would begin work after marriage – it has already been shown that even many women who worked before marriage ceased to do so once they had a husband. In short, by determining the proportion of men in each occupation whose wives did not work, it is possible to generate a third ranking of occupations, this time measuring one salient element of a bourgeois life style and also indirectly measuring the wherewithal on which such a life style was based.

Before describing the scales generated by these three indicators of social status, some technical problems of scale construction should be discussed. The first problem is the large number and great disparity in size of the occupations practiced in Marseille. The marriage registers contain literally hundreds of distinct occupational titles, ranging from common occupations like shoemaking (*cordonnier*) to rare specialties like cartography (*cartographe*) and from very specific titles like carriage painter (*peintre en voitures*) to vague and general titles like clerk (*commis*) or laborer (*journalier*). The occupational code used in preparing the data for computer analysis recognized over 700 occupations, and even then some occupations had to be included in miscellaneous categories. From this very long list of titles a condensed list of 80 occupations has been devised. This list includes a separate entry for all the common occupations and groups the remaining ones into relatively homogeneous categories. A complete list of coded occupational titles, grouped into the 80 categories composing the condensed list of occupations, is given in Appendix B.

For the purpose of reliably estimating the status of an occupation, it is important that calculations be based on a sufficiently large number of cases. For example, if it is known that 30 out of a sample of 60 shoemakers could sign their names on their marriage acts, one can be much more confident that something like half the city's shoemakers were literate than if it is known that 2 out of a sample of 4 could do so. This is because the possibility that an observed proportion is due purely to chance factors is much greater when dealing with a very small sample than when dealing with a relatively large one. To limit the influence of random variation in the status measures, those occupations represented by fewer than 7 grooms in the marriage register samples were grouped into larger miscellaneous categories. This means that all the occupations for which status scores are calculated are represented by a minimum of 7 cases, and usually by considerably more than 7.[7] Applying this criterion to the data sets from 1821–2, 1846–51, and 1869 results in a different list of occupations for each. Due in part to differences in the number of cases in the three data sets, in part to chance variation in the incidence of marriage in a given occupation in a given year, and in part to real changes in the size of occupational groups over time, some occupations that appear in sufficient numbers in one data set are extremely rare in another. For the 1846–51 data set, the largest of the three, it was possible to calculate scores for 76 separate occupations; for 1869 the number of occupations had to be reduced to 65, and for 1821–2 to only 58.

A second problem to be solved in creating scales is that the characteristics on which each of the rankings is based varied over time. To take the most notable case, the proportion of grooms able to sign their marriage acts rose from 62 percent in 1821–2 to 86 percent in 1869. Variation across the years in the other status criteria is less striking, but is nevertheless present. This variation presents a serious problem, for the meaning of a given percentage score is different in one year than in another. An occupation with a literacy rate of 75 percent would be well above the norm in 1821–2, but well below the norm in 1869. What is needed to compare scores across years is a measure of the relative rather than the absolute positions of occupations with respect to the status criteria. The most convenient way of constructing such a measure is to perform the statistical procedure known as standardization. To standardize a distribution is to set its mean equal to 0 and its standard deviation equal to 1. All scores above the mean are then positive, and all below the mean are negative. In 1821–2 the literacy distribution for 58 occupations has a mean of 62 percent and a standard deviation of 28 percent. An occupation with a literacy rate of 34 percent in 1822 (that is, 62 percent minus 28 percent) would therefore have a standardized score of −1.00. Because the comparable literacy distribution for 1869 has a mean of 86 percent and a standard deviation of 14 percent, an occupation with a literacy rate of 72 percent in 1869 (that is, 86 percent minus 14 percent) would have a standardized score of −1.00. This indicates that the relative position of an occupation with a literacy rate of 34 percent in 1822 is the same as the relative position of an occupation with a literacy rate of 72 percent in 1869. Putting scales into standardized form not only makes it possible to make exact comparisons across the years; it also makes it possible to compare an occupation's standing on one status criterion to its standing on another. Because of the great convenience of being able to make such comparisons, all the occupational rankings are standardized.[8] To make them easier to read, they are then converted to numerical scores ranging from 0 to 100, with a mean of 50.[9]

The literacy scale is formed by tabulating the proportion of grooms in each occupation who could sign their names on their marriage acts and then converting these proportions to standardized numerical scores. In 1821–2, literacy rates ranged from 14 percent for fishermen to 100 percent for no fewer than

11 occupations. The mean literacy rate, as mentioned above, was 62 percent. In 1821–2, the distribution of literacy rates was spread rather evenly across the entire range of variation. By 1846–51, the mean literacy rate had risen to 75 percent and the bottom of the range, still represented by fishermen, had risen to 26 percent. Although the number of occupations with no illiterate grooms had remained essentially constant at 12, a much higher proportion of the cases were now clustered at the upper end of the range. By 1869, these trends had been accentuated. The mean had risen to 86 percent; the bottom of the range, although still occupied by fishermen, had finally risen to 59 percent; and by now nearly a third of the occupations had achieved 100 percent literacy.

The rankings generated from these data are presented in Table 4.1. Inspection of the results shows no great surprises: The upper end of the scale is dominated by bourgeois occupations, the middle by artisans, and the bottom by agricultural workers, sailors, fishermen, and unskilled laborers. The main defect of this scale is that it obviously distinguishes far better at the bottom of the social hierarchy than at the top, where a large number of occupations are piled together in the 100 percent literate category. Inspection of the ranking also reveals that there is a rather close correspondence between the ranks of occupations across the years. This observation can be given much greater precision by determining the coefficient of correlation between the scores of the three different time periods. The product-moment correlations were extremely high: .91 for 1821–2 and 1846–51, .89 for 1846–51 and 1869, and .89 for 1821–2 and 1869.[10] The statistical measure, then, confirms what inspection of the scores already makes apparent: Although the general level of education rose dramatically between 1821 and 1869, the relative literacy levels of different occupations changed only slightly.

Construction of the nonemployed bride scale is analogous in all respects. For each set of grooms with a given occupation, the proportion of their brides who were not employed (*sans profession*; *rentières* or *propriétaires*) was tabulated. Unfortunately, the occupation of brides was not stated in the marriage registers of 1821–2, so this scale could not be constructed for those years. In 1846–51, the mean proportion of nonemployed brides was 27 percent. The distribution ranged all the way from 0 percent (for shepherds, mine and quarry workers, woolen workers, and rope and sail makers) to 100 percent (for military officers, other businessmen, and medical and legal professionals). In 1869 the mean was 23 percent, and the range was still from zero (fishermen, shepherds, stonecutters, cabinetmakers, and ship caulkers) to 100 percent (legal professionals). In both years, the distributions were clustered toward the low end of the scale. As with the literacy scale, the raw percentages were converted to standardized scores with a mean of 50. The resulting rankings are given in Table 4.2. As will be clear from an inspection of the rankings, this scale differentiates better at the top of the status hierarchy than at the

Table 4.1. *Literacy scale*

1821–2		1846–51		1869	
Occupation	Score	Occupation	Score	Occupation	Score
Barber	64	Artistic professional	62	Artistic professional	60
Clerk	64	Clerk	62	Cabinetmaker	60
Customs clerk	64	Customs clerk	62	Café keeper	60
Jeweler, watchmaker	64	Hatter	62	Confectioner	60
Legal professional	64	Legal professional	62	Customs clerk	60
Merchant	64	State employee	62	Hatter	60
Medical professional	64	Medical professional	62	Housepainter	60
Military officer	64	Military officer	62	Jeweler, watchmaker	60
Other professional	64	Other professional	62	State employee	60
Printer	64	Other professional	62	Medical professional	60
Ship captain	64	Ship captain	62	Merchant	60
Small manufacturer	64	Small manufacturer	62	Octroi clerk	60
Woodworker	62	State official	62	Other professional	60
State official	62	Tapestry weaver	62	Printer	60
Shopkeeper	62	Merchant	61	Ship captain	60
Proprietor	62	Proprietor	61	Small manufacturer	60
Café keeper	62	Octroi clerk	60	State official	60
Octroi clerk	61	Barber	60	Stonecutter	60
Tailor	61	Cabinetmaker	60	Tapestry weaver	60
Joiner	60	Rentier	60	Wine shop keeper	60
Housepainter	59	Shopkeeper	60	Clerk	59
Coachman	59	Employee	60	Shopkeeper	58
Hatter	57	Jeweler, watchmaker	59	Joiner	58
Locksmith	56	Printer	59	Cook, waiter	58
Cabinetmaker	55	Light-metal worker	58	Proprietor	58

Occupation		Occupation		Occupation	
Cook, waiter	55	Packer	58	Employee	58
Miscellaneous service worker	55	Café keeper	58	Miscellaneous service worker	57
Soldier	55	Housepainter	58	Other businessman	57
Shoemaker	54	Crate maker	57	Butcher	57
Employee	54	Miscellaneous service worker	57	Woodworker	57
Packer	54	Tailor	57	Barber	57
Miscellaneous artisan	53	Joiner	56	Tailor	57
Baker	52	Locksmith	56	Locksmith	56
Cooper	52	Longshoreman	56	Miscellaneous artisan	55
Machinist	51	Peddler	56	Legal professional	54
Light-metal worker	51	Woodworker	56	Light-metal worker	54
Wine shop keeper	50	Caulker	55	Cooper	53
Crate maker	48	Wine shop keeper	54	Packer	53
Miscellaneous	48	Forge worker	54	Miscellaneous builder	52
Rope, sail maker	48	Miscellaneous artisan	54	Baker	52
Miscellaneous building worker	48	Machinist	54	Coachman	52
Longshoreman	47	Confectioner	53	Crate maker	51
Stonecutter	47	Baker	53	Caulker	51
Carpenter	46	Soldier	53	Stonemason	50
Gardener	46	Cook, waiter	52	Machinist	50
Stonemason	44	Butcher	52	Carpenter	47
Soap maker	43	Carpenter	51	Shoemaker	46
Caulker	43	Basket maker	51	Gardener	46
Tanner	42	Miscellaneous builder	50	Shepherd	46
Miscellaneous unskilled worker	42	Shepherd	50	Longshoreman	45
Seaman	42	Stonecutter	50	Forge worker	44
Peddler	40	Shoemaker	50	Miscellaneous unskilled worker	43
Sugar refiner	39	Turner	48	Tanner	42
Shepherd	39	Coachman	48	Miscellaneous maritime worker	42
Carter	38	Tanner	48	Rope, sail maker	40
Day laborer	37	Cooper	47	Wagon driver	40

Table 4.1. Literacy scale (cont.)

1821–2		1846–51		1869	
Occupation	Score	Occupation	Score	Occupation	Score
Cultivator	35	Miscellaneous unskilled worker	47	Seaman	37
Fisherman	32	Innkeeper	46	Day laborer	36
		Sugar refiner	45	Cultivator	34
		Rope, sail maker	44	Loader	32
		Stonemason	44	Miscellaneous	32
		Miscellaneous	44	Flour miller	31
		Woolen worker	43	Tile maker	29
		Loader	42	Carter	25
		Wagon driver	40	Fisherman	22
		Gardener	40		
		Seaman	39		
		Flour miller	38		
		Miscellaneous maritime worker	38		
		Day laborer	37		
		Tile maker	36		
		Carter	35		
		Soap maker	34		
		Miner	34		
		Cultivator	28		
		Fisherman	20		

Table 4.2. *Nonemployed-bride scale*

1846–51		1869	
Occupation	Score	Occupation	Score
Legal professional	79	Legal professional	80
Medical professional	79	Merchant	79
Military officer	79	Other professional	77
Other businessman	79	Other businessman	77
Merchant	78	Proprietor	77
Proprietor	75	Ship captain	72
Other professional	74	Medical professional	69
Rentier	73	Artistic professional	67
Ship captain	72	State official	67
State official	72	Jeweler, watchmaker	63
Innkeeper	63	Shopkeeper	62
Clerk	63	Clerk	59
Tapestry weaver	62	Employee	58
Employee	61	Confectioner	57
Shopkeeper	61	Café keeper	54
Artistic professional	60	Small manufacturer	52
Small manufacturer	60	Tapestry weaver	52
Wine shop keeper	57	Woodworker	51
Crate maker	57	Wine shop keeper	51
Jeweler, watchmaker	57	Hatter	51
Printer	55	Crate maker	50
Packer	54	Cooper	49
Barber	53	Housepainter	49
Woodworker	53	Packer	49
Longshoreman	53	Joiner	48
Hatter	52	Longshoreman	48
Caulker	51	Machinist	48
Café keeper	51	Locksmith	48
Confectioner	51	Light-metal worker	48
Cabinetmaker	50	Tailor	47
Stonecutter	50	Miscellaneous builder	47
Machinist	50	Butcher	47
Housepainter	49	Loader	47
State employee	49	Cook, waiter	47
Miscellaneous	49	Octroi clerk	47
Peddler	49	Rope, sail maker	47
Soldier	48	Miscellaneous artisan	46
Miscellaneous unskilled worker	48	Tile maker	46
Butcher	48	Barber	46
Turner	48	State employee	46
Cooper	47	Printer	45
Miscellaneous artisan	47	Miscellaneous service worker	45

Table 4.2. (cont.) *Nonemployed-bride scale*

1846–51		1869	
Occupation	Score	Occupation	Score
Baker	47	Forge worker	45
Sugar refiner	47	Miscellaneous maritime	
Miscellaneous service		worker	44
worker	47	Miscellaneous	44
Locksmith	47	Customs clerk	44
Customs clerk	46	Wagon driver	44
Joiner	46	Flour miller	44
Miscellaneous builder	46	Baker	44
Tile maker	46	Tanner	44
Cook, waiter	46	Carpenter	43
Fisherman	46	Miscellaneous unskilled	
Basket maker	45	worker	43
Tailor	45	Stonemason	43
Stonemason	45	Gardener	43
Tanner	44	Seaman	43
Seaman	44	Cultivator	43
Shoemaker	44	Coachman	43
Light-metal worker	44	Shoemaker	42
Forge worker	43	Carter	42
Loader	43	Day laborer	42
Carpenter	43	Cabinetmaker	41
Wagon driver	43	Caulker	41
Octroi clerk	43	Fisherman	41
Cultivator	43	Shepherd	41
Flour miller	42	Stonecutter	41
Gardener	42		
Carter	42		
Coachman	41		
Day laborer	41		
Soap maker	41		
Miner	39		
Rope, sail maker	39		
Shepherd	39		
Woolen worker	39		

bottom. Once again, the rankings are very similar across the years: The correlation coefficient is .96, even higher than the coefficient for the literacy scale. The bride's lack of employment appears to be a highly stable indicator of social status.

Construction of the prestige scale was slightly more complicated than that of the literacy and nonemployed-bride scales. Rather than calculating the proportion of all business, professional, and rentier witnesses at weddings of men in a given occupation, their proportion has been calculated separately for first, second, third, and fourth witnesses. These four scales were standardized in the usual way and then summed and restandardized to form the final prestige scale. This seemingly complex procedure was chosen over the more direct method because it was much more convenient to perform by computer, given the packaged programs available at the time it was carried out. The two alternative methods would, of course, produce virtually identical results. The mean proportion of witnesses who were professionals, businessmen, or rentiers was constant at 19 percent in 1821–2, 1846–51, and 1869, and the ranges of the distributions were broad in every year. At the bottom in 1821–2 were peddlers, stonecutters, and housepainters with 0 percent; in 1846–51 woolen workers with 2 percent; and in 1869 loaders with 4 percent. Legal professionals were alone at the top in each distribution: Their proportion of elite witnesses was 84 percent in 1821–2, 95 percent in 1846–51, and 85 percent in 1869. The rankings generated by this scale are presented in Table 4.3. Even more than the nonemployed-bride scale, the prestige ranking differentiates better at the top of the hierarchy than at the bottom, where many occupations have relatively similar scores. Once again, the interyear correlations are extremely high: .95 for 1821–2 and 1846–51, .95 for 1846–51 and 1869, and .92 for 1821–2 and 1869. As with the other rankings, this scale also seems to measure a highly stable dimension of occupational status.

The attempt to generate three status rankings of Marseille's occupations has clearly succeeded: The high correlation of the rankings across the years seems to indicate that each scale measures a stable dimension of occupational status. But how closely were these dimensions related to each other? Should the three types of scales be considered independent measures of a unified status hierarchy? And if so, might they be combined into a single summary occupational-status scale? These questions can conveniently be approached by measuring the intercorrelations of the different scales. In the case of the nonemployed-bride and prestige scales, the correlation coefficients are once again extremely high: .90 in 1846–51 and .93 in 1869. The correlations between nonemployed-bride and literacy scales are more moderate: .66 in 1846–51 and .57 in 1869. Between literacy and prestige, the correlations are slightly lower but still substantial: .55 in 1821–2, .45 in 1846–51, and .42 in 1869.

How should these results be interpreted? The prestige and nonemployed-bride scales are so highly correlated that it seems reasonable to assert that they measure essentially the same underlying status hierarchy. But the correlations of these two scales with the literacy scale is of a much lower order. Here two hypotheses present themselves. The most obvious one is that the literacy scale measures a distinct but related dimension of occupational status. The alternative hypothesis is more complex, but no less plausible. It has been noted that the literacy scale distinguished rank better at the bottom of its range than at the top, where a sizable number of occupations had literacy rates either at or very close to 100 percent. By contrast, both the prestige and

Table 4.3. *Witness scale*

1821–2		1846–51		1869	
Occupation	Score	Occupation	Score	Occupation	Score
Legal professional	90	Legal professional	95	Legal professional	94
Merchant	86	Merchant	87	Merchant	86
Medical professional	80	Medical professional	84	Medical professional	82
Military officer	78	Other businessman	81	Other professional	79
Ship captain	76	Military officer	76	Proprietor	78
Other professional	74	Proprietor	74	Other businessman	78
Proprietor	67	State official	73	Ship captain	68
Clerk	64	Ship captain	72	State official	64
Shopkeeper	62	Rentier	70	Jeweler, watchmaker	60
State official	60	Other professional	68	Rope, sail maker	57
Jeweler, watchmaker	56	Employee	63	Small manufacturer	57
Miscellaneous	55	Shopkeeper	58	Shopkeeper	56
Small manufacturer	55	Clerk	58	Clerk	55
Employee	53	Jeweler, watchmaker	57	Wine shop owner	55
Soldier	53	Miscellaneous	55	Employee	52
Customs clerk	53	Small manufacturer	55	Packer	52
Miscellaneous service worker	51	Artistic professional	53	Tapestry weaver	50
Tailor	51	Tapestry weaver	53	Miscellaneous	50
Gardener	50	Gardener	51	Artistic professional	50
Cultivator	48	Innkeeper	51	Confectioner	50
Wine shop keeper	48	Café keeper	51	Fisherman	50
Miscellaneous	47	Baker	50	Caulker	49
Packer	47	Sugar refiner	50	Tanner	49
Carpenter	47	Cabinetmaker	50	Café keeper	49
Barber	47	Tile maker	50	Light-metal worker	48

Occupation		Occupation		Occupation	
Fisherman	47	Soldier	50	Miscellaneous builder	48
Miscellaneous artisan	47	Printer	49	Joiner	48
Light-metal worker	47	Cultivator	49	Gardener	48
Joiner	47	Miscellaneous builder	49	Cabinetmaker	48
Rope, sail maker	47	Loader	48	Cultivator	48
Sugar refiner	46	Packer	48	Longshoreman	48
Octroi clerk	46	Light-metal worker	48	Locksmith	48
Soap maker	46	Locksmith	48	Woodworker	47
Baker	46	Butcher	48	Crate maker	47
Caulker	46	Barber	47	Forge worker	47
Shoemaker	46	Rope, sail maker	47	Miscellaneous artisan	47
Locksmith	45	Customs clerk	46	Tile maker	47
Seaman	45	State employee	46	Housepainter	47
Machinist	45	Seaman	46	Miscellaneous maritime worker	47
Woodworker	45	Crate maker	46	Seaman	46
Café keeper	45	Flour miller	46	Flour miller	46
Stonemason	45	Basket maker	46	Cooper	46
Cooper	45	Miscellaneous artisan	46	Machinist	46
Crate maker	45	Caulker	46	Tailor	46
Tanner	45	Cooper	46	Miscellaneous service worker	46
Day laborer	44	Stonemason	46	Printer	46
Coachman	44	Coachman	46	Baker	46
Miscellaneous unskilled worker	43	Woodworker	46	Stonecutter	46
Cook, waiter	43	Machinist	46	Barber	45
Hatter	43	Housepainter	46	Cook, waiter	45
Carter	43	Longshoreman	46	Coachman	45
Longshoreman	43	Tailor	45	Stonemason	45
Shepherd	42	Wine shop owner	45	Carpenter	45
Printer	41	Joiner	45	Butcher	44
Cabinetmaker	41	Miscellaneous unskilled worker	45	Hatter	44
Housepainter	39	Octroi clerk	45	Customs clerk	44

Table 4.3. *Witness scale (cont.)*

1821–2		1846–51		1869	
Occupation	Score	Occupation	Score	Occupation	Score
Stonecutter	39	Hatter	44	State employee	44
Peddler	39	Day laborer	44	Miscellaneous unskilled worker	44
		Soap maker	44	Wagon driver	44
		Cook, waiter	44	Octroi clerk	44
		Miscellaneous maritime worker	44	Shoemaker	43
		Stonecutter	44	Carter	43
		Wagon driver	44	Day laborer	42
		Fisherman	43	Shepherd	42
		Shoemaker	43	Loader	42
		Peddler	43		
		Miscellaneous service worker	43		
		Carpenter	43		
		Confectioner	43		
		Tanner	43		
		Forge worker	43		
		Turner	43		
		Carter	43		
		Shepherd	42		
		Miner	42		
		Woolen worker	41		

nonemployed-bride scales distinguished rank very effectively at the top but
not at the bottom. Given these characteristics of the measures, it is hardly
surprising that their intercorrelations were only moderate. It is therefore quite
possible that all the scales measure an essentially unitary underlying status
hierarchy, but that imperfections of the measures impose a limit on the scales'
intercorrelations. For example, if it had been possible to measure not only
literacy rates of occupations but their mean years of schooling, it is likely
that the correlation of this measure with prestige and nonemployed bride
would be much higher. At the very least, such a measure would certainly
place the legal and medical professions well ahead of occupations such as
clerks or tapestry weavers, who shared their 100 percent literacy rates in
1846–51. In summary, it is possible that the relatively low correlations of
the literacy scale with the other two scales result primarily from the ''ceiling
effect'' inherent in the literacy measure.

  With the data available for mid-nineteenth-century Marseille, it is impossible to choose between these alternative hypotheses. In fact, it is probably
not very important to do so, for the scales are all positively correlated to a
substantial degree. Given these positive correlations, it seems justifiable to
combine the scales into a single scale of occupational status. There are three
arguments for doing so. First it will be convenient to have a single summary
measure of occupational status to use in later chapters of this book, rather
than always having to present three separate calculations – whose results
would normally be very similar in any case. Second, because the different
scales discriminate status best at opposite extremes of the hierarchy, a scale
that combines them should discriminate relatively well along the entire range
of the hierarchy. Finally, the measurement errors that are inevitably present
on each of the scales will tend to be canceled out when the scales are combined.[11]

  Because the nonemployed-bride scale is present only for 1846–51 and 1869,
and because it correlates so highly with the prestige scale, the summary
measure of occupational status will be composed of only the literacy and
prestige scales. This will yield a scale that can be used for all three data sets.[12]
The summary scale is formed by simply adding the scores on the two scales
together and restandardizing the resulting distribution. The results of this
operation are presented in Table 4.4. The correlation of the summary status
scales across the years is extremely high: .95 for 1821–2 and 1846–51, .95
for 1846–51 and 1869, and .93 for 1821–2 and 1869. This summary scale
of occupational status is probably the best single measure of the status of
occupations in nineteenth-century Marseille and will therefore be used for
calculations of status in the remainder of this book.

Interpretation

What do the summary scales reveal about occupational stratification in nineteenth-century Marseille? First, as has already been remarked, the high in-

tercorrelations of the scores from year to year indicate a great deal of stability in the relative status of occupations. Of course there were appreciable changes in the scores of some individual occupations from year to year. But, for most occupations, the changes were not very great. This stability was particularly notable at the extremes of the scale. The top three occupations were the same every year: legal professions were first, merchants second, and medical professions third. In fact, of the 13 occupations with scores above .75 in 1821–2, 12 never fell below .75 in any year. The analogous figure for 1846–51 was 14 out of 17, and for 1869 13 out of 14. Using this principle of selection, it is possible to single out 14 occupations that scored above .75 every year they appeared in the scales. These were the legal and medical professions and other professions; merchants, ship captains, and other business occupations; military officers and state officials; property owners and rentiers; retail tradesmen, small manufacturers, clerks, and jewelers and watchmakers. These were, year in, year out, the high-status occupations.

There was more flux at the bottom, but here, too, certain occupations were perennials. Five of the 9 occupations with scores below − .75 in 1821–2 never rose above − .75 in any year, and this was true of 10 out of the 12 trades below − .75 in 1846–51 and of 8 out of 11 in 1869. The 10 trades that never rose above − .75 were tile makers, flour millers, and woolen workers; carters and wagon drivers; seamen and fishermen; day laborers, cultivators, and miners. These were the perennial low-status occupations. It would, then, be possible to divide Marseille's occupations into three broad status levels, with 14 perennial high-status occupations, accounting for about 20 percent of the adult male population, at the top; 10 perennial low-status occupations, accounting for between 20 and 25 percent, at the bottom; and a large intermediate group, accounting for about 60 percent, in between.

These three status levels bore no exact correspondence to the occupational categories discussed in the last chapter. There were, however, distinct and relatively stable differences between the mean status scores of the different categories. This can be seen in Table 4.5. Throughout the half-century covered by this study, the bourgeois occupational categories had distinctly higher mean-status scores than the remaining categories, and the rank of the four bourgeois categories was unchanged: Businessmen and professionals were at the top, followed by rentiers, clerical employees, and small businessmen. The mean scores of artisans and service workers were near the middle of the range in all years, and in all years the bottom was occupied by unskilled workers, maritime workers, and agriculturalists. Mean scores for the small miscellaneous category were, appropriately, extremely unstable. But, overall, one is struck by the stability of the scores of occupational categories. Generally speaking, the various types of work performed in nineteenth-century Marseille continued to have about the same relative standing late in the century as in its early years.

There were some changes in mean scores over time, but most of these

Table 4.4. *Summary scale*

1821–2		1846–51		1869	
Occupation	Score	Occupation	Score	Occupation	Score
Legal professional	80	Legal professional	83	Legal professional	78
Merchant	78	Merchant	77	Merchant	77
Medical professional	74	Medical professional	76	Medical professional	75
Military officer	74	Other businessman	74	Other professional	72
Ship captain	72	Military officer	72	Proprietor	71
Other professional	71	Proprietor	71	Other businessman	70
Proprietor	66	State official	70	Ship captain	66
Clerk	66	Ship captain	70	State official	64
Shopkeeper	64	Other professional	67	Jeweler, watchmaker	62
State official	63	Rentier	67	Small manufacturer	60
Jeweler, watchmaker	61	Employee	63	Wine shop keeper	59
Small manufacturer	61	Clerk	62	Clerk	58
Customs clerk	60	Shopkeeper	61	Shopkeeper	58
Barber	57	Small manufacturer	60	Tapestry weaver	56
Tailor	56	Jeweler, watchmaker	60	Employee	56
Woodworker	56	Artistic professional	59	Artistic professional	56
Soldier	54	Tapestry weaver	58	Confectioner	56
Employee	54	Cabinetmaker	56	Café keeper	55
Café keeper	54	Café keeper	55	Cabinetmaker	55
Octroi clerk	54	Customs clerk	55	Housepainter	54
Joiner	54	Printer	55	Joiner	54
Printer	53	State employee	55	Printer	53
Miscellaneous service worker	53	Barber	54	Stonecutter	53
Coachman	52	Hatter	54	Woodworker	53
Miscellaneous	52	Packer	54	Customs clerk	52

Table 4.4. *Summary scale (cont.)*

1821–2		1846–51		1869	
Occupation	Score	Occupation	Score	Occupation	Score
Packer	51	Light-metal worker	54	Hatter	52
Locksmith	51	Octroi clerk	53	Packer	52
Hatter	50	Locksmith	52	State employee	52
Miscellaneous artisan	50	Crate maker	52	Octroi clerk	52
Shoemaker	50	Housepainter	52	Miscellaneous service worker	52
Housepainter	49	Baker	51	Locksmith	52
Wine shop keeper	49	Soldier	51	Tailor	52
Cook, waiter	49	Tailor	51	Cook, waiter	52
Baker	49	Joiner	51	Barber	51
Light-metal worker	49	Longshoreman	51	Light-metal worker	51
Cooper	48	Woodworker	50	Miscellaneous artisan	51
Machinist	48	Caulker	50	Butcher	51
Cabinetmaker	48	Miscellaneous service worker	50	Miscellaneous builder	50
Gardener	48	Miscellaneous artisan	50	Caulker	50
Miscellaneous builder	48	Wine shop keeper	50	Cooper	50
Rope, sail maker	47	Peddler	50	Crate maker	49
Crate maker	46	Butcher	50	Baker	49
Carpenter	44	Machinist	49	Coachman	48
Longshoreman	44	Miscellaneous builder	49	Rope, sail maker	48
Soap maker	44	Miscellaneous	48	Machinist	47
Stonemason	44	Forge worker	48	Stonemason	47
Caulker	44	Innkeeper	48	Gardener	46
Tanner	43	Basket maker	48	Longshoreman	46
Stonecutter	43	Confectioner	48	Carpenter	45
Seaman	42	Cook, waiter	48	Tanner	44

Miscellaneous unskilled worker	42
Sugar refiner	42
Cultivator	40
Day laborer	39
Carter	39
Shepherd	39
Peddler	38
Fisherman	38

Sugar refiner	47
Carpenter	47
Stonecutter	46
Coachman	46
Cooper	46
Shoemaker	46
Shepherd	45
Miscellaneous unskilled worker	45
Turner	45
Rope, sail maker	45
Gardener	45
Tanner	45
Loader	44
Stonemason	44
Tile maker	42
Seaman	41
Flour miller	41
Wagon driver	41
Woolen worker	40
Miscellaneous maritime worker	39
Day laborer	39
Soap maker	37
Carter	37
Cultivator	36
Miner	35
Fisherman	28

Forge worker	44
Shoemaker	44
Miscellaneous maritime worker	43
Shepherd	43
Miscellaneous unskilled worker	42
Wagon driver	40
Seaman	40
Miscellaneous	39
Cultivator	39
Day laborer	37
Flour miller	37
Tile maker	35
Loader	34
Fisherman	33
Carter	31

Table 4.5. *Mean summary occupational-status scores, by occupational category*

Occupational category	Marriage registers, 1821–2	Marriage registers, 1846–51	Marriage registers, 1869
Business and professional	76	75	74
Rentier	66	69	71
Sales and clerical	62	61	57
Small business	59	57	57
Artisan	48	49	49
Unskilled	41	39	37
Service	51	48	50
Maritime	42	39	39
Agriculture	40	39	43
Miscellaneous	46	50	39

changes were small enough to make their significance doubtful. Only in the cases of rentiers, sales and clerical employees, and unskilled workers, where the net change from 1821–2 to 1869 was over 4, can it be assumed that the changes were meaningful. It has been noted that rentiers were a declining proportion of Marseille's population over this half-century, presumably in part because Marseille's bourgeois classes came to value work more and leisured opulence less. That the status of rentiers rose while their numbers fell does not belie this interpretation. Rather, it implies that the decline of rentiers took place mainly among men of middling to mediocre rank; that a leisured life style was abandoned above all by those who could afford it least. The falling status of clerical workers, which took place most dramatically after midcentury, was paralleled by a rise in their proportion of the population, which was also most dramatic after midcentury. As more and more people came to be capable of writing and ciphering, and as clerical jobs came to be more common and more routine, the status of clerical work declined. In 1821–2, the clerical category had a clearly higher average status than small business and was not far below rentiers. By 1869, the average statuses of clerical and small-business occupations were virtually identical, and both were now far below rentiers. The status gulf between the *grande bourgeoisie* and the *petite bourgeoisie*, in short, had clearly widened. The declining status of unskilled workers coincided with an increase in their proportion of the population. More importantly, perhaps, it also coincided with an increasing tendency for unskilled workers to list their occupations as *journalier*, rather than specifying a particular trade. Declining status, that is, seems to have been associated with a decline in job security or at least with a declining sense of job security. As measured by either standing in the community or identification with a particular trade, the gulf between artisans and unskilled workers appears to have widened, not narrowed, over the half-century from 1820 to 1870.

Although it is possible to speak of the status of occupational categories in general, it must be recognized that the status scores of occupations within a category varied considerably and that they overlapped with those of occupations in other categories. This can be seen clearly in Table 4.6, where occupations and their summary status scores are listed by category. The only categories that corresponded clearly to status levels were the businessmen and professionals and the rentiers. In every year, business and professional occupations dominated the top end of the scale, and only the artistic professions – dancers, musicians, actors, and the like – ranked below the top ten occupations in the city.[13] Rentiers and property owners were also comfortably within the top ten every year. In other categories, the overlap was always considerable. Both sales and clerical and small-business occupations ranged from quite elevated to distinctly mediocre status. Service occupations ranged rather narrowly over the middle of the distribution. All the unskilled, maritime, and agricultural occupations had scores below zero, but their ranges overlapped considerably with artisan occupations.

Artisans, by far the most numerous category of occupations, had a very wide range, from jewelers and watchmakers, who ranked above most clerical and small-business occupations, to a few trades whose scores overlapped with the top end of the unskilled-worker category. But there is, as usual, a problem with the artisans. Once again, figures for artisan occupations include a significant number of men who were in fact masters, and this surely tended to inflate the scores of these occupations. As Table 4.7 demonstrates, there was a definite tendency for artisan trades with high ratios of workers to masters to have lower status scores than trades with few workers per master. Presumably this is due, at least in part, to the high proportion the relatively high-status masters among the men included in calculations for the small-scale trades. Had it been possible to isolate artisan workers from masters, the range of status scores for artisan trades would have been lower and narrower. But the scores of artisan occupations would still have overlapped both with small-business and clerical occupations at the top and with unskilled, maritime, and agricultural occupations at the bottom. There would have been a noticeable tightening of ranks toward the lower end of the artisan range, but the relative position of artisans in the scale would not have changed significantly.

Functional occupational categories, then, did not correspond perfectly with status levels. Yet it is also true that each category had a characteristic position on the scale and that the scores of its component occupations tended to cluster around this position. Although several artisan occupations had higher scores than the lowest of the clerical or small-business occupations, even the lowest bourgeois occupations had scores above the artisan mean. Again, artisan and

Table 4.6. *Summary status scores of occupations, by occupational category*

1821–2		1846–51		1869	
Occupation	Score	Occupation	Score	Occupation	Score
Businessmen and Professional					
Legal professional	80	Legal professional	83	Legal professional	78
Merchant	78	Merchant	78	Merchant	77
Medical professional	74	Medical professional	76	Medical professional	75
Military officer	74	Other businessman	74	Other professionals	72
Ship captain	72	Military officer	72	Other businessman	70
Other professional	71	State official	70	Ship captain	66
State official	63	Ship captain	70	State official	64
		Other professional	67	Artistic professional	56
		Artistic professional	59		
Rentier					
Proprietor	66	Proprietor	70	Proprietor	71
		Rentier	67		
Sales and clerical					
Clerk	66	Employee	63	Clerk	58
Customs clerk	60	Clerk	62	Employee	56
Employee	54	Customs clerk	55	Customs clerk	52
Octroi clerk	45	State employee	55	State employee	52
		Octroi clerk	53	Octroi clerk	52
Small business					
Shopkeeper	64	Shopkeeper	61	Small manufacturer	60
Small manufacturer	61	Small manufacturer	60	Wine shop keeper	59
Barber	57	Café keeper	55	Shopkeeper	58
Café keeper	54	Barber	54	Café keeper	55
Wine shop keeper	49	Wine shop keeper	50	Barber	51
		Innkeeper	48		

Artisan

Artisan		Artisan		Artisan	
Jeweler, watchmaker	61	Jeweler, watchmaker	60	Jeweler, watchmaker	62
Tailor	56	Tapestry weaver	58	Tapestry weaver	56
Woodworker	56	Cabinetmaker	56	Confectioner	56
Joiner	54	Printer	55	Cabinetmaker	55
Printer	53	Hatter	54	Housepainter	54
Packer	51	Packer	54	Joiner	54
Locksmith	51	Light-metal worker	52	Printer	53
Hatter	50	Locksmith	52	Stonecutter	53
Miscellaneous artisan	50	Crate maker	52	Woodworker	53
Shoemaker	50	Housepainter	52	Hatter	52
Housepainter	49	Baker	51	Packer	52
Baker	49	Tailor	51	Locksmith	52
Light-metal worker	49	Joiner	51	Tailor	52
Cooper	48	Longshoreman	51	Light-metal worker	51
Machinist	48	Woodworker	50	Miscellaneous artisan	51
Cabinetmaker	48	Caulker	50	Butcher	51
Miscellaneous builder	48	Miscellaneous artisan	50	Miscellaneous builder	50
Rope, sail maker	47	Butcher	50	Caulker	50
Crate maker	46	Machinist	49	Cooper	50
Carpenter	46	Miscellaneous builder	48	Crate maker	49
Longshoreman	44	Forge worker	48	Baker	49
Stonemason	44	Basket maker	48	Rope, sail maker	48
Caulker	44	Confectioner	47	Machinist	47
Tanner	43	Carpenter	46	Stonemason	47
Stonecutter	43	Stonecutter	46	Longshoreman	46
		Cooper	46	Carpenter	45
		Shoemaker	45	Tanner	44
		Turner	45	Forge worker	44
		Rope, sail maker	45	Shoemaker	44
		Tanner	44		
		Stonemason	44		

Table 4.6. *Summary status scores of occupations, by occupational category (cont.)*

1821–2		1846–51		1869	
Occupation	Score	Occupation	Score	Occupation	Score
Service					
Miscellaneous service worker	53	Miscellaneous service worker	50	Miscellaneous service worker	52
Coachman	52	Cook, waiter	48	Cook, waiter	52
Cook, waiter	49	Coachman	44	Coachman	48
Unskilled worker					
Soap maker	44	Sugar refiner	47	Miscellaneous unskilled worker	42
Miscellaneous unskilled worker	42	Miscellaneous unskilled worker	45	Wagon driver	40
Sugar refiner	42	Loader	44	Day laborer	37
Day laborer	39	Tile maker	42	Flour miller	37
Carter	39	Flour miller	41	Tile maker	35
		Wagon driver	41	Loader	34
		Woolen worker	40	Carter	31
		Day laborer	39		
		Soap maker	37		
		Carter	37		
		Miner	35		
Maritime					
Seaman	42	Seaman	41	Miscellaneous maritime worker	43
Fisherman	38	Miscellaneous maritime worker	39	Seaman	40
		Fisherman	28	Fisherman	33
Agriculture					
Gardener	48	Shepherd	45	Gardener	46
Cultivator	40	Gardener	45	Shepherd	43
Shepherd	39	Cultivator	36	Cultivator	39
Miscellaneous					
Soldier	54	Soldier	51	Miscellaneous	39

Table 4.7. *Relationship of summary status scores to average size of firm, artisan occupations, 1846–51*

	Status scores		
Ratio of workers to masters	above .20	.20 to − .20	below − .20
10 to 1 or greater	2	5	5
Between 4 to 1 and 10 to 1	3	2	5
4 to 1 or smaller	5	3	0

Source: The ratios of workers to masters were calculated from the "Enquête sur le travail industriel et agricole," 1848–49, *Archives Nationales*, C947. Of the 33 artisan occupations for which status scores are available in 1846–51, figures on the number of workers and masters are available for only 30.

unskilled occupations overlapped, but the majority of the unskilled occupations were below even the lowest of the artisan trades, and the highest unskilled occupations fell considerably short of the artisan mean. What this signifies is that the commonplace divisions of occupations into blue- and white-collar strata or into skilled or unskilled trades bear a substantial correspondence to the realities of occupational status in nineteenth-century Marseille. Such divisions are not very precise and would lead to mistaken conclusions about status in some individual cases. But they nevertheless mark off broad strata of the population quite effectively. Dividing up occupations according to function – whether into broad strata like white- and blue-collar or into more refined groupings like the ten occupational categories used in this study – also tends to divide them into status groupings. Different types of economic functions, that is, tend to be associated with different levels of rewards – in both income and status.

What conclusions can be drawn from this look at the status of occupations in nineteenth-century Marseille? Perhaps the most important conclusion is methodological. It is possible to construct reliable and statistically sound scales of occupational status on the basis of historical data, and such scales need not be limited to those classes of the population who owned enough property to be taxed. This conclusion should be of interest both to historians and to sociologists. Sociologists working on problems of occupational status have confined their research almost exclusively to contemporary societies, where they can produce the necessary data by familiar techniques of survey research. They have assumed that sufficiently detailed and comprehensive information could not exist before there were sociologists around to collect it. The successful construction of occupational-status scales for nineteenth-century Marseille should help to expose this solipsistic fallacy: Quantifiable data that can be used to approach this and many other sociological issues exist in abundance, not only for nineteenth-century France but for many other past societies as well. The real reason that quantitatively minded sociologists have avoided research on historical societies is not an absence of appropriate data, but a present-mindedness that has limited their curiosity about the past. A quantitative sociological analysis based on historical sources like French marriage registers is no more difficult and probably less expensive than analogous research using survey methods to study contemporary America. Given sociologists' vast duplication of effort in studies of contemporary society, it seems likely that such historical research will often be more illuminating than research in the conventional ahistorical mode. In contrast to sociologists, historians who have studied social stratification usually recognize the abundance of available data. The weak point in their efforts has usually been timidity about using the systematic statistical techniques that would enable them to order the data more adequately. As a self-conscious effort to apply sociological techniques to historical data, this exercise should help to indicate to both sides the potential advantages of a closer alliance between history and sociology.

The major substantive conclusion must be that the scores of occupations were remarkably stable over time. The by now tedious recitation of correlation coefficients on the order of .9 allows of no other interpretation. This does not mean that all was quiet on the occupational front. The status scores of some occupations and even of some occupational categories changed significantly during the half-century covered by these figures. Moreover, as has been seen in the last chapter, some occupations grew while others shrank, and the overall shape of the occupational structure changed significantly. But, in spite of some exceptions, the relative ranking of the different occupations within the changing structure was on the whole quite constant. That this should have been true during a period of rapid urbanization, of industrial revolution and economic development, of three major changes in political regime, and of important changes in social and political ideology, is a fact worth remarking. It seems to indicate one important continuity underlying the sweeping social changes that took place during the nineteenth century.[14]

5   The urban framework

While our other great cities, Bordeaux, Rouen, Lyon, Nantes, have certain traits of similarity between them, Marseille resembles only itself. Contemplated from the block of arid rocks that shelter its port, its tile roofs form an immense reddish tapestry on which the sun of the Midi pours in torrents its brilliance and its warmth. Nowhere an oasis of verdure where the eyes can rest; even the surrounding countryside is bare; the pale olive trees and delicate-foliaged almond trees which surround the numerous villas on the outskirts of Marseille are not enough to enliven the spectacle. Inside the walls of the city there is no grandiose monument to captivate one's admiration; but the sea is there, with its majesty. It curls about in all directions, as if to embrace the city.[1]

Such was the exterior aspect of Marseille as described by a visitor in the early 1850s: a city of tile, stone, plaster, and pavement, only rarely embellished by trees, whose beauty owed little to human artifice and much to the brightness of the sun, the sparkling blue of the sea, and the stark white of the surrounding mountains. But the peculiar charm of Marseille always owed more to the rich variety of its population and the striking contrasts of its different quarters than to its architecture or its natural setting. As the visitor remarked:

In its immense perimeter, Marseille contains the most astonishing contrasts: here the opulent solitude of the allées de Meilhan and the cours Bonaparte, there the extreme animation of la Cannebière and the port; and a little farther, the indigence stacked up around the place de Linche and the montée du Saint-Esprit, in narrow little streets containing degenerate elements of more than one kind, and too long forgotten in the midst of this vast scene where everything announces labor and wealth.[2]

Historical development of the city

A tour through the various and sharply contrasting quarters of Marseille is also a tour through the city's long history and therefore should begin at the beginning. It was in the shelter of the hill guarding the northern side of the port that a colony of Greeks founded Marseille in the sixth century B.C., and it was on this same hill that the city remained throughout the Middle Ages. To this day the old city, the portion of the city once contained by the ancient and medieval walls, bears the imprint of its Greek founders: Its main thoroughfare, Grande Rue, and many of its lesser streets still follow the lines traced by its original Greek inhabitants.[3] In the Middle Ages, Marseille was fortified by walls on the north and east and by a steep cliff leading down to the sea on the west, and the port basin that formed its southern perimeter was well guarded by a fortress at its narrow inlet. Throughout the Middle Ages, needs of defense predominated over the needs of commerce or comfort, and whatever expansion took place was constrained to do so within the limits of the ramparts. Hence the characteristics of the old city that have lasted to this day: narrow, dark, cavernous streets, and small irregular, crowded, low-ceilinged multistory dwellings built helter-skelter along the steep hillside. But if residents of the old city suffered from overcrowding and hazardous sanitary conditions, they were partially repaid by the intimacy, variety, and color of their teeming environment. A walk through what remains of the old city today constantly turns up surprises. Here, a gently sloping street falls sharply downward, and the flat paving is replaced by steep steps; there, a cavernous alley suddenly opens onto a spectacular view of the port or the sea, or a wide and sunny street imperceptibly narrows into a dark and cool *impasse*. The very names of the streets in the old city have a kind of poetry and enchantment. To be sure, some names that now seem quaint were mere identifications of streets by familiar objects or by the occupations carried out on them: thus the rue Fontaine du Gros Cannon or the rue Foie de Boeuf. Others have an unintended irony, such as the montée du Saint-Esprit. Some, however, have a quality of pure fancy: the rue des Festons Rouges and the rue de la Guirlande; the rue de la Lune Blanche and the rue de la Lune d'Or; and the ultimate fantasy of the rue Pierre Qui Rage and the rue Pavé d'Amour.

By the end of the seventeenth century, Marseille had outgrown its medieval limits, and new walls were built, approximately doubling the area of the city. Both the perimeter of the old city and the line of the new walls can be seen very clearly in Figure 5.1, a plan of Marseille dating from the 1830s. The seventeenth-century walls had by then been replaced by broad, tree-shaded boulevards except in the extreme southwestern corner of the city. Within this perimeter, the old city is marked off from the new by the broad street running east–west from the head of the port – the famous Cannebière – and by the thoroughfare extending north from the eastern extremity of la Cannebière.

Most of the land in the new quarters that were created by the seventeenth-century extension of the walls was relatively flat; consequently, the streets in the new quarters were broader and were laid out more geometrically than in the old city. The spacious and comfortable new quarters attracted the more opulent classes of the population, who fled the old city, leaving behind the humble classes of workers, artisans, shopkeepers, sailors, and fishermen.[4] Except for the narrow strip of land along the southern edge of the port, which became an industrial quarter in the eighteenth century, the entire new city remained much more opulent and much less crowded than the old city.[5] This difference may be seen by contrasting the types of houses in these two parts of the city. The typical house in the area enclosed by the seventeenth-century walls was wide enough to have three windows in the front and rear. In the

Figure 5.1. Marseille in the 1830s. Courtesy Archives de la Chambre de Commerce de Marseille.

old city most houses were only two windows wide, and some had barely room enough for a single aperture. The difference is also made apparent by population statistics. In 1790, some 49,967 people lived in the old city, while only 27,118 lived in the slightly larger area contained by the new walls;[6] in other words, the density of population was about twice as high in the old city as in the new. By 1790, however, the city had outgrown its walls once again, and some 29,494 people, or over one quarter of the population, lived outside the perimeter of the ramparts.[7] To be sure, some of them were peasants living at a considerable distance from the city proper, but most of them inhabited new suburban quarters, especially to the east and south of the city walls, but also to the north. The new suburban quarters were generally extensions of the quarters that lay within the walls; thus the extramural developments to the south and east were predominantly bourgeois, and that to the north predominantly plebian. These extramural developments are clearly evident in Figure 5.2, which depicts Marseille near the end of the First Empire.

Between 1790 and the late 1820s there was almost no outward extension of the city. The population did not increase during the Revolution and Empire, and in the first years of the Restoration most new houses were constructed on land within the built-up area that had been confiscated from the church during the Revolution.[8] The most important change that came about during the Revolution and Empire was the beginning of the demolition of the ramparts, which had lost their military significance and now constituted a serious obstacle to the flow of traffic. The process of demolition was completed on the eastern perimeter during the Empire, but dragged on into the 1830s and 1840s in the north and south.[9] Outward extension of the city began once again in the late 1820s, principally toward the south and east, but toward the north as well. Although the southern extension was predominantly bourgeois, the new quarters in the north, east, and southeast were predominantly working class. This was partly due to the development of industry in the suburbs. During the Old Regime, industry had been concentrated primarily in the upper part of the old city and along the southern side of the port. Between the 1820s and 1840s, new industrial quarters developed in the suburbs to the north and southeast of the city, with sugar-refining and oil-pressing factories concentrated in the north and mechanical and metallurgical factories in the southeast.[10]

The extent of expansion of the city by the middle of the century can be seen by comparing Figure 5.2 with Figure 5.3. The plan in Figure 5.2 depicts Marseille near the end of the First Empire, when the built-up area extended only a little beyond the perimeter of the seventeenth-century walls. This had been the geographical extent of Marseille since the late eighteenth century, and there was very little change before the middle 1820s. By 1847, when the plan in Figure 5.3 was drawn, the southern and eastern suburbs had expanded prodigiously; so much that nearly half the built-up area of Marseille now lay outside the line of the seventeenth-century walls. Such rapid extension of the city made this a period of feverish activity for the building industry. Between 1826 and 1846 an average of 250 houses was built each year. Nearly all of them were the *maisons à trois fenêtres* already typical of housing outside the old city – three windows wide in front and rear and three or four stories high, with a single staircase, generally accommodating one family on each floor.[11]

The outward extensions of the city in the first half of the nineteenth century were novel neither in the direction of growth nor in the type of houses constructed. Physically, Marseille in 1850 was still recognizable as the Marseille of 1789, only grown larger; the physiognomy of the older districts was unchanged, and growth of new quarters was in the anticipated directions. The era of the Second Empire, however, changed the shape and face of the city far more fundamentally. The construction of new port basins along the northern coastline radically shifted the commercial center of gravity northward,

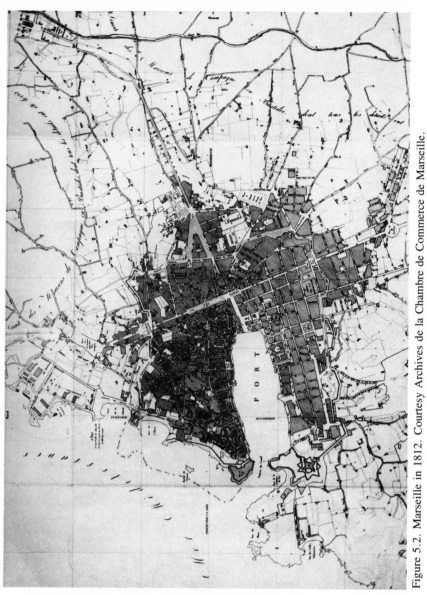

Figure 5.2. Marseille in 1812. Courtesy Archives de la Chambre de Commerce de Marseille.

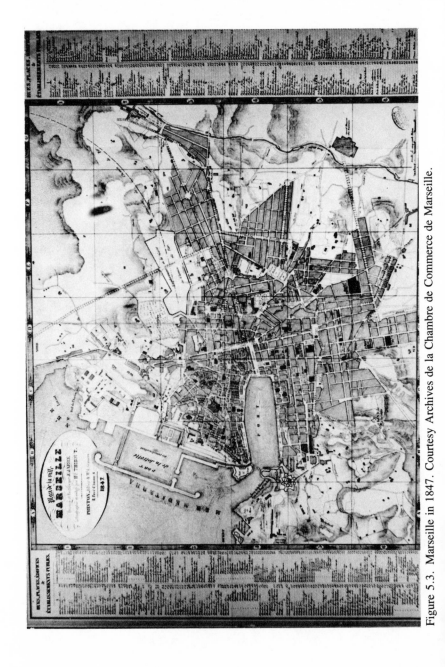

Figure 5.3. Marseille in 1847. Courtesy Archives de la Chambre de Commerce de Marseille.

and most of Marseille's new factories were also built in close proximity to the new ports, to assure ready access to low-cost transportation. As a result, during the Second Empire, the northern suburbs became Marseille's preeminent industrial quarter, eclipsing the industrial settlements in the upper old city, in the southeastern suburbs, and on the southern shore of the old port. At the same time, vast reconstruction projects and extensive monumental building changed the physical aspect of the older quarters of the city. Because of the opening of new port facilities along Marseille's northern coast, the main advance of built-up area in these years was neither to the east nor to the south, as during the past two centuries, but to the north. The extension of Marseille in this period can be seen clearly by comparing Figure 5.3 with Figure 5.4, a plan of Marseille in 1874. The most prominent difference is a vast expansion of built-up area extending from the northern edge of the old city and proceeding along the coast, parallel to the new port basins. There were also new extensions to the south and east, and even to the west, on the steep and rocky promontory that jutted into the sea south of the old port. But the outstanding feature of Marseille's urban expansion during the Second Empire was the opening up of vast new quarters in the north.

The city also experienced significant reconstruction projects, some of which have already been described in Chapter 2. The most important was construction of the rue Impériale, a man-made canyon sliced through the old city to link up the head of the old port with the new. But there were others, including the construction of the cours Lieutaud, which created a broad new north–south thoroughfare from the railway station to the southern edge of the city, and the lengthening of la Cannebière to create a thoroughfare from the head of the port to the eastern suburbs. The construction of these streets necessitated destruction of a large number of houses, but it also created the basis of an urban communications network that served Marseille well for nearly one hundred years without major alterations. The Second Empire also ended the monopoly of the *maison à trois fenêtres*. Although many such structures were erected in the new quarters built during the Second Empire, this era was more notable for the city's first large blocks of apartments. The most spectacular – and the most financially disastrous – were the block-long, six-story apartments lining the rue Impériale, which the Pereire brothers were unable to rent at a sufficient profit. But large multiple-unit apartment houses also appeared elsewhere: in the new northern suburbs, along the cours Lieutaud, and scattered about throughout the newly built-up areas. At the same time the appearance of the city was changed by the erection of several monumental public buildings: official buildings like the Préfecture and the Palais de Justice, cultural centers like the new Bibliothèque and the Palais des Beaux Arts, and new churches like the Cathedral, the Eglise des Reformées, and Notre Dame de la Garde. By 1870, Marseille had assumed the shape and the aspect it was to wear without major alteration through the first half of the twentieth century.

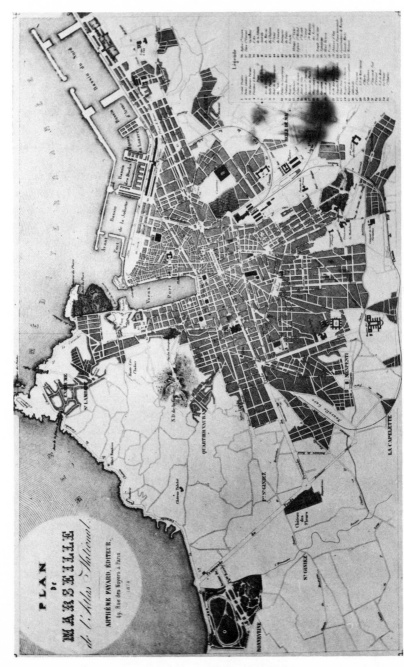

Figure 5.4. Marseille in 1874. Courtesy Archives de la Chambre de Commerce de Marseille.

The changes wrought by the Second Empire can be seen clearly by comparing Figure 5.5 – a view of Marseille around 1850 – with Figure 5.6 – a view of Marseille in the 1880s. The lithograph in Figure 5.6 in fact exaggerates the size and prominence of virtually all the monumental constructions of the Second Empire.

Social characteristics of neighborhoods

What were the social characteristics of Marseille's various neighborhoods, and how did they change as the city grew in the nineteenth century? An answer to these questions will require a close examination of the 10 percent sample of the *listes nominatives* of the census of 1851 and of the marriage registers of 1821–2, 1846–51, and 1869. The weaknesses of both these samples of the population have been touched on in Chapter 3 and are explored in some detail in Appendix A. Most of the conclusions reached in reference to the occupational structure are also valid for an analysis of neighborhood patterns. The census gives a far more comprehensive listing of the population, but it omits a significant number of unmarried males, most of whom presumably lived in rooming houses. Moreover, although it was possible to estimate the occupational distribution of these missing males, there is no basis on which to estimate their distribution in different neighborhoods. The marriage registers, on the other hand, represent only the settled young-adult population, entirely omitting children and transients and underrepresenting older people. In this chapter, the analysis will begin with the 1851 census data, which, in spite of their imperfections, yield a picture of the city's neighborhoods that is not only accurate in most essentials but also extremely detailed. This will be followed by an analysis of data from the marriage registers, which will make it possible to check the accuracy of the census findings and to discuss changes over time. The census data, however, are unsatisfactory for describing the distribution of women's occupations in the city's neighborhoods. Because different census takers varied enormously in the degree to which they reported women's occupations, some districts had implausibly low proportions of women reported as employed. For example, according to the census, 63 percent of the women were not employed in the poor neighborhood bordering the port in the old city (district 1 in the maps and tables below), whereas only 51 percent lacked employment in the opulent quarter just east of the central commercial district (district 5 in the maps and tables). Given that employment of women was much rarer among the wealthy than among the poor, the figure for district 1 is clearly the result of massive underreporting. Because the reporting of women's occupations varied so sharply from district to district the remarks about women's occupations in the following pages are based on the marriage registers of 1846–51 rather than on the census of 1851.

The first task is to delimit Marseille's neighborhoods. On the basis of street-

Figure 5.5. View of Marseille about 1850. Courtesy Musée du Vieux Marseille.

Figure 5.6. View of Marseille in 1886. Courtesy Musée du Vieux Marseille.

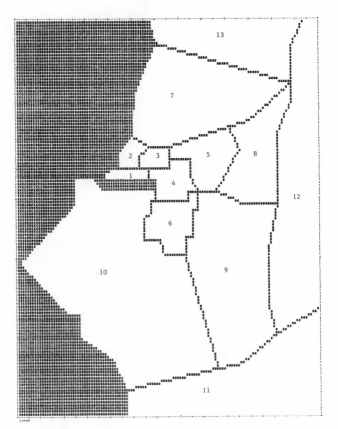

Figure 5.7. Marseille's districts.

by-street data from the census of 1851, the city has been divided into thirteen
districts that were as internally homogeneous as possible in their occupational
composition. The districts are presented in the computer-generated map in
Figure 5.7. In drawing the district boundaries, administrative boundary lines
between *arrondissements* were followed whenever possible. However, in only
five cases were *arrondissements* sufficiently homogeneous to be used with
no alterations of boundaries: urban districts 2 and 3 and the rural districts 11,
12, and 13 in the maps and tables below. It must be remembered that these
thirteen districts are based on the characteristics of the population in 1851; a
similar attempt to draw neighborhood boundaries in 1821 or 1869 would
surely have led to somewhat different results. But these neighborhoods were
sufficiently distinct in 1821–2 and 1869 – as well as in the middle of the
century – to make them appropriate units of analysis for the entire half-century
covered by this study.

A glance at Table 5.1 and at the maps in Figures 5.8 and 5.9 will show that the districts of Marseille varied considerably in their socio-occupational composition in 1851. These differences can be summarized most conveniently by calculating mean scores of occupational status for each district. These scores appear on line 14 of Table 5.1 and are presented visually in Figure 5.9. The feature that stands out most prominently on the map is a high-status belt stretching both east and south from the head of the port, composed of districts 4, 5, and 6. These relatively opulent quarters encompassed the better part of the area joined to Marseille by the seventeenth-century extension of the walls, but reached well beyond the line of the walls both to the east and south. These quarters were in sharp contrast to the old city, districts 1, 2, and 3, where mean status scores were much lower, and they also stood out only slightly less sharply from quarters 7, 8, 9, and 10, the less opulent industrial suburbs. Finally, the rural quarters, districts 11, 12, and 13, had the lowest mean status scores of all. The mean status scores of Marseille's districts give only the roughest and most general orientation to the city's neighborhoods at midcentury. To get a sense of each district's particular qualities and texture requires a much closer examination of the census data.

The old city

In 1851, the old city included four more or less distinct neighborhoods. The first of these, the area at the northeastern corner of the old port, was part of the commercial center of Marseille. Because it was socially indistinguishable from the rest of the central commercial district, it will be discussed as a part of district 4 below.

District 1 was Marseille's maritime quarter. According to the census of 1851, it was the home of 51 percent of the city's seamen, 55 percent of its fishermen, and 42 percent of the workers in other maritime occupations – boatmen, pilots, etc. It was mainly this heavy concentration of men in the maritime trades that gave district 1 the lowest mean occupational-status score of any of Marseille's urban districts. The other common occupational groups in district 1 were skilled and unskilled workers, who together made up another 45 percent of the adult male population. Bourgeois of all sorts were extremely scarce, comprising only 13 percent of the adult males, the lowest proportion in any of Marseille's urban districts (see Table 5.1). The distribution of women's occupations completes the portrait of a poor maritime neighborhood. Few young women in district 1 (22 percent) did not work for a living (see Table 5.2). The proportion of women in small business was high – largely accounted for by fish sellers – as were the proportions in unskilled labor and the "other craft" category – largely straw plaiters, cigar makers, and sail makers. The proportion in domestic service was unusually low. District 1 also had other characteristics typical of maritime quarters anywhere in the

Table 5.1. *Occupational composition of districts, active male population over 17, census of 1851 (in percent)*

	District													Total
Occupation	1	2	3	4	5	6	7	8	9	10	11	12	13	
1. Business and Professional	3	1	2	9	20	21	3	7	3	2	1	1	1	6
2. Rentier	1	2	2	3	13	11	3	6	4	2	4	10	2	5
3. Sales and clerical	4	5	5	14	25	24	7	16	8	8	2	2	2	10
4. Small business	5	6	6	15	14	6	10	7	8	9	2	3	6	8
5. Artisan	32	47	45	42	18	20	36	40	44	48	17	28	32	37
6. Service	2	2	3	4	4	9	4	1	3	4	5	1	6	3
7. Unskilled	13	31	28	8	4	6	31	17	21	18	31	14	15	18
8. Maritime	36	4	4	3	—	1	1	2	1	7	6	—	6	5
9. Agriculture	1	1	2	1	1	1	4	2	7	1	30	40	30	7
10. Miscellaneous	3	3	3	1	1	1	1	2	1	1	2	1	—	1
Elite (1 + 2)	4	3	4	12	33	32	6	13	7	4	5	11	3	11
Bourgeois (1 + 2 + 3 + 4)	13	14	15	41	72	62	23	36	23	21	9	16	11	29
Workers (5 + 6 + 7 + 8)	83	84	80	57	26	36	72	60	69	77	59	43	59	63
Summary occupational-status score	45	47	48	54	61	60	48	53	49	48	43	45	43	50
Number of males over 17	430	337	829	878	376	371	274	281	631	237	179	384	360	5,607

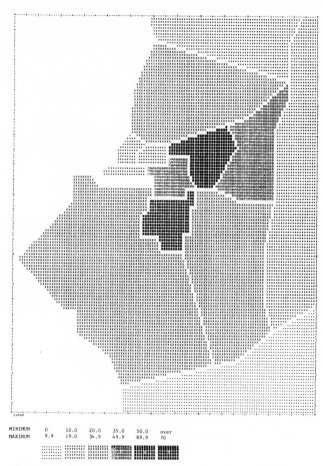

MINIMUM   0   10.0   20.0   35.0   50.0   over
MAXIMUM   9.9   19.0   34.9   49.9   69.9   70

Figure 5.8. Districts by percent bourgeois, census of 1851.

world. As one would expect of a district that included many itinerant seamen, a relatively high proportion of its adult males (some 17 percent) lived alone in rooming houses or hotels (see Table 5.3). This conclusion is, of course, based on the weakest aspect of the census data – data on transients – and therefore must be stated only tentatively. But it certainly fits with expectations. Perhaps even more characteristic of a maritime quarter was the high concentration of prostitutes: To judge from the census sample, district 1 had 330 registered prostitutes, out of some 380 in the city as a whole. It also had a very high proportion of foreigners, who made up about a fifth of the adult population and nearly a quarter of the adult male population (see Table 5.4). Among the foreigners, Italians – the most impoverished of Marseille's im-

MINIMUM   under   45.0   47.6   50.0   53.0   over
MAXIMUM   45   47.5   49.9   52.9   55.9   56

Figure 5.9. Districts by mean occupational-status score, census of 1851.

migrants – were particularly common. Finally, as will be shown in Chapter 8, district 1 had an extremely high crime rate. District 1 was, then, a more or less typical maritime quarter: poor, rough, cosmopolitan, and dangerous.

The two remaining neighborhoods of the old city, districts 2 and 3, had much in common. They were perched side by side on the ridge of the hill that guarded the old port, and together they constituted the upper portion of the old city. Their mean status scores were relatively low, although higher than that of the neighboring district 1. Both districts were overwhelmingly working class: Workers made up 84 percent of the active adult male population in district 2 and 80 percent in district 3. Skilled workers were the largest single male occupational category in both districts, but the districts were more

Table 5.2. *Bride's occupation by district, marriage registers of 1846–51 (in percent)*

Bride's occupation	District													Total
	1	2	3	4	5	6	7	8	9	10	11	12	13	
Not employed	22	15	14	35	39	31	23	34	26	20	18	21	12	25
Rentière	0	1	0	3	8	5	0	4	2	2	0	1	1	2
Business and professional	0	1	0	1	1	1	1	1	0	1	0	1	0	1
Small business	11	6	8	9	4	3	4	4	5	6	0	2	6	6
Needle trades	30	35	34	26	15	25	38	28	33	29	30	23	28	29
Laundry	7	4	6	6	7	4	10	9	10	5	7	17	22	8
Other crafts	10	14	9	2	1	2	5	3	4	24	0	0	1	6
Domestic service	4	5	6	13	22	25	9	8	10	9	3	7	5	6
Unskilled	15	18	22	8	2	3	9	8	7	6	16	5	8	11
Agriculture	0	0	1	1	1	0	2	1	3	1	24	22	17	9
Miscellaneous	0	0	0	0	0	0	0	0	0	0	2	1	1	0
Number of cases	277	211	432	514	298	260	167	109	315	126	67	169	162	3,107

Table 5.3. *Selected characteristics of districts, census of 1851*

District	Percent of males over 17 living alone	Ratio of males to females
1	17	87
2	8	94
3	21	104
4	23	91
5	8	61
6	12	73
7	4	99
8	6	81
9	11	96
10	8	112
11	17	112
12	8	107
13	5	122
Total	13	92

notable for their heavy concentrations of unskilled workers, who made up 31 percent of the adult males in district 2 and 29 percent in district 3. Correlatively, both districts had very small bourgeois populations: Bourgeois made up only 14 percent of district 2's adult males and only 15 percent of district 3's. The two districts also had similar patterns of female employment. They had the lowest proportions of nonemployed young women, the highest proportions of unskilled workers, and very low proportions of domestic servants – all unmistakable signs of poverty. They also had, like district 1, high proportions in the "other crafts." But in spite of all these similarities between districts 2 and 3, there were also striking differences. In district 3, of the enumerated adult males 21 percent lived alone in hotels or rooming houses, whereas only 8 percent lived alone in district 2. This finding may simply be due to the inaccuracy of data on the rooming-house population, but it seems to fit with other differences between the two quarters. District 3 also had the highest proportion of foreigners in its adult population (21 percent) of any district in Marseille and nearly all of them were Italians. District 2 had only 10 percent foreign and 9 percent Italian – barely above the citywide proportions. District 3 was also more densely populated. Although the two districts had approximately equal surface areas, district 3 had a total population of some 23,520, whereas district 2 had only half as many people: 11,770. Finally, to anticipate Chapter 8, district 3 had the highest crime rate of any district in the city – higher even than the maritime quarter – whereas the crime rate in district 2 was at about the citywide average. Although both districts were

Table 5.4. *Percentage of foreigners by district, census of 1851*

District	Male			Female			All adults		
	Italian	Rest of world	Total foreign	Italian	Rest of world	Total foreign	Italian	Rest of world	Total foreign
1	21	2	23	13	1	14	17	2	19
2	11	1	12	7	1	8	9	1	10
3	24	2	26	15	1	16	20	1	21
4	7	5	12	4	3	7	5	4	9
5	3	3	6	2	1	3	3	2	5
6	3	5	8	2	5	7	2	5	7
7	3	2	5	1	1	2	2	1	3
8	1	0	1	3	1	4	3	1	4
9	6	3	9	3	3	6	4	3	7
10	5	2	7	3	1	4	4	2	6
11	13	1	14	1	1	2	7	1	8
12	2	1	3	0	1	1	1	1	2
13	4	1	5	4	1	5	4	1	5
Total	9	3	12	5	2	7	7	2	9

distinctly poor and working class, district 3 was a severely overcrowded slum district with a high proportion of transients and foreigners and a very high rate of crime. District 2, by contrast, was a respectable working-class neighborhood.

The central commercial district

In the decades following the construction of new city walls in the late seventeenth century, the commercial center of Marseille migrated eastward and southward out of the old city into the plain at the head of the port. By the middle of the nineteenth century, the new commercial center of the city had expanded over much of the originally opulent residential district contained within the seventeenth-century walls. This area, together with the immediately adjacent portion of the old city, formed the central commercial district labeled as district 1 in the maps and tables. The mean status score of district 4 was well above average, but was lower than in the most opulent neighborhoods, districts 5 and 6. The social composition of district 4 was extremely mixed: Bourgeois and workers were more evenly balanced than in any other neighborhood of Marseille. Not surprisingly, the central commercial district had the highest proportion of small businessmen of any district in the city: Twenty-eight percent of the city's male shopkeepers resided here, most of them either above or behind their shops. The female occupational distribution had analogous characteristics: a high proportion of nonemployed women, a proportion of domestics above all but opulent districts 5 and 6, and a high proportion in small business. But in the central district no occupational group was dominant. In some cases rich merchants, unskilled laborers, artisans, and shopkeepers lived intermingled on the same street or even on different floors of the same houses. Elsewhere in the district, immediately adjacent streets would differ sharply in social composition: Walking along a street inhabited chiefly by well-to-do merchants and professional men, one could turn the corner and suddenly be surrounded by humble laborers and artisans. However, most of the workers living in the central commercial district were artisans – only 8 percent of the adult males and 8 percent of the females were unskilled workers.

District 4 had one attribute in common with the old-city districts: It had a high proportion of transients. Indeed, 21 percent of the adult males counted in district 4 lived alone in rooming houses and hotels – the highest proportion of any district in Marseille. But the central district's transients, to judge from admittedly doubtful figures, were not the poor itinerant unskilled laborers who filled the rooming houses of the old city. Unskilled workers accounted for only 7 percent of the males living alone in district 4, whereas 43 percent were skilled workers and another 23 percent were bourgeois. The central district was also relatively cosmopolitan: It had the highest proportion of foreigners of any district outside the old city. But in district 4 the proportion of Italians was unusually low, whereas the proportion of non-Italian foreigners was unusually high (see Table 5.4). Non-Italian foreigners living in Marseille tended to be in relatively high-status jobs, and it was these skilled and prosperous foreigners, ranging from artisans to international merchants and bankers, who congregated in the central commercial district, whereas the predominantly unskilled Italians were relegated to the old city. The central commercial district therefore seems to have been relatively cosmopolitan and transient, but it was a cosmopolitanism and transiency born of prosperity rather than of desperation.

The opulent quarters

Stretching to the east and south of the central commercial district were Marseille's opulent quarters, districts 5 and 6. Although contiguous at only one point, on the southeast corner of the central commercial district, these districts were very similar in character. Their mean status scores were far above those of any other district. They were also the only districts in which the majority of the adult males were bourgeois: Seventy-two percent were bourgeois in district 5 and 62 percent in district 6. Particularly notable was the number of men in elite occupations, who made up nearly a third of the total in both districts. The proportion of workers was correspondingly low, and the proportion of unskilled laborers particularly low: only 4 percent in district 5 and 6 percent in district 6. To judge from the census figures, neither district had many transients or foreigners, although it is notable that a high proportion of the foreigners who did live there were non-Italians, especially in district 6. The female occupational distributions also reflected the prosperity of these districts. The proportions of nonemployed women were high: 39 percent, the highest in the city, in district 5, and 31 percent in district 6. They also had the highest proportion of *rentières*: 8 percent in district 5 and 5 percent in district 6. According to both these measures, district 5 was the more opulent of the two. District 6, however, had the city's highest proportion of domestic servants – 25 percent, as against 22 percent in district 5. The large number of domestics accounts for another peculiarity of these sections: a pronounced imbalance between males and females. The ratio of adult males to females for the *listes nominatives* sample as a whole was 92 to 100, whereas the ratio was 73 in district 6 and only 61 in district 5[12] (see Table 5.3). In short, districts 5 and 6 differed sharply from any others in the city. They were prosperous islands of bourgeois contentment in an essentially plebian city.

The working-class suburbs

Encircling the entire city were a series of working-class suburbs, districts 7, 8, 9, and 10. The majority of the active adult males in all four districts were workers, with the proportions ranging from 60 percent in district 8 to 77 percent in district 10. Among females, the proportion of domestics and unskilled workers was intermediate, between those of the old city and those of the bourgeois quarters. The same was true of the proportion not employed, except in district 8, which had the second highest rate in the city. These districts were predominantly working class in character, but they were all highly respectable neighborhoods. They had few transients (the proportion of adult males living alone was below the citywide average in every district), few foreigners (from only 3 percent of the adults in district 7 to 7 percent in district 9) and relatively low crime rates. By contrast with the crowded, transient, and cosmopolitan neighborhoods of the old city, and especially with slum districts 1 and 3, the working-class suburbs were comfortable, stable, safe, and ethnically homogeneous.

But in spite of these common characteristics, each of the working-class suburbs had its own social personality. District 8, which lay immediately to the east of opulent district 5, was the most prosperous of the working-class suburbs and was also the newest: Nearly all its area had been farmland as recently as the early 1820s. Its mean occupational-status score was the fourth highest in the city, and it had a very substantial bourgeois minority, that is, 36 percent of all active adult males. It also had a high proportion of nonemployed women, that is, 34 percent of the total, second only to district 5, and a high proportion of *rentières*. But if the development of district 8 was influenced by its proximity to district 5, it was a distinctly less opulent neighborhood: Workers made up 60 percent of the active male population, and a substantial proportion of these workers were unskilled. Skilled building workers were particularly prominent in district 8, probably in part because much of the city's new housing was being constructed there at midcentury. All in all, district 8 was intermediate between opulent, bourgeois districts 5 and 6 and the less prosperous of the working-class suburbs, districts 7, 9, and 10. But it had more in common with the working-class suburbs than with the bourgeois quarters.

District 7, which lay immediately to the north of the old city, was the most plebian of the working-class suburbs and had the lowest mean occupational-status score among them. It actually had a substantial bourgeois minority (23 percent of its active adult males), but these were more than balanced off by a very large contingent of unskilled workers. Unskilled workers comprised 31 percent of district 7's active adult males, as high a proportion as any district in the city. District 7 was the main site of Marseille's sugar-refining and oil-pressing factories, which presumably accounted for its very large unskilled population. Skilled workers, who made up 36 percent of the active adult males, barely outnumbered unskilled workers; in no other urban district was the ratio of unskilled to skilled workers so high. Among women, the only distinction of district 7 was that it had the highest proportion of workers in the needle trades (38 percent). Despite the heavy concentration of male un-skilled laborers, district 7 was overwhelmingly French and overwhelmingly stable. Only 3 percent of its population were foreigners – the lowest of any urban district – and only 4 percent of the enumerated adult males lived alone – the lowest proportion of any district in Marseille, urban or rural. District 7 seems to have been a curious neighborhood, at once quite poor and quite respectable.

District 10, the southern shore of the old port, was the oldest of the working-class suburbs; indeed, it was in some respects not a suburb at all, in that most of its built-up area in 1851 lay within the line of the seventeenth-century walls. It had been an industrial neighborhood since the eighteenth century, when it became the center of Marseille's soap industry. But despite the presence of factory industry, and despite the highest proportion of workers of any of the suburbs (77 percent of the active adult males), it had relatively few unskilled workers – only 18 percent of the active adult males. It also had a remarkable concentration of women in the "other craft" category (24 per-cent). District 10 was, above all, a skilled working-class quarter, with workers in trades related to maritime activity particularly prominent: ship caulkers and carpenters, packers and longshoremen, and both male and female rope and sail makers.

District 9, which stretched south and east from the southeastern corner of the seventeenth-century wall, had by far the largest population of the working-class suburban districts in 1851. Among these districts, it was intermediate in its proportion of workers to bourgeois, in its proportion of unskilled to skilled workers, and in its female occupational distribution. It was the center of Marseille's mechanical industry and therefore had a high proportion, about a third, of the city's skilled mechanical and metallurgical workers. Like neighboring district 8, it had an unusually high proportion of workers in the building trades because, like district 8, it was the site of a disproportionate share of new housing construction in this period. It also stood out from the other suburbs in its relatively high proportion of agriculturalists. Although all the suburban districts included open land, only in district 9 does it seem to have been cultivated intensively. All in all, however, district 9 seems to have been more or less typical of the working-class suburbs as a whole.

The outlying countryside

The commune of Marseille covered an area of some 150 square kilometers, of which the built-up area of the city proper covered only a small fraction. The commune was so extensive, in fact, that nearly half its total area was made up of uninhabitable mountainous terrain. (Figure 5.10, a plan of the commune of Marseille in 1848, brings this out clearly.) The commune of Marseille included many acres of farmland and more than a dozen semirural

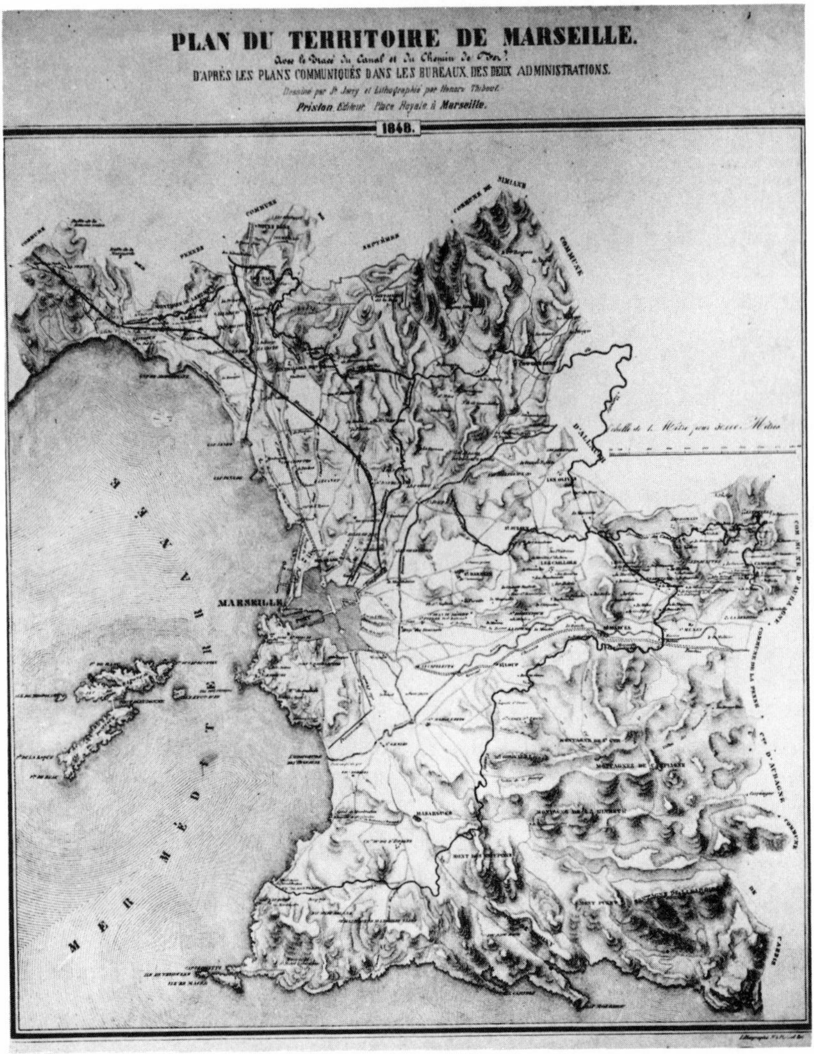

Figure 5.10. The commune of Marseille, 1848. Courtesy Archives de la Chambre de Commerce de Marseille.

villages, the largest of which – Mazargues – had a population of over 2,000 in 1851. But this outlying countryside, although predominantly rural, was strongly influenced by the city. Only a little over a third of the active adult males and about a fifth of young adult females listed agriculture as an occupation. It is likely that some of the men giving *propriétaire* and *journalier* as their occupations actually made their livings from agriculture, but, even adjusting for this possibility, the proportion of the population employed in agriculture would remain considerably less than half the total. Several of Marseille's industries – heavy chemicals, brick and tile manufacture, and flour milling – were located exclusively in the countryside or in small semirural villages in remote parts of the commune. For this reason the percentage of unskilled workers in the outlying countryside was nearly as high as in the commune as a whole. In addition, a substantial number of skilled workers also resided in the countryside. As a result, a higher proportion of the active adult males were engaged in industry than in agriculture in all three of the rural districts. The urban economy thus extended into the predominantly rural areas of the commune. This fact is attested not only by the high proportion of nonagricultural occupations, but also by the nature of the agriculture carried on in the commune. Originally most of the crops grown were the same as in adjoining areas of Provence – principally vines and olives. During the nineteenth century, however, the traditional crops were increasingly replaced by dairy and meat products, fruits, and vegetables, which were sold to the expanding urban population.[13]

District 11, which lay along the seacoast to the south of Marseille, was the most heavily industrialized of the rural districts. Thirty-one percent of its active adult males were unskilled laborers – as high a proportion as in any of the urban districts. Most of these were employed in the large chemical works on the commune's far southern shore. These same factory workers account for the high concentration of Italian males, who made up 13 percent of the district's adult male population, and for the large proportion of transients. These workers were nearly all young single men, most of them Italians, who were housed in barracks on the factory grounds. A high proportion of the women in this district also were unskilled laborers, most of them probably employed in the same factories. District 11 had an appreciable number of fishermen, who lived scattered up and down the coastline. District 13, which lay along Marseille's northern coast, was very similar to district 11. It also had a large working-class population and a sizable contingent of fishermen. Its chief difference from district 11 was that most of its workers were artisans rather than unskilled laborers. District 13, along with district 12, had a high proportion of laundresses, presumably there to take advantage of the open country to lay their clothes out to dry. District 12, which was Marseille's landlocked rural district, had the largest agricultural population, accounting for 40 percent of the active adult males. One also suspects that a healthy proportion of the district's numerous *propriétaries* were engaged in agriculture. Conversely, the district's working-class population was the smallest of the rural districts, and there was only a negligible number of men in maritime occupations.

Stability and change

Such were the neighborhoods of Marseille in 1851. How had they changed and how were they to change over the half-century covered by this study? To answer these questions, it is necessary to examine data from the marriage registers. The first step, which serves as a check on both the marriage-register and census data, is a comparison of the midcentury neighborhood patterns that emerge from these two sources. The marriage registers of 1846–51 generally yield results quite similar to the 1851 census results. A comparison of mean occupational-status scores derived from census and marriage registers shows only minor differences (see Table 5.5 and Figures 5.9 and 5.12). At least when using this measure of overall neighborhood quality, the marriage registers give a close approximation of the census findings. The same conclusion emerges from a more detailed examination of occupational distributions generated by the two sources. (Compare Tables 5.1 and 5.7.) The most notable differences between the census and marriage-register distributions are those already remarked in Chapter 3: Skilled workers are significantly overrepresented on the marriage registers and unskilled workers and rentiers are significantly underrepresented. But these distortions are rather evenly spread across all districts of Marseille. Thus data from the marriage registers tend to make each district too high in skilled workers and too low in unskilled workers and rentiers, but the relative standing of the districts is rarely perceptibly different than indicated by the census data. Indeed, the only really striking difference is readily explained: The marriage registers indicate that only 11 percent of the grooms in district 11 were unskilled workers, whereas according to the census unskilled workers made up 31 percent of active adult males. Most of the unskilled workers in question were young, unmarried transients from Italy who worked in the chemical plants near the southern border of the commune. These workers were nearly all housed in barracks near the plants, and nearly all of them returned to Italy with their savings after a few months or years of labor, consequently making no impression in the marriage registers. The essential reliability of the marriage-register data is also confirmed by figures on the proportion foreign born. Although the marriage registers indicate somewhat higher proportions of foreign born than the census, the relative standing of districts is once again very similar to the census. (Compare Tables 5.4 and 5.11.)

All in all, the marriage registers of 1846–51 and the census of 1851 agree

Table 5.5. *Mean occupational-status scores of districts, 1821–2 to 1869*

	Districts													City
	1	2	3	4	5	6	7	8	9	10	11	12	13	
Marriage registers, 1821–2	49	47	48	54	60	56	50	50	50	51	44	44	43	50
Marriage registers, 1846–51	47	46	47	54	57	59	48	52	49	49	46	44	43	50
Marriage registers, 1869	45	48	48	53	58	57	47	52	51	49	46	46	43	50
Census, 1851	45	47	48	54	61	60	48	53	49	48	43	45	43	50

quite closely. This is heartening, for it seems to imply that both sources give reasonably accurate pictures of Marseille's neighborhoods. Although neither source can be trusted to give precise estimates of, say, the percentage of the active male population of a district in a given occupation, or the percentage of foreigners in the population of a given district, both can probably be trusted to indicate reliably whether a neighborhood stands high or low in its percentage of rentiers, of unskilled workers, of foreigners, etc. Similarly, the apparent accuracy of the 1846–51 marriage registers increases confidence in the accuracy of the 1821–2 and 1869 marriage registers. At the very least, it seems likely that most changes that took place in the social characteristics of brides and grooms living in these neighborhoods were reflections of changes taking place in their overall adult populations.

Probably the most important of all changes taking place in Marseille's neighborhoods between 1821 and 1869 was a change in their absolute and relative populations. The marriage registers, of course, give only a very rough estimate of the populations of districts, because they measure only the number marrying in a given year, not the total population. If the ratio of population to marriages had been constant both over time and from district to district, this would not constitute a difficulty. The problem, of course, is that it was not. The rate of marriages per thousand varied considerably from year to year. For example, it was about 8.0 in 1821, about 8.5 in 1822, about 7.8 in 1846, about 8.9 in 1851, and about 7.7 in 1869. (These marriage rates are calculated by dividing the number of marriages by the best available estimates of the total population. The 1821–2 rates are based on the 1821 census total, the 1846 and 1851 rates on the 1846 and 1851 census totals, and the 1869 rate on the 1866 census totals.) Even in these five sample years, the marriage rate varied by as much as 15 percent. The variation is reduced, however, when 1821–2 and 1846–51 are treated as single units. The effective rates per thousand for the sample units are then 8.25 for 1821–2, 8.35 for 1846–51, and 7.7 for 1869, or a variation of only about 1 percent from 1821–2 to 1846–51 and about 8 percent from 1846–51 to 1869. This means that using the numbers of marriages in a district as an index of its population will tend to understate the population of districts in 1869 relative to 1821–2 and to 1846–51 by about 8 percent.

In addition, marriage rates must also have varied from district to district. One way of checking the likely extent of such variation is to compare the percentages of Marseille's brides and grooms living in each district with the percentage of the population living in the districts as indicated by the 1851 *listes nominatives*. This comparison indicates considerable variation (see Table 5.6). Generally speaking, in 1846–51 the old city and central commercial district had more brides and grooms than would be expected from their weight in the *listes nominatives* sample, and the suburbs and outlying countryside fewer. The reasons for this pattern are by no means clear, and there is no

Table 5.6. *Estimates of population of districts*

	1	2	3	4	Subtotal, old city, and central commercial district	5	6	Subtotal, opulent districts	7	8	9	10	Subtotal, working-class suburbs	11	12	13	Subtotal, outlying districts	Total, Marseille
1. Estimated population from census of 1851	13,890	11,770	23,520	27,090	76,270	14,640	13,150	27,790	8,180	9,900	20,100	7,610	45,790	5,430	12,430	10,170	28,030	177,880
Percent	7.8	6.6	13.2	15.2	42.8	8.2	7.4	15.6	4.6	5.6	11.3	4.3	25.7	3.1	7.0	5.7	15.8	
2. Brides and grooms per year, marriage registers of 1821–2 Number	202	148	308	373	1,031	156	78	234	54	12	97	64	227	63	128	110	301	1,793
Percent	11.2	8.3	17.2	20.8	57.5	8.7	4.4	13.1	3.0	0.7	5.4	3.6	12.7	3.6	7.1	6.1	16.8	
3. Brides and grooms per year, marriage registers of 1846–51 Number	280	212	434	516	1,442	243	227	470	161	107	328	127	723	76	169	168	413	3,048
Percent	9.2	7.1	14.2	16.9	47.4	8.0	7.4	15.4	5.3	3.5	10.7	4.1	20.6	2.4	5.5	5.5	13.4	
4. Brides and grooms per year, marriage registers of 1869 Number	249	281	351	489	1,370	374	366	740	374	332	608	256	1,570	132	284	289	705	4,385
Percent	5.6	6.4	8.0	11.4	31.4	8.5	8.3	16.8	8.5	7.6	13.9	5.8	35.8	3.0	6.5	6.6	16.1	

way of knowing whether it represents some enduring difference or some aberration peculiar to these years. In any case, the variation in marriage rates from district to district that these figures implies is sufficiently large that not too much weight should be placed on changes in the number of brides and grooms over the years unless those changes were quite substantial.

Given these caveats, what do the marriage-register data show (see Table 5.6)? Most obviously, they show that the proportion of the population living in the old city and the central commercial district declined sharply as the city grew. In 1821–2 a sizable majority of Marseille's brides and grooms lived in districts 1, 2, 3, and 4. By 1846–51, the proportion had dropped to less than half, and by 1869 to less than a third. Most of the gains were made by the working-class suburbs, districts 7, 8, 9, and 10, which together rose from about an eighth of the total in 1821–2 to over a third in 1869. The share of the bourgeois quarters rose much more slowly, whereas that of the outlying countryside fell from 1821–2 to 1851 as the city's built-up area came to encompass a larger proportion of the commune's total population and then rose again by 1869 as industrial suburbs began to stretch into previously rural areas.

Despite their declining share of Marseille's population, however, the old city and the central districts seem to have grown in absolute numbers, at least until the middle of the century. Even though these districts were already crowded in 1821–2, their number of brides and grooms per year rose by nearly 40 percent between then and 1846–51. Between 1846–51 and 1869, the number of brides and grooms fell in districts 1, 3, and 4, but rose again in district 2. For the four districts combined, the fall was about 5 percent. But since Marseille's marriage rate was about 8 percent lower in 1869 than in 1846–51, this slight decline probably means no fall in the districts' populations. Indeed, it may mean an increase in crowding in real terms; the new rue Impériale ran through districts 3 and 4, and a large number of dwellings were destroyed during its construction. In 1869 a population of more or less constant size was living in a considerably smaller number of houses. The growth of Marseille's population in the nineteenth century resulted not only in an expansion of housing on the periphery, but in an increased density of population in the already teeming quarters of the old city and the central commercial district. In part this was the result of new building in these areas; old houses were torn down and replaced by larger new ones, and former church property was sold and covered with new dwellings. But there was probably also an increase in crowding in the older buildings, with more people living in each room and buildings being subdivided into more and more tiny chambers. The marriage-register data thus alert us to what must have been an extreme case of overcrowding by the middle of the nineteenth century.

But if the old city and the central district grew during the nineteenth century, their rate of growth was far lower than in the newer parts of the city. Growth was most rapid in the working-class suburbs, which more than tripled from 1821–2 to 1846–51 and doubled again by 1869. Overall, the number of brides and grooms in district 7, 8, 9, and 10 increased by 693 percent from 1821–2 to 1869. From 1821–2 to 1846–51, growth was most rapid in districts 8 and 9. Between 1846–51 and 1869, district 8 was still the fastest growing, but district 7, benefiting from construction of the new port basins, now grew more rapidly than the southern suburbs. The bourgeois quarters, districts 5 and 6, grew less rapidly, but their population more than tripled in the half-century from 1821–2 to 1869. Between 1821–2 and 1846–51, district 6 grew by 291 percent, a rate exceeded only by districts 7, 8, and 9. It was quite densely built by then, however, and its growth rate slowed over the next two decades. Rural districts 11, 12, and 13 also grew more rapidly than the old city and the commercial center. From 1821–2 to 1869, their number of brides and grooms increased by 234 percent. Most of the growth was concentrated in the last two decades, a period when industrial development of the outlying regions was extremely robust.

In a half-century that saw such important changes in the absolute and relative sizes of Marseille's districts, one might also expect important changes in their social characteristics. Yet social characteristics were remarkably stable. As Table 5.5 and Figures 5.11, 5.12, and 5.13 demonstrate, changes in the mean status scores of the districts were relatively slight. The same conclusion emerges from a detailed examination of the distribution of male occupations by neighborhood (see Tables 5.7, 5.8, and 5.9). From 1821–2 to 1846–51, changes were generally very minor, except in the outlying rural districts, where the proportion engaged in agriculture fell dramatically and there was a corresponding rise in the proportion of workers. In the urban districts, the most important changes were in district 10, which lost most of its initially sizable contingent of businessmen and professionals, and in district 6, which became considerably more bourgeois. There were more substantial changes from 1846–51 to 1869. Workers continued to displace agriculturalists in the rural districts. Maritime workers came to be concentrated more heavily than ever in district 1. The proportion of small businessmen dropped in districts 4 and 5 and rose significantly in several other districts: 3, 6, 8, 9, and 10. Apparently, small business followed the city's population outward. In addition, the proportion of bourgeois rose in the upper old city, districts 2 and 3. The rise in district 3 might be accounted for by residents of the new rue Impériale, but there were no major reconstruction projects to explain the rise in district 2.

The distribution of women's occupations by district also remained relatively stable from 1846–51 to 1869 – except that the proportion of domestic servants rose nearly everywhere and the proportions of agriculturalists and unskilled laborers underwent a general decline (see Table 5.10). Small businesswomen continued to be concentrated in the old city and the central commercial district;

MINIMUM	under	45.0	47.6	50.0	53.0	over
MAXIMUM	45	47.5	49.9	52.9	55.9	56

Figure 5.11. Districts by mean occupational-status score, marriage registers, 1821–2.

laundresses were still especially numerous in the rural suburbs; the needle trades continued to be spread remarkably evenly across the city; and the "other crafts" continued to be common in the old city, although their extraordinary concentration in district 10 had vanished. The proportions of nonemployed women and of domestic servants followed the same broad patterns as in 1846–51, but there were some changes. Although the proportion of nonemployed women dropped citywide, it rose to 44 percent of the total in district 5 by 1869. By contrast, in district 6, the other opulent district, nonemployed women made up only 27 percent of the total. This low figure, however, was

MINIMUM   under   45.0   47.6   50.0   53.0   over
MAXIMUM   45   47.5   49.9   52.9   55.9   56

Figure 5.12.   Districts by mean occupational-status score, marriage registers, 1846–51.

partially explained by the extraordinarily high proportion of domestic servants in district 6's female population: 43 percent. In fact, if the domestic servants in district 6 are eliminated from the calculation, 46 percent of all the remaining women were without occupations and only 54 percent employed. On the whole, the correspondence between a district's prosperity and the proportion of its females engaged in domestic service was less clear in 1869 than in 1846–51. By 1869, even the slum districts of the old city had between 13 and 19 percent of their females employed in domestic service, and the proportion reached 30 percent in distinctly working-class suburban district 10.

MINIMUM   under   45.0   47.6   50.0   53.0   over
MAXIMUM   45   47.5   49.9   52.9   55.9   56

Figure 5.13. Districts by mean occupational-status score, marriage registers, 1869.

This suggests that some of the women who reported their occupations as domestic servants in 1869 may not have been live-in domestics but instead lived with their families. This would fit with the fact that a much higher proportion of domestics in 1869 than in 1846–51 were natives of the city.

As might have been expected from the physical development of the city, changes in the occupational characteristics of Marseille's neighborhoods were more significant between 1846–51 and 1869 than between 1821–2 and 1846–51. More surprising is that these extensive projects did not seem to have the effects generally attributed to Haussmann's rebuilding of Paris in these same

Table 5.7. *Groom's occupation by district, marriage registers of 1821–2 (in percent)*

Occupation	District 1	2	3	4	5	6	7	8	9	10	11	12	13	Total
1. Business and professional	7	2	1	8	18	20	—	—	4	13	2	2	1	7
2. Rentiers	—	1	1	3	9	5	8	—	1	—	2	2	4	3
3. Sales and clerical	9	5	5	10	25	14	10	23	16	10	6	1	2	8
4. Small business	4	4	5	13	12	5	6	—	4	4	—	4	2	6
5. Artisan	38	60	63	56	23	39	52	46	49	44	18	19	11	43
6. Service	—	1	1	3	1	5	2	8	—	1	2	—	—	1
7. Unskilled	9	15	15	3	3	5	17	15	11	12	9	6	6	9
8. Maritime	29	9	6	3	3	1	—	—	2	12	9	—	3	8
9. Agriculture	1	1	1	1	3	4	6	8	11	3	52	66	71	14
10. Miscellaneous	3	2	2	—	3	2	—	—	2	1	—	—	—	1
Elite (1 + 2)	7	3	2	11	27	25	8	—	5	13	4	4	5	10
Bourgeois (1 + 2 + 3 + 4)	20	12	12	34	64	44	24	23	25	27	10	9	8	24
Workers (5 + 6 + 7 + 8)	76	85	85	65	30	50	71	69	62	69	38	25	20	61
Number of cases	212	139	302	345	73	81	52	13	98	70	119	106	86	1,761

Table 5.8. Groom's occupation by district, marriage registers of 1846–51 (in percent)

Occupation	District 1	2	3	4	5	6	7	8	9	10	11	12	13	Total
1. Business and professional	4	1	1	8	16	18	1	4	3	6	1	—	1	5
2. Rentier	—	—	1	4	9	5	2	5	2	2	2	3	1	3
3. Sales and clerical	7	2	7	11	16	30	10	17	8	7	8	2	4	10
4. Small business	4	6	5	15	10	7	7	7	7	6	4	5	2	7
5. Artisan	43	62	52	47	34	30	45	48	53	48	36	30	40	45
6. Service	3	1	1	5	6	3	2	3	3	3	1	13	2	3
7. Unskilled	8	20	26	6	7	5	25	10	17	17	11	15	12	14
8. Maritime	30	6	3	2	—	—	2	2	1	7	2	1	2	5
9. Agriculture	—	2	1	1	—	1	5	3	4	1	35	40	35	7
10. Miscellaneous	1	—	3	1	1	1	1	1	2	3	—	1	1	1
Elite (1 + 2)	4	1	2	12	25	23	3	9	5	8	3	3	2	8
Bourgeois (1 + 2 + 3 + 4)	15	9	14	38	51	60	20	33	20	21	15	10	8	25
Workers (5 + 6 + 7 + 8)	84	89	82	60	47	38	74	63	74	75	50	49	56	67
Number of cases	284	213	435	517	188	194	155	105	342	128	84	169	174	2,988

136

Table 5.9. *Groom's occupation by district, marriage registers of 1869 (in percent)*

Occupation	1	2	3	4	5	6	7	8	9	10	11	12	13	Total
1. Business and professional	1	3	6	10	20	13	2	4	7	2	—	1	1	6
2. Rentier	—	—	—	2	5	5	—	2	1	3	—	1	1	2
3. Sales and clerical	10	15	7	18	26	22	19	25	15	10	5	7	6	15
4. Small business	8	3	11	11	10	11	5	6	10	8	3	3	1	7
5. Artisan	28	47	41	38	28	26	43	41	45	52	37	37	38	39
6. Service	2	2	4	11	5	18	3	3	5	3	3	7	1	5
7. Unskilled	10	12	24	7	3	4	22	14	13	18	20	13	26	14
8. Maritime	41	17	5	3	2	.	2	2	1	2	1	2	8	5
9. Agriculture	—	—	1	—	1	—	3	1	2	2	31	29	17	6
10. Miscellaneous	—	1	1	—	—	1	1	1	1	—	—	—	1	1
Elite (1 + 2)	1	3	6	12	25	18	2	6	8	5	—	2	2	8
Bourgeois (1 + 2 + 3 + 4)	19	21	24	41	61	51	26	37	33	23	8	12	9	30
Worker (5 + 6 + 7 + 8)	81	78	74	59	38	48	70	60	64	75	61	59	73	63
Number of cases	115	144	164	236	163	157	198	164	312	136	147	147	106	2,158

Table 5.10. *Bride's occupation by district, marriage registers of 1869 (in percent)*

Bride's occupation	District													Total
	1	2	3	4	5	6	7	8	9	10	11	12	13	
Not employed	16	17	18	30	44	27	12	33	23	17	12	12	9	23
Rentière	1	1	0	2	1	1	1	0	1	0	0	1	1	1
Business and professional	1	1	2	1	1	1	0	1	1	0	2	1	0	1
Small business	10	7	10	8	2	5	7	5	6	5	4	3	6	6
Needle trades	34	41	32	27	21	19	35	34	37	39	26	36	39	32
Laundry	7	7	4	5	5	2	4	4	5	8	12	13	13	6
Other crafts	8	5	6	1	3	1	5	5	3	6	0	0	1	3
Domestic service	17	13	19	22	23	43	28	16	18	18	30	22	21	22
Unskilled	6	9	8	4	1	1	7	4	6	6	4	7	7	5
Agriculture	1	0	1	0	0	0	1	0	0	1	12	5	2	1
Miscellaneous	0	0	1	0	0	0	1	0	0	0	0	0	0	0
Number of cases	134	138	187	253	211	209	178	168	296	120	57	137	142	2,230

years. "Haussmannization" is supposed to have increased the residential segregation of bourgeois and workers in Paris; in Marseille it seems to have caused a partial reintegration of the neighborhoods in the old city. But all in all, the remarkable thing is that changes in the character of Marseille's neighborhoods were so slight. In spite of massive growth of population and built-up areas all along the periphery of the city, and in spite of huge construction projects that reoriented the city's commercial axis and destroyed large numbers of dwellings, Marseille's neighborhoods still retained the same social character in 1869 that they had in the early 1820s, before the city's rapid growth began. In spite of some minor shifts in the proportions of some occupations, the portraits of Marseille's neighborhoods drawn from the census of 1851 can stand without significant retouching for the entire half-century from 1820 to 1870.

The marriage registers also contain one kind of information that is lacking in the census. The census indicates the national origin of all foreigners living in Marseille, but does not give the origins of those residents born in France. The marriage registers, on the other hand, give the place of birth of every groom and bride, thus making it possible to distinguish French-born immigrants to Marseille from natives of the city. When the city was growing as rapidly as it did in the half-century covered by this study, migration was massive. The marriage registers make it possible to discern how the city's neighborhoods were affected by the migratory influx, and how the immigrants' settlement patterns changed over time. As a glance at Table 5.11 will reveal, the most obvious change between 1821–2 and 1869 was a huge increase in the proportion of Marseille's population born outside the city. The proportion of natives dropped from 65 percent in 1821–2 to only 35 percent in 1869. Furthermore, the increase of the immigrant population was felt in all quarters of the city. In 1821–2 no district was less than half native born; in 1869 only two were more than half native born. None of the city's neighborhoods could escape the effects of Marseille's immense influx of migration, a process that was of fundamental importance to the city's social history in the era, and one that will be discussed in some detail in the following chapters. But at the same time, neighborhoods were affected differently at different times.

Throughout the half-century under study, the outlying districts had distinctly fewer immigrants than the urban districts. In large part this reflects the continuing presence of agriculturalists, of whom the vast majority were native born. Within the urban agglomeration, however, different districts had relatively high proportions of immigrants at different times (see Figures 5.14, 5.15, and 5.16). In 1821–2, there were only two neighborhoods with more than 40 percent immigrants: the central commercial district and district 5, the bourgeois quarter immediately to the east. District 8, which also had over 40 percent immigrants, was represented by only 24 cases in 1821–2, not enough to make these figures reliable. The neighborhoods with the highest proportion

Table 5.11. Birthplace by district, brides and grooms combined (in percent)

District	1821–2				1846–51				1869			
	Marseille	Other France	Italy	Rest of world	Marseille	Other France	Italy	Rest of world	Marseille	Other France	Italy	Rest of world
1	61	31	6	2	50	33	16	1	36	48	15	1
2	69	25	5	1	56	30	12	2	36	52	11	1
3	60	33	6	1	39	40	19	2	24	59	14	3
4	56	36	7	1	34	52	8	6	28	61	7	4
5	53	32	3	12	36	54	4	6	33	61	2	4
6	63	27	4	6	36	52	4	8	23	66	4	2
7	64	29	4	3	51	42	5	2	32	59	8	1
8	54	42	0	4	43	47	7	3	37	54	5	4
9	66	28	2	4	37	51	9	3	30	60	7	3
10	62	29	6	3	52	35	10	3	42	46	10	2
11	83	16	1	0	73	21	5	1	58	30	11	1
12	88	11	0	1	67	31	3	2	51	39	8	2
13	89	11	0	0	68	29	2	1	42	47	10	1
Total	65	29	4	2	45	43	9	3	35	54	8	3

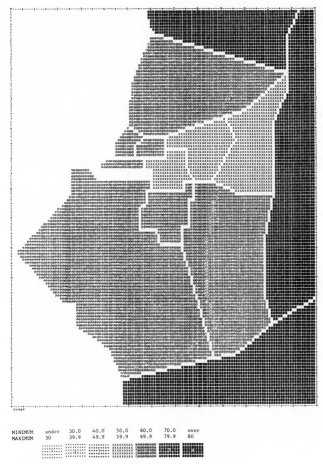

MINIMUM   under   30.0   40.0   50.0   60.0   70.0   over
MAXIMUM   30   39.9   49.9   59.9   69.9   79.9   80

Figure 5.14. Districts by percent natives, 1821–2.

of natives were two working-class quarters: district 2 in the old city and district 9 on the southeastern periphery. By 1846–51 and 1869, this config-uration had changed considerably. District 4 continued to have a high pro-portion of immigrants, and district 2 to have a high proportion of natives. But district 9, originally a preserve of native Marseillais, had among the highest proportion of immigrants in 1846–51 and 1869; districts 3 and 6 went from about average proportions of natives in 1821–2 to the lowest proportions in 1869; districts 1 and 10 went from average proportions of natives in 1821–2 to near the top in the later periods. This rather jumbled pattern of change over time would seem to indicate the irresistible force of the migratory influx:

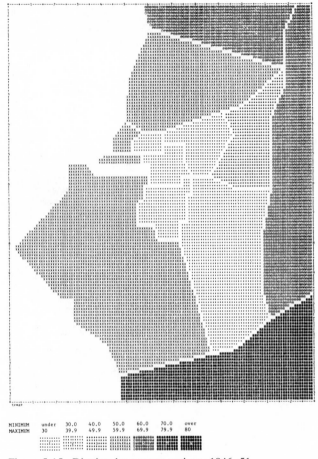

MINIMUM   under   30.0   40.0   50.0   60.0   70.0   over
MAXIMUM   30   39.9   49.9   59.9   69.9   79.9   80

Figure 5.15. Districts by percent natives, 1846–51.

No neighborhood could resist effectively for long. The only general pattern that seems to stand out in the flux is a tendency for the coastal districts 1, 2, 7, and 10 to emerge as the native-dominated quarters by midcentury and to retain this character to an attenuated extent in 1869 – except for district 7, which was transformed fundamentally in this latter period by the construction of new port basins and industries.

The figures on foreign-born immigrants form a somewhat more coherent picture (see Table 5.11). In 1821–2 the number of foreign born was very small and the patterns of concentration not very clear – except for the non-Italian foreigners, who were concentrated to a remarkable extent in districts 5 and 6, the bourgeois quarters. But by 1846–51 clearer patterns had emerged,

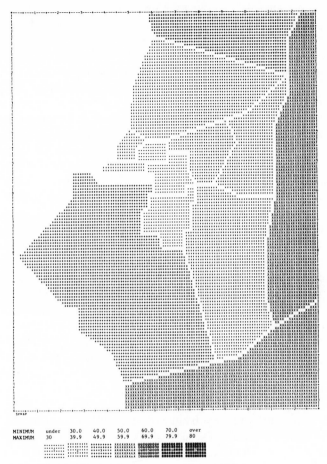

Figure 5.16. Districts by percent natives, 1869.

and these held with only minor changes in 1869 as well. Italians were concentrated in the working-class districts, 1, 2, and 3, and other foreigners in the more opulent districts, 4, 5, and 6. The most striking change over time was a sharp rise of Italian immigrants in the outlying districts, from virtually none in 1821–2, to fewer than 5 percent in 1846–51, to about 10 percent, or higher than the citywide average, in 1869. This rise is presumably attributable to the growth of factory industry in the once-rural periphery of the city.

Perhaps the most surprising finding of this chapter is the remarkable stability in the social character and occupational composition of Marseille's neighborhoods. Extensive new developments were built all around the city's periphery to accommodate its rapidly growing population, and these changed the shape and the physical aspect of the city fundamentally. But the social characteristics of the newly constructed neighborhoods so closely resembled those of the contiguous older neighborhoods that the social and occupational map of the city was scarcely altered by the new construction. In 1869, as in 1821–2, the city was comprised of four socially distinct areas: the old city, which was a crowded and poor working-class quarter; an opulent belt, occupying the central commercial district at the head of the port and stretching to the south and to the east; a series of peripheral, predominantly working-class, suburbs; and an outer ring of largely rural countryside. The most important changes that took place during the half-century of rapid city growth were changes in distribution of population. The working-class suburbs grew enormously, while the opulent quarters grew at a moderate rate and the already crowded old city and central district grew much more slowly. But the growth of the city's population filled up and extended the already existing social framework of Marseille's neighborhoods, rather than producing a new spatial arrangement of social classes and categories.

If the stability of neighborhood characteristics was remarkable, the most notable feature of Marseille in this half-century was the sheer extent and rapidity of its growth. Its population nearly tripled from 1821 to 1872, and its built-up area more than doubled. So intense was Marseille's growth that the already overcrowded quarters of the old city and central commercial district actually gained population between the 1820s and the middle of the century and probably became even more crowded by the end of the 1860s. The density of population increased in all parts of the commune, as existing houses came to accommodate more and more people, as open spaces in the formerly built-up area were filled with new buildings, as farmland was covered over by streets and dwellings, and as the number of houses and factories in the outlying rural areas of the commune increased. At the same time, in all the city's districts the proportion of native-born Marseillais fell precipitously, as an unending stream of immigrants from the rest of France and beyond poured into the city to fill the unquenchable demand for new labor and new talent. The historian of Marseille, contemplating the results of his calculations, may be impressed by the underlying continuity of Marseille's neighborhood structure, but a Marseillais who lived through these years would doubtless have been far more impressed by the crowding, the receding of green spaces, the noise and the bustle of traffic, and the increasing cosmopolitanism of the city's population.

One such Marseillais, Victor Gelu, had already formed such impressions by 1851.

The sight of this countryside, once so smiling, but now needlessly disemboweled by the vandals of real-estate speculation to make room for satanic foundries, unhealthy factories, sordid little streets with their huts full of hooligans, has always broken my heart. . . . Oh Marseille of my youth, where are you. . . ? Where are those sandy beaches where I cavorted under the summer sun? Where are those coves, those tranquil bays in which, without fear of the tempest's blast, we went to frolic like a band of joyous tritons for days on end, with the crowd of my little comrades? Beaches, bays and coves now lie buried more than a kilometer inside the earth that filled them up.[14]

. . . And another thing that saddened me in my promenades was to meet along my way only Piedmontais, *Gavots* [a slang term for persons from the Alpine regions, with about the same connotations as our hillbilly], *Auvergnats*, or other unsavory *Franciots* [that is, speakers of French rather than the local dialect of Provençal]. "Alas," I cried, in the bitterness of my soul. . . . "There are probably no more than fifteen thousand real Marseillais among the three hundred thousand souls who live in Marseille today."[15]

Perhaps most Marseillais would look upon these changes more favorably; after all, they could be seen as signs of prosperity and progress, rather than of destruction and degradation. But nearly all must have been far more impressed with the changes wrought by the rapid growth of their city than by the continuities that the historian can discern beneath the flux. And they were right: The most important feature of the social history of nineteenth-century Marseille was its monumental and unrelenting growth in area and in population.

6 The demography of urban growth

By what processes and with what rhythms did the massive increase in Marseille's population take place? This chapter attempts to chart and analyze the demographic components of Marseille's population growth. The population of Marseille was virtually stagnant for the first two decades of the nineteenth century – and had been essentially stagnant since the outbreak of the French Revolution, thanks to the great maritime depression of the Revolutionary and Napoleonic war years. It was not until the 1820s that a significant upturn began, and not until the later twenties that genuinely rapid growth was launched (see Table 6.1). From the 1820s on, the growth was relentless. In no five-year period between 1821 and 1872 did population actually fall. And when, as in 1836–41 or 1846–51, the rate was lower than usual, the next five-year period showed unusually rapid growth. What were the sources of this relentless growth of Marseille's population? Did it result mainly from the internal demographic situation of the city with death rates falling while birth rates rose or remained high? Or did growth result mainly from migration? The first step toward answering these questions is to assess the balance of births and deaths in the city.

Births, deaths, natural increase, and migration

Figure 6.1 charts the number of births and deaths per year from 1806 to 1872. The figures for births show a decline during the last years of the Empire, a rather constant rise from 1814 to 1855, a sudden spurt between 1855 and 1859, and very little change thereafter. The figures for deaths are far more irregular, yielding a much more jagged line. The number of deaths clearly varied much more sharply from year to year than the number of births. Generally speaking, deaths were above births during the Empire, below births from the late teens to the late twenties, above births again through the late thirties, and generally below births thereafter, with the notable exception of occasional years of very high mortality. Much of the jaggedness of the death line was caused by visitations of epidemic disease. The heavy mortalities of the first two and a half decades were caused by typhoid in 1813 and by smallpox in 1828. All but one of the much deadlier and more frequent peaks in mortality from the middle 1830s to the early 1870s were caused by cholera

146

Table 6.1. *Population of Marseille, 1801–72*

Population		Annual rate of increase
1801	111,130	−0.3
1816	106,872	0.5
1821	109,483	1.3
1826	115,943	3.3
1831	132,330	3.2
1836	148,597	1.5
1841	156,060	5.4
1846	183,186	2.4
1851	195,138	7.7
1856	233,817	5.4
1861	260,910	4.8
1866	300,131	2.1
1872	312,868	

Sources: The figure for 1801 is from Charles H. Pouthas, *La Population française pendant la première moitié du XIXe siècle* (Paris, 1956), p. 98, and that for 1816 is from Joseph Mathieu, *Marseille: statistique et histoire* (Marseille, 1879), p. 6. In both cases the figure used is the largest available estimate. The figures from 1821 on are generally available census figures. They may be found, for example, in F. L. Charpin, *Pratique religieuse et formation d'une grand ville: Le Geste du baptême et sa signification en sociologie religieuse* (Paris, 1964), in Gaston Rambert, *Marseille: la formation d'une grande cité moderne: Etude et géographie urbaine* (Marseille, 1934), p. 270; or in Hyppolyte Mireur, *Le Mouvement comparé de la population à Marseille, en France et dans les états de l'Europe* (Paris, 1889), pp. 14–18.

– in 1835, 1837, 1849, 1854–5, and 1865. The dismal peak of 1871 was caused by smallpox.

The curves for births and deaths show very little difference between births and deaths in Marseille through the 1830s. Thereafter, births outnumbered deaths in most years. But the excess of births over deaths that accumulated over normal years tended to be wiped out by catastrophic mortalities that struck at least once a decade. Owing to very similar numbers of births and deaths in the earlier years, and owing to occasional years of very high mortality from the middle 1830s on, very little of the growth of Marseille's population in the first three quarters of the nineteenth century can be attributed to a surplus of births over deaths. This surplus, which demographers call the "natural increase" in the population, was very low in this period. In the entire 66 years from 1806 to 1872, only 14,012 more people were born in Marseille than died.

Assessing changes in Marseille's demographic behavior over time requires

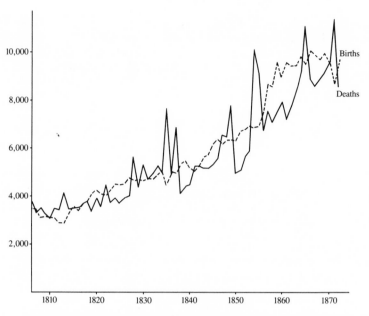

Figure 6.1. Births and deaths per year, 1806–72. From Joseph Mathieu, *Marseille, statistique et histoire* (Marseille, 1879), pp. 34–5.

examination of rates rather than absolute figures for births, deaths, and natural increase. Because available figures for the total population of Marseille must be used to construct rates, some remarks on the nature and reliability of the figures are in order. Figures for the total population of Marseille from 1801 to 1816 are highly unreliable and involve a great deal of guesswork. For example, the population of Marseille in 1801 is listed in different sources as 90,500, 102,219, and 111,130,[1] and figures given for 1806, 1811, and 1816 are almost equally disparate. All the figures from 1821 on are published census results. Of course, the accuracy of these figures is not entirely certain either, but it seems reasonable to assume that the margin of error in the census figures is probably considerably smaller. On the other hand, the figures for births and deaths from 1806 on are derived from the civil registries of vital events and appear to be relatively accurate.[2] This means that acceptably reliable birth and death rates can be constructed only from 1821 on, whereas those from 1806 to 1821 are more dubious. For this reason, in the tables that follow, maximum and minimum birth and death rates are given for these earlier years, based on the lowest and the highest available estimates of the total population.

The demography of urban growth 149

Table 6.2. *Birth and death rates, France and Marseille, 1807–72*

	Average annual birth rates per 1,000			Average annual death rates per 1,000		
	France	Marseille	Marseille as % of France	France	Marseille	Marseille as % of France
1807–11	31.3	(31.7)	(101)	25.9	(33.3)	(129)
		(34.6)	(110)		(36.2)	(140)
1812–16	31.6	(31.3)	(99)	26.3	(34.5)	(131)
		(32.2)	(105)		(36.3)	(138)
1817–21	31.8	(36.7)	(115)	25.3	(34.2)	(135)
		(37.3)	(117)		(34.8)	(138)
1822–6	31.2	38.7	124	25.0	34.9	140
1827–31	30.2	37.6	125	25.0	39.1	156
1832–6	29.4	34.4	117	25.0	38.6	151
1837–41	28.2	34.1	121	23.8	32.9	138
1842–6	28.0	34.2	122	22.7	31.3	138
1847–51	20.7	33.6	126	23.7	32.5	137
1852–6	25.9	32.4	125	24.2	35.0	145
1857–61	26.7	36.5	137	23.8	30.0	126
1862–6	26.5	34.2	129	22.5	32.3	143
1867–72	25.4	31.1	122	25.9	30.4	117

Source: The figures for birth and death rates in France are from E. Levasseur, *La Population française*, 2 vols. (Paris, 1891), vol. 2, pp. 6–9.

The birth and death rates given in the charts and tables are average *annual* rates for the five-year periods. Because there was sometimes a large difference between the total population of Marseille at the beginning and end of the five-year periods, calculations are based on the mean of the population at the beginning and end of each five-year census interval. For example, because the population of Marseille grew from 156,000 in 1841 to 183,186 in 1846, the average of these two figures, 169,593, has been used for calculating birth, death, natural increase, and migration rates for the period 1842–6.[3]

When Marseille's vital figures are converted into rates, it is clear that the low rate of natural increase was attributable mainly to high mortality. In fact, Marseille's birth rates were 15 to 37 percent higher than the national average, except during the First Empire, when they were about equal to the national average. Death rates, however, were consistently much higher than the national average, by a margin ranging from 25 to 56 percent. Marseille clearly remained a very unhealthy place throughout the first three-quarters of the nineteenth century (see Table 6.2). The birth rate was relatively low during the First Empire: between 31 and 35 per 1,000 in 1807–11 (depending on what estimate of the total population is used) and between 31 and 32 per 1,000 in 1812–16. The low birth rate probably reflects a lack of confidence in the future as well as in the absence of some marriage-age men, who were serving in the Imperial armies. With the return of peace, the birth rate rose to 36.7 in 1817–21 and remained high for the following decade. It then fell to 34.4 in 1832–6 and fluctuated around that level until 1867–72, when it fell to 31.1 – perhaps in response to the disruptions of the Franco-Prussian War and the Commune. Death rates were higher than birth rates from 1807 to 1816 and remained at about the same level until 1827–31, when they rose to just under 40 per thousand. Death rates remained high in the next period, 1832–6, partly because of the cholera epidemic in 1835. In 1837–41, the death rate dropped to 32.9, below the level of the first quarter of the century, and fluctuated with no clear trend between then and 1872. Resulting from the interplay of birth and death rates were three periods of natural increase in population: 1817–26, 1837–51, and 1857–72. These were partially offset by three periods of natural decrease: 1807–16, 1827–36, and 1852–6 (see Table 6.3).

From 1821 (the first census giving an acceptably reliable figure for total population) to 1872, the natural increase in population was only 9,284. Yet in these same five decades the population of Marseille rose from 109,438 to 312,868, a gain of 203,430 inhabitants. The large gap between these two figures was filled by migration. The net flow of migration into Marseille over this entire fifty-year period was thus 194,146, or the difference between the total increase in population (203,430) and the amount of increase accounted for by a surplus of births over deaths (9,284). It should be stressed that this figure of 194,146 is the figure for the *net* migration into Marseille in these years, or the difference between the movement of people into the city and the movement of people out of the city. Research on nineteenth-century Boston has shown how much the actual flow of migration may surpass the net flow. In Boston during the decade of the 1880s, total immigration into the city was more than twelve times as great as net immigration. Some three times as many families lived in Boston at *some* time during the 1880s as lived there at any *single* time in the decade.[4] Although comparable figures are not available for Boston in other decades, there is no reason to think the 1880s should have been extraordinary. Unfortunately, the kind of data used in the Boston study (annual city directories) are not available for Marseille, so no estimation of the total flow of migration can be made. But all studies that have attempted to measure population stability, in both Europe and North America, have found that nineteenth-century urban dwellers were extremely mobile. The flow of in- and out-migration between 1855 and 1864 in the German city Frankfurt-am-Main was not quite as dizzying as that in Boston in the 1880s, but it too was very high. Twice as many individuals lived in Frankfurt in that

Table 6.3. Birth rates, death rates, and rates of natural increase, Marseille, 1807–72

	Total births	Average annual birth rate per 1,000	Total deaths	Average annual death rate per 1,000	Natural increase (+) or decrease (−)	Average annual rate of natural increase per 1,000
1807–11	15,993	(31.7) (34.6)	16,783	(33.3) (36.2)	−790	(−1.6) (−1.6)
1812–16	16,073	(31.3) (32.2)	18,111	(34.5) (36.3)	−2,037	(−3.2) (−3.9)
1817–21	19,838	(36.7) (37.3)	18,511	(34.2) (34.8)	+1,326	(2.5) (2.5)
1822–6	21,816	38.7	19,655	34.9	+2,161	3.8
1827–31	23,381	37.6	24,285	39.1	−904	−1.5
1832–6	24,152	34.4	27,171	38.6	−3,019	−4.2
1837–41	25,949	34.1	24,963	32.9	+986	1.3
1842–6	29,011	34.2	26,555	31.3	+2,456	2.9
1847–51	31,820	33.6	30,747	32.5	+1,083	1.1
1852–6	34,773	32.4	37,525	35.0	−2,752	−2.6
1857–61	45,185	36.5	37,115	30.0	+8,070	6.5
1862–6	48,009	34.2	45,387	32.3	+2,622	1.9
1867–72	57,216	31.1	55,878	30.4	+1,344	0.7

Table 6.4. *Net migration into Marseillle, 1817–72*

	Total growth of population	Growth attributable to natural increase	Growth attributable to migration	Average annual migration rate per 1,000
1822–6	6,460	2,161	4,299	7.6
1827–31	16,387	−904	17,291	27.8
1832–6	16,267	−3,019	19,286	27.4
1837–41	7,463	986	6,477	8.6
1842–6	27,126	2,456	24,670	29.1
1847–51	11,952	1,083	10,869	11.5
1852–6	38,633	−2,752	41,385	42.3
1857–61	27,039	8,070	18,969	16.5
1862–6	39,221	2,625	36,596	27.2
1867–72	12,733	2,344	10,389	5.7

decade as lived there at any single time.[5] In a wide range of nineteenth-century cities – Omaha, Poughkeepsie, and Boston in the United States, Hamilton in Canada, and Bochum in Germany – the proportion of the population living in a city that continued to live there ten years later was only 30 to 50 percent.[6] As all these figures make plain, net immigration figures grossly understate the real flow of migration. Yet even the net immigration figures tell a striking story: Fully 94 percent of Marseille's growth from 1821 to 1872 must be attributed to net immigration. It was only by attracting a large and continuing stream of immigrants that Marseille achieved its impressive growth in population.

The size of this migratory stream varied considerably over time, as Table 6.4 and Figure 6.2 make clear. The annual rate of net migration into Marseille was particularly high in 1827–36, 1842–6, and 1852–66; it was more moderate in 1822–6, 1837–41, 1847–51, and 1867–72. But in no period between 1822 and 1872 (nor for that matter between 1872 and the Second World War)[7] did the number of people moving away from Marseille surpass the number of people arriving.

The proportion of immigrants in the population

Figures for net immigration are useful both to set a lower limit for the total volume of immigration and to indicate probable fluctuations in the flow of immigration over time. But they do not tell us what weight immigrants had in the overall population at any point in time. To answer this question other kinds of sources must be used. The census does not indicate the places of birth of the city's population until 1861, and even then only the department

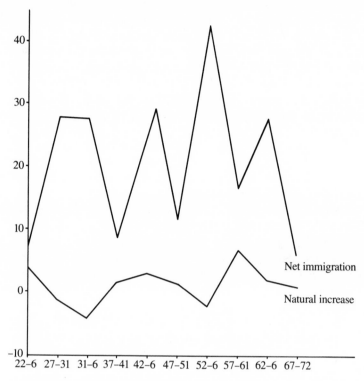

Figure 6.2. Natural increase and net immigration, rates per thousand, 1822–6 to 1867–72.

of birth is given – meaning that it is impossible to distinguish between natives of the city and immigrants who moved to Marseille from other localities within the department. In 1872 no information on birthplace was recorded, and not until 1881 is a figure given for the proportion of the population actually born in the city. In both 1861 and 1866 the proportion of the population born in the Bouches-du-Rhône (Marseille's department) was 59 percent. In 1876 the proportion had fallen somewhat to 54 percent, but by 1881 it had risen again to 59 percent. In this latter year the proportion of the population born in the city proper was 50 percent.[8] It is difficult to know how much of the fluctuation in these figures can be accounted for by real changes in the proportion of immigrants in the population and how much by measurement errors, but it appears that persons born in Marseille's department accounted for somewhere between 54 and 60 percent of the population from 1861 to 1881. If it can be assumed that the proportion of immigrants from the Bouches-du-Rhône was more or less constant at its 1881 level of 8 to 9 percent, the proportion of the city's population made up by native Marseillais must have been between 45 and 51 percent.

These census figures are of only limited utility. In the first place, they concern only the final decade of the period covered by this study. In addition, they do not distinguish birthplaces by age, so that the figures include both adults and children in a single aggregate proportion. Most children in any city, even where rates of immigration are very high, are likely to have been born in the city: very few children migrate on their own initiative, and many children of immigrant young adults will actually be born in the new residence rather than the premigration residence. As a result, the proportion of immigrants is normally much higher in the adult population than in the preadult population. Thus the census figures are not very useful for estimating the proportion made up by immigrants in the adult population, and it is this latter proportion that is of greatest social significance.

These problems of the census figures can be avoided by using birthplace data from the marriage registers – although only at the cost of adding new problems. The marriage registers have the advantage of including only adults. They have the added advantage of providing figures for 1821–2, 1846–51, and 1869, thus spanning the entire half-century covered by this study. The problem, by now a familiar one, is that they do not accurately reflect the composition of the adult population (see the discussion in Appendix A). The population of brides and grooms was considerably younger than the adult population as a whole, marriage registers omitted those who remained unmarried, and the registers also missed those residents of the city who married women from other localities and celebrated the wedding at the bride's home town.

More seriously, from the point of view of estimating the proportion of immigrants in the population, was the fact that the marriage registers did not include immigrants who married before settling in Marseille. This omission from the data set makes the marriage registers underrepresent immigrants by an unknown but possibly substantial amount. In this, as in most societies demographers have studied, migration seems usually to have been undertaken by persons between the ages of 15 and 35. At least in the 1860s and 1870s, migration into Marseille seems to have been particularly concentrated in the late 20s.[9] This means that the age of migration was roughly similar to the usual age of marriage, which was between 25 and 30 for men and 20 and 25 for women. It seems likely that migration was most commonly undertaken by unmarried men and women and that marriage usually marked the beginning of a more settled existence. But because migration was still quite common in the late 20s and early 30s, it must be assumed that a substantial proportion of immigrants was already married when they arrived in Marseille. This means that they do not appear in the marriage-register data sets, and that migration figures based on the marriage registers will systematically underestimate the proportion of immigrants in the population.

In spite of these problems and shortcomings, the marriage-register data are indispensable for forming an adequate picture of migration into Marseille, especially for the period before 1861, when no other data are available. In 1821–2, on the eve of Marseille's rapid influx of immigration, 61 percent of Marseille's grooms and 69 percent of its brides had been born in the city, whereas immigrants accounted for 39 percent of grooms and 31 percent of brides. These figures seem to indicate two conclusions. First, they show that native Marseillais were a solid majority of the city's adults in the years before the massive population rise. But at the same time, they indicate that a substantial level of immigration was already a well-established feature of Marseille's social life even before the spectacular expansion that began in the 1820s. Taking into account that the marriage registers underestimate the true proportion of immigrants in the young adult population, it appears that better than two-fifths of the city's young men and at least a third of its young women had been born outside Marseille. A sizable immigrant population was thus already evident in the early 1820s.

By the middle of the nineteenth century, after two decades of rapid population growth and heavy net immigration, the weight of immigrants in the population was much greater. In 1846–51, only 43 percent of the grooms and 47 percent of the brides were natives of Marseille, whereas immigrants now rose to 57 percent and 53 percent. Allowing once again for the underrepresentation of immigrants in these figures, by the middle of the century at least three-fifths of the city's young men and substantially over half of its young women had been born outside the city. Immigrants now were the solid majority, whereas native Marseillais had been reduced to a minority in their own city. By 1869 these tendencies had become more pronounced. Now only 33 percent of the grooms and 36 percent of the brides were natives, whereas immigrants made up 67 percent of the grooms and 64 percent of the brides. When adjusted for the underrepresentation of immigrants, these figures reveal a population dominated by immigrants to an even greater extent than it had been dominated by natives some fifty years earlier. A good seven-tenths of the city's young men had been born outside the city, and no fewer than two-thirds of its young women. Marseille had become a city of immigrants.

That the proportion of immigrants had risen sharply from 1821–2 to the middle of the century is hardly surprising. Before 1821 the population had been essentially stagnant for over thirty years, and net immigration had consequently been insignificant. But from 1821 to 1851 some 83,000 more persons had moved to Marseille than had moved away. This large increase in the net inflow of immigrants produced a much higher proportion of immigrants in the population. But the further rise in the weight of immigrants in the population that took place between the middle of the century and 1869 is not so easy to explain. Net immigration was only very slightly higher in the 1860s than in the 1840s, so this factor alone should not explain the large increase in the proportion of immigrants. Rather, it seems most likely that the rise in the proportion of immigrants and corresponding fall in the proportion of natives must have resulted from an increasing volatility of the native-born population. If so, the relatively constant rate of net immigration between the 1840s and 1860s must actually have been the outcome of an increasing total flow of immigration that was canceled out by an increasing flow of native Marseillais out of their native city. Although the evidence is by its nature inconclusive, it suggests that the third quarter of the century – perhaps not coincidentally the period when the basic French rail network was laid – saw a declining attachment to the home community on the part of both rural-born and urban-born people.

In any case, the major conclusions to be drawn from the marriage-register data are clear. The proportion of immigrants in the population increased prodigiously in the half-century following 1820. Marseille began the half-century as a city dominated by a native-born adult population but ended it as a city dominated by immigrants, in which better than two of every three adults had migrated to Marseille from either near or distant parts. In the composition of its population, Marseille had ceased to be a hometown community.

Part II
Mobility

The changes in Marseille's social structure that have been charted in Chapters 2 through 6 had one inescapable consequence: an increase in the mobility of individuals. Marseille's booming economy and changing occupational structure meant a growing demand for labor in general and for certain types of labor in particular. Given a demographic structure that produced only a small differential between births and deaths, and consequently a very low rate of natural increase in population, the rising demand for labor could only be met by an influx of individuals from outside the city. Chapter 7 will attempt to describe the process of migration into Marseille: to chart the changing characteristics of the immigrants and to indicate something of their experience of migration. Chapter 8 will examine the records of criminal courts to assess the common claim that migration was a potent source of personal and social disorder in nineteenth-century cities.

Chapters 9 and 10 will examine another variety of individual mobility that arose out of changes in Marseille's social structure: social mobility. Economic growth and changes in occupational structure meant that young men and women had increasing opportunities to occupy social and occupational statuses different from those of their families of origin. Because the population of Marseille did little more than reproduce itself, many of the young men and women who were to fill the new positions were bound to be drawn from the countryside, where few of their families were engaged in urban occupations of any kind. This meant an increasingly poor fit between the occupational backgrounds of the labor force and the requirements for labor in Marseille. The consequence was rising social mobility. What was less certain, however, was how opportunities for mobility would be distributed among natives, immigrants, and individuals from different occupational backgrounds.

Chapter 9 discusses the changing levels and processes of social mobility among men; Chapter 10 continues the analysis for women. For men, the most important determinant of social status was occupation. The analysis of men's social mobility will therefore concentrate on the ways in which men's occupations differed from those of their fathers. For women, the question of social mobility is more complex. Getting a good job was certainly an important step toward achieving a satisfactory status, but for most women the main determinant of their adult status was not their own occupation but that of the men they married. An analysis of women's social-mobility patterns will,

157

consequently, require not only a comparison of women's occupations with those of their fathers, but also a comparison of their fathers' and husbands' occupations. These chapters will show that men's and women's social-mobility patterns differed in a number of ways. They will also reveal one important similarity: Among both men and women, immigrants played a special role in the process of social mobility.

7 Migration

In the half-century following 1820, Marseille became a city of immigrants. To the extent that immigrants differed significantly from natives, their increasing predominance in the population must have had important consequences for Marseille's social life. But, popular and professional preconceptions notwithstanding, it is by no means self-evident what the social effects of immigration were. Traditionally, immigration into cities like nineteenth-century Marseille was assumed to have been a profoundly disruptive process that led to a deterioration of social order and mental well-being in the urban population. The dominant metaphor for rural–urban migration, among both professional historians and the educated public at large, is uprooting. Immigrants are said to be uprooted from well-integrated native communities and cast into an impersonal, mechanical urban world. Bereft of kin and community ties, immigrants suffer from personal disarray and social disorganization, and, although many are eventually assimilated into urban society, the process leaves many casualties. This conception of migration is embedded in a long and pervasive tradition of sociological thought, most notably represented in this country by Robert E. Park,[1] a tradition that has been assimilated by historians.[2]

The social history of nineteenth-century France has been especially dominated by this gloomy view of migration. Louis Chevalier's *Classes laborieuses et classes dangereuses*,[3] which is by far the most widely read book on the subject, presents what is probably the most luridly pessimistic account of migration anywhere in the scholarly literature of history. He treats immigration to Paris and the social conditions it allegedly created there as not only abnormal, but, to use his own favorite term, "pathological." According to Chevalier, most of the serious social problems of nineteenth-century Paris – poverty, crime, suicide, mental illness, even class hatred – can be traced to excessive migration. In fact, a close reading of Chevalier's book reveals that his inferences about the pathological effects of migration are almost entirely speculative; they are based more on his theoretical presuppositions and on the opinions of current observers than on any analysis of the actual nature and experience of migration.[4] But the overwhelmingly positive reception this curious book has received, in both France and the English-speaking world, indicates the strength of popularly held preconceptions about migration and the need for a more cautious and empirical approach to the problem.

Although many historians have accepted the traditional gloomy view of

159

migration, studies by historical demographers have put migration in a new light. These scholars have found migration to be an important feature of nearly all the populations they have studied, back as far as adequate data are available.[5] The fact that migration has been widespread in all parts of Europe at least since the fourteenth or fifteenth century challenges the assumption, implicit in the traditional view, that premodern rural societies were usually immobile and that high levels of migration are a peculiarly modern affliction. The historical demographers, with rare exceptions,[6] treat migration as an expected and normal feature of all populations, a feature no more alarming than births, deaths, or marriages. Although this attitude supplies a healthy corrective to the older gloomy view, demographers have generally been far more concerned simply to measure levels of migration – and to determine the numerical importance of migration in the growth or decline of the populations they study – than to assess its broader impact on society.[7] Their work has not, therefore, directly confronted the common historical view that migration was both a symptom and a cause of social disarray.

On the other hand, empirical work by sociologists and anthropologists suggests that most migration in contemporary societies, both in highly in-dustrialized countries and in Third World countries, has not been of the extreme uprooting kind. In recent times, migration has commonly taken place in the context of larger family or kinship groups and has not necessarily broken ties with the migrant's community of origin. Moreover, those who migrated often were considerably better qualified for the urban labor market than those who did not migrate, and migrants frequently had already obtained jobs in the place of destination before undertaking to move.[8] Historical studies of nineteenth-century European and American cities are also beginning to undermine the traditional gloomy view of migration. Perhaps the best-known are studies of international migration, which show that immigrants have quickly established stable and socially dense communities in the cities where they have settled.[9] A few studies have recently appeared that provide the same kind of detailed quantitative assessment of migration as that offered here for Marseille – studies that analyze the pre- and postmigration characteristics of a large number of individual migrants to assess the overall nature of the migration process. This work has tended to undermine the traditional gloomy view, showing that migration usually took place in the context of mediating institutions and that migrants were rarely demoralized by the experience.[10]

The arguments presented in this chapter will join this growing chorus of criticism of the traditional view of migration. But it will also attempt to go beyond the traditional problematic. Because recent scholars have been so busy demonstrating that migration is a stable and orderly process and that immi-grants are not social and psychological cripples, they have sometimes failed to ask what the effects of migration actually *were*. This chapter will try to demonstrate that different categories of immigrants had very different experiences – that male immigrants differed from females, long-distance immigrants from short-distance immigrants, Italian-born immigrants from both French-born and other foreign-born immigrants, immigrants early in the nineteenth century from those who migrated later. Finally this chapter and the remaining three chapters will also argue that immigrants in general differed systematically and significantly from natives, although not always in the ways predicted by the traditional theory.

The difficulties that immigrants could be expected to face in the city depended on two considerations. First, what was the extent of *uprooting*? Was the immigrant torn loose from solidary social ties with family and friends and therefore turned into a vulnerable social isolate? Or did the immigrant retain ties with the home community or have friends and family in the city who were ready to help his or her adjustment to urban life? Second, what were the immigrants' *resources*? Was immigration selective? Did immigrants have skills, occupational experience, or business connections that would help them to find good jobs in the city? Had they migrated directly from the countryside, or did they already have some experience of urban life? Information provided in Marseille's marriage registers can be used to measure both uprooting and resources. Although the conclusions are not always unambiguous, the patterns that emerge from the data imply that most migration into Marseille, both in the 1820s when migration was moderate in volume and later in the century when it was massive, was selective, took place within the context of mediating institutions of some sort, or both.

Migration in 1821–2

What was the pattern of immigration in 1821–2, before the rapid growth of Marseille's population had begun? The geographical origins of Marseille's immigrants can be determined from the birthplaces of brides and grooms reported in the marriage registers. An examination of these data shows that migration in the early 1820s was limited not only in scale, but also in range (see Table 7.1). Nineteen percent of the immigrant grooms and 24 percent of the immigrant brides came from the Bouches-du-Rhône, the department of which Marseille was the *chef-lieu*. Another 29 percent of the men and 31 percent of the women came from the departments of the Var and the Basses-Alpes, which together with the Bouches-du-Rhône made up the former province of Provence. Provence, in short, accounted for 48 percent of the males and 55 percent of the females who had immigrated to Marseille. Another 14 percent of the men and 17 percent of the women had been born in six other nearby departments: the Hérault, the Gard, the Vaucluse, the Drôme, the Isère, and the Hautes Alpes. These six departments, together with the three departments of Provence, seem to have constituted the major migrational hinterland of Marseille. (See Figure 7.1 for the boundaries of Provence and

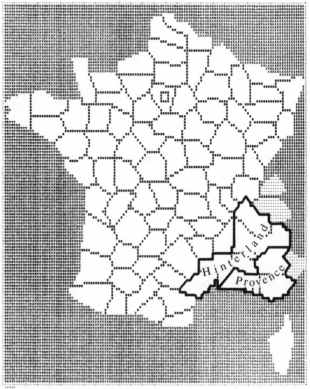

Figure 7.1. France, with Provence and Marseille's migrational hinterland (dotted departments were annexed to France in 1860).

of the migrational hinterland.) Another 18 percent of the male immigrants and 9 percent of the females had come from more distant regions of France, and the remaining 19 percent of both sexes were foreign born. Italians accounted for 13 percent of both the male and female immigrants, and the remaining 6 percent of each sex came from the rest of Europe – chiefly Switzerland, Savoy, Spain, and Germany – or from more distant regions of the world.

Although some immigrants traveled great distances to Marseille, in general the range of migration in 1821–2 was relatively short. Nearly half the men and over half the women were from Provence, and 63 percent of the men and 72 percent of the women came from nine departments in southeastern France that were both geographically and culturally close to Marseille. Migration from Provence was extremely dense, and it therefore stands to reason that immigrants from this area were likely to have kin or friends in Marseille

Table 7.1. *Birthplace of immigrants to Marseille,*
marriage registers of 1821–2 (in percent)

	Grooms	Brides
Bouches-du-Rhône	19	24
Other Provence	29	31
Total Provence	48	55
Other hinterland	14	17
Other France	19	9
Italy	13	13
Rest of world	6	7

who could help them find jobs and housing, provide a circle of friendship, and otherwise ease their adaptation to city life. Because they had migrated over short distances, it was also relatively easy for them to retain ties with their families and home communities. Furthermore, they all spoke dialects of Provençal that were closely related to the dialect of Marseille, and they had other cultural similarities with the Marseillais. For many of these immigrants, migration was probably a relatively painless affair. Men and women from the remainder of the migratory hinterland shared most of these advantages with the Provençaux, although usually to a lesser degree. They too had migrated relatively short distances, though generally farther than the Provençaux, and their dialects and cultural traditions were also reasonably close to those of Marseille. Immigration from these departments was less dense, but probably still substantial enough to create some sort of supportive network for new immigrants.

The problems facing immigrants from the remaining areas of France were presumably more severe. Although many were from southern France and therefore had some cultural and linguistic affinities with the Marseillais, this was generally less true than for migrants from within Marseille's hinterland. The distances from their home communities were also greater, and the sparseness of migration to Marseille from these areas greatly reduced the likelihood of having kin and friends in the city. These observations are even more true of foreign-born immigrants. With the exception of the Savoyards and French-speaking Swiss, virtually all these men and women arrived in Marseille ignorant of Provençal, and, unless they had previously migrated to other French cities, they probably had only limited experience of French language and culture. Except for Italians from the coastal regions between Nice and Genoa, who were present in relatively large numbers, it was rare for them to have had many kin or home-town friends in Marseille. We might expect their adaptation to life in Marseille to have been particularly difficult as a consequence.

Although most immigration was short in range, it often involved a jarring change in social environment. Because the marriage registers indicate both the commune and department of birth for all brides and grooms born in France, it is possible to determine how many of the French-born immigrants began their lives in cities and therefore had some prior experience of urban life. (The birthplace information for the foreign-born was not exact enough to make such a calculation possible.) Among the French-born immigrants, only 19 percent of the men and 21 percent of the women had been born in a city with a population of 20,000 or more, and very few of these cities were actually comparable in size to Marseille. The remaining 81 percent of the men and 79 percent of the women had been born either in small marketing or manufacturing towns or in essentially agrarian villages, none of which gave immigrants much preparation for the pace, complexity, and impersonality of a city as large as Marseille. Of course some of the rural born may have moved to other cities before coming to Marseille, but surely most of them had considerably less urban experience than men and women born in cities.

Figures on the geographical and rural–urban origins of Marseille's immigrants are ambivalent in their implications. Most migration was short in range, and this implies a minimum of uprooting. But most immigrants were not from cities, which implies that their adjustment to life in Marseille may have been relatively difficult. To reach more definite conclusions about the character of Marseille's immigration, other factors than these must be examined.

One factor often alleged to soften the impact of migration is the maintenance of bonds between immigrants and their families. The immigrant who can turn to family members or kin in the city, or who remains in touch with those back home, is probably less likely to fall prey to anomie and disorientation than the immigrant who is isolated from family and kin. The marriage registers, fortunately, contain one item that makes it possible to assess immigrants' family attachments. The present residence of the father and mother of both spouses – or, when a parent had died, his or her place of death – was normally entered onto the marriage act. In 1821–2, this information was omitted in some 15 percent of the cases for grooms' parents and in 11 percent of the cases for brides' parents; in later years the rate of omission was considerably higher. But in spite of the problem of occasional omission, this information can be used to construct a rough measure of the immigrants' family and kinship networks in the city.

When an immigrant's parents are found to live in Marseille or to have been in Marseille at the time of their death, this indicates that the son's or daughter's immigration did not sever family ties. The presence of parents in Marseille could logically have resulted from several different sequences of migration. One possibility is that the son or daughter came to Marseille with his or her parents when still a child. A second is that a grown son or daughter initially immigrated to Marseille and then worked and saved money to bring along the rest of the family. A third possibility is that the parents came to live with their immigrant son or daughter in Marseille only when they were too old or feeble to care for themselves. But all these different sequences share a common element: The bonds of family solidarity that linked parents and adult children clearly survived the process of migration. Of course the residence of parents in Marseille is a far from perfect indicator of the strength and density of immigrants' kinship relations in Marseille. Many men and women whose parents remained behind in their birthplaces must also have had other relatives in Marseille – brothers, sisters, aunts, uncles, cousins. Moreover these figures obviously say nothing about the quality of kinship bonds. But the parents' residence serves adequately as a kind of minimum indicator of an immigrant's ties of kinship.

Among all immigrant grooms, 23 percent had parents who either lived in Marseille or had died there. It is known that the parents of another 53 percent either currently lived or had died elsewhere, most commonly in the son's birthplace. In the remaining 24 percent of the cases, the parents' residence was not indicated on the marriage act. Some of the parents on whom information is lacking may have lived or died in Marseille, but it seems far more likely that they did not; after all, determining the whereabouts of a man or woman's parents was much easier if the parents lived in Marseille than if they did not.[11] It therefore seems most prudent to assume that the proportion of parents known to have lived or died in Marseille is quite close to the actual figure. The proportion of parents living or having died in Marseille was considerably higher among immigrant brides than among immigrant grooms: 35 percent, as against 46 percent known to be living or to have died elsewhere, and 19 percent for whom information is lacking. This would seem to indicate that parents had stronger feelings of protectiveness about their daughters than about their sons and were therefore less likely to send daughters off to the city alone. As a result, female immigrants were more likely than male immigrants to have kinfolk in the city to whom they could turn in times of trouble.

The proportion of brides and grooms whose parents resided in Marseille also varied according to the immigrants' geographical origins (see Table 7.2). In general, as might have been expected, immigrants from nearby regions were more likely to have parents in Marseille than those who migrated from more distant regions. Immigrant grooms from Provence had parents in Marseille in 26 percent of the cases, followed by other hinterland with 21 percent, other France with 14 percent, and non-Italian foreigners with only 5 percent. But Italian-immigrant grooms were a striking exception to this tendency: They were the most likely of any group to have parents in Marseille, which they did in 31 percent of the cases. Among immigrant brides, the Italians were

Table 7.2. *Percentage of immigrant brides and grooms with parents in Marseille, 1821–2*

Birthplace	Grooms	Brides
Provence	26	38
Other hinterland	21	23
Other France	14	25
Italy	31	40
Other foreign	5	41

second only to women from other foreign countries in the proportion of parents living in Marseille, and that by an insignificant margin. Among Italian brides the proportion was 40 percent, among other foreigners 41 percent, among Provençales 38 percent, among women from the rest of the hinterland 23 percent, and among women from the rest of France 25 percent. The conclusions to be drawn from these figures seem clear. First, among all categories of female immigrants and most categories of male immigrants, it was not uncommon for migration to be undertaken in family units that included both parents and children. And second, immigrants from Italy were more likely to have migrated in family units than any other immigrant group. Because this measure of family ties is strictly a lower-bound estimate of the proportion of immigrants benefiting from kinship ties, it seems clear that kinship must have played a major role in cushioning the impact of migration in Marseille, particularly for females and Italians.

Another factor that should have mitigated the disruptive effects of migration was the possession of high status, wealth, or marketable skills – or resources that would help an immigrant find a comfortable place in urban society. It has been noted, of course, that the vast majority of Marseille's French-born immigrants were not born in cities, and, given these predominantly rural origins, it might be expected that most of them were sons and daughters of peasants. If so, most would presumably be poor and few would be able to enter the urban labor market with skills that were much in demand. But to judge from the data available in the marriage registers, the occupational backgrounds of Marseille's immigrants were surprisingly urban in character. The marriage registers give occupations of both the brides' and grooms' fathers; however, these data are incomplete in two respects. First, the father's occupation is not reported for 23 percent of the grooms and 16 percent of the brides, and the rate of nonreporting was even higher among immigrants: 39 percent for grooms and 31 percent for brides. Second, as has been seen, 23 percent of the immigrant grooms and 35 percent of the immigrant brides are reported as either having parents living in Marseille or having parents who died there. In most cases, occupations reported for these men's and women's fathers were probably the occupations they exercised in Marseille, rather than the occupations they exercised in their home communities before migrating. To find few peasants among these men would hardly be surprising. Thus, to determine the socio-occupational milieux from which Marseille's immigrants came, the figures must be limited to those immigrant brides and grooms whose parents had not themselves migrated to Marseille. After eliminating the cases in which the father's occupation is lacking and those in which the parents had themselves immigrated, occupational background data exist for only 42 percent of the immigrant grooms and 37 percent of the immigrant brides. The figures extracted from these data can therefore only be regarded as approximations and are subject to potentially large margins of error. Even so, they are instructive.

According to these data, only 21 percent of Marseille's immigrant grooms came from peasant backgrounds. Skilled trades, rather than agriculture, was the most common occupational background, accounting for 29 percent of male immigrants, and other working-class occupations – unskilled labor, service trades, and maritime occupations – accounted for the backgrounds of another 8 percent. As surprising as the small contingent of peasants' sons was the very large number of immigrants from nonmanual or bourgeois backgrounds. Fully 38 percent of the immigrant grooms were from nonmanual backgrounds, and of these the majority had fathers with elite occupations. Twelve percent were from business and professional families, and 13 percent were sons of rentiers. The remaining 13 percent had fathers in small-business or clerical occupations.

The significance of this pattern of socio-occupational backgrounds among immigrant grooms is made clearer by comparing it to the patterns of native-born Marseillais (see Table 7.3). In the first place, the proportion of grooms from agricultural backgrounds was actually higher among natives of the city than among immigrants: 24 to 18 percent. Working-class occupations were substantially more common among natives than among immigrants. Fifty-four percent of native-born grooms had fathers in manual labor, as against 37 percent of immigrants. The difference between natives and immigrants was particularly pronounced for skilled trades, which were the background of 40 percent of native grooms. Bourgeois backgrounds, however, were far more common among immigrants than among natives. Thirty-eight percent of the immigrant grooms had bourgeois fathers, as against only 20 percent of native grooms. And for elite backgrounds the advantage of immigrants was decisive: 25 percent for immigrants as against only 10 percent for natives. The difference between the occupational backgrounds of natives and immigrants was also reflected in their fathers' mean occupational-status scores: 49 for natives and 54 for immigrants.

The occupational backgrounds of immigrant brides did not have such an

Table 7.3. *Occupational backgrounds of natives and immigrants in 1821–2 (in percent)*

	Grooms		Brides	
Father's occupation	Natives	Immigrants	Natives	Immigrants
1. Business and professional	6	12	6	11
2. Rentier	4	13	4	7
3. Sales and clerical	3	4	3	2
4. Small business	7	9	8	4
5. Artisan	40	29	39	22
6. Service	1	1	1	0
7. Unskilled	4	4	5	5
8. Maritime	9	3	8	4
9. Agriculture	24	21	23	42
10. Miscellaneous	2	4	3	3
Elite (1 + 2)	10	25	10	18
All bourgeois (1 + 2 + 3 +4)	20	38	19	24
Father's mean occupational-status score	49	54	49	50
Number of cases	888	273	1,100	200

urban cast. Forty-two percent of the immigrant brides were daughters of cultivators, that is, fewer than half, but more than came from any other socio-occupational milieu. Artisan trades were next, accounting for 22 percent of the cases, and unskilled and maritime occupations combined accounted for another 9 percent. Bourgeois backgrounds were less common among female than among male immigrants, but still accounted for 24 percent of the cases – appreciably above the 19 percent among native-born brides. And, as with men, the immigrants were especially likely to come from elite backgrounds. But the mean occupational-status scores of native and immigrant brides' fathers were essentially equal: 49 and 50, respectively (see Table 7.3).

These characteristics were true even of immigrants born in communes with populations under twenty thousand. As a glance at Table 7.4 will demonstrate, immigrants born in cities were more likely to be from artisan or bourgeois backgrounds than those born in smaller communities. But even among the small-town and village immigrants, the more "urban" occupational back-grounds were still strikingly prominent: Fully 28 percent of the rural-born grooms were sons of artisans, and 37 percent were sons of bourgeois. Indeed, men from elite backgrounds were more prominent among the rural-born than the urban-born immigrants. Twenty-four percent of the brides from smaller communities were daughters of skilled workers, but the percentage from bourgeois families was lower (17 percent) or essentially the same as for native-

Table 7.4. *Occupational backgrounds of rural-born and urban-born immigrants in 1821–2 (includes only French-born) (in percent)*

Father's occupation	Grooms		Brides	
	Rural	Urban	Rural	Urban
1. Business and professional	11	9	4	18
2. Rentier	14	11	7	4
3. Sales and clerical	5	6	1	3
4. Small business	7	19	4	14
5. Artisan	28	38	24	21
6. Service	0	0	0	0
7. Unskilled	4	4	5	11
8. Maritime	4	0	3	11
9. Agriculture	20	6	49	18
10. Miscellaneous	3	7	3	2
Elite (1 + 2)	25	20	11	22
All bourgeois (1 + 2 + 3 +4)	37	45	17	39
Number of cases	197	47	148	28

born brides. In part, the "urban" cast of the "rural" immigrants to Marseille reflects the nature of settlement patterns in Mediterranean France – a pattern characteristic of much of the Mediterranean basin. The villages in this region were almost never purely agricultural, but were relatively large "urbanized villages" or "agro-towns," in which agriculturalists, artisans, shopkeepers, professionals, and wealthy landowners lived side by side. Moreover, during the nineteenth century these "urbanized villages" tended to lose their elite populations by what Maurice Agulhon has called a "rural exodus from above."[12]

Of course all these figures are open to doubt on the grounds that the marriage-register data on fathers' occupations are incomplete. Perhaps the fathers whose occupations were not reported, or whose reported occupations were exercised in Marseille rather than in their home communities, were nearly all poor peasants, and the surprisingly "urban" and top-heavy occupational distribution is only an artifact of the inadequate instrument of measurement. But independent evidence on immigrants' literacy rates argues strongly against this supposition. In spite of the fact that they came predominantly from small communities where schooling was presumably less available than in major cities like Marseille, immigrant grooms had much higher rates of literacy than native-born grooms. Native grooms had a rate of only 56 percent; immigrant grooms whose parents had also immigrated to Marseille had a rate of 65 percent; and those immigrants who had come without their parents had the highest rate of all, 72 percent. These literacy figures are particularly valuable because they include all the immigrants in the marriage registers, even those whose fathers' occupations were not reported. Immigrant grooms whose fathers' occupations were not reported had a slightly lower literacy rate than those whose fathers' occupations were reported (67 percent as against 72 percent), but they, too, stood far above native-born grooms. These literacy figures make it highly improbable that the immigrant grooms whose premigration occupational backgrounds are unknown were recruited from the bottom of the rural social hierarchy. Rather, they would seem to confirm the general accuracy of the conclusions drawn from the occupational figures.

Among the brides, literacy figures tell a quite different story. Immigrant brides who had migrated without their parents had a literacy rate of 28 percent, below the native rate of 34 percent, whereas those immigrants whose parents resided in Marseille had a rate of 35 percent, slightly above the native rate. In addition, immigrant brides whose fathers' occupations were unknown were appreciably less likely to be literate than those whose occupations were known: 21 as against 34 percent. It is thus possible that the missing brides' fathers may have included a disproportionately large number of peasants. If this is true then the superiority of the social backgrounds of immigrant grooms over immigrant brides is actually understated in Table 7.4.

But, all in all, it seems likely that the figures on the occupational backgrounds of immigrants are not far from the truth. To judge from these figures, migration into Marseille before the era of massive population growth was a highly selective affair, although it was far more selective among men than among women. Most of the immigrants seem to have been from small towns and villages, but they generally came from the middle and upper levels of small-town and village society, not from the rural poor. A sizable majority of the immigrant grooms and nearly half the immigrant brides were children of village artisans, shopkeepers, substantial landowners, small-town notaries, doctors, or government officials. They came from families whose horizons and connections spread well beyond the local small-town or village society. One expects that their decisions to move to Marseille were typically prompted less by the goad of poverty or unemployment in their home communities than by the lure of greater opportunities or a more interesting life in the city. Most of the male immigrants already possessed skills – or capital – that were in demand in the urban market. Although the move to a new urban environment doubtless had its anguish and its difficulties for them, in most cases it probably had its rewards as well. Female immigrants had distinctly poorer resource endowments. They came from lower and more rural backgrounds, and they had very high illiteracy rates. Their problems of adjustment should, therefore, have been greater than those of male immigrants. Nevertheless, an optimistic overall conclusion seems justified for both men and for women. At least in the years before the massive growth of Marseille's population, immigration was less a barbarian invasion than a controlled and moderate circulation of talent from the periphery to the urban center.

But what about the immigrants whose resources were poor? After all, nearly 70 percent of the women and 30 percent of the men were illiterate, and sons and daughters of peasants were by no means rare. Perhaps the experiences of these illiterate and rustic immigrants was less rosy. But there was another feature of Marseille's immigration pattern that must have softened the impact of migration on many of these rustic and illiterate immigrants: Most of them came from geographically and culturally proximate regions. Among male immigrants, 69 percent of the illiterates and 82 percent of the peasants' sons (as against 62 percent of all immigrants) came from the nine southeast departments designated as Marseille's migratory hinterland. Among women, the figures were 78 percent of the illiterates and 92 percent of the peasants' daughters, as against 72 percent of all immigrants.

As these figures imply, there were important differences between short-distance and long-distance immigration. This can be seen by examining Tables 7.5, 7.6, and 7.7, which give the socio-occupational origins and the literacy rates of brides and grooms born in Marseille, in Provence, in the remainder of the migratory hinterland, elsewhere in France, in Italy, and in the rest of the world.[13] For grooms, migration seems to have fallen into three quite distinct patterns. The first pattern was that of Provençal immigrants. Their socio-occupational backgrounds were very similar to those of native Marseillais: Slightly fewer of them were from skilled and maritime backgrounds than were natives, and slightly more were sons of rentiers and professionals or businessmen, but the overall similarity was striking. Their fathers' mean occupational status was above that of native Marseillais, but by a relatively small margin. The rate of literacy among the Provençal immigrants was also above that of the native Marseillais, but was below that of most other immigrant groups.

The second pattern of migration was that of Italians. The number of Italians whose fathers' premigration occupations were reported in the marriage registers is rather small, but it suggests immigration of a distinctly plebian character. Peasants' sons were more common among the Italian immigrants than in any other group. Sons of artisans and bourgeois were relatively rare and were nearly equaled by sons of unskilled workers, seamen, and fishermen. And the status score of Italian immigrants' fathers, at 46, was the lowest of any group. The Italians were the only immigrant group in Marseille whose distribution of socio-occupational backgrounds was actually lower than that of natives. But in spite of their overwhelmingly plebian background, men born in Italy were as likely to be able to sign their marriage registers as native Marseillais – that is, in 56 percent of the cases. Given the generally humble socio-occupational backgrounds of the Italians, this substantial rate of literacy

Table 7.5. *Occupational backgrounds of grooms, by birthplace, 1821–2 (in percent)*

Father's occupation	Birthplace					
	Marseille	Provence	Other hinterland	Other France	Italy	Rest of world
1. Business and professional	6	10	17	8	—	50
2. Rentier	4	13	17	14	15	6
3. Sales and clerical	3	3	17	6	—	—
4. Small business	7	5	17	17	—	6
5. Artisan	40	31	21	32	15	19
6. Service	1	—	—	2	—	—
7. Unskilled	4	6	—	2	15	—
8. Maritime	9	3	4	3	8	—
9. Agriculture	24	27	8	8	39	13
10. Miscellaneous	2	2	—	8	8	6
Elite (1 + 2)	10	23	34	22	15	56
Bourgeois (1 + 2 + 3 + 4)	20	31	68	45	15	62
Mean summary status score	51	52	60	56	46	63
Number of cases	888	157	24	63	13	16

implies that the immigrants were probably considerably better educated than most of the compatriots they left behind. Immigration from Italy, in short, was probably more selective in terms of education than of occupational background.

The third pattern of migration was shared by all the remaining immigrant groups: those from the "hinterland," those from the rest of France, and the non-Italian foreign born. The means status scores of the fathers of immigrants in all these groups were substantially above both those of fathers of native Marseille and those of fathers of immigrants from Provence. Among all these groups, sons of peasants, unskilled workers, seamen, and fishermen were scarce. Artisans' sons were more common, accounting for about a fifth of the men in each of these categories. But among all of these immigrants, sons of bourgeois were predominant, making up 68 percent of immigrants from the "hinterland" and 62 percent of the non-Italian foreign born.

Women's migration also varied according to geographical origin, but the patterns were somewhat different than for men. As with men, the socio-occupational backgrounds of the short-distance immigrants were lower than those of other immigrants, but in the case of women this was characteristic

Table 7.6. *Occupational backgrounds of brides, by birthplace, 1821–2 (in percent)*

Father's occupation	Birthplace					
	Marseille	Provence	Other hinterland	Other France	Italy	Rest of world
1. Business and professional	6	5	—	19	38	60
2. Rentier	4	6	8	5	7	20
3. Sales and clerical	3	2	—	5	—	—
4. Small business	8	4	4	14	—	—
5. Artisan	39	19	31	38	14	10
6. Service	1	—	—	—	—	—
7. Unskilled	5	7	—	5	—	—
8. Maritime	8	5	8	—	—	—
9. Agriculture	22	51	42	5	43	—
10. Miscellaneous	3	17	8	9	—	10
Elite (1 + 2)	10	11	8	29	45	80
Bourgeois (1 + 2 + 3 + 4)	21	16	12	43	45	80
Mean summary status score	51	54	53	58	55	72
Number of cases	1,100	129	26	21	14	10

Table 7.7. *Percent literate by birthplace, brides and grooms, 1821–2*

	Marseille	Provence	Hinterland	Other France	Italy	Rest of world	All immigrants
Men	56	65	80	89	56	79	72
Women	34	18	26	80	30	64	29

of immigrants from all Marseille's hinterland, not only those from Provence. The mean status scores of the fathers of immigrants from both Provence and other hinterland areas were considerably below those of other groups. The proportion from peasant backgrounds was high – half for immigrants from Provence and two-fifths for immigrants from the rest of the hinterland, much higher than for male immigrants from either region. Bourgeois backgrounds were less common among brides from the hinterland than among native brides. Literacy rates were also low among both groups: 24 percent for brides from

Provence and 26 percent for brides from the rest of the hinterland. In summary, short-distance immigration of women tended to include a high proportion of illiterates and peasants' daughters, although women from higher socio-occupational backgrounds were by no means uncommon. Immigration from the remainder of France and from foreign countries other than Italy was much the same among women as among men. Agricultural backgrounds were even rarer among women migrating from these areas than among men, and bourgeois backgrounds were extremely common, accounting for 80 percent in the rest-of-the-world category. Mean status backgrounds were high, and so was literacy. The Italian immigration pattern was quite different for women than for men. As among Italian-born males, agricultural backgrounds were common, and only a quarter of the Italian-born women were literate. But six of the fourteen Italian brides whose father's premigration occupation is known were daughters of rentiers, businessmen, or professionals. At least among women whose parents had not migrated to Marseille, immigration of Italian women seems to have been less plebian in character than immigration of Italian men.

All in all, these figures on geographical variations in migration patterns seem to confirm and extend the conclusions already put forward about the nature of migration to Marseille before the era of massive population growth. Most long-distance immigration was undertaken by people well prepared for urban life – by their socio-occupational backgrounds, their education and skills, and in many cases, one suspects, by their personal or family wealth and connections. Their horizons and contacts were presumably wide enough that the decision to move to Marseille was only one of a number of alternative choices, a decision that was fixed upon for well-considered reasons – because of good connections, because relatives or friends had already settled there, and the like. Short-distance immigration was somewhat different. To be sure, many of the young men and women who moved to Marseille from nearby areas of southeastern France came from the same kinds of social backgrounds as the long-distance immigrants. But short-distance immigration included a substantial number of peasants' sons and daughters and a disproportionate share of illiterates as well. For many of them, the move to Marseille was probably less a rationally calculated choice from a number of alternative possibilities than an escape to the one big city that lay within their horizon.[14] Yet the very fact that Marseille lay firmly within their horizon must have eased the transition to urban life. Short-distance migration meant retained ties with home folk, greater familiarity with the dialect and customs of the Marseillais, and, because short-distance migration was relatively dense, the probable existence of a supportive community of friends and relatives in the city itself. Thus the very groups of immigrants whose occupational and educational backgrounds did not prepare them well for life in the city benefited from the compensatory advantages of cultural affinity and density of supportive social bonds.

There were two partial exceptions to these generalizations. The first is Italian immigrants, particularly Italian males, whose geographically and culturally distant origins were not compensated for by superior occupational and educational backgrounds. For this reason, it would appear that immigration from Italy may have been more trying than most immigration into Marseille. It must be remembered, however, that Italians seem to have had the densest kinship networks in Marseille of any of the city's immigrant groups. This feature of Italian immigration must have helped to mitigate some of the effects of low occupational backgrounds and of cultural and geographical distance.

The second exception is female immigrants, to whom these generalizations apply less fully than to males. It has been noted in several connections that female immigrants were generally less well prepared for urban life than male immigrants. Their rates of literacy were very low, even lower than the rates of native Marseillaises; the proportion from agricultural backgrounds was higher among female than among male immigrants; and high rates of immigration of peasants' daughters were spread over the entire migrational hinterland of Marseille, rather than being essentially limited to Provence, as among men. These findings all imply that migration may typically have been more disorienting and painful among women than among men. It is true, of course, that over one-third of the female immigrants had parents in Marseille and that their immigration therefore frequently took place within a protective family environment. But this still leaves a large number of female immigrants, most of them illiterate, many of them peasants' daughters, who had to find their way in the city without the help of their families.

This does not necessarily mean that they were bereft of all social attachments in Marseille. One very likely possibility is that many of these poor, illiterate, rustic young women worked as domestic servants in the households of wealthy residents of Marseille. Traditionally, it was very common for young women from peasant families to migrate to cities by obtaining places as domestic servants. The young women's employers got her labor at a very low rate, well below what would be required to attract city girls. At the same time, the girls' parents were placing her in a respectable household, where she would live and work under the authority and protection of the mistress and master of the house. Under these circumstances, it was common for the young woman to send a portion of her wages home to her parents – a sign that physical separation by no means implied dissolution of family ties. As for the young woman, she could learn city ways while living in a sheltered niche, and if she eventually became dissatisfied with her low wages and lack of freedom in domestic service, she could find a job in the needle trades or some other branch of industry. By then she would have learned to cope with city ways and could make the transition to living on her own with much less difficulty than when she was fresh off the farm.[15] Domestic service did not always work so satisfactorily, of course. The master and mistress of the house could be harsh and callous, and in some cases the servant girl might be subjected to sexual exploitation by her master. If she became pregnant, it would normally mean dismissal from her position, expulsion from her own family, and, all too often, the ultimate degradation of living as a prostitute.[16] But most of the time domestic service was a satisfactory arrangement, one that provided peasant girls with protection and security while enabling them to contribute to the resources of their own family, to accustom themselves to city life, and to save a little money for a dowry. Unfortunately, the marriage registers of 1821–2 do not indicate brides' occupations, so it is impossible to know how common it was for country girls to become domestic servants. But there is evidence that it was very common indeed in 1846–51 and 1869, and one suspects that it was very common in the early 1820s as well. Although the lack of evidence makes any conclusion speculative, it seems very likely that the immigration of peasant girls from Marseille's hinterland frequently took place through the mediating institution of domestic service.

But the fact remains that female immigration was quite different in character from male immigration. To explain these differences would require more evidence and different sorts of evidence than that available in the marriage registers. But the marriage-register evidence suggests some speculations. One suspects that the motives that lay behind immigration were usually different for women than for men. For men, the most common motive was probably ambition – to find better-paying and more rewarding work and a better social position than was available in the small town or village. For women, ambition was probably a less common motive for migration. In the first place, given nineteenth-century sex roles, ambition was supposed to be a male rather than a female attribute; it referred to the public world of striving and competition, and this was almost exclusively a male world. The woman's place was in the home, and her part was to subordinate herself to the interests of the family – of her father's family before marriage and of her husband's family thereafter. If this is true, then one suspects that migration to the city was usually undertaken in the interest of the girl's family. If an unmarried daughter could find work in the city, she reduced the number of mouths to be fed at home and may also have been able either to send some money to her family or to save up enough for a modest dowry – in either case relieving the economic burdens on her parents.[17]

These kinds of motivations would imply just the sort of differences between male and female migration that have been observed for Marseille. Male immigrants would be mainly those who could expect to benefit most from migration – those who were prepared to succeed in the city by high occupational backgrounds, acquired skills and wealth, or, lacking these, at least an elementary education. Female immigrants, on the other hand, would include a large number of women from poor families who most needed their daughters' supplementary earnings. Furthermore, because female immigration presumably was not usually undertaken to achieve upward mobility, there would be no reason for migration to be associated with literacy among women. Finally, migration that was intended to aid the immigrant's family rather than to advance the status and the earnings of the immigrant should often have been only a temporary affair, to be ended when the girl had accumulated a dowry and reached the age of marriage. Although it is uncertain how frequent this type of short-term immigration actually was, there is some evidence that it was common at least among domestic servants. As was remarked in Chapter 3, domestics seem to have been nearly three times as prominent in the population at large as in the population of young women getting married, which seems to imply that many domestics returned to their native communities to marry, rather than staying on in Marseille permanently.

If these speculations are correct, it would imply that ties between immigrant girls and their families were generally quite strong, even when the parents did not migrate to Marseille with their daughters. Nevertheless, bonds that were stretched so far may sometimes have grown slack, and young women removed from parental supervision may frequently have fallen on bad times. In this connection, it would be extremely useful to have figures on the number of illegitimate births to young immigrant women, for seduction and abandonment was probably the most common demoralizing experience suffered by young women in nineteenth-century cities. But the birth records in Marseille's archives unfortunately do not contain information on the mother's place of birth for either legitimate or illegitimate births.

There remain, then, many unanswered questions. But, generally speaking, the more closely patterns of migration into Marseille in the early 1820s are examined the more apparent it becomes that migration usually took place within the context of mediating institutions – that socially isolated, atomized, and disorienting forms of migration were the exception rather than the rule.

Migration in 1846–51 and 1869

Immigration in 1821–2 was, of course, limited in volume. The population was growing very slowly, and immigration into the city was only a little more than sufficient to counterbalance emigration from the city. But from the later 1820s on, the volume of immigration increased markedly as the city began its long period of rapid population growth. In the two years 1821 and 1822, only 349 male immigrants and 313 female immigrants got married in Marseille. For the two years 1846 and 1851, the numbers had soared to 1,275 male and 1,179 female immigrants. And in the single year 1869, the number of male immigrants marrying was 1,295 and the number of females 1,214.

Table 7.8. *Birthplace of immigrants to Marseille, brides and grooms (in percent)*

Birthplace	Men			Women		
	1821–2	1846–51	1869	1821–2	1846–51	1869
Bouches-du-Rhône	19	15	10	24	13	10
Other Provence	29	20	15	31	25	14
Total Provence	48	35	25	55	38	24
Other hinterland	14	16	20	17	22	25
Other France	19	24	35	9	19	37
Italy	13	18	15	13	16	10
Rest of world	6	7	4	7	5	4

To judge from these figures, the number of immigrants living in Marseille nearly quadrupled between the early 1820s and midcentury and more than doubled again in the next two decades. This immense rise in the volume of immigration also entailed important changes in its character. The traditional sources and channels of migration were necessarily limited in capacity; so large an increase in migration implied the tapping of new sources of supply. By using data from the marriage registers of 1846–51 and 1869, it is possible to determine Marseille's patterns of immigration in the era of rapid population growth and to compare the new patterns with those of 1821–2.

Increase in the volume of immigration was accompanied by an increase in its range (see Table 7.8). In 1821–2, 19 percent of immigrant grooms and 24 percent of immigrant brides had been born in the Bouches-du-Rhône; in 1846–51 these proportions had dropped to 15 and 13 percent, and by 1869 to 10 percent for both men and women. The proportions migrating from the rest of Provence also fell over time; from 29 percent for immigrant grooms and 31 percent for immigrant brides in 1821–2, to 20 and 25 percent in 1846–51, and to 15 and 14 percent in 1869. In 1821–2 nearly half Marseille's immigrant grooms (48 percent) and over half the immigrant brides (55 percent) had been born in Provence; by 1869 the proportion had dropped to about a quarter for both men and women (25 and 24 percent, respectively). By 1869, Provence had ceased to be the predominant source of Marseille's immigrants. When one adds to these immigrant Provençaux the equally Provençal natives of Marseille, the change is even more striking. In 1821–2, 80 percent of Marseille's grooms and 86 percent of its brides had been born somewhere in Provence. By 1846–51, this proportion had dropped to 63 percent of the grooms and 67 percent of the brides, and by 1869 it had slipped further to 50 percent of the grooms and 52 percent of the brides. Once a city where non-Provençaux were a rarity, Marseille had become only half-Provençal by 1869.

The declining proportion of immigrants who came from Provence did not result from a drying up of the sources. On the contrary, in absolute terms the number of immigrants moving to Marseille from Provence increased over time. On the marriage registers of 1821–2, there were 315 grooms and 299 brides who had migrated to Marseille from Provence, or an average of 158.5 grooms and 149.5 brides per year. In the two years 1846 and 1851, the totals had risen to 595 grooms and 627 brides, or a yearly average of 297.5 grooms and 313.5 brides. In 1869, the figures for the single year had risen still farther to 369 grooms and 338 brides. Immigrants continued to stream into Marseille from Provence; indeed, the stream rose in volume as the city's needs grew. But the importance of its contribution was diluted by a flood of immigrants from more distant areas of France.

Immigration from the rest of the hinterland accounted for a growing proportion of immigrants, rising from 14 percent of immigrant grooms and 17 percent of immigrant brides in 1821–2, to 16 and 22 percent in 1846–51, and to 20 and 25 percent in 1869. But it was immigration of French men and women from beyond the hinterland that increased most rapidly. From 19 percent of immigrant grooms and only 9 percent of immigrant brides in 1821–2, the other French category rose to 24 and 19 percent in 1846–51 and to 35 and 37 percent in 1869. On the other hand, the proportion of foreign born among the immigrants was no higher in 1869 than in 1821–2, although it was higher in 1846–51. The great new influx of immigration, in short, came above all from within the country but from beyond the nearby departments that had traditionally sent large contingents of young men and women to Marseille.

The increasing range of immigration can be seen clearly in Figures 7.2 through 7.8, which depict the proportion of Marseille's population born in each of the departments of France. In 1821–2, only the three departments that made up the old province of Provence accounted for over 3 percent each of Marseille's brides and grooms. Another two, the Hautes-Alpes and the Vaucluse, each accounted for more than 1 percent of the brides, and for grooms the Hérault must be added to the list. A few remaining nearby departments accounted for a liberal sprinkling of brides or grooms, but most of the country's departments contributed either no one or only a single bride or groom. This situation had already changed markedly by 1846–51. The Hautes-Alpes had joined the group of departments accounting for over 3 percent of Marseille's brides and grooms. Four departments – the Gard, the Hérault, the Isère, and the Vaucluse – now accounted for between 1 and 3 percent of grooms, and three – the Drôme, the Isère, and the Vaucluse – for an equivalent proportion of brides. The number of departments accounting for between .5 and 1 percent of the population also increased dramatically. In 1869 the same

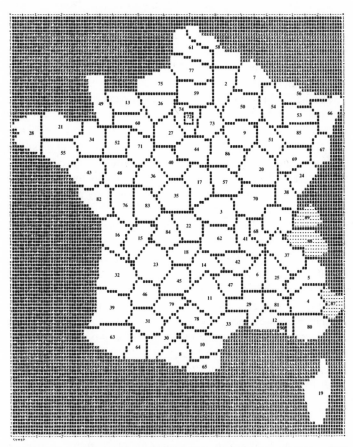

Figure 7.2. The departments of France: **1** Ain; **2** Aisne; **3** Allier; **4** Alpes (Basses); **5** Alpes (Hautes); **6** Ardèche; **7** Ardennes; **8** Ariège; **9** Aube; **10** Aude; **11** Aveyron; **12** Bouches-du-Rhône; **13** Calvados; **14** Cantal; **15** Charente; **16** Charente-Inférieure; **17** Cher; **18** Corrèze; **19** Corse; **20** Côte-d'Or; **21** Côtes-du-Nord; **22** Creuse; **23** Dordogne; **24** Doubs; **25** Drôme; **26** Eure; **27** Eure-et-Loir; **28** Finistère; **29** Gard; **30** Haute-Garonne; **31** Gers; **32** Gironde; **33** Hérault; **34** Ille-et-Vilaine; **35** Indre; **36** Indre-et-Loire; **37** Isère; **38** Jura; **39** Landes; **40** Loire-et-Cher; **41** Loire; **42** Haute-Loire; **43** Loire-Inférieure; **44** Loiret; **45** Lot; **46** Lot-et-Garonne; **47** Lozère; **48** Maine-et-Loire; **49** Manche; **50** Marne; **51** Haute-Marne; **52** Mayenne; **53** Meurthe; **54** Meuse; **55** Morbihan; **56** Moselle; **57** Nièvre; **58** Nord; **59** Oise; **60** Orne; **61** Pas-de-Calais; **62** Puy-de-Dôme; **63** Basses-Pyrénées; **64** Hautes-Pyrénées; **65** Pyrénées-Orientales; **66** Bas-Rhin; **67** Haut-Rhin; **68** Rhône; **69** Haute-Saône; **70** Saône-et-Loire; **71** Sarthe; **72** Seine; **73** Seine-et-Marne; **74** Seine-et-Oise; **75** Seine-Inférieure; **76** Deux-Sèvres; **77** Somme; **78** Tarn; **79** Tarn-et-Garonne; **80** Var; **81** Vaucluse; **82** Vendée; **83** Vienne; **84** Haute-Vienne; **85** Vosges; **86** Yonne; **87** Alpes Maritimes; **88** Savoie; **89** Haute-Savoie; **90** Marseille.

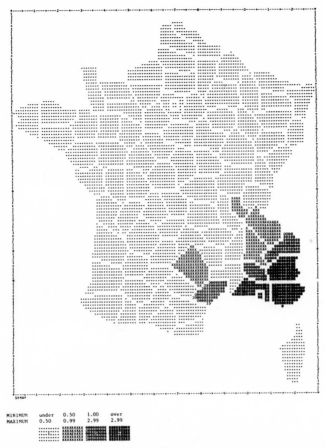

Figure 7.3. Percentage of Marseille's grooms born in department, 1821–2.

four departments contributed over 3 percent of Marseille's grooms, but the number of departments contributing between 1 and 3 percent rose to thirteen: the Ardeche, the Ariège, the Aude, Corsica, the Drôme, the Gard, the Haute-Garonne, the Hérault, the Isère, the Tarn, the Vaucluse and two new departments acquired from the Kingdom of Sardinia in 1860 – the Alpes-Maritimes and Savoie. For brides, the Var slipped from the group of departments contributing over 3 percent but was replaced by the Vaucluse and the Ardeche, and ten departments contributed between 1 and 3 percent: the Var, the Ariège, Corsica, the Gard, the Haute-Garonne, the Hérault, the Isère, the Tarn, the Alpes-Maritimes, and Savoie.

This expansion of the range of migration can be seen even more clearly by measuring immigration as a proportion of the population of the home department. When this is done the differences between 1821–2 and 1869 stand

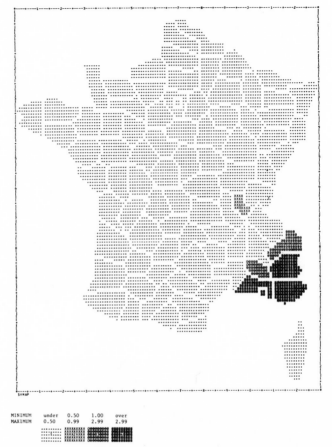

Figure 7.4. Percentage of Marseille's brides born in department, 1821–2.

out in the most striking fashion (see Figures 7.9 through 7.14). The rates given in these calculations are the number of individuals who married in Marseille in each year for every hundred thousand persons in the population of their departments of origin. In the years 1821 and 1822, these rates were above ten per one hundred thousand only for the Bouches-du-Rhône, the Var, and the Basses-Alpes in the case of grooms, and only for the Bouches-du-Rhône, the Var, the Basses-Alpes, and the Hautes-Alpes in the case of brides. In addition, rates between three and ten per one hundred thousand obtained for the Hautes-Alpes and the Vaucluse among grooms and for the Vaucluse among brides.

By 1846 and 1851, the Hautes-Alpes joined the departments with over ten grooms per hundred thousand, and the Vaucluse was added to the list for brides. In addition, there were now five departments with between three and

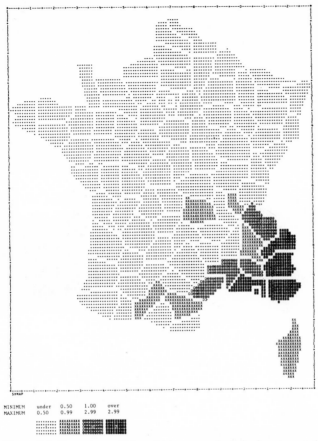

Figure 7.5. Percentage of Marseille's grooms born in department, 1846–51.

ten grooms per hundred thousand and six with equivalent proportions of brides. By 1869, the list of departments with over ten grooms per hundred thousand had grown to twelve, as had the list with over ten brides per hundred thousand. Furthermore, the number of departments with between three and ten grooms per hundred thousand had risen to twelve, and the number with three to ten brides per hundred thousand had risen to ten. Thus, from 1821–2 to 1869, the number of departments with high rates of emigration to Marseille rose from five for both men and women in 1821–2 to 24 for men and 22 for women in 1869. In 1821–2, the area of relatively intense immigration to Marseille was confined to the extreme southeastern corner of France; by 1869 this area had spread out to encompass all of Provence, Languedoc, the Alpine region, the lower Rhône valley, and most of the Pyrénées and the Massif

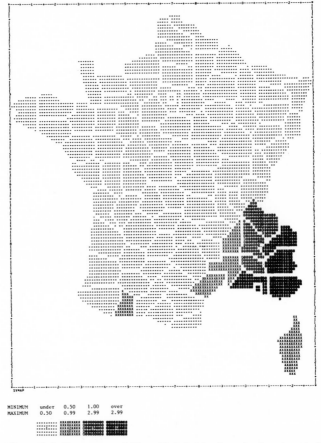

MINIMUM   under   0.50   1.00   over
MAXIMUM   0.50   0.99   2.99   2.99

Figure 7.6. Percentage of Marseille's brides born in department, 1846–51.

Central. By 1869, Marseille had clearly become a major pole of attraction for young men and women throughout a wide area of southern France.

This expansion of the range of immigration implies that problems of uprooting may well have been more common later in the century than in the early 1820s. It was true, at least, that fewer of the immigrants lived within a few days of their home communities and that fewer of them had linguistic and cultural affinities with the Marseillais. It also appears that kinship ties in Marseille declined as the range and volume of immigration increased (see Table 7.9). In 1821–2, 23 percent of immigrant grooms and 35 percent of immigrant brides had parents in Marseille; by 1851,[18] the figures were 17 and 22 percent, and in 1869 they were essentially unchanged at 15 and 24 percent. As these figures indicate, family ties continued to be considerably

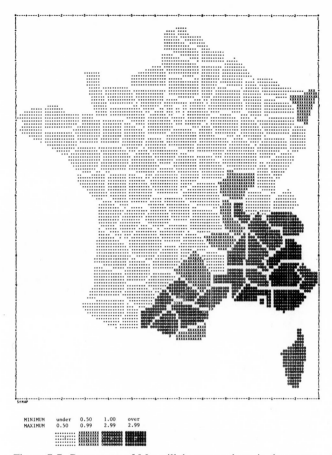

MINIMUM under 0.50 1.00 over
MAXIMUM 0.50   0.99 2.99 2.99

Figure 7.7. Percentage of Marseille's grooms born in department, 1869.

more common for female than for male immigrants; there was still a tendency for immigration of young women to take place in a sheltered family context.

In 1821–2, Italians had been more likely to have family ties in Marseille than any other group of immigrants – among both women and men. Although Italians' proportion of family ties remained above average, Provençal immigrants had moved to first place among men by 1851 and among women as well by 1869. Immigration within a family context remained reasonably common for Italians, but the role of the family in Italian immigration seems to have been on the wane. There is, however, a problem with these figures, for the proportion of cases in which the parents' residence or place of death is unknown increased over time from 15 percent for grooms and 11 percent for brides in 1821–2 to 27 and 22 percent in 1851 and to 35 and 29 percent in 1869. It is therefore possible that at least some of the decline in the

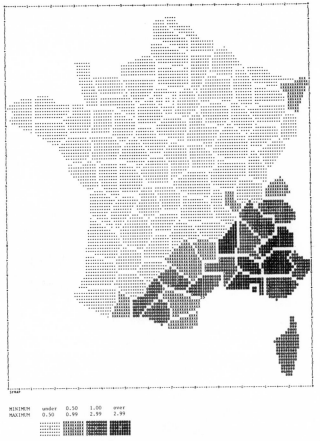

Figure 7.8. Percentage of Marseille's brides born in department, 1869.

proportion of parents of immigrants known to be living in Marseille is due to a decline in the quality of the data. Furthermore, it must be remembered that these figures give only a lower-bound estimate of kinship ties in Marseille. But it still seems likely that the importance of family based migration declined somewhat over time. If this is true, it must be seen as intensifying the effects of increased geographical range. Not only did more immigrants come from greater geographical and cultural distance, but they seem to have been more likely to come as single individuals, rather than as part of a larger family group.

As immigration to Marseille grew in volume, it expanded not only its geographical range, but its social range as well. One sign of increasing social range was that fewer immigrants came from cities later in the century than in 1821–2, in spite of the fact that the urban population now made up a higher

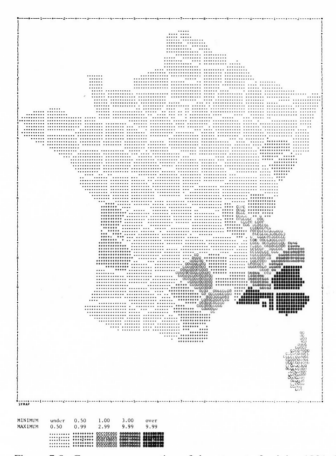

MINIMUM   under   0.50   1.00   3.00   over
MAXIMUM   0.50   0.99   2.99   9.99   9.99

Figure 7.9. Grooms as proportion of department of origin, 1821–2 (rates per 100,000).

proportion of the total French population. In 1821–2, 19 percent of the grooms and 21 percent of the brides who had immigrated to Marseille from elsewhere in France had been born in cities over 20,000. In 1846–51, the proportions had dropped to 15 percent of grooms and 12 percent of brides, and in 1869, after another two decades of rapid growth of France's urban population, the proportions were still only 16 and 15 percent. What these figures show is that during the course of the nineteenth century the paths of migration that led to Marseille penetrated ever more deeply into the countryside. As a result, prior urban experience was even rarer among immigrants later in the century than it had been in the early 1820s.[19]

This rise in the proportion of rural-born immigrants signaled a much more striking change in the occupational backgrounds of immigrants. As in 1821–

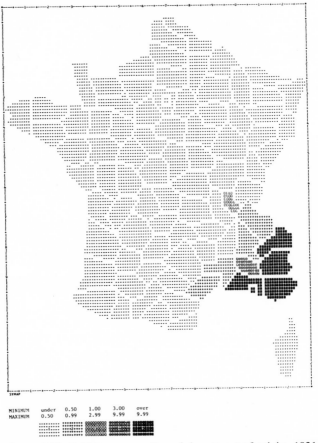

MINIMUM	under	0.50	1.00	3.00	over
MAXIMUM	0.50	0.99	2.99	9.99	9.99

Figure 7.10. Brides as proportion of department of origin, 1821–2 (rates per 100,000).

2, this conclusion is based on the occupations of immigrants' fathers as reported in the marriage registers. In both 1851 and 1869, the occupations of the grooms' and brides' fathers were given in virtually all the cases, so the figures are far more complete than the 1821–2 figures. Furthermore, the fact that fewer of the parents of immigrant brides and grooms had themselves immigrated to Marseille than in the early 1820s means that the premigration occupational backgrounds can be determined accurately for over four-fifths of all immigrant grooms and over three-quarters of all immigrant brides. This means that the figures on the occupational backgrounds of Marseille's immigrants in 1851 and 1869 are much more worthy of confidence than those for the earlier period.[20]

The general course of change in occupational backgrounds among male

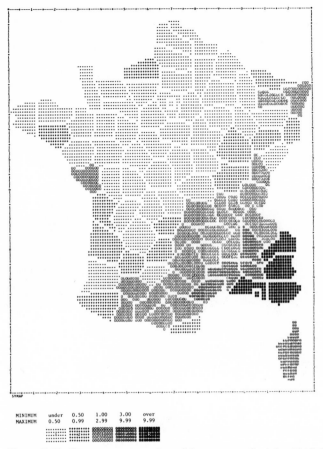

MINIMUM   under   0.50   1.00   3.00   over
MAXIMUM   0.50   0.99   2.99   9.99   9.99

Figure 7.11. Grooms as proportion of department of origin, 1846–51 (rates per 100,000).

immigrants was downward (see Table 7.10). This can be seen clearly in the mean occupational-status scores of immigrants' fathers, which fell from 54 in 1821–2 to 49 in 1851 and 46 in 1869. One of the most important changes was a rise in the proportion from peasant backgrounds. From only 21 percent of immigrants grooms in 1821–2, peasants' sons came to account for 33 percent in 1851 and 38 percent in 1869. At the same time, the proportion from artisan backgrounds fell from 29 percent in 1821–2 to 26 percent in 1851 and 20 percent in 1869. The fall of the proportion from bourgeois backgrounds was equally striking: from 38 percent in 1821–2, to 24 percent in 1851, and to 20 percent in 1869. This fall was particularly steep for sons of businessmen, professionals, and rentiers. In 1821–2, no fewer than a quarter of immigrant grooms came from these elite occupational backgrounds. By

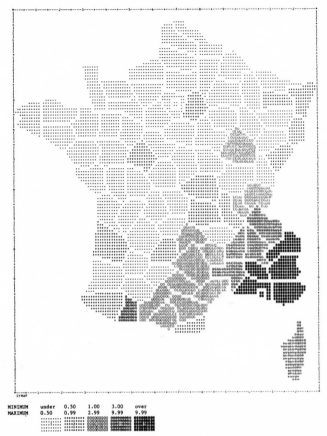

Figure 7.12. Brides as proportion of department of origin, 1846–51 (rates
per 100,000).

1851, the proportion had dropped to 15 percent and by 1869 to only 9 percent.
Finally, the weight of unskilled laborers' sons in the immigrant population
rose from 4 percent in 1821–2, to 7 percent in 1851, and to 12 percent in
1869. Between 1821–2 and 1869, the balance of social backgrounds had been
reversed. Rather than being dominated by men whose fathers were bourgeois
or artisans, male immigration came to be dominated by sons of peasants and
unskilled laborers.

For female immigrants, the contrast was not nearly so sharp, primarily
because they had frequently come from lower-status backgrounds even in
1821–2. Indeed, the differences between men's and women's socio-occupational backgrounds, which had been quite pronounced in 1821–2, had all
but disappeared by 1869 (compare Tables 7.3 and Table 7.11). By 1869, the
proportion of immigrant brides from peasant backgrounds was 46 percent,

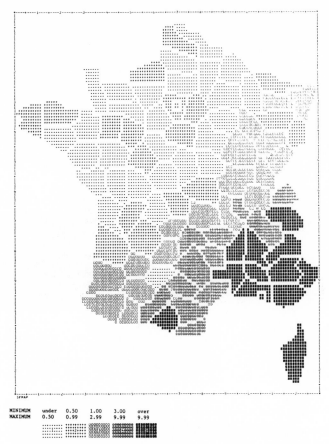

MINIMUM   under   0.50   1.00   3.00   over
MAXIMUM   0.50   0.99   2.99   9.99   9.99

Figure 7.13. Grooms as proportion of department of origin, 1869 (rates per 100,000).

only slightly above the levels of 1821–2. The proportion of artisans' daughters also remained essentially constant, but the proportion from bourgeois backgrounds fell from 24 percent in 1821–2 to 13 percent in 1869, and the proportion from elite backgrounds plummeted from 18 percent to only 4 percent. The main increases, besides the peasants' daughters, were among daughters of unskilled workers and among women from miscellaneous backgrounds, the latter consisting principally of illegitimates and foundlings. Among female as well as male immigrants the balance of socio-occupational backgrounds definitely declined during the course of the century. This is registered by a fall in the mean occupational-status scores of immigrant brides' fathers from 50 in 1821–2 to 47 in 1851 and 44 in 1869.

As a comparison of Table 7.4 and 7.12 will show, these changes in the

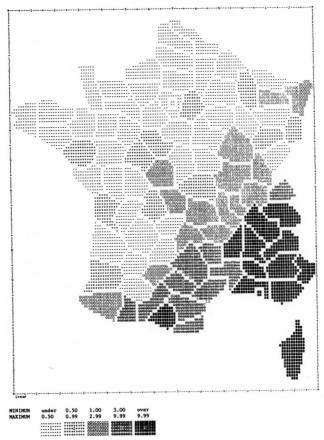

Figure 7.14. Brides as proportion of department of origin, 1869 (rates per 100,000).

socio-occupational composition of immigration took place both among immigrants from villages and small towns and among those from cities. Among urban-born immigrants, the proportion of bourgeois and skilled backgrounds fell and the proportion of unskilled backgrounds rose. In addition, the proportion from miscellaneous backgrounds rose very sharply, especially among female immigrants. This rise was attributable almost entirely to immigrants whose fathers were unknown – that is, to illegitimates and foundlings. Because the social backgrounds of these immigrants must be counted among the most humble of all, it is clear that there was a general downward drift in the level of backgrounds of urban-born immigrants. The most important changes among rural-born immigrants were a striking rise in the proportion of men from

Table 7.9. *Percentage of brides and grooms with parents in Marseille, by birthplace (in percent)*

	Marseille	Provence	Other hinterland	Other France	Italy	Rest of world	All immigrants
Grooms							
1821–2	87	26	21	14	30	5	23
1851	82	28	11	7	23	6	17
1869	76	22	17	10	17	5	15
Brides							
1821–2	87	38	23	26	40	42	35
1851	83	26	11	20	31	11	22
1869	81	34	24	17	31	15	24

Table 7.10. *Occupational backgrounds of native and immigrant grooms, 1851 and 1869 (in percent)*

	1851		1869	
Father's occupation	Natives	Immigrants	Natives	Immigrants
1. Business and professional	6	5	6	3
2. Rentier	7	10	7	7
3. Sales and clerical	5	4	5	4
4. Small business	7	5	7	5
5. Artisan	37	26	38	20
6. Service	1	1	1	2
7. Unskilled	8	7	11	12
8. Maritime	7	2	8	2
9. Agriculture	19	33	13	39
10. Miscellaneous	4	6	4	6
Elite (1 + 2)	13	15	13	9
All bourgeois				
(1 + 2 + 3 + 4)	25	24	25	20
Number of cases	690	799	703	1,228

peasant backgrounds and an equally striking fall in the proportion of both male and female immigrants from bourgeois backgrounds. Particularly notable was the fall in elite backgrounds, which had sunk to a fraction of their 1821–2 proportions by 1869. Skilled backgrounds also became somewhat less common among the rural-born male immigrants as the proportion of peasants' sons rose.

The rising proportion of peasant backgrounds and the falling proportion of

Table 7.11. *Occupational backgrounds of native and immigrant brides, 1851 and 1869 (in percent)*

	1851		1869	
Father's occupation	Natives	Immigrants	Natives	Immigrants
1. Business and professional	8	2	7	2
2. Rentier	4	9	7	2
3. Sales and clerical	5	3	6	5
4. Small business	10	6	9	4
5. Artisan	33	23	36	21
6. Service	1	1	1	1
7. Unskilled	9	7	15	9
8. Maritime	7	2	4	1
9. Agriculture	16	38	11	46
10. Miscellaneous	7	9	4	9
Elite (1 + 2)	12	11	14	4
All bourgeois				
(1 + 2 + 3 + 4)	27	20	29	13
Number of cases	768	732	816	1,067

bourgeois and artisan backgrounds among the rural-born immigrants could have come about by either or both of two processes. It may reflect above all a change in the mix of village as opposed to small-town origins among the immigrants, with the populations of small and strictly agrarian settlements entering the migratory stream on a much larger scale. Or it may be that the size and character of the home communities remained more or less constant, but more and more peasants living in these communities became willing to pull up stakes. In either case, it is clear that the social range of immigration extended markedly during the half-century between 1820 and 1870 and that this extension took place in both urban and rural areas. Migration became a truly mass phenomenon.

Having said this, however, some important qualifications must be added. The change in the socio-occupational composition of migration did not result from reduced migration rates among the artisan and bourgeois social categories who had sent Marseille the bulk of its immigrants in 1821–2. On the contrary, migration from these sources rose impressively between 1821–2 and 1846–51 and rose again between 1846–51 and 1869. The old, socially selective processes of migration went on and did so at a higher level than ever before. But the old stream of selective migration was joined and diluted by a new and ever-growing stream of peasant and plebian migration. The result was a mixture whose composition differed from that of 1821–2, one in which sons and daughters of skilled workers and bourgeois were no longer a majority and in which immigrants' social origins were now generally lower than those of

Table 7.12. *Occupational backgrounds of rural-born and urban-born immigrants, 1851 and 1869 (includes only French-born) (in percent)*

Father's occupation	Grooms, 1851		Grooms, 1869		Brides, 1851		Brides, 1869	
	rural	urban	rural	urban	rural	urban	rural	urban
1. Business and professional	4	12	2	8	1	7	1	8
2. Rentier	12	9	7	9	10	3	1	4
3. Sales and clerical	4	4	4	6	4	3	4	8
4. Small business	5	11	5	8	4	14	8	11
5. Artisan	26	35	19	33	22	42	22	24
6. Service	1	0	2	2	1	3	1	2
7. Unskilled	5	5	8	10	6	3	7	8
8. Maritime	1	2	1	3	1	2	1	3
9. Agriculture	37	7	47	7	41	9	53	10
10. Miscellaneous	5	15	5	14	10	14	7	21
Elite (1 + 2)	16	21	9	17	11	10	2	12
Bourgeois (1 + 2 + 3 + 4)	25	35	18	31	19	27	9	31
Number of cases	516	82	841	146	529	59	804	119

the natives of Marseille. However, immigration was still by no means a movement of the disinherited and destitute, even as late as 1869. Men and women from bourgeois and artisan backgrounds still made up a substantial portion of the immigrants, and there is evidence that even the immigrants from more humble backgrounds were far from the dregs of society. Among men, rates of literacy were marginally higher for immigrants than for natives in 1851: 76 percent both for immigrants whose parents lived in Marseille and for immigrants whose parents had stayed behind, as against 75 percent for natives. In 1869 the rate for immigrant males whose parents had not themselves immigrated was 85 percent, only slightly below the 88 percent for both natives and immigrants whose parents lived in Marseille. Given the lower distribution of socio-occupational backgrounds among immigrants than among natives in these years, these figures indicate that migration continued to be quite educationally selective.

It is also possible to compare the literacy rates of French-born immigrants with national literacy rates, and this comparison demonstrates that male immigrants who settled in Marseille were actually considerably more likely to be literate than the compatriots they left behind in their native towns and villages. Estimates of literacy for the entire adult-male population of France put the rates at 69 percent in 1854 and 75 percent in 1869.[21] These figures, like the Marseille figures, are based on the proportion of grooms capable of signing their marriage acts. Because they are national averages, they certainly contain a higher proportion of peasants than appear in the samples of Marseille's immigrants and are therefore not directly comparable to the Marseille figures. But the remarkable thing is that in both 1851 and 1869 even the sons of peasants and unskilled workers among French-born immigrants to Marseille had higher rates of literacy than the French male population as a whole; their rates were 70 and 71 percent in 1851 and 83 and 80 percent in 1869. Because the national average for sons of peasants and unskilled workers was surely well below the general average, this comparison implies that peasants' sons and unskilled workers' sons who settled in Marseille were far more likely to be literate than those who remained behind in their birthplaces. This comparison also points up an interesting contrast between immigration in 1821–2 and later in the century. In 1821–2, peasants' sons and unskilled workers' sons who immigrated to Marseille had literacy rates below the national average of 54 percent:[22] 52 percent for peasants' sons and only 30 percent for unskilled workers' sons. This implies that as migration became less occupationally selective, it actually became more educationally selective. Once again, the data seem to caution against seeing migration in dismal terms. Even in the period when the bulk of immigrants came from occupational backgrounds giving them few skills that were in demand in an urban economy, their educational preparation was generally good. In this sense, male immigrants to Marseille were still an impressive lot.

As in 1821–2, so in 1846–51 and 1869, the question of literacy looks quite

Table 7.13. *Percent literate by region of birth*

	Grooms			Brides		
	1821–2	1851	1869	1821–2	1851	1869
Born Marseille	56	75	88	34	48	75
Born Provence	65	71	85	20	31	55
Born other hinterland	80	83	90	22	33	61
Born other France	89	89	88	63	46	58
Born Italy	56	53	67	24	15	33
Born rest of world	79	85	97	68	74	85
All French-born immigrants	73	79	88	28	36	58
All native Marseillais	62	75	86	33	42	65
French population[a]	54	69	75	35	53	63

[a] The figures for the French population are from E. Levasseur, *La Population française*, 2 vols. (Paris, 1891), vol. 2, pp. 478, 491. The figures are for the years 1816–20, 1854, and 1869.

different for women than for men. In each of these periods, immigrant brides were less likely to be literate than native-born brides. In 1821–2, the rates were 28 percent for immigrants and 34 percent for natives; in 1851, 36 percent for immigrants and 48 percent for natives; and in 1869, 56 percent for immigrants and 75 percent for natives. Until 1869, even the natives' rates were slightly below the national average, and in 1869 the rate for French-born immigrants was still below the national average.[23] This continuing discrepancy between male and female immigrants could be taken to indicate that differences between men's and women's motives for migration persisted in the 1840s, 1850s, and 1860s, even though the occupational backgrounds of male and female immigrants came to be more and more alike.

As in 1821–2, literacy rates of immigrants from different geographical regions varied considerably (see Table 7.13). Italian-born immigrants continued to have the lowest rates and other foreign-born immigrants continued to have high rates. But differences among French-born immigrants, which had been quite pronounced in 1821–2, became smaller and smaller over time, and by 1869 there were no noticeable differences between those born in Provence, in the hinterland, and in the rest of France, either for men or for women. This growing similarity in the literacy rates of French immigrants who migrated over long and short distances signals another fundamental change in Marseille's migration pattern. One of the distinctive features of immigration into Marseille in the era before massive population growth had been the contrast between long- and short-range migration. In 1821–2, long-distance migration had been dominated by men and women from high-status backgrounds, whereas short-distance migration included many sons and

Table 7.14. *Father's occupational-status scores by birthplace*

	Grooms			Brides		
Birthplace	1821–2	1851	1869	1821–2	1851	1869
Marseille	49	49	49	49	50	50
Provence	52	48	48	46	46	43
Other hinterland	60	47	45	47	45	45
Other France	56	52	46	48	50	44
Italy	46	44	43	55	43	41
Rest of world	63	52	51	72	53	51
All immigrants	54	49	46	50	47	44

daughters of peasants. But as the social and geographical range of migration increased, these differences began to disappear. This is demonstrated clearly in Table 7.14, which gives the mean occupational-status scores of grooms' fathers and brides' fathers in 1821–2, 1851, and 1869. There are two notable trends in the table. First, the mean status background of immigrants of both sexes from every geographical area declined steadily over time. By 1869, the mean status background of all immigrants except non-Italian foreigners had fallen to below those of natives, and the non-Italian foreigners stood only slightly above the Marseillais. Second, the differences between immigrants from different areas became less pronounced.

The increasing similarity of backgrounds of immigrants from different areas is equally apparent in Tables 7.15 through 7.18, which give the socio-occupational origins of immigrants by their birthplaces. In 1821–2, male immigrants from Provence had a much higher proportion of agricultural backgrounds and a much lower proportion of bourgeois backgrounds than any long-distance immigrants except the Italians. By 1851, the difference between immigrants from Provence and the rest of the hinterland had vanished, and the difference between these and the longer-distance immigrants had become much less distinct, although the longer-distance immigrants were still somewhat more likely to come from bourgeois backgrounds and somewhat less likely to come from peasant backgrounds. By 1869, however, there were essentially no important differences among the French-born immigrants, although the non-Italian foreign born continued to come from more distinguished origins than the French born. As in 1821–2, the Italian immigrants continued to be far more plebian in background than any others both in 1846–51 and in 1869, and they continued to have a particularly high proportion of unskilled laborers' sons among them.

The pattern of women's migration from these different geographical regions was very similar to that of men, more so than it had been in 1821–2. Female immigrants from beyond the hinterland remained distinct from the nearby

Table 7.15. *Occupational background by birthplace, grooms, 1851 (in percent)*

Father's occupation	Marseille	Provence	Other hinterland	Other France	Italy	Rest of world	All immigrants
1. Business and professional	5	4	4	6	4	12	5
2. Rentier	6	11	8	13	4	13	10
3. Sales and clerical	5	2	7	4	5	3	4
4. Small business	7	6	4	7	2	4	5
5. Artisan	37	24	22	33	23	25	26
6. Service	2	1	2	1	0	0	1
7. Unskilled	8	7	3	4	17	3	7
8. Maritime	8	2	0	2	3	2	2
9. Agriculture	18	37	43	22	39	29	33
10. Miscellaneous	4	6	6	7	3	9	15
Elite (1 + 2)	11	15	12	19	8	25	15
Bourgeois (1 + 2 + 3 + 4)	23	23	23	30	15	32	24
Number of cases	642	245	125	231	130	68	799

Table 7.16. *Occupational background by birthplace, grooms, 1869 (in percent)*

Father's occupation	Marseille	Provence	Other hinterland	Other France	Italy	Rest of world	All immigrants
1. Business and professional	6	5	2	2	1	13	3
2. Rentier	7	11	3	6	3	8	7
3. Sales and clerical	5	5	5	4	3	2	4
4. Small business	7	4	6	6	4	10	5
5. Artisan	38	19	21	22	15	20	20
6. Service	1	2	2	2	1	3	2
7. Unskilled	11	8	7	9	28	15	12
8. Maritime	7	3	1	1	4	0	2
9. Agriculture	14	38	48	40	34	22	39
10. Miscellaneous	4	5	5	8	6	7	6
Elite (1 + 2)	13	16	5	8	4	21	10
Bourgeois (1 + 2 + 3 + 4)	25	25	16	18	11	33	19
Number of cases	703	334	200	453	181	60	1,228

Table 7.17. *Occupational background by birthplace, brides, 1851 (in percent)*

Father's occupation	Marseille	Provence	Other hinterland	Other France	Italy	Rest of world	All immigrants
1. Business and professional	8	1	1	3	3	8	2
2. Rentier	4	12	9	9	2	16	9
3. Sales and clerical	5	2	3	6	3	2	3
4. Small business	10	4	5	7	6	6	6
5. Artisan	33	20	21	33	14	33	23
6. Service	1	1	2	1	0	2	1
7. Unskilled	9	6	2	11	12	6	7
8. Maritime	7	1	1	1	6	0	2
9. Agriculture	16	44	50	15	48	22	38
10. Miscellaneous	7	8	8	15	5	4	9
Elite (1 + 2)	12	13	10	12	5	24	11
Bourgeois (1 + 2 + 3 + 4)	27	19	18	25	14	32	20
Number of cases	772	225	193	170	95	49	732

Table 7.18. Occupational background by birthplace, brides, 1869 (in percent)

Father's occupation	Marseille	Provence	Other hinterland	Other France	Italy	Rest of world	All immigrants
1. Business and professional	7	3	1	2	1	12	2
2. Rentier	7	1	3	2	0	8	2
3. Sales and clerical	6	4	6	5	0	8	5
4. Small business	9	2	5	4	5	8	4
5. Artisan	36	23	21	23	12	20	21
6. Service	1	0	0	1	1	0	1
7. Unskilled	15	9	5	7	31	6	9
8. Maritime	4	2	1	1	2	0	1
9. Agriculture	11	49	51	43	37	29	46
10. Miscellaneous	4	7	7	11	10	10	9
Elite (1 + 2)	14	4	4	4	1	20	4
Bourgeois (1 + 2 + 3 + 4)	29	10	14	13	6	36	13
Number of cases	1,460	223	271	429	93	51	1,067

immigrants through 1846–51, but by 1869 all the French-born immigrants had essentially the same patterns. And like their male counterparts, females who immigrated from Italy generally came from very humble occupational backgrounds, whereas those who came from other foreign countries tended to come from higher backgrounds than the French born.

Thus, one of the essential features that had marked immigration into Marseille in the period before massive population growth was all but effaced by 1869. This increasing similarity in the social character of long- and short-distance immigration implies important changes in the nature of immigrants' experiences. In 1821–2, virtually all the immigrants who traveled over great distances were men and women whose social backgrounds prepared them adequately for successful adaptation to city life. It was only among immigrants from Provence, and also from the rest of the hinterland for females, that large numbers of peasants' sons and daughters were to be found. In 1821–2, immigrants whose social backgrounds gave them little preparation for urban life generally had other advantages that helped to ease the transition: Their native culture and dialect was similar to that of Marseille, they were close enough to their natal villages to maintain regular contact with the home folk, and they presumably found sizable communities of their compatriots in Marseille when they arrived.

By 1846–51, and even more clearly by 1869, this was no longer true. There were now masses of rustic young men and women flocking to the city from all over France. To many of them, Marseille's customs and dialect must have been utterly foreign, and there were usually not large numbers of their compatriots in the city. Furthermore, the difficulty of keeping in touch with families and home communities that were hundreds of kilometers away must have increased the immigrants' sense of isolation – although the completion of the French rail network in the 1860s must have eased this problem considerably. All this implies that the problems of uprooting and disorientation, which seem to have been minimal in the years before large-scale migration began, were probably much more important from the late 1820s on. It can be stated with certainty that by 1851 a substantial proportion of Marseille's immigrants had neither the advantages conferred by cultural and geographical proximity nor those conferred by relatively high social backgrounds. As a result, their experiences in adapting to life in Marseille must have been particularly trying.

Data on literacy, however, indicate that these conclusions must be qualified to a certain extent. In 1851, illiteracy was very common among peasants' sons who had immigrated from Provence and from Italy, but not among peasants' sons who immigrated from elsewhere. Only 56 percent of Provençal peasants' sons, and only 47 percent of Italian peasants' sons, were literate, whereas those who came from other areas were literate in 81 percent of the cases. Indeed, in 1851, immigrants from Provence accounted for over 44 percent of the illiterate peasants' sons in the marriage-register sample. Thus, many of the immigrants whose disadvantaged backgrounds were compounded by illiteracy had migrated only over short distances. In 1869, Provençal peasants' sons were still considerably less likely to be literate than other non-Italian peasants' sons, but even they were literate in 77 percent of the cases, as against 63 percent for the Italians and 83 percent for other immigrants. By 1869, a combination of illiteracy and a rustic socio-occupational background had become something of a rarity among male immigrants, except among those who came from Italy. Among women, however, a combination of rustic background and illiteracy remained very common indeed. In 1851, only 18 percent of all immigrant peasants' daughters were literate, and rates of literacy were very low among all except the non-Italian foreign born. By 1869 the rate of literacy among peasants' daughters had risen substantially to 48 percent. But it was just as common for peasants' daughters who immigrated over long distances to be illiterate as for the short-distance immigrants. Among peasants' daughters, other disadvantages do not usually seem to have been compensated for by literacy.

There is also some evidence that extension of the geographical range of migration was accompanied by a growth in the significance of immigrant communities in Marseille. An examination of the marriage registers indicates a marked tendency for men and women born in a given geographical region to choose marriage partners from the same region. Among French-born immigrants, we can determine the proportions of brides and grooms whose spouses were born in their department of origin. As Tables 7.19 and 7.20 demonstrate, these proportions were already substantial in 1821–2 (11 percent of all immigrant grooms and 15 percent of all immigrant brides) and rose steadily (to 19 percent) for both sexes by 1869. Among women, those whose parents had immigrated with them to Marseille were no less likely to have grooms from their home departments than those whose parents had not come with them. It therefore appears that many of the families that left their native towns and villages as a unit retained important ties with the friends and kinsmen they left behind and also sought out the company and friendship of compatriots when they settled in Marseille. Among men, those who had immigrated with their parents were less likely to marry compatriots than those who left parents behind, although the differences between these two types of immigrants declined over time. This difference between men and women may have arisen out of sex-role differences in courtship: Males were probably more independent from their families than females when it came to choosing a spouse.

It is true that only a minority of immigrants had spouses from their home departments. It remained very common for French-born immigrants to marry natives of Marseille rather than compatriots of their own home departments – not surprisingly, for there were many more natives of Marseille to choose

Table 7.19. *Percent of grooms with brides from same department, by birthplace (French-born immigrants)*

Region of birth	1821–2			1851			1869		
	Parents in Marseille	Parents not in Marseille	All immigrants	Parents in Marseille	Parents not in Marseille	All immigrants	Parents in Marseille	Parents not in Marseille	All immigrants
Provence	7	17	14	12	18	16	12	17	16
Other hinterland	0	11	9	7	22	20	10	21	19
Other France	6	4	4	6	11	10	21	21	21
All French-born immigrants	5	13	11	10	16	15	14	20	19

Table 7.20. *Percent of brides with grooms from same department, by birthplace (French-born immigrants)*

Birthplace	1821–2			1851			1869		
	Parents in Marseille	Parents not in Marseille	All immigrants	Parents in Marseille	Parents not in Marseille	All immigrants	Parents in Marseille	Parents not in Marseille	All immigrants
Provence	18	17	17	16	20	19	22	19	20
Other hinterland	5	12	10	14	15	15	16	17	17
Other France	17	9	11	14	13	13	22	20	21
All French-born immigrants	16	14	15	15	16	16	20	19	19

from. But it is remarkable that by 1869 French men and women who came from departments beyond Marseille's hinterland were as likely to have spouses born in their home departments as born in Marseille – at a time when none of these departments accounted for more than 2.1 percent of the city's young men and 3.4 percent of its young women, whereas 33 percent of its young men and 36 percent of its young women were natives of Marseille. This astonishing fact seems to indicate either the existence of tightly knit immigrant communities within Marseille or the persistence of ties between the immigrants and their home communities – and most probably both.

It is also remarkable that the proportion of marriages uniting compatriots rose over time. This was in part because the pool of available young men and women from the more distant departments swelled as the range of immigration into Marseille increased. But an increase in long-distance migration would not automatically lead to higher rates of departmental endogamy; higher rates could be expected to result only if the long-distance immigrants formed communities of compatriots once they arrived in Marseille. What these figures seem to attest is that increased immigration solidified the supportive communities into which immigrants were received when they came to Marseille. Hence, although long-distance immigrants were more numerous in 1851 and 1869 than they had been in 1821–2, and although they were more likely to have come from rustic occupational backgrounds and seem to have been less likely to migrate in family units, they also seem to have been more likely to find supportive communities of compatriots once they arrived.

To judge from this same kind of data, foreign-born immigrants also seem to have formed their own communities in Marseille. In 1821–2, 23 percent of the Italian grooms had Italian brides and 27 percent of the Italian brides had Italian grooms – at a time when Italians constituted only 5 percent of the male and 4 percent of the female young-adult populations. In 1851, when the proportion of Italians in the population had more than doubled, 50 percent of the Italian grooms and 60 percent of the brides married compatriots. In 1869 when the proportion of Italians in the population had dropped once again to an intermediate level, 33 percent of the Italian grooms and 53 percent of the brides married fellow Italians. In all three time periods, Italians married fellow Italians over five times more frequently than would be predicted from their numbers in the population. Even though the pool of young Italian men and women was quite limited, Italians were very likely to marry other Italians. This fact, together with the Italians' marked tendency to migrate in family groups, points to the existence of a particularly tightly knit Italian immigrant community.

Other foreigners had a very different marriage pattern. They were quite likely to marry other non-Italian foreigners: in 1821–2, 28 percent of the grooms and 32 percent of the brides did so, and in 1851 the rates were similar, that is, 27 percent of grooms and 35 percent of brides. In 1869, rates were lower, but still substantial, at 21 and 24 percent. Given that non-Italian foreign-born immigrants never accounted for over 4 percent of the city's young men and 3 percent of its young women, it is clear that the foreign born had a distinct preference for foreign-born mates. Initially, however, the non-Italian foreign-born immigrants seem to have had little particular preference for mates from their own countries of birth. The proportion who took spouses born in their own country was only 2 percent for grooms and 3 percent for brides in 1821–2. By 1846–51, it had risen to 6 percent for grooms and 11 percent for brides, and by 1869 to 13 percent for grooms and 14 percent for brides. Up to the middle of the nineteenth century, foreigners who came to Marseille from other countries than Italy seem to have constituted one big immigrant community. By 1869, this big immigrant community seems to have been breaking down into a series of distinct national communities.

These ties between compatriots were particularly common among the very groups of immigrants who most needed supportive communities. As Table 7.21 shows, departmental endogamy was generally more common among illiterate than among literate immigrants. Furthermore, among male immigrants, peasants' sons had rates of departmental endogamy higher than those of men from any other occupational background in every year. Among women, peasants' daughters had the highest rates in 1869 and were above the average rates in every year. It appears that ties to home folk, to communities of compatriots in Marseille, or to both, were especially strong among illiterate and rustic immigrants.

Another mediating institution that softened the shock of migration was domestic service. In both 1851 and 1869, many young women from rustic backgrounds came to Marseille as domestics. Of the 278 immigrant peasants' daughters who got married in 1851, 100, or 36 percent, were employed in domestic service at the time of their marriage. Because many immigrant girls probably worked in Marseille as domestics but returned to their native village to marry, and others began their stay in Marseille as domestic servants and then went on into more lucrative or independent occupations after they had established themselves in the city, this figure of 37 percent certainly under states the proportion of peasants' daughters who passed through domestic service. The real figure was probably at least one-half. Looking at the problem from a different angle, it is clear that peasants' daughters constituted the main source of supply of domestic servants. Fifty-two percent of all the domestic servants in the marriage registers of 1851 were immigrant daughters of peasants. Furthermore, virtually all the city's domestic servants were immigrant. Only 4 percent had been born in Marseille. This seems to confirm the notion that domestic service provided a kind of surrogate family life for young women. Girls who were born in Marseille and could live at home almost never became domestic servants; they moved directly into freer and better paying occupations.

Table 7.21. *Percent of spouses from same department of birth, by literacy (French-born immigrants)*

Region of birth	1821–2			1851			1869		
	Parents in Marseille	Parents not in Marseille	All immigrants	Parents in Marseille	Parents not in Marseille	All immigrants	Parents in Marseille	Parents not in Marseille	All immigrants
Grooms									
Literate	5	11	9	10	15	15	13	18	17
Illiterate	8	18	15	11	16	16	31	28	23
Brides									
Literate	10	16	14	7	12	11	18	16	17
Illiterate	18	14	15	24	18	21	26	23	23

In 1869, the proportion of peasants' daughters who were in domestic service had risen to 50 percent, but the proportion of all domestic servants who were immigrant peasants' daughters had fallen somewhat to 49 percent. Both these changes seem to be accounted for by a rise in the proportion of young women employed as domestic servants at the time of marriage, from 11 percent of all brides in 1846–51 to 22 percent in 1869. With rising demand for domestic servants, young women born in Marseille came to account for 14 percent of the city's domestics in 1869, although a large majority – the remaining 86 percent – were still immigrants. But in spite of all these changes, the overall conclusion must be the same for both 1846–51 and 1869: A substantial proportion of immigrant women and a particularly large proportion of immigrant peasants' daughters began their lives in Marseille as domestic servants. Domestic service, which placed young women in a protective familial environment, was and remained a major channel of immigration into the city.

We can get one closer glimpse at how this channel of migration operated from data on departmental endogamy. No other young women were as likely to marry young men from their home departments as domestic servants. In 1851, when only 16 percent of all French-born immigrant brides married men born in their departments, the rate for French-born immigrant domestic servants was 22 percent. And in 1869, when the overall rate was 19 percent, the domestic servants' rate was 27 percent. This suggests that young women whose sweethearts had immigrated to Marseille often followed them to the city by becoming domestic servants. One suspects that the young man characteristically secured a position in domestic service for his fiancée and that both then saved enough money to set up a household on their own. This pattern of migratory courtship was of course a minority phenomenon even among domestic servants. But it graphically illustrates the way in which domestic service could serve as a way station for rustic young women who determined to live in the city.

Continuity and change

A comparison of Marseille's immigration patterns in 1821–2 with those of 1846–51 and 1869 reveals both continuities and changes. Surely the most significant change was the sheer increase in volume of immigration. To judge from the marriage registers, there were nearly eight times as many immigrants living in Marseille in 1869 as there had been a half-century earlier. So vast an increase in numbers would in itself constitute a major transformation, even if the social origins of the immigrant population had remained constant. But the immigrants' origins changed as well: Not only were there many more immigrants, but these immigrants were likely to have come from greater geographical and cultural distances, were more likely to be sons and daughters of peasants or unskilled workers, and were less likely to have had prior urban experience. The immigrants who came to Marseille in the early 1820s were easily assimilable both by reason of their small numbers and by reason of their relatively high skills and cultural similarities. But the thousands of young peasants' sons and daughters who flocked to Marseille from all over the country in the 1840s, 1850s, and 1860s posed a problem of a different order. Their adaptation to urban life was likely to be difficult: They often lacked skills that were in demand in an urban economy; they were unused to the impersonality and the pace of the city; and, because they had often come over great distances, they might be expected to have been out of touch with friends and family and to be uncomfortable with the manners, customs, and dialect of the Marseillais. The problems of uprooting, loneliness, despair, poverty, and disorientation that such authors as Handlin and Chevalier have made so central in their accounts of immigration would seem to have been far more serious in the 1840s, 1850s, and 1860s than they had been in the early 1820s, before the massive growth of Marseille's population began.

Although the psychological and social problems associated with uprooting were probably intensified as the volume and range of migration increased, it would be incorrect to see these problems as either crippling or universal among the later immigrants. In the first place, immigration of the old type not only continued but increased in volume. A significant proportion of the immigrants continued to come from nearby regions and from the advantaged social strata that had traditionally sent large contingents to Marseille. The changed social composition of immigration resulted not from the replacement of the old type of immigration by a new type, but from the addition of a new type to the old. Furthermore, even the new type of immigration – the movement into Marseille of low-status immigrants from more distant regions of the country – generally took place by orderly and controlled processes, and often did so within the context of mediating institutions. The figures indicate that even sons of peasants and unskilled workers who migrated to Marseille were surprisingly likely to be literate, particularly if they migrated from beyond Provence. Hence, although they may have come from occupational backgrounds that did little to prepare them for success in the urban labor market, their educational preparation was generally good. Second, a substantial proportion of immigration continued to take place in family units, with the result that immigrants frequently had kin living in the city on whom they could rely. Third, the proportion of immigrants who married men or women from their own birthplaces actually rose over time. This would seem to indicate both that they maintained extensive ties with their home communities and that they formed immigrant communities in Marseille once they had arrived. This practice was particularly common among illiterates and among peasants' sons and daughters, which seems to indicate that immigrant communities were strongest among those immigrants who needed them most. Finally, female immigrants, and particularly peasants' daughters, often began their careers in Marseille in the mediating institution of domestic service. If the new migration of the 1830s through the 1860s posed greater problems of assimilation and adaptation than the migration of the early 1820s, it certainly does not seem to have been the pathological phenomenon that Louis Chevalier has described for Paris in this same era.

The evidence examined so far, however, deals more with the origins of immigrants than with what became of them once they arrived in the city. Immigrants may have been well prepared for the urban labor market and may often have maintained ties with their families, home communities, and compatriots who had migrated to Marseille. But none of these factors necessarily assured them of success or happiness in the city. Nor did it mean that immigrants, however well adjusted to urban life, would be just like native Marseillais, or just like other immigrants who came to Marseille from other areas. The following three chapters explore such questions further. Chapter 8 examines the records of Marseille's criminal courts to see if immigrants and natives had different patterns and levels of criminality. Chapters 9 and 10 examine the intergenerational social-mobility experiences of both men and women, assessing, among other things, the differential mobility patterns of natives and immigrants. Both chapters show important differences between various categories of immigrants as well. Migration, it turns out, had significant effects – but sometimes not the effects that might have been expected.

8 Dangerous classes?

One commonly offered explanation for criminal behavior is a weak attachment of individuals to the norms and values of their communities.[1] From this perspective, it is reasonable to expect a positive association between migration and criminality. Migration could undermine the solidity of immigrants' values in at least two ways. First, it may have attenuated the bonds between immigrants and their home communities more rapidly than new bonds could be established in the postmigration community. Second, the values and standards of the pre- and postmigration communities may have been mutually inconsistent, leaving the immigrant uncertain and confused. In either case, one would expect immigrants' moral restraints against criminal behavior to be weaker than natives' and therefore that immigrants would have higher crime rates. This chapter investigates the overall patterns of criminality in nineteenth-century Marseille – the relationship of crime to age, sex, occupation, and residence, as well as to migration. But its chief purpose is to discover the extent and nature of links between migration and criminality.

When a person was brought to trial in the criminal courts of Marseille, the name, age, sex, place of residence, occupation, and birthplace of the accused were recorded onto a register, along with a description of the crime or misdemeanor with which the person was charged, a record of the court's judgment, and, if the judgment was guilty, an indication of the penalty imposed. Although the registers are missing for some years, they are available in quantity for the period just preceding the middle of the nineteenth century. Because these registers include birthplace data, they can be used to investigate the differential crime rates of immigrants and natives. There were two different courts that dealt with offenses committed in Marseille: The *tribunal correctionnel*, which was located in Marseille and had only the commune of Marseille as its jurisdiction, and the *cour d'assise*, located in Aix-en-Provence, which had as its jurisdiction not only Marseille, but the rest of the department of the Bouches-du-Rhône.[2] Less serious crimes or misdemeanors (such as begging, vagrancy, ordinary assault, or tax evasion) were tried in the *tribunal correctionnel*, more serious crimes (such as stabbings, homicide, or counterfeiting) in the *cour d'assises*. Theft, by far the most common offense in Marseille in these years, could be tried in either of these courts, depending on the scale and seriousness of the theft. The range of offenses brought before these two courts was very broad: everything from infanticide to bigamy to

213

Table 8.1. *Criminal convictions by sex*

	Theft, *tribunal correctionnel*	Theft, *cour d'assises*	Assault	Vagrancy	Begging
Male					
Number	1,086	190	61	119	208
Percent	89	87	80	98	93
Female					
Number	132	29	15	2	16
Percent	11	13	20	2	7

usury to insulting police officers to hunting without a license. Most of these offenses occurred far too infrequently to be of any use in assessing statistically the impact of migration on crime. For this purpose, it proved more useful to examine the patterns of only four relatively common categories of crimes – theft, begging, vagrancy, and assault – where the numbers were large enough to allow for elementary statistical manipulations. The theft figures are based on 1844–50, the begging and vagrancy figures on 1848–50, and the assault figures on 1848 only.

Determinants of crime: sex, age, and occupation

Criminality was, of course, influenced by many things other than migration. The most important single determinant of criminality was sex. Women were far less likely than men to be convicted (or accused) of any of the categories of crimes analyzed in this study (see Table 8.1). Women generally made up no more than an eighth of those convicted. They were most common among those guilty of assaults, where they accounted for a fifth of the cases, and least common among the vagrants, of whom they made up only a fiftieth. There were so few female criminals, in fact, that only for thefts were their numbers sufficient to allow meaningful statistical breakdowns. For this reason, only women convicted of theft will be included in the analysis hereafter.

A second important determinant of criminality was age. Crime rates are generally very low among young children, rise sharply during the teens or twenties, and then decline steadily with age.[3] In modern industrial societies, the highest crime rates are usually in the late teens; in nineteenth-century Marseille, the highest rates occurred in the twenties. Different types of crimes, however, had different age profiles. The youngest criminals were those convicted of theft and vagrancy. As Figure 8.1 makes clear, theft rates were highest between 18 and 22, for both men and women, and for those tried in the *cour d'assises* as well as those tried in the *tribunal correctionnel*.[4] The youngest of all, however, were men tried in the *tribunal correctionnel*, where some 27 percent were under 18 and the mean age was 24.7. Those tried in the *cour d'assises* – who were accused of more serious thefts – were somewhat older. Only 10 percent were under 18, and the mean age was 25.3. A substantial proportion of the women convicted of theft in the *tribunal correctionnel* were very young – 16 percent were under 18. But female thieves were less concentrated into the teens and early twenties than male thieves, so their mean age was older: 28.7. Men convicted of vagrancy had an age profile very similar to those convicted of theft in the *tribunal correctionnel*. Twenty-eight percent were under 18, and the mean age was 25.0. Other crimes had less youthful age profiles. The peak rate for assault was among the 23–7 age group, and there was no sharp fall-off in rates until 33–7. Very few of the men convicted of assault were under 18, and the mean ages of those convicted was 29.8. Convicted beggars had a very flat age profile. There were few convicted beggars under 18, but rates were quite constant from 18–22 to 58–62. The mean age of beggars was much higher than that of other criminals: 41.3. With the exception of begging, then, crime was mainly an activity of the young – of the teens and early twenties in the case of theft and vagrancy, and of the late teens and the twenties in the case of assault. It must also be assumed that most of the criminals were unmarried. This is of course implied by their youth. Moreover, studies of criminality have consistently found that single persons of any age are more likely to commit crimes than married persons of the same age.[5] Unfortunately, Marseille's crime records do not indicate marital status, but there is no reason to think that Marseille's criminals would have deviated from this general pattern.

Another important determinant of crime was occupation. As Tables 8.2 and 8.3 demonstrate, occupations differed a great deal in their rates of criminality. These tables give the percentage of convicted criminals falling into different occupational categories and then compare these percentages with each occupation's percentage in the population as a whole. The result is an occupation-specific rate, expressed as a ratio, for each type of crime. A rate below 1.0 means that criminals in an occupational category were underrepresented relative to their proportion in the population, and a rate of over 1.0 means they were overrepresented. Criminality was clearly related to wealth and status. The two elite occupational categories had very low crime rates, except in the case of assault, where businessmen and professionals had a slightly above-average rate. Rentiers, in fact, were convicted of none of the crimes tabulated in this study. The petite bourgeoisie had higher rates than the elite, but with only one exception – assault, once again – were well below the citywide average. Workers, by contrast, had rates near or above 1.0, with artisans generally very close to 1.0 and other workers generally higher. Agriculturalists had generally moderate but very inconsistent rates, and miscel-

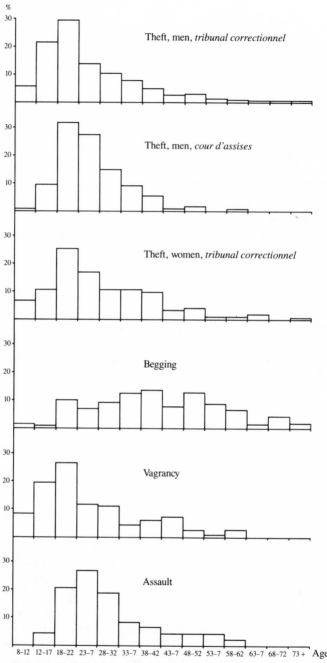

Figure 8.1. Criminal convictions by age category.

Table 8.2. *Criminal convictions by occupation, men*

	Business and professional	Rentier	Sales and clerical	Small business	Artisan	Unskilled	Service	Maritime	Agriculture	Miscellaneous	No occupation	Number of cases
1. Percent theft, tribunal correctionnel	0.8	—	2.5	2.2	27.5	29.3	6.2	16.8	2.6	5.3	6.8	1,084
2. Ratio of 1 to 11	0.1	0.0	0.3	0.3	0.8	1.7	1.9	3.2	0.4	4.1	1.1	
3. Percent theft, cour d'assises	1.1	—	1.6	3.7	44.4	27.0	7.9	7.9	3.2	3.2	1.1	189
4. Ratio of 3 to 11	0.2	0.0	0.2	0.5	1.3	1.6	2.4	1.5	0.5	2.5	0.2	
5. Percent assault	6.6	—	3.3	9.8	29.5	19.7	3.3	13.1	—	11.5	3.3	61
6. Ratio of 5 to 11	1.2	0.0	0.4	1.3	0.9	1.2	1.0	2.5	0.0	8.8	0.5	
7. Percent vagrancy	0.8	—	0.8	0.8	34.7	23.7	4.2	11.9	6.8	5.1	11.0	118
8. Ratio of 7 to 11	0.1	0.0	0.1	0.1	1.0	1.4	1.3	0.3	1.0	3.9	1.8	
9. Percent begging	—	—	1.9	1.9	32.7	28.4	5.8	7.2	9.6	4.8	7.7	208
10. Ratio of 9 to 11	0.0	0.0	0.2	0.3	1.0	1.7	1.8	1.4	1.5	3.7	1.2	
11. Percent of male population over 17, census of 1851 (augmented)	5.4	4.2	8.9	7.3	34.4	17.1	3.3	5.2	6.6	1.3	6.2	

laneous occupations – ex-soldiers, refugees, street entertainers, peddlers, those employed in various stopgap and makeshift occupations – consistently had the highest rates of any category.

In spite of this clear overall pattern, the relationship between poverty and criminality was far from perfect, and different types of crimes had different occupational profiles. Not surprisingly, the crimes related most directly to poverty were vagrancy and begging. Virtually none of the beggars or vagrants were from bourgeois occupations; artisans were right on the citywide average; and unskilled workers, service workers, sailors, agriculturalists, and the miscellaneous occupations were above average. Men with no occupation were also overrepresented among the vagrants and beggars. This should come as no surprise, because both offenses are basically a consequence of being without gainful employment or other means of support. Most of the men who gave an occupation were probably unemployed at the moment they were picked up for begging or vagrancy. The difference between them and the men who called themselves *"sans profession"* was that the former still considered themselves cooks, agricultural laborers, masons, quarrymen, or day laborers, whereas the latter had been unemployed so long that they no longer thought of themselves as having an occupation at all.

In the case of theft, the pattern was more complicated. To begin with, it differed for more serious and less serious thefts. Petty thefts – those tried before the *tribunal correctionnel* – were committed above all by the poor. Unskilled workers, maritime workers, and men with occupations in the miscellaneous category made up less than a quarter of the population but accounted for over half the convicted petty thieves. Artisans, by contrast, were below the citywide average with a rate of 0.8. In the case of more serious thefts – those tried before the *cour d'assises* – artisans had rates only a little below those of unskilled workers and sailors. Skilled workers, in other words, had an affinity for skilled thefts. Service workers, who ranked about equal to artisans in occupational status, also had higher rates for serious than for petty thefts, whereas unskilled workers had virtually equal rates and sailors and men in the miscellaneous category had considerably higher rates for petty thefts than for serious ones. Agriculturalists, another relatively impoverished category, who had average vagrancy rates and above-average begging rates, had low rates of theft, both petty and serious. Finally, those without occupations were slightly overrepresented among petty thieves but nearly absent among the thieves tried in the *cour d'assises*. In short, those convicted of petty theft were consistently more down and out than those convicted of more serious thefts.

Figures for assault are based on a small number of cases (61) and therefore must be taken skeptically. Assault figures are also suspect for another reason. Even more than other crimes, they suffer from very selective reporting. Many exchanges of blows and even knife wounds are regarded as purely private matters. The figures for assault convictions are as much an indication of the victims' readiness to seek legal redress as they are an index of acts of physical violence. This combination of few cases and selective reporting may explain the rather unusual occupational profile of the men convicted of assault. Only maritime workers and the miscellaneous category had rates substantially above the citywide average. Assault was the only category of crime for which we have figures that showed no clear relationship between crime and poverty. Small businessmen and businessmen and professionals had rates as high as unskilled workers and service workers, and agriculturalists were absent entirely.

Women convicted of theft in the *tribunal correctionnel* were the only female criminals numerous enough to allow a meaningful occupational breakdown. Table 8.3, which displays this breakdown, is constructed analogously to Table 8.2. Women's crime rates show some relation to the wealth and status of occupational groups, but not so clearly as in the case of men. As row 3 of Table 8.3 demonstrates, women with bourgeois occupations had fewer convictions than would be expected from their proportion in the population, as did women who did not work, who were, more often than not, from relatively prosperous families. But with the exception of females employed in agriculture, who were entirely absent from the register of convicted thieves, all other groups had crime rates over 1.0. This was true even of *rentières* and small businesswomen, whose cognate groups, the rentiers and small businessmen, had very low rates. This contrast, however, simply shows how different the female and male occupational worlds were. *Rentières* were often very poor women, trying to scrape by on a tiny pension, and small businesswomen were often poor market vendors of foodstuffs rather than owners of substantial shops. Neither group was clearly distinguished in income or status from manual workers.

The two female occupational groups with the highest theft rates were domestic servants and members of the needle trades. But before concluding that there were particularly demoralizing circumstances in these occupations, one other factor should be considered. The needle trades and domestic service were above all occupations of younger, single women. (See Table 3.6 for the marital-status distributions of female occupations.) Crime rates were much higher among young women than older women, and we may presume that they were also much higher among unmarried than married women. It may well be that the high theft rates imputed to women employed in domestic service and the needle trades are purely a function of their concentration in a particularly crime-prone demographic category. This bias may be checked by calculating theft rates based only on never-married females over 17, rather than on all females over 17. When this is done, the theft rates look quite different: Rates for the needle trades and domestic service are substantially reduced and are now comparable to those of unskilled workers and other crafts (see Table 8.3). But this method of calculation also introduces some

Table 8.3. Convictions for theft by occupation, women

	Not employed	Rentière	Business and professional	Small business	Needle trades	Other crafts	Domestic service	Unskilled	Agriculture	Misc.	No. cases
1. Percent convictions for theft	14.7	4.7	0.8	9.3	21.7	7.8	31.8	7.8	0.0	1.6	129
2. Percent of female population over 17, census of 1851	53.8	3.6	1.1	5.9	9.9	6.5	11.2	6.3	1.1	1.1	6,524
3. Ratio of 1 to 2	0.3	1.3	0.7	1.6	2.2	1.2	2.8	1.2	0.0	1.5	
4. Percent of single females over 17, census of 1851	33.5	2.8	1.3	4.0	15.5	8.1	26.4	5.4	0.4	2.5	2,250
5. Ratio of 1 to 4	0.4	1.7	0.6	2.3	1.4	1.0	1.2	1.4	0.0	0.6	

new distortions. It attributes the highest theft rates to *rentières* and small businesswomen, for exactly the inverse of the reason that the initial calculations showed high rates for domestic service and the needle trades: Both the small business and the *rentière* category were composed primarily of older women, either married or widowed. The safest conclusion, in the end, is that female occupations can be divided into only two groups: the bourgeois, the agriculturalists, and those who did not work, who had very low rates; and all other categories, which had moderately high rates.

Migration and crime

Migration was not the only social determinant of crime, but it was nevertheless an important one. This can be seen by an inspection of Tables 8.4 to 8.7. Tables 8.4 and 8.5 compare the crime rates of men and of women born in Marseille, Provence, Marseille's migratory hinterland, the rest of France, Italy, and the rest of the world. The rates are calculated by comparing the percentage of convicted criminals born in each of these regions with the proportion of the adult population born there, as determined by the marriage registers of 1846–51.

The first conclusion that emerges from these tables is that for every type of crime and for both sexes, all categories of immigrants had higher crime rates than native Marseillais. Immigration and crime were clearly and positively linked. Among males (see Table 8.4), crime rates had a strong tendency to rise with the distance of the migration. In every case except thefts tried in the *cour d'assises*, immigrants from Provence had lower rates than immigrants from the hinterland, who in turn had lower rates than those from more distant areas of France. The crime rates of foreign-born men were less consistent. Italians had very high rates of theft but lower rates of assault, vagrancy, and begging than Frenchmen from beyond Marseille's hinterland, whereas non-Italian foreigners had high rates of all crimes. The overall fit between distance of migration and crime is remarkable. This would seem to be a striking confirmation of the argument, advanced in Chapter 7, that immigrants who came to Marseille from long distances ran a greater risk of disorientation and demoralization than those who were still a few days' walk from home.

The main exception to this pattern is the Italians, whose theft rates were equal to or higher than those of the more distant foreigners, but whose assault, vagrancy, and begging rates were more like those of men from Marseille's hinterland. The assault rates must, as usual, be regarded skeptically. They may simply indicate that when Italians got into fights it was usually with other members of the Italian community, who preferred to seek private vengeance rather than get involved with the police – especially considering that the police were openly prejudiced against Italians. The Italians' relatively low rates of vagrancy and begging can probably be explained by two factors. Many beggars

Table 8.4. *Criminal convictions by birthplace*

	Marseille	Provence	Hinterland	Other France	Italy	Rest of world	No. cases
1. Percent theft, tribunal correctionnel	20.1	14.9	11.8	20.2	23.5	9.6	1,057
2. Ratio of 1 to 11	0.5	0.7	1.3	1.5	2.3	2.4	
3. Percent theft, cour d'assises	21.1	18.9	10.8	13.5	27.6	8.1	185
4. Ratio of 3 to 11	0.5	0.9	1.2	1.0	2.7	2.0	
5. Percent assault	20.0	15.6	13.3	31.1	11.1	8.9	45
6. Ratio of 5 to 11	0.5	0.8	1.5	2.3	1.1	2.2	
7. Percent vagrancy	10.1	16.8	10.9	34.5	13.4	14.3	119
8. Ratio of 7 to 11	0.2	0.8	1.2	2.5	1.3	3.6	
9. Percent begging	14.9	14.4	11.5	32.7	18.8	7.7	208
10. Ratio of 9 to 11	0.3	0.7	1.3	2.4	1.8	1.9	
11. Percent of grooms, marriage registers of 1846–51	43.0	20.0	8.9	13.8	10.3	4.0	

and vagrants were simply men who were out of work, out of money, and incapable of getting home, where parents or relatives could help them. Here Italians, in spite of their poverty, had two advantages. First, to judge from the marriage registers, nearly a quarter of the Italian-born immigrants had parents living in Marseille, a rate well above that of all other immigrant groups except those born in Provence. This meant that they were more likely to be able to turn to relatives in Marseille when they were out of work. Second, although Italians were more culturally distant from Marseille than Frenchmen born outside the hinterland, most of them came from Piedmont or the Genoese littoral, which could be reached by either boat or foot more quickly and easily than inland cities or villages in northern or central France. Italians, on the whole, were geographically closer to their families than long-distance French immigrants.

Female criminality was also related to the distance of migration (see Table 8.5). Natives had by far the lowest theft rates, and immigrants from Provence had rates well below those of other immigrants. The highest rates were among women who had been born in the hinterland, although the rates of those born in the rest of France, Italy, and other foreign countries were all higher than the rates of immigrants born in Provence. On the whole, the women's theft statistics fit the pattern established by the men: Natives were far less likely to be criminals than any category of immigrants, and immigrants from greater

Table 8.5. *Convictions for theft by birthplace, women;* tribunal correctionnel

	Marseille	Provence	Hinterland	Other France	Italy	Rest of world	No. cases
1. Percent of convictions	20.3	19.5	25.0	16.4	14.8	3.9	128
2. Percent of brides, marriage registers, 1846–51	47.1	20.3	11.5	9.9	8.5	2.8	3,103
3. Ratio of 1 to 2	0.4	1.0	2.2	1.7	1.7	1.4	

cultural and geographical distances were more likely to be criminals than those from nearby Provence.

One might also expect immigrants without prior urban experience to have had higher rates of criminality than those who were long accustomed to city life. This expectation is not borne out by Marseille's crime statistics. Tables 8.6 and 8.7 give the percentage of offenders and the crime rates for native Marseillais, for immigrants born in communes with populations of less than 20,000, and for those born in communes with populations of over 20,000. The figures are based only on men and women born in France. Rural-born male immigrants actually had lower crime rates than urban-born immigrants, except in the case of begging (see Table 8.6). The differences between the rural and urban born were not very important in the case of theft, but they were striking in the case of both vagrancy and assault. Why urban-born rates should have been so high for assaults and vagrancy is far from obvious. One might speculate that a willingness to seek judicial redress for violent wrongs was more common among urban than rural populations, but this hardly fits the low assault rate of the native Marseillais. In the case of vagrancy, one might hypothesize the existence of an urban casual employment circuit followed by young men from one city to another – with the vagrancy arrests representing a kind of residue of those who ran out of luck and funds too far from home. But, however plausible, this hypothesis must remain entirely speculative for the moment. The reason for higher begging rates among rural-born than among urban-born men is equally obscure. The pattern among female thieves (see Table 8.7) also argues against the assumption that prior experience of urban life prepares against the dislocation of migration: Theft rates of urban-born female immigrants were nearly twice as high as among the rural born. Whatever advantages immigrants may have gained from a long

Table 8.6. *Criminal convictions by rural or urban birth, French-born men*

	Rural	Marseille	Other urban	No. cases
1. Percent theft, *tribunal correctionnel*	55	31	13	1,057
2. Ratio of 1 to 11	1.3	0.6	1.6	
3. Percent theft, *cour d'assises*	52	36	12	117
4. Ratio of 3 to 11	1.2	0.7	1.5	
5. Percent assault	44	25	31	36
6. Ratio of 5 to 11	1.0	0.5	3.8	
7. Percent vagrancy	51	15	34	86
8. Ratio of 7 to 11	1.2	0.3	4.2	
9. Percent begging	72	21	7	203
10. Ratio of 9 to 11	1.7	0.4	0.9	
11. Percent of grooms, marriage registers of 1846–51	42	50	8	2,556

Table 8.7. *Convictions for theft by rural or urban birth, French-born women*

	Rural	Marseille	Other urban	No. cases
1. Percent of convictions	61.5	25.9	12.5	104
2. Percent of brides, marriage registers, 1846–51	53.1	41.2	5.7	2,754
3. Ratio of 1 to 2	1.2	0.6	2.2	

experience of urban life, a protection against the temptation of criminality was not one of them.

Because criminality was strongly related to occupation as well as migration, it would be possible for the difference between natives and immigrants, or between different groups of immigrants, to be a result of differences in their occupational distributions. If, for example, foreign-born immigrants were more likely to be unskilled workers, service workers, and sailors than were people from other birthplaces, it might have been their concentration in these occupational groups, rather than the fact that they had migrated from foreign countries, that accounted for their higher crime rates. This possibility is examined in Table 8.8, which shows figures on males convicted of theft in the *tribunal correctionnel*, controlling simultaneously for occupation and place of birth.[6] Table 8.8 gives both the number of thieves with a given combination of birthplace and occupation and a theft rate based on a comparison of the percent of all convicted thieves in a given occupational and birthplace category with the percent of men in that category in the population at large, as estimated

Table 8.8. Convictions for theft by occupation and birthplace, men, tribunal correctionnel

| | Occupation | | | | | | | | | | |
Place of birth	Business and professional	Rentier	Sales and clerical	Small business	Artisan	Unskilled	Service	Maritime	Agriculture	Miscellaneous	Total
Marseille											
Number	0	0	4	1	80	61	5	23	4	4	182
Rate	0.0	0.0	0.1	0.0	0.3	1.6	1.7	1.1	0.1	2.0	0.4
Provence											
Number	1	0	4	6	52	44	12	17	8	6	150
Rate	0.1	0.0	0.2	0.4	0.7	1.4	2.0	1.9	0.5	3.0	0.8
Hinterland											
Number	2	0	4	4	46	27	15	8	4	6	116
Rate	0.7	0.0	0.3	0.5	1.2	2.2	2.5	8.0	1.3	6.0	1.3
Other France											
Number	1	0	9	6	51	42	11	64	4	13	201
Rate	0.1	0.0	0.3	0.5	0.9	3.9	2.8	10.8	4.0	1.8	1.5
Italy											
Number	3	0	3	4	41	125	14	23	7	15	235
Rate	1.0	0.0	0.8	1.0	1.3	3.1	2.8	2.3	2.3	5.0	2.3
Rest of world											
Number	1	0	1	2	23	14	9	44	1	4	99
Rate	0.2	0.0	0.2	0.5	1.3	3.5	2.2	45.0	a	a	2.5
Total											
Number	8	0	25	23	293	313	66	179	28	48	983
Rate	0.3	0.0	0.3	0.3	0.7	2.3	2.4	3.7	0.4	3.5	

*a*There were no grooms from the ''rest of world'' in these occupational categories in the marriage registers of 1846 and 1851.

by the marriage registers of 1846 and 1851. (The census, which has more accurate occupational figures, cannot be used for this purpose because it does not give birthplaces.) The method of constructing this table can be made clearer by an example. Sixty-one unskilled workers born in Marseille were convicted of theft. This constituted 6.2 percent of all convicted male thieves. But unskilled workers born in Marseille made up only 3.9 percent of the grooms in the marriage registers of 1846 and 1851. The crime rate for unskilled workers born in Marseille, hence, was 6.2 divided by 3.9, or 1.6. This means that they were 60 percent more common in the population of petty thieves than in the population at large. The crime rates for all occupational and birthplace categories were calculated analogously.

Inspection of Table 8.8 makes it clear that occupation and migration had independent effects on criminality. Distant immigrants generally had higher theft rates than natives or nearby immigrants, within each occupational category as well as for the population as a whole. And wealthier occupations nearly always had lower theft rates than poorer occupations, within each of the birthplace categories as well as for the entire population. The overall relationship between migration and criminality was definitely not the result of occupational differences between natives and immigrants. Table 8.8 does, however, modify some conclusions and reveal some exceptional cases.

Perhaps the most important modification concerns the difference in theft rates of French-born and foreign-born immigrants. For the population at large, foreign-born rates were well above those of French-born immigrants. (See the "total" column of Table 8.8.) But a close inspection of Table 8.8 reveals a quite different pattern. Provençal-born immigrants had consistently lower rates than other immigrants, but the differences between the hinterland, other France, Italy, and rest-of-world categories were generally small and inconsistent. Italian-born bourgeois had higher rates than other bourgeois, but the rates of Italian artisans, unskilled workers, and service workers were about equal to those of French immigrants from beyond Provence, and the rates of Italian maritime workers were substantially lower. The reason that Italian immigrants as a whole had such high rates is that so many of them were concentrated in crime-prone occupational categories: unskilled labor, service workers, and maritime workers. This, as will be seen in Chapter 9, was a consequence both of their low socio-economic backgrounds in Italy and of their poor chances for social mobility in Marseille. In other words, the Italians' high crime rates did not result from the special strains caused by adapting Italian ways to the French setting but from their poverty. The case of the other foreign-born immigrants was different. Their theft rates were not very different either from those of Italians or from those of French immigrants born outside Provence – except in the maritime category, where their rate was a staggering 45.0. In short, it would be incorrect to conclude that special problems of linguistic and cultural adjustment made migration from foreign countries particularly disorienting. Rather, the high crime rates of Italians can be accounted for by poverty and those of other foreigners by the special case of maritime workers.

The extraordinary theft rate of non-Italian foreign-born sailors points up the one major inconsistent case in Table 8.8: the maritime workers. Whereas crime rates for other occupational categories were more or less equal for all immigrants from beyond Provence, the maritime workers' rates were wildly erratic. True to form, maritime workers from Marseille had the lowest rates, and Provençal immigrants' rates were above natives' but below other immigrants'. Thereafter, all regularity ceased. The theft rate of maritime workers from the hinterland was an extraordinarily high 8.0; that of maritime workers from the rest of France was higher yet, at 10.8; and that of maritime workers from foreign countries other than Italy was a truly astronomical 45.0. Yet the Italian rate was quite moderate – only 2.3. How can this pattern be explained? In the first place, the marriage-register data, on which the calculations of rates are based, are not very appropriate for maritime workers. The marriage registers include only those maritime workers who married a women in Marseille and who therefore presumably regarded Marseille as their home port. Although some sailors from distant areas of the world married and established a home in Marseille, most of Marseille's resident maritime population was from relatively nearby. Forty-three percent of the sailors who got married in Marseille in 1846 and 1851 had been born in Marseille. Another 19 percent were from Provence, and 20 percent were from Italy – with rare exceptions, from nearby port cities along the coast from Nice to Genoa. All the rest of the world, the port cities of northern France and foreign ports from Buenos Aires to Liverpool, Seville, and Constantinople accounted for only 18 percent.

But the maritime workers living in Marseille at a given point in time, and therefore those at risk for criminal activity, were composed of both Marseille-based sailors and those who were merely passing through during the course of their voyages. This latter group were of the most diverse origins. Whether ashore only while their ships were unloaded and loaded, or laying over between engagements, the temporary population of maritime workers at any time was bound to be substantial. Ashore after days or weeks at sea, they were a notoriously unruly lot and probably contributed disproportionately to criminal activities of all sorts. The sailors whose wives and families lived in Marseille may have been equally unruly in the distant ports they visited, but while in Marseille they were in the bosom of their families, resting from their dangerous labors and renewing ties with loved ones. The problem with the maritime theft rates in Table 8.8 is that thieves – probably drawn largely from the temporary population – are assigned rates based only on the resident population. To a certain extent, then, the high theft rates of the non-Provençal and non-Italian immigrant maritime workers is a statistical artifact. Because these categories were amply represented in the temporary maritime population but very rare among those maritime workers who married and settled in Marseille, their rates were considerably inflated. But it remains likely that visiting sailors from these categories actually were more likely to commit thefts than those from Provence or Italy. They were, after all, much farther from home. To the extent that theft was an outcome of being broke, friendless, and far from relatives, one should expect mariners far from their home ports to have had higher rates than those who were only a day or two's sail from home. In any case, the furloughed mariners represent a very special problem, for they were the only sizable group of residents who were neither employed nor seeking employment in Marseille. They were, in a sense, not really immigrants, but only visitors to the city.

Crime and domicile

The extraordinary role of the temporary maritime population in Marseille's theft statistics raises a broader question. Were other temporary migrants also prominent among convicted criminals? Criminals tried in the *tribunal correctionnel* were required to state their place of residence in Marseille, and these data can be used to approach the question of temporary migration.[7] This question is made all the more significant because temporary immigrants were essentially missed by the marriage registers – the main source of information about migration for this study. Criminal statistics can be used to make some assessment of the problems faced by this significant but otherwise virtually unknowable category of immigrants.

As Table 8.9 demonstrates, criminals were by no means drawn equally from all quarters of the city. Crime rates were generally low in the bourgeois quarters (districts 5 and 6) and in the outlying, quasi-agricultural quarters (districts 11, 12, and 13). The highest crime rates were in working-class quarters. But the rates of the working-class quarters varied considerably. Rates for most crimes were highest in district 1 (the maritime quarter), district 3 (the slum quarter in the old city), and district 4 (the central commercial district, a mixed bourgeois and working-class quarter). They were generally at an intermediate level in the remaining working-class neighborhoods: districts 2, 7, 8, 9, and 10. The neighborhoods with high crime rates were not necessarily the poorest. District 3 had a high proportion of unskilled workers, and district 1 had the lion's share of the city's maritime workers. But districts 2, 7, and 11, which had the highest proportions of unskilled workers in the city, had low or moderate crime rates. (For the occupational composition of districts in 1851, see Table 5.1.) But the high-crime districts had one thing in common: A high proportion of their adult-male populations lived in rooming houses (see Table 5.2).[8] The figures suggest that it was less poverty than a large itinerant population that led to high rates of crime.

Table 8.9. *Criminal convictions by district*

	1	2	3	4	5	6	7	8	9	10	11	12	13	No. cases
1. Percent thefts, males	13.2	6.9	29.6	18.7	3.9	1.9	5.1	2.4	9.0	3.1	0.7	2.0	3.5	743
2. Ratio of 1 to 11	1.7	1.0	2.2	1.2	0.5	0.3	1.1	0.4	0.8	0.7	0.2	0.3	0.6	
3. Percent thefts, females	13.9	8.3	24.1	22.2	8.3	3.7	3.7	4.6	6.4	0.9	—	0.9	2.7	132
4. Ratio of 3 to 11	1.8	1.3	1.8	1.5	1.0	0.5	0.8	0.8	0.6	0.2	—	0.1	0.5	
5. Percent assaults	15.9	2.3	15.9	36.4	11.4	—	4.5	—	4.5	2.3	—	—	6.8	44
6. Ratio of 5 to 11	2.0	0.3	1.2	2.4	1.4	—	1.0	—	0.4	0.5	—	—	1.2	
7. Percent vagrancy	14.3	4.8	33.3	14.3	9.5	—	—	9.5	—	—	—	4.8	—	21
8. Ratio of 7 to 11	1.8	0.7	2.5	0.9	1.2	—	—	1.7	—	—	—	0.7	—	
9. Percent begging	7.8	4.3	66.1	8.7	1.7	0.9	4.3	0.9	5.2	—	—	—	—	115
10. Ratio of 9 to 11	1.0	0.7	5.0	0.6	0.2	0.1	0.9	0.2	0.5	—	—	—	—	
11. Percent of population, census of 1851	7.8	6.6	13.2	15.2	8.2	7.4	4.6	5.6	11.3	4.3	3.1	7.0	5.7	17,788

District 3, the slum district of the old city, emerges from Table 8.9 as the preeminent criminal neighborhood of Marseille. It had the highest rates of male theft convictions, begging, and vagrancy, and it was tied for the highest rate of female theft convictions. Only in the case of assaults – which once again had the least explicable pattern – was district 3 not at the top. Much of district 3's lugubrious superiority was due to the population of two streets, the rue de la Couronne and the rue de l'Echelle. Perched on the top of the hill overlooking the port, these two streets were lined by the city's poorest rooming houses. Although these two streets accounted for only 0.7 percent of the city's population, they contributed 9 percent of male theft convictions, 19 percent of vagrancy convictions, and no less than 43 percent of convictions for begging.

All these figures are for convicted criminals who had a stated domicile in Marseille. There were many, however, who had none. Some of these were listed simply as living ''in Marseille'' with no domicile specified, some as ''without fixed domicile,'' and others as having domiciles elsewhere than in Marseille. The latter two categories presumably were made up of transients. Those listed as living ''in Marseille'' but without specified domicile may have been transients, but it is also possible that this designation merely reflected a certain carelessness on the part of the police and recording officials, who may have neglected to determine or write down these persons' addresses. Inspection of the geographical origins of convicted thieves in the ''in Marseille'' group lends plausibility to the hypothesis of simple carelessness. Whereas the ''without fixed domicile'' and ''domiciled outside Marseille'' groups came disproportionately from the ''other France'' and ''rest-of-world'' categories, and had only rarely been born in Marseille, thieves listed as living ''in Marseille'' had a profile of geographical origins barely indistinguishable from that of thieves with specified domiciles in the city. It therefore seems most prudent to assume that those who are indicated as having domiciles outside Marseille or as having no fixed domicile were genuine transients but that the ''in Marseille'' category were not.

The transients, commonly referred to as the ''floating population'' by nineteenth-century officials, were generally temporary immigrants who worked in Marseille for a time, living in rooming houses or wherever they could find shelter. It is perhaps not surprising that such people made up 77 percent of the men convicted of vagrancy or 28 percent of those convicted of begging. But they also made up 15 percent of the male thieves, 7 percent of the female thieves, and 8 percent of the males convicted of assault. If the nondomiciled criminals are added to the hardly less ''floating'' population of the rue de la Couronne and the rue de l'Echelle – leaving aside numerous others who doubtless lived in rooming houses elsewhere – they made up 22 percent of convicted male thieves, 58 percent of convicted beggars, and 88 percent of convicted vagrants.

The figures on domiciles suggest that although criminality may have been related to migration in general, it was especially common among the most footloose of the immigrants: those whose residence in Marseille had been brief and was probably intended as only temporary, who had no permanent domicile, or who lived in a tiny chamber in a commercial rooming house. Rather than creating a permanent "dangerous class" trapped in the city slums by crushing poverty and demoralization, the picture painted by Chevalier and the nineteenth-century observers on whom he relied,[9] immigration seems to have created a temporary dangerous class. It was probably temporary in two senses. First, its members were drawn from the most mobile portion of the population – poor, single young men, traveling from city to city in search of employment. Second, it was also temporary in the sense that a high propensity to criminality characterized only a certain phase of life. Once a man had passed the age of 25 or 30 and married, his likelihood of engaging in criminal activity fell dramatically. It appears, moreover, that most offenders were not habitual criminals. Eighty-one percent of the male thieves and the same proportion of male vagrants had had no earlier conviction, and the rate was even higher for those convicted of begging (90 percent) and assault (93 percent). For most, commission of a crime was probably a more or less isolated event in a period of personal, residential, and economic instability, not an irreversible decline into the world of criminality.

The main exception to these generalizations was female thieves, whose proportion of prior convictions was a much higher 39 percent. This, combined with the fact that a higher proportion of female than male thieves was older than 27 (41 percent as against 30 percent), seems to indicate that criminality may have been a way of life for a higher proportion of the small population of female criminals than of the larger population of male criminals. And the fact that a lower proportion of female than male thieves was part of the "floating" population implies that many of these "hardened" female criminals were relatively permanent residents of the city. One might hypothesize two reasons for these differences between males and females. First, because criminality was so much rarer among women than men, and so much farther from conventional feminine role definitions, one might expect those women who were so unconventional, audacious, or depraved as to engage in criminal activity to have done so more deliberately than men and therefore also to have been more likely to repeat their offenses. The idea that women were less casual criminals than men is given further plausibility by the fact that 18 percent of all thefts committed by women, as against 15 percent of those committed by men, were deemed serious enough to be tried in the *cour d'assises*. Second, once a woman had been convicted of a crime, she was more likely than a male criminal to be marked as a transgressor of community norms, certainly in the eyes of the community and perhaps even in her own eyes. This, too, would have increased the likelihood that she would commit further offenses. Once a woman had crossed the line into criminality, she probably found it harder than a man to find her way back. At the same time, women's relative lack of mobility meant that they were more likely than men to live out their criminal lives in Marseille.

Transiency, migration, and crime

The crime statistics shed significant light on the problem of migration. First, they provide a warning that the picture of migration derived from the marriage registers may not be valid for all immigrants. The fact that temporary immigrants had much higher crime rates than immigrants who had more settled domiciles in Marseille implies that the most volatile immigrants – those missed in the marriage registers – were probably also the most subject to disorientation. It is impossible to say why, precisely, the temporary immigrants had such high crime rates, although a few plausible hypotheses present themselves. One obvious hypothesis is that the transients' high crime rates derived from their lack of integration into the local community. It is probable that a larger proportion of the transients than of the domiciled population had recently arrived in Marseille and that therefore they were more likely to be without networks of friends and family in the city. And even if they had been in Marseille for some time, their nomadic life styles would make it hard for them to form durable social bonds with the more settled population. Adrift socially and morally, as well as residentially, they might be expected to lack the usual defenses against criminal behavior. A second hypothesis would attribute the high rates of criminality to the flocking of certain types of individuals – the impoverished, the chronically maladjusted, the insane, the antisocial; in short, society's "losers" – into the floating population. According to the first hypothesis, the social experience of "floating" would turn individuals into criminals. According to the second, a significant proportion of the individuals who became "floaters" may already have been engaged in criminal activities. Yet another hypothesis would stress the importance of a rooming-house criminal subculture that would actively recruit "floaters" into crime. These three hypotheses are not mutually exclusive. It would be quite possible to imagine a core of social-misfit floaters who constituted a rooming-house criminal subculture that recruited substantial numbers of hitherto honest but disoriented young and unattached immigrants into crime. The high rate of crime among temporary immigrants may have been the result of any one of these three mechanisms, of some combination of them, or of some quite different social process. Given the thinness of the data at hand, any attempt to pin down the causes would be pure speculation.

But that the temporary floating immigrant population differed substantially from the population of more settled immigrants seems beyond dispute. The crime statistics make it possible to discern a somber underside of migration, one marked by poverty, instability, loneliness, and criminality. Most of the men and many of the women caught up in this syndrome probably departed from Marseille after relatively brief stays, leaving no trace in the marriage registers. On the whole, the unfortunate experiences of such people do not seem to have immobilized them in Marseille's slums, turning them into a permanent "dangerous class." Indeed, those immigrants who had bad experiences in Marseille may eventually have found more secure jobs, married, and settled down in other cities, leaving their failures behind them. The evidence now available gives us no way of knowing their ultimate fates.

It was among the "floating" population that immigration had the most spectacular effect on criminality. But all measures, for all types of crimes, also indicate that immigrants in general were more likely to commit crimes than natives and that immigrants who had come to Marseille from greater distances were more likely to do so than those born in nearby Provence. Uprooting does appear to have weakened moral constraints on criminal behavior, not only among "transients" but among the more settled immigrant population as well. Migration meant a break with the community in which a man or woman had been raised; even when the immigrants were well prepared for city life, the tremendous range of new possibilities and the lack, or the weakness, of family and community constraints meant that they were more open to criminal activities than men and women who had been born in Marseille. Migration did not lead inexorably to crime. But it did weaken some of the constraints that might otherwise have kept immigrants from committing crimes. Thus, in spite of all the mitigating features discussed in Chapter 7 – selectivity of migration, the presence of family ties and of communities of immigrants in the city, the good overall educational preparation of the immigrants – migration still carried a significant risk of disorientation and criminality.

9 Social mobility: men

The immigrants who moved into Marseille between the early 1820s and the late 1860s had to find positions in the city's changing occupational structure. Their ability to find good jobs – secure, well-paying, high in status – constitutes one important gauge of their migration experience. Were the best jobs monopolized by native Marseillais, with immigrants relegated to the lower reaches of the occupational hierarchy? Or did the immigrants' ambition, restlessness, and prior educational preparation allow them to match or better their native-born competitors? This chapter examines the shifting patterns of men's social mobility in nineteenth-century Marseille. It attempts to show how the changing shape of the male occupational structure interacted with the changing recruitment of young men into the labor force – above all with rising immigration – to create particular patterns of upward and downward mobility, of opportunity and blockage, of movement across class boundaries and recruitment from within. The following chapter will take up the distinct but related question of women's social mobility.

Studies of social mobility have become a major genre of historical research in the past two decades.[1] Interest in the question of social mobility has been particularly strong among American social scientists and historians, who seem to consider occupational mobility the prime test of a society's openness or rigidity and, therefore, of its vitality and justice. This fixation on occupational mobility flows naturally from the pervasive American ideology of competitive individualism that is neatly summed up in the phrase "equality of opportunity." But the issue is not only an American concern, as is demonstrated by the existence of a large number of European mobility studies,[2] or, for that matter, by the famous slogan of the French Revolution – "*la carrière ouverte aux talent*" (the career open to talent). An analysis of men's social mobility will make it possible to assess the openness of Marseille's male occupational structure and determine whether its openness increased or decreased over time, to examine both the persistence and the permeability of the urban social hierarchy in an era of massive population growth and economic transformation.

Sociologists normally distinguish two different kinds of occupational mobility. The first is *inter*generational mobility – changes in occupation from one generation to the next. The second is *intra*generational mobility – changes in a person's occupation during the course of his or her lifetime. The method normally used by historians to investigate intragenerational mobility involves

234

tracing individuals from one census to subsequent censuses, noting changes in occupation over the years. In Marseille the poor quality of the census data and the sheer size of the city's population made this procedure impracticable. The marriage-register data, which allow comparisons of grooms' occupations with their fathers' occupations, can be used to measure only intergenerational, not intragenerational, mobility. This is, of course, a serious limitation. There are some indications that intragenerational mobility, and particularly upward intragenerational mobility, may have been appreciable. The mean age of small businessmen, rentiers, and businessmen and professionals in the census of 1851 was considerably higher than that of men in the clerical and working-class categories (see Table 9.1). These differences could have resulted from a number of different processes, but they suggest some amount of net mobility from working-class and clerical occupations to professional and property-owning occupations during the course of men's careers. Likewise, the occupational distribution for men marrying at the age of 30 or more was higher than that of younger grooms in each of the marriage-register data sets used in this study (see Table 9.2). Again, although the inference is not certain, these figures suggest some net upward intragenerational mobility. But it is impossible, on the basis of the data at hand, to learn precisely how much intragenerational mobility there may have been.

If there was a tendency for men's occupational standing to improve during their careers, this would also introduce a bias into measurements of inter-generational mobility. Because the grooms were usually young men near the beginning of their careers, whereas their fathers were older men near the end of their careers, the marriage-register data should tend to underestimate upward intergenerational mobility and overestimate downward mobility. The figures on occupational mobility, then, are incomplete and probably biased downward. But the marriage-register data do give comparable figures on intergenerational mobility for three periods during the nineteenth century and are certainly worth a careful examination.

Before examining these data, two technical points must be made. First, it must be remembered that in 1821–2 the groom's father's occupation was not reported in 23 percent of the cases. This means that the intergenerational-mobility figures given for 1821–2 are incomplete and therefore less reliable than the data for 1846–51 and 1869. Second, comparing rates of occupational mobility in Marseille over time is complicated by the fact that the city's boundaries included large areas of primarily agricultural suburbs. As has been seen in Chapter 5, the rural population of the commune declined sharply between 1821–2 and 1869. Hence, the population of Marseille in the early years of the century included a sizable rural sector, whereas later in the century the rural sector was relatively small. This change in the mix of the population confounds an analysis of changing mobility patterns, for occupational mobility was lower in the rural than in the urban districts of the city – primarily because

Table 9.1. *Mean age by occupation, men, census of 1851*

	Business and professional	Rentier	Sales and clerical	Small business	Artisan	Service	Unskilled	Maritime	Agriculture	Miscellaneous	All occupations
Mean age	43.1	54.8	37.8	41.3	35.6	33.3	35.5	37.1	41.7	30.6	37.6

Table 9.2. *Groom's occupational distribution by age at marriage (in percent)*

Occupational category	1821–2		1846–51		1869	
	Under 30	30 and above	Under 30	30 and above	Under 30	30 and above
1. Business and professional	3.7	13.5	3.1	8.8	6.9	7.3
2. Rentier	0.8	5.1	1.4	4.1	0.9	2.8
3. Sales and clerical	8.3	13.1	9.1	12.6	16.3	18.0
4. Small business	7.1	7.3	7.2	8.9	7.7	9.7
5. Artisan	59.0	39.6	52.9	40.2	44.4	33.6
6. Service	0.1	2.2	2.5	3.6	5.6	5.7
7. Unskilled	9.7	8.0	14.6	13.3	11.9	14.1
8. Maritime	7.1	8.4	5.9	4.7	5.0	6.4
9. Agriculture	2.2	1.8	1.5	2.0	0.8	1.5
10. Miscellaneous	1.3	1.1	1.5	1.6	0.4	1.0

sons of suburban cultivators tended very strongly to remain in agricultural occupations. To remove this confounding influence, the figures on occupational mobility presented in this chapter include only residents of the urban districts of the city, districts 1 through 10. This is, then, an analysis of strictly urban mobility patterns.

Occupational mobility, as many students of the subject have demonstrated, must be seen within its demographic and economic context.[3] The rapid growth of Marseille's economy and population between the 1820s and 1870 should have been conducive to relatively high rates of social mobility. As the economy grew, the number of available jobs increased at all levels of the occupational structure, making it relatively easy for men to change jobs frequently and hence to move up or down in the occupational hierarchy. In a stagnating economy, there would have been fewer opportunities to change jobs, and men should have been less likely to experience mobility in either an upward or a downward direction.

Moreover, expansion of the economy and population created a growing gap between the distribution of men's occupational backgrounds and the distribution of occupations practiced in the city. This is evident in Table 9.3. In 1821–2, there was a reasonably good fit between the occupational background of men entering the labor market and the jobs available to them, although there was a shortfall of men from artisan and clerical backgrounds and an oversupply of men from agricultural backgrounds. In 1846–51, the fit was worse, and in 1869 worse again. This judgment can be given greater rigor by calculating indices of dissimilarity between fathers' occupations and sons' occupations for each year. The index of dissimilarity, which states what percentage of cases would have to be shifted to other categories to make two distributions equal, rose from 20.7 to 26.8 to 34.2.[4] The most important factor in this increasingly poor fit was, of course, the influx of peasant immigrants into Marseille in later years. The increasingly poor fit meant that a growing volume of intergenerational mobility was required simply to fill the gaps between backgrounds and available positions. It should therefore be expected that levels of mobility would be higher later in the century than earlier.

Finally, the gap between backgrounds and available positions tended to increase the amount of upward mobility from working-class and peasant backgrounds to the bourgeoisie. In 1821–2 there were more men with bourgeois backgrounds than bourgeois positions available for them to fill; in 1846–51 the two were essentially in equilibrium; and in 1869 there were considerably more bourgeois jobs than men from bourgeois backgrounds. Hence, there is reason to expect that upward mobility into the bourgeoisie would become more common over time and downward mobility from the bourgeoisie less common.

Most of this discussion of mobility will focus on movement from one occupational category or stratum to another. But it is also possible to measure

Table 9.3. *Profile of male labor market (in percent)*

Occupational category	Men married 1821–2			Men married 1846–51			Men married 1869		
	1. Groom's occupation	2. Groom's father's occupation	3. Excess of demand over supply $(1-2)$	4. Groom's occupation	5. Groom's father's occupation	6. Excess of demand over supply $(4-5)$	7. Groom's occupation	8. Groom's father's occupation	9. Excess of demand over supply $(7-8)$
1. Business and professional	6.3	8.7	-2.4	5.8	6.1	-0.3	7.1	4.9	2.2
2. Rentier	1.9	6.7	-4.8	2.6	8.0	-5.4	1.8	8.1	-6.3
3. Sales and clerical	9.6	4.0	5.6	10.6	5.2	5.4	17.1	5.3	11.8
4. Small business	7.1	9.0	-1.9	8.0	6.6	1.4	8.6	6.4	2.2
5. Artisan	53.9	42.3	11.6	47.3	33.2	14.1	39.4	27.8	11.6
6. Service	1.2	1.4	-0.2	3.0	1.6	1.4	5.7	1.3	4.4
7. Unskilled	9.3	5.8	3.5	14.1	9.4	3.7	12.9	12.3	.6
8. Maritime	7.4	8.6	-1.2	5.4	5.2	0.2	5.7	4.3	1.4
9. Agriculture	2.1	10.1	-8.0	1.7	20.0	-18.3	1.1	24.9	-23.8
10. Miscellaneous	1.3	3.5	-2.2	1.6	4.8	-3.2	0.7	4.8	-4.1
All bourgeois $(1 + 2 + 3 + 4)$	24.9	28.4	-3.5	27.0	25.9	1.1	34.6	24.7	9.9
Index of dissimilarity	20.7			26.7			34.2		
Number of cases	1,036	1,036		2,561	2,561		1,785	1,785	

the total extent of occupational mobility of any kind by determining the proportion of men whose occupational titles were different from their fathers'. Mobility of this kind rose markedly in Marseille between 1821–2 and 1869. In 1821–2, over a third of Marseille's men had the same occupation as their fathers; by 1846–51 the proportion had dropped to under a quarter; and by 1869 it had fallen to a sixth. Some of this decline in the inheritance of occupations resulted from the rising proportion of peasants' sons, few of whom could hope to find jobs in agriculture in Marseille. But, as Table 9.4 demonstrates, the decline was felt in nearly all categories of occupational background. Except for sons of service workers and of businessmen and professionals, men from all types of occupational origins were less likely to follow their fathers' occupations in 1869 than they had been a half-century earlier. In this most basic sense, intergenerational occupational mobility clearly increased as the century progressed.

Before examining mobility between different occupational categories, one familiar and vexing technical problem of the data must be confronted. As was pointed out at some length in Chapter 3, occupational figures derived from the marriage registers do not satisfactorily distinguish between masters and employees in the artisan trades; a significant number of masters gave no occupational designation that would distinguish them from workers employed in the same trade. This imprecision is potentially important in a study of occupational mobility, for it means that a substantial amount of movement between the status of worker and that of employer will be missed. The reporting of both fathers' and sons' occupation suffers from the same defect. Taking occupational titles at face value will result in four different kinds of errors: (1) Some men whose fathers were workers but who themselves became small employers will incorrectly be counted as experiencing no upward mobility. (2) Some workers whose fathers were small employers will incorrectly be counted as experiencing no downward mobility. (3) Some men with bourgeois occupations whose fathers were small employers will incorrectly be counted as upwardly mobile workers' sons. (4) Some small employers whose fathers were in bourgeois occupations will incorrectly be counted as downwardly mobile. There is no way of knowing a priori whether the combined effects of these measurement errors will be to inflate or deflate the amount of mobility that actually occurred.

The alternative to taking occupational designations at face value is, once again, to construct corrected figures. These figures are based on the assumption that the husbands who actually identified themselves as artisan masters were typical of the remaining unidentified masters, and, similarly, that the fathers who were identified as artisan masters were typical of the artisan master fathers who remained unidentified. This can be used to generate a modified mobility matrix that corrects for the errors of classification by removing an appropriate number of cases from the skilled-workers category and placing them in the

Table 9.4. *Occupational inheritance by father's occupational category (percent sons with same occupation as father)*

	Business and professional	Rentier	Sales and clerical	Small business	Artisan	Service	Unskilled	Maritime	Agriculture	Miscellaneous	All categories
1821–2	23.6	15.9	22.0	22.6	47.6	6.7	31.7	38.2	17.3	28.6	34.2
1846–51	27.6	8.3	12.1	22.0	36.5	2.5	34.3	33.3	3.9	1.6	22.4
1869	23.0	5.6	14.9	18.3	26.7	8.7	26.9	32.9	2.0	0.0	16.4

small-businessmen category. (For an explanation of the mechanics of this procedure, see Appendix C.) It is quite possible that the men actually identified as small employers in the artisan trades differed significantly from those not identified as such. But applying this correction to the mobility figures should give an indication of the scale and direction of the errors introduced by the initial misclassifications.

In fact, these corrections generally result in only negligible changes in rates of mobility between occupational categories, except in the case of small businessmen, where the corrections result in a sharp decline in rates of downward mobility. Because more concrete and less hypothetical figures seem preferable to figures that have been modified by complicated calculations, and because the corrected figures would result in few significant changes in argument, only *uncorrected* figures are given in this chapter. In those few cases where use of the corrected figures would result in a different conclusion, this fact is noted in the text. The corrected figures, which are presented in Appendix C, should in fact increase our confidence in the rough accuracy of the mobility matrices used in the text.

Mobility and the urban occupational hierarchy

The overall patterns of occupational mobility in Marseille are revealed in Tables 9.5, 9.6, and 9.7, which give the percentage distribution of sons' occupations for each category of fathers' occupations. The tables also include (in row 11) figures for the percentage of grooms from a given occupational background who held bourgeois positions at the time of their marriage. These figures provide a convenient summary measure of different groups' mobility.

The mobility tables reveal that downward mobility from bourgeois occupational backgrounds was appreciable in all three time periods. Even sons of businessmen and professionals had failed to achieve bourgeois occupations in 19 percent of the cases in 1821–2, and, although the rate of downward mobility tended to fall somewhat thereafter, it was still 14 percent in 1869. Rates of downward mobility were higher for men coming from other categories of bourgeois backgrounds. Sons of rentiers fell to manual positions in 23 percent of the cases in 1821–2, in 36 percent in 1846–51, and in 24 percent in 1869. Furthermore, men coming from both these elite occupational backgrounds very frequently found jobs in small-business or clerical occupations, rather than in the elite category. In fact, sons of rentiers were more likely to hold jobs in the petite bourgeoisie than in the elite in all three periods. Only sons of businessmen and professionals managed to retain elite status in half or more of the cases. Their likelihood of doing so rose from 50 percent in 1821–2 to 57 percent in 1846–51 and 61 percent in 1869.

According to the uncorrected mobility figures, downward mobility was much more common for men born into the petite bourgeoisie than for those

Table 9.5. *Father's occupation by son's occupation, 1821–2 (in percent)*

	Father's occupation										
Son's occupation	Business and profes- sional	Rentier	Sales and clerical	Small business	Arti- san	Ser- vice	Un- skilled	Mari- time	Agri- culture	Miscel- laneous	Total
1. Business and professional	44	17	5	6	1	—	—	—	—	3	6
2. Rentier	7	17	—	1	—	—	—	—	—	—	2
3. Sales and clerical	23	28	37	15	4	20	3	2	4	8	10
4. Small business	7	14	5	30	4	—	2	2	8	3	7
5. Artisan	12	17	44	40	81	53	42	30	48	42	54
6. Service	—	1	—	3	1	7	5	—	2	—	2
7. Unskilled	—	3	7	—	6	—	45	18	17	14	9
8. Maritime	6	1	2	2	4	13	2	47	2	11	7
9. Agriculture	—	—	—	—	—	7	—	—	17	8	2
10. Miscellaneous	1	—	—	2	—	7	2	—	3	11	1
11. All bourgeois (1 + 2 + 3 + 4)	81	76	47	52	9	20	5	4	11	14	25
Number of cases	90	69	41	93	438	15	60	89	105	36	1,036

243

Table 9.6. *Father's occupation by son's occupation, 1846–51 (in percent)*

Son's occupation	Father's occupation										Total
	Business and professional	Rentier	Sales and clerical	Small business	Artisan	Service	Un-skilled	Maritime	Agri-culture	Miscellaneous	
1. Business and professional	47	19	9	5	1	—	—	2	—	4	6
2. Rentier	10	11	2	3	1	—	1	2	1	—	3
3. Sales and clerical	22	20	31	14	5	15	3	3	11	10	11
4. Small business	4	13	7	33	6	8	3	2	6	7	8
5. Artisan	10	27	40	33	73	48	39	33	38	43	47
6. Service	—	3	3	2	2	8	2	1	5	9	3
7. Unskilled	1	2	3	5	7	18	46	9	26	14	14
8. Maritime	2	2	4	4	3	2	3	49	3	6	5
9. Agriculture	—	—	—	1	—	—	—	—	7	2	2
10. Miscellaneous	3	2	1	—	1	2	2	—	2	5	2
11. All bourgeois (1 + 2 + 3 + 4)	83	63	48	55	13	23	7	8	17	21	
Number of cases	156	205	132	168	849	40	242	132	513	124	2,561

Table 9.7. *Father's occupation by son's occupation, 1869 (in percent)*

Son's occupation	Father's occupation										
	Business and professional	Rentier	Sales and clerical	Small business	Artisan	Service	Un-skilled	Maritime	Agriculture	Miscellaneous	Total
1. Business and professional	55	28	4	10	2	—	1	3	1	1	7
2. Rentier	6	10	—	2	1	—	—	—	1	2	2
3. Sales and clerical	21	24	40	15	14	9	6	5	21	20	17
4. Small business	5	14	9	31	7	4	5	3	7	8	9
5. Artisan	10	16	36	28	63	52	42	33	31	37	39
6. Service	2	5	4	4	4	22	4	1	11	4	6
7. Unskilled	1	2	—	4	6	9	36	7	21	16	13
8. Maritime	—	1	5	2	3	4	5	49	4	10	6
9. Agriculture	—	—	—	2	—	—	1	—	3	1	1
10. Miscellaneous	—	—	1	3	—	—	1	—	1	—	1
11. All bourgeois (1 + 2 + 3 + 4)	86	76	53	58	24	13	12	10	30	31	35
Number of cases	87	144	94	115	496	23	219	76	445	86	1,785

born into the elite. Over half of clerical employees' sons had failed to achieve bourgeois occupations in both 1821–2 and 1846–51, and nearly half had failed to do so in 1869. The uncorrected downward-mobility rates of small businessmen were lower, but not by much: 47, 45, and 42 percent. The corrected figures, however, change the picture drastically. They indicate no significant change for clerical employees' sons but indicate much lower rates for small businessmen's sons: 26 percent in 1821–2, 25 percent in 1846–51, and 31 percent in 1869. These corrected rates, if accurate, would mean that the mobility experience of small businessmen was actually far more like that of rentiers' sons than of clerical employees' sons. This evidence that small businessmen's sons had a more favorable mobility experience than clerical employees' sons is particularly interesting in light of the clerical employees' higher scores on the occupational-status scales developed in Chapter 4. As salaried employees, clerical workers seem to have been considerably less able to pass their advantages on to their sons than were the more solid, property-owning small businessmen.

However, neither small businessmen's sons nor clerical workers' sons had much success in rising into elite positions in 1821–2 or 1846–51. Small businessmen's sons had attained positions in the elite category in 7 percent of the cases in 1821–2 and in 8 percent in 1846–51; for clerical workers' sons, the rates were 5 and 11 percent. In 1869 the experiences of sons of small businessmen and clerical workers diverged. The percentage of small businessmen's sons with elite occupations rose slightly to 12, whereas that of clerical workers fell to only 4. In this case, the corrected figures tell essentially the same story. This would appear to confirm the picture of the clerical workers that was elaborated in Chapters 3 and 4; the vast bureaucratization of Marseille's commerce that increased the number of clerical workers, routinized their work, and lowered their status in the 1850s and 1860s also decreased their chances for intergenerational upward mobility.

In summary, the mobility experiences of sons of bourgeois was marked by appreciable rates of downward mobility in all categories of bourgeois backgrounds and by low rates of upward mobility from the petite bourgeoisie to the elite. Some of the downward mobility revealed in these figures may have been only temporary; data on the age distribution of occupations suggests a significant amount of upward mobility in the course of men's careers. Some sons of rich merchants may have spent time as clerks before becoming partners in their fathers' firms; some sons of shopkeepers may have practiced skilled trades until they inherited the family store. But the figures for downward mobility are high enough that much of this downward mobility was probably not made up later in men's careers. Nor was there any significant change in rates of downward mobility over time. The proportion of men from all bourgeois backgrounds not having bourgeois occupations at the time of their marriage was 34 percent in 1821–2, 37 percent in 1846–51, and 32 percent in 1869.

These rates are comparable to those found in most contemporary industrialized societies. It is particularly notable that rates of downward mobility failed to fall significantly as the demographic situation became more favorable. High rates of downward mobility in 1821–2 can be explained largely by the surplus of young men from bourgeois backgrounds. But by 1869 young men from bourgeois backgrounds were scarce, not overabundant. That the proportion obtaining bourgeois jobs did not rise significantly seems to signal an important increase in the openness and competitiveness of Marseille's occupational system.

Increasing openness is much more evident in the figures for upward mobility from the working class into the bourgeoisie. The proportion of workers' sons obtaining bourgeois occupations rose steadily between the early 1820s and late 1860s. For all categories of workers' sons combined, the rates of upward mobility into the bourgeoisie rose from 8 percent in 1821–2 to 12 percent in 1846–51 and 19 percent in 1869. It is important to note, however, that mobility from working-class to elite occupations remained extremely rare, even in 1869. Those who moved from working-class backgrounds into the bourgeoisie did so by obtaining clerical and small-business jobs; they did not become professionals or merchants or rentiers. The pinnacle of the occupational hierarchy remained virtually inaccessible to those who began their lives below the petite bourgeoisie. But if the range of upward mobility remained limited, the overall increase was truly impressive. Where only one workers' son in twelve rose to a bourgeois occupation around 1820, one in five did so fifty years later. This represented a fundamental change in the life chances, and presumably in the expectations, of Marseille's workers.

These figures on working-class mobility document the change from an occupational structure with only minimal opportunities for upward mobility to a much more open structure by the late 1860s. In part, no doubt, this change is a reflection of the growing gap between the number of opportunities for bourgeois jobs in Marseille and the number of men from bourgeois backgrounds available to fill them. But it is doubtful whether changes in levels of supply and demand could by themselves have created such impressive changes in rates of upward mobility – just as they certainly cannot account for the failure of downward mobility from the bourgeoisie to decline over time. Rather, the evidence suggests a general freeing of restrictions in the labor market, resulting in a far more open occupational structure in the 1850s and 1860s than in the early nineteenth century.

The rising trend of mobility into the bourgeoisie holds for all categories of workers' sons except sons of service workers, and the figures for service workers are based on such a small number of cases as to be of doubtful validity. Artisans' sons, not surprisingly, had consistently higher rates of upward mobility than sons of unskilled workers and maritime workers: 8 percent in 1821–2, 14 percent in 1846–51, and 24 percent in 1869. The most striking thing about artisans' sons in 1821–2 was that so few of them were mobile in any direction. Fully 81 percent of them remained in the artisan trades. Nearly half (48 percent) were actually employed in the same trade as their fathers (see Table 9.4). In 1821–2, the predominant experience of artisans' sons was of striking occupational stability rather than occupational mobility. This tendency of artisans to remain in their fathers' trade and occupational category was weakened but by no means obliterated during the next half-century. In 1846–51, artisans' sons were employed as artisans in 73 percent of the cases and in the same trade as their fathers in 36 percent. By 1869, the percentages were lower, but still substantial: 63 and 27. The increasing flow of artisans' sons out of the artisan category was directed exclusively upward. Downward mobility into unskilled or maritime occupations was low and essentially constant: 10 percent in 1821–2 and 1846–51 and 9 percent in 1869. In 1821–2, downward mobility was slightly more common than upward mobility for those few artisans' sons who ventured beyond the artisan category. By 1869, upward mobility was far more common than downward mobility. Artisans' sons seem to have abandoned the security of the well-organized and moderately prosperous skilled trades only when they could be quite sure of finding positions in the petite bourgeoisie.

Sons of unskilled and maritime workers had considerably lower rates of mobility into the bourgeoisie than sons of artisans: 5, 7, and 12 percent in 1821–2, 1846–51, and 1869 for unskilled workers' sons; and 4, 8, and 10 percent for maritime workers' sons. These rates were about half the rates achieved by artisans' sons. They confirm what the occupational-status scales have already indicated: Artisans stood significantly higher than unskilled and maritime workers in the social structure of nineteenth-century Marseille. Sons of both types of workers had strong tendencies to remain in their fathers' occupational categories. Unskilled workers' sons became unskilled workers in 45 to 46 percent of the cases in 1821–2 and 1846–51, with the percentage falling to 36 in 1869. The proportion of maritime workers' sons who remained in the maritime occupational category remained essentially constant at nearly one-half. Many sons of unskilled and maritime workers also achieved positions in the artisan trades. Unskilled workers' sons had higher rates of mobility into artisan trades than maritime workers' sons – about 40 percent as against about 30 percent in each of the years for which we have information. Overall rates of upward mobility, defined as movement into either bourgeois or artisan occupations, rose slightly over time for both groups, from 47 percent to 46 percent to 54 percent for unskilled workers' sons, and from 34 percent to 41 percent to 43 percent for maritime workers' sons.

This analysis of the intergenerational-mobility experiences of men from working-class and bourgeois backgrounds points to both important changes and important continuities from the early 1820s to the late 1860s. It has already been remarked that overall mobility, measured by the movement of men into occupations different from those of their fathers, increased significantly between the early 1820s and the late 1860s. But not all this movement was in either an upward or a downward direction. Some movement was lateral; it was what sociologists call "horizontal" rather than "vertical" mobility. Downward mobility, whether from the bourgeoisie to the working class, or from artisan to unskilled labor, remained essentially constant over these years, as did upward mobility from the unskilled and maritime categories to the artisan category. None of these forms of vertical mobility increased significantly. Nor did mobility from the petite bourgeoisie to the elite show any clear trends. Among sons of small businessmen, rates climbed slowly upward, but among sons of clerical employees they first rose and then fell back to their initial level. In fact, virtually *all* the increase in vertical mobility was concentrated into a single pathway – the one that led up from the working class into the petite bourgeoisie, where rates nearly tripled. Here, and here alone, did vertical mobility between urban occupational categories increase impressively from the early 1820s to the late 1860s.

Even with this important rise in movement from the working class to the petite bourgeoisie, mobility patterns continued to bear the imprint of a clear hierarchy of occupational stratification. Sons of unskilled and maritime workers continued to have significantly lower chances than artisans' sons of rising to bourgeois jobs. Artisans' sons, by the late 1860s, had managed to gain an appreciable access to clerical and small-business positions, but virtually never found their way into the elite. Sons of clerical workers and small businessmen attained elite status significantly more often than did sons of artisans. But even they managed to climb into the elite only rarely; most of the elite positions were reserved for men born into the elite. From the beginning to the end of the period covered in this study, upward occupational mobility moved stepwise, and rarely more than one step at a time, from unskilled and maritime workers at the bottom, to artisans, to small businessmen and clerical employees, and finally to the businessmen, professionals, and rentiers who commanded the summit. The only important change in this hierarchy of urban occupations was that the height of the step separating the working class from the petite bourgeoisie was considerably reduced between the early 1820s and late 1860s, allowing many more workers' sons to scramble up to the modest eminence of the petite bourgeoisie at the end of the Second Empire than had done so during the Restoration.

Peasants' sons

The most remarkable example of upward mobility actually came from *outside* this urban occupational hierarchy. In all the periods for which information has been recorded, sons of peasants had considerably higher rates of mobility into the bourgeoisie than workers' sons. In 1821–2, the proportion of peasants' sons who had bourgeois occupations at the time of their marriage was 11 percent. This rate, however modest, was nevertheless higher than the rates for all workers' sons and artisans' sons, both of which were only 8 percent. As workers' sons' rates of mobility into the bourgeoisie rose impressively over time, peasants' sons' rates also rose, enabling them to maintain this lead. Eighteen percent of peasants' sons had bourgeois occupations in 1846–51, as against 12 percent of all workers' sons and 14 percent of artisans' sons. In 1869, the peasants' sons' rate had risen to 30 percent, still appreciably higher than the 19 percent rate attained by all workers' sons or the 24 percent attained by sons of artisans.

The peasants' sons' high rates of upward mobility are surprising. One would expect peasants' sons to have had little experience to prepare them for competition in the urban labor market. In this respect, the advantages would seem to lie with sons of workers, most of whom were from urban backgrounds. Moreover, peasants' sons were less likely than workers' sons to have attained literacy. In 1821–2, only 42 percent of the peasants' sons who got married in Marseille were able to sign their marriage registers, as against 58 percent of all workers' sons. Their disadvantage was even greater in comparison with artisans' sons, who were literate in 63 percent of the cases. The workers' advantage in literacy rates was maintained over time, although the differences became smaller as overall literacy rates rose. In 1846–51, the rates were 66 percent for peasants' sons, 72 percent for all workers' sons, and 84 percent for artisans' sons. In 1869 they were 84 percent for peasants' sons, 88 percent for all workers' sons, and 94 percent for artisans' sons. Yet in all these years, peasants' sons found their way into the bourgeoisie more often than even the much better qualified artisans' sons.

Some of the surprising success of the peasants' sons could have been due to the social and economic heterogeneity of the agricultural category. Different "peasants' sons" could have been from quite different backgrounds. Most of them designated their fathers' occupation by the broad term "cultivator," or used the equally vague "agriculturalist," although a few specified winegrower, shepherd, or gardener. There were also some who added the term "proprietor" to their father's title, designating their father's occupation as "cultivator-proprietor," "winegrower-proprietor," etc. The addition of the term "proprietor" meant that the father owned at least some of the land he worked, although it could in principle designate anything from the owner of a tiny, inadequate patch of ground to a wealthy peasant who had managed to become a substantial landowner – what the Russians called a "kulak" and the French called a *"coq du village"* (cock of the village). Unfortunately, the reporting of proprietor status was very uneven. In 1821–2, only 6 of the 105 men who reported their fathers as having agricultural occupations indicated that their fathers were proprietors. In 1846–51, such an indication was made by 81 of 513 peasants' sons, but in 1869 *none* of the 445 did so. It is possible that this change reflects a real change in the backgrounds of the peasants' sons, but it seems far more likely to be a change in reporting occupations. Probably a significant number of the agriculturalist fathers not designated as proprietors by their sons in 1869 and in 1821–2, and perhaps even in 1846–51, were in fact owners of their land.

In any case, it is interesting that in both the periods for which agricultural-proprietor fathers were reported, sons of the proprietors had much higher rates of mobility into the bourgeoisie than sons of nonproprietors. In 1821–2, 3 out of 6, or 50 percent, of proprietors' sons held bourgeois occupations, whereas only 7 out of 83, or 8 percent, of the nonproprietors' sons did so. In 1846–51, the differences were less striking, but nonetheless sizable: 34 percent for the now much larger group of proprietors' sons and 17 percent for the nonproprietors' sons. Thus, what data are available seem to show considerably higher rates of mobility among sons of prosperous landowning peasants than among others. Peasant proprietors' sons probably had significantly greater resources – some sort of prior training or perhaps a modest capital – that gave them an advantage in the urban labor market. Their literacy rates were certainly higher than those of nonproprietors' sons. Of the 6 proprietors' sons, 100 percent were literate in 1821–2, as against only 39 percent of the nonproprietors' sons. In 1846–51, 75 percent of the proprietors' sons were literate, as against 65 percent of the nonproprietors' sons.

These differences in literacy surely help explain the different rates of mobility into the bourgeoisie on the part of proprietors' and nonproprietors' sons. But sorting out the experiences of proprietors' sons by no means explains away the overall differences between workers' sons and peasants' sons. Even the nonproprietors' sons did very well by comparison with workers' sons. In 1821–2, the nonproprietors' sons had a literacy rate of only 39 percent, as against 58 percent for all workers' sons. Yet the nonproprietor peasants' sons had bourgeois occupations in 8 percent of the cases, the same proportion as among the much better qualified workers' sons. In 1846–51, the comparison is equally revealing. Nonproprietor peasants' sons were literate in only 65 percent of the cases, as against 72 percent for all workers' sons and 84 percent for artisans' sons. Yet the nonproprietors' sons had bourgeois jobs in 17 percent of the cases, as against 12 percent for all workers' sons and 14 percent for artisans' sons. Even the least privileged peasants' sons, whose educational qualifications were distinctly inferior to those of workers' sons, found bourgeois jobs at equal or higher rates. Whatever the reasons may have been, peasants' sons seem to have had a special knack for mobility into the bourgeoisie of Marseille.

Of course, only a minority of peasants' sons entered bourgeois occupations, even as late as 1869. They found jobs in a wide range of other occupations. As the city proper expanded into the fields and gardens that once covered the outlying areas of the Commune of Marseille, only a diminishing number of peasants' sons could find employment in agriculture: 17 percent in 1821–2, 7 percent in 1846–51, and 3 percent in 1869. Most became manual workers: 69 percent in 1821–2, 73 percent in 1846–51, and 67 percent in 1869. Peasants' sons seem to have been particularly responsive to changing patterns of demand within the manual sector. The proportion entering the artisan trades fell sharply, from 48 to 39 to 31 percent. This fall corresponded to a decline in the proportion of artisans in the labor force, but did so disproportionately. The decline in the artisans' proportion of the male labor force was about 10 percent, whereas the decline in artisan positions among the peasants' sons was nearly 20 percent. There was a similar, but inverse, pattern in the service occupations. The proportion of service workers in the male labor force increased from about 2 percent to about 6 percent, whereas the proportion of peasants' sons in service occupations rose from 2 percent in 1821–2 to 5 percent in 1846–51 and 11 percent in 1869. Finally, the proportion of peasants' sons working in unskilled labor rose sharply from 17 percent in 1821–2 to 26 percent in 1846–51, a period when the proportion of unskilled workers in the male labor force rose from 10 percent to 15 percent, and then fell back to 21 percent in 1869, when the proportion of unskilled workers had stabilized at 15 percent. Peasants' sons, in other words, not only responded to the changing opportunities in the market for manual labor, but responded *disproportionately*. This is in sharp contrast with the behavior of unskilled and maritime workers' sons, who continued to enter artisan occupations at a constant rate even though opportunities in the artisan sector were declining, and who entered service occupations at a low and essentially constant rate even though opportunities in the service sector were rising. Peasants' sons seem to have been more sharply attuned to the changing structure of opportunities in the labor market than other men from low-status backgrounds.

This responsiveness to the market can also be seen in the changing distribution of the bourgeois occupations filled by peasants' sons. Like workers' sons, peasants' sons virtually never reached the elite occupational categories of rentiers or businessmen and professionals. But much more of their increase in upward mobility was concentrated in the expanding clerical category. The proportion of peasants' sons who found positions as small businessmen remained essentially constant between the early 1820s and late 1860s, whereas the proportion who became clerical employees soared from 4 percent in 1821–2 to 11 percent in 1846–51 and 21 percent in 1869. Although the proportion of artisans' sons and unskilled and maritime workers' sons who entered clerical occupations also rose over time, the rise was not nearly so steep, and more of the overall rise in upward mobility of these categories was accounted for by mobility into small business than was the case for peasants' sons. Once again, peasants' sons were more responsive than workers' sons to changes in the structure of occupational opportunities.

This unusual responsiveness of peasants' sons was undoubtedly the secret of their surprisingly high rates of upward mobility. This can be seen most clearly by contrasting peasants' sons with artisans' sons. Given their substantial educational advantages and prior experience of urban life, it seems certain that sons of artisans could have entered bourgeois occupations in greater proportion than peasants' sons had they joined wholeheartedly in the pursuit of bourgeois jobs. But artisans' sons who entered the labor market in Marseille did so with traditions and expectations that directed their gaze toward the familiar occupations exercised by their fathers. As both their own rates of literacy and the opportunities for bourgeois positions improved, more and more of them broke out of the artisan category. But for many who would have been capable of entering the petite bourgeoisie, the familiarity and security of the corporately structured artisan trades continued to have a strong appeal. The situation of peasants' sons was utterly different. Peasants' sons who took up residence in Marseille had, with rare exceptions, already decided to abandon their ancestral occupation. They had no "natural" place to look in the urban labor market and were therefore more sensitive than sons of artisans or other workers to whatever opportunities might offer themselves. Hence, in spite of their disadvantages in urban experience and educational qualifications, peasants' sons plucked a disproportionate share of the new bourgeois jobs that opened up in Marseille from 1820 to 1870. Because of their distance from the urban occupational world they found in Marseille, peasants' sons behaved more like "rational economic men" in the labor market than did sons of manual workers, who had already absorbed the assumptions of the existing urban occupational hierarchy.

Literacy and mobility

Current studies of occupational mobility consistently show that education is one of the prime determinants of occupational placement. This was true of nineteenth-century urban society as well.[5] The professions, for example, were only available to those who had completed the requisite higher education, and even the lesser ranks of the bourgeoisie – small business and clerical occupations – were virtually closed to those who had not attained at least the ability to read, write, and calculate. Even as early as 1821–2, over 95 percent of the men employed in each of Marseille's bourgeois occupational categories was literate (see Table 9.8). The fact that literacy was a virtual prerequisite for bourgeois occupations, together with the fact that literacy was rising rapidly in the subbourgeois population in the nineteenth century, poses a question about the process of occupational mobility in Marseille. To what extent can the rise in upward mobility into the bourgeoisie between the early 1820s and late 1860s be accounted for by a rise in the level of qualifications of the subbourgeois population?

An examination of literacy rates of men from different occupational back-

Table 9.8. *Percentage of sons literate, by occupation*

	1821–2	1846–51	1869
Business and professional	100	99	98
Rentier	95	99	97
Sales and clerical	97	99	100
Small business	96	94	99
Artisan	65	82	90
Service	83	80	95
Unskilled	27	51	69
Maritime	38	45	65
Agriculture	23	50	80
Miscellaneous	46	80	67
Total	67	79	89

Table 9.9. *Percentage of sons literate, by father's occupation*

	1821–2	1846–51	1869
Business and professional	100	99	99
Rentier	96	97	100
Sales and clerical	90	95	96
Small business	94	93	94
Artisan	63	84	94
Service	60	72	96
Unskilled	45	67	79
Maritime	36	51	72
Agriculture	42	66	84
Miscellaneous	56	71	85
Total	67	79	89

grounds certainly suggests that increasing literacy was a major factor in the rising rate of upward mobility (see Table 9.9). In 1821–2, the gap in literacy between sons of bourgeois and sons of workers and peasants was very sizable. Whereas virtually all sons of bourgeois were literate, illiteracy for other groups ranged from nearly 40 percent among artisans' sons to nearly 65 percent among sons of maritime workers. By 1846–51, this literacy gap had begun to close, and by 1869 it had closed even farther. In 1869, sons of artisans and service workers had literacy rates indistinguishable from those of men from petit bourgeois backgrounds, and even sons of unskilled workers, maritime workers, and peasants were literate in some four-fifths of the cases. The most important change in patterns of vertical mobility in nineteenth-century Marseille was a narrowing of the gap that divided the bourgeoisie from the rest of the population. This change in mobility patterns was paralleled by, and doubtless in part caused by, a remarkable narrowing of the literacy gap.

One way of specifying the effect of literacy on changing mobility rates is to separate out the mobility experience of literates from those of illiterates. If rising rates of upward mobility were entirely accounted for by rising literacy, then the mobility rates of *literate* workers and peasants would be constant across the years. Table 9.10 gives figures for the percentage of literate and illiterate sons from different occupational backgrounds who found jobs in the bourgeoisie in each period. These figures show that illiterates virtually never found bourgeois occupations – even illiterate sons of bourgeois remained in the bourgeoisie (usually as small businessmen) only rarely. The figures also indicate that rising literacy in the subbourgeois population was an important source of the overall increase in rates of upward mobility, especially between 1821–2 and 1846–51, but they indicate that the increase cannot be explained by changes in literacy alone.

Between 1821–2 and 1846–51, rates of mobility into the bourgeoisie rose substantially for sons of peasants, artisans, unskilled workers, and maritime workers alike. But when only literate sons are considered, the differences between 1821–2 and 1846–51 were much diminished. For literate sons of peasants, rates of mobility into the bourgeoisie increased from 19 to 24 percent, not nearly as steep an increase as for all peasants' sons. For sons of workers, the results were even more striking. For literate sons of artisans, the rates rose only from 13 to 16 percent. The rise for literate maritime workers' sons was comparable, from 12 to 15 percent. And for literate un-skilled workers' sons, there was no rise at all. For all these categories, most of the increase in mobility into the bourgeoisie between 1821–2 and 1846–51 was a result of higher literacy levels. Among those who satisfied the basic literacy requirements, access to bourgeois occupations was scarcely easier in the middle of the nineteenth century than it had been in the early 1820s. Between 1846–51 and 1869, the patterns changed. Over this span, only a little of the increase in mobility into the bourgeoisie can be accounted for by rising literacy among workers' and peasants' sons. Literate sons of workers and peasants experienced much higher increases in rates of upward mobility between 1846–51 and 1869 than during the previous period.

An examination of the effects of literacy changes on mobility changes reveals two quite different processes accounting for the overall rise in mobility into the bourgeoisie. In the period from the early 1820s to the middle of the century, the rising rates of upward mobility were mainly a function of rising literacy. Mobility rose because more of the men from subbourgeois back-grounds had acquired the requisite education to obtain bourgeois jobs, not because access to those jobs became easier for those who were qualified. From the middle of the century to 1870, it was quite the opposite. Rising education accounted for only a small fraction of the overall rise in upward mobility. In these years access to bourgeois jobs on the part of literate men from nonbourgeois backgrounds expanded impressively, especially in the

Table 9.10. *Percentage of sons with bourgeois occupations, by father's occupation and literacy*

Father's occupation	1821–2			1846–51			1869		
	Literate	Illiterate	Total	Literate	Illiterate	Total	Literate	Illiterate	Total
1. Business and professional	81	—	81	86	0[a]	84	86	100[a]	86
2. Rentier	79	33[a]	76	66	0[a]	64	76	—	76
3. Sales and clerical	49	25[a]	46	51	0[a]	48	56	0[a]	53
4. Small business	56	0[a]	53	58	18	55	62	20[a]	58
5. Artisan	13	1	8	16	4	14	26	0	24
6. Service	33[a]	0[a]	20	31	0	22	14	0[a]	13
7. Unskilled	11	0	5	11	1	7	16	0	12
8. Maritime	12	0	4	15	0	8	14	0	10
9. Agriculture	19	6	11	24	5	18	35	4	30
10. Miscellaneous	25	0	14	31	0	25	37	0	31
All bourgeois (1 + 2 + 3 + 4)	69	15	66	66	7	63	70	16	68
All workers (5 + 6 + 7 + 8)	13	0	8	15	2	12	22	0	19
Total	36	2	25	33	3	27	38	3	35
Number of cases	689	347	1,036	2,018	534	2,552	1,558	196	1,754

[a]Based on fewer than 10 cases.

clerical occupations. To put it otherwise, the rise in upward mobility in the 1850s and 1860s was largely a by-product of the burgeoning, in precisely these years, of private and public bureaucracies.

Migration and mobility

So far, the occupational-mobility patterns of native Marseillais have not been distinguished from those of immigrants. Yet there is reason to believe that the experiences of natives and immigrants might be quite different. In most respects, the advantages would seem to lie with the natives. Thanks to their long residence in Marseille they should have had both a better understanding of the urban labor market and a much more highly developed network of contacts for finding a desired job. On the other hand, the highly selective character of migration that was documented in Chapter 7 might mean that immigrants made up in qualifications or ambition for what they lacked in local contacts. These possibilities can be assessed by comparing the mobility patterns of natives and immigrants in each of the sample years. This is done in Table 9.11. This table gives figures for the percentage of sons from different occupational backgrounds who held bourgeois jobs at the time of their marriage, rather than full ten-by-ten mobility matrices. This is done both for the sake of simplicity and because many of the cell totals in the ten-by-ten tables are too small to yield reliable figures. The figures are for natives of Marseille and for two groups of immigrants – those born in Italy and those born in either France or a foreign country other than Italy.[6]

The mobility patterns of these two groups of immigrants contrasted sharply. Although non-Italian immigrants generally fared well in Marseille's labor market, the Italians did very badly. The figures for Italians are sometimes based on a small number of cases, particularly in 1821–2, but the pattern is nevertheless clear. For almost every category of father's occupation in all three periods, Italians had much higher rates of downward mobility and much lower rates of upward mobility than the rest of the population. Clearly, Italians were laboring under special handicaps. To begin with, they faced serious problems of linguistic and cultural adjustment: As a rule they spoke neither French nor Provençal when they arrived in Marseille, and their values and work habits had been formed in an economically backward country. Furthermore, as was seen in Chapter 7, their rates of literacy were below those of natives, French migrants, and other foreign-born migrants alike. There is no doubt that by purely objective criteria they were, on the average, less qualified than their French-born competitors.

But there is also evidence of widespread and open prejudice against Italians – prejudice that surely entered into decisions about hiring and firing. The evidence of prejudice comes from many sources: from the working-class memorialist François Mazuy, who, although hostile to all non-Marseillais,

Table 9.11. *Percentage of sons with bourgeois occupations, by father's occupation and migration*

Father's occupation	1821–2			1846–51			1869		
	Natives	Non-Italian immigrants	Italian immigrants	Natives	Non-Italian immigrants	Italian immigrants	Natives	Non-Italian immigrants	Italian immigrants
1. Business and professional	82	80	—	88	84	67[b]	95	83	0[a]
2. Rentier	85	69	100[a]	76	58	56[a]	84	73	57[a]
3. Sales and clerical	39	59[b]	0[a]	52	48	36[b]	55	53	42[a]
4. Small business	58	41	—	70	45	10[b]	65	59	12[a]
5. Artisan	6	15	0	10	20	5	20	28	14
6. Service	27[b]	0[a]	—	18[b]	32[b]	0[a]	0[a]	17	—
7. Unskilled	7	4	0[a]	5	14	2	5	22	2
8. Maritime	4	0[b]	17[a]	7	22	0[b]	12	11[b]	0[b]
9. Agriculture	7	19	0	7	22	8	6[b]	34	7
10. Miscellaneous	5	29[b]	0[a]	14	29	0[a]	5	30	0[a]
All bourgeois (1 + 2 + 3 + 4)	67	65	75[a]	72	59	44	76	67	33
All workers (5 + 6 + 7 + 8)	6	12	5	9	20	3	16	25	6
Total	21	33	12	26	32	10	35	38	10
Number of cases	674	329	33	1,010	1,245	295	537	1,075	173

[a]Based on fewer than 10 cases.
[b]Based on 10 to 19 cases.

reserved his harshest comments for Italians;[7] from the Justices of the Peace, who in preparing their report for a parliamentary inquiry into labor conditions blandly assumed that Italians could maintain an adequate standard of living on 50 percent to 25 percent less income than Frenchmen;[8] from the police, who quite unjustifiably considered Italians to be dangerous political radicals and a perpetual threat to public order, and who kept them under special surveillance;[9] from a treatise on begging in Marseille, whose author attributed the problem to the laziness and viciousness of the city's Italian immigrants.[10] The precarious position of Marseille's Italian community was made tragically apparent in the weeks following the Revolution of 1848, when they were assaulted and forced to leave their jobs by unemployed French workers. The authorities, unable to suppress the agitation against the defenseless Italians, could finally do nothing but send several boatloads of jobless men and their families back to their homeland.[11] Italians labored under a double disadvantage. They were not only less qualified, on the average, than their competitors; they were also treated prejudicially even when their qualifications were equally good. As a result, upward mobility was difficult to attain and downward mobility was very common. The Italians' position as an exploited minority is evident in Marseille's mobility figures.

The story was quite different for non-Italian immigrants. On the whole, their mobility experience was at least as favorable as that of native Marseillais. Among men from bourgeois backgrounds, natives had the advantage, but among men from working-class and agricultural backgrounds, it was immigrants who came out on top. Non-Italian immigrants from bourgeois backgrounds were consistently more likely to fall into manual occupations than natives from comparable social origins. Among sons of rentiers and small businessmen, the advantage of the natives was substantial in every year; among sons of businessmen and professionals, the advantage of the natives was slight in 1821–2, but it grew steadily thereafter. In the property-owning categories of the bourgeoisie, then, natives had significantly lower rates of downward mobility than immigrants. The exception to this pattern of native advantage was the one non-property-owning bourgeois category: clerical employees. Among sons of clerical employees, immigrants did substantially better than natives in 1821–2 and only slightly worse thereafter.

These figures seem to confirm the hypothesis, put forth earlier in this chapter, that the possession of property constituted a crucial barrier against downward mobility from the bourgeoisie to manual occupations. Men from bourgeois backgrounds who migrated to Marseille left their family's property behind. Some were probably second or third sons who had no prospect of inheriting the family business anyway; others may have preferred trying their luck in the big city to the secure mediocrity of a small-town proprietor's life. Of course, immigrants from proprietary backgrounds may very well have brought along some money that helped give them a start in Marseille, but physical separation from the family's property seems to have entailed an element of risk. Some measure of the degree of risk can be obtained by comparing the rates of downward mobility among sons of small businessmen and sons of clerical employees. Among immigrants, sons of clerical employees had considerably lower rates of downward mobility than sons of small businessmen in 1821–2 and substantially equal rates in 1846–51 and 1869. This rough equality is what one might expect from the two occupational categories that made up the petite bourgeoisie, categories that, moreover, had approximately equal occupational-status scores. But among natives, the picture was quite different: Sons of small businessmen had rates of downward mobility nearly 20 percent below those of clerical employees' sons in 1821–2 and 1846–51 and 10 percent below in 1869. Or to put it another way: All sons of clerical workers and immigrant sons of small businessmen had about the same rates of downward mobility, but native sons of small businessmen, who had access to the local family property, were consistently more likely to remain in the bourgeoisie. To judge from this comparison, the superior intergenerational security of status enjoyed by native-born sons of Marseille's bourgeoisie was probably a function of their superior access to family property.

On the question of upward mobility from working-class and agricultural to bourgeois occupations, the picture is reversed: Here it was the non-Italian immigrants who did best. The immigrants' advantage was most pronounced among men from agricultural backgrounds. Non-Italian immigrant sons of peasants were the supreme leaven of nineteenth-century Marseillais society; they consistently had the highest rates of upward mobility in the city. In 1821–2, 19 percent of them had obtained bourgeois jobs, and the proportion climbed to 22 percent in 1846–51 and 34 percent in 1869. This was in sharp contrast to the agriculturalists' sons who were born in Marseille, whose rates of mobility were low and constant: 7 percent in both 1821–2 and 1846–51 and 6 percent in 1869. In part, the natives' rates were so low because more native-born than immigrant sons of agriculturalists followed their fathers' occupations. But only in part: The proportion of native-born agriculturalists' sons who worked outside agriculture was already 75 percent in 1821–2, and it rose to 78 percent in 1846–51 and 82 percent in 1869. Apparently all but a few of these men were either unwilling or unable to find positions in Marseille's expanding bourgeoisie at a time when immigrant sons of peasants were rising into the bourgeoisie at ever more impressive rates. In fact, in 1846–51 and 1869 even Italian-born peasants' sons had slightly higher rates of upward mobility than natives.

Among men from working-class backgrounds, the differences between natives and non-Italian immigrants were neither as clear nor as consistent. But overall it was the immigrants who held the edge. The differences between natives and immigrants were inconsistent among sons of maritime workers and service workers. Among maritime workers, the non-Italian immigrants held a large advantage in 1846–51 but did slightly worse than natives in 1821–2 and 1869. Among sons of service workers – whose numbers were in any case so small as to give us figures of only doubtful validity – natives had a big advantage in 1821–2, and immigrants had a big advantage in 1846–51 and 1869. But among the much larger groups of men who were sons of unskilled workers and of artisans, the overall advantage of the non-Italian immigrants was clear. The only exception was for sons of unskilled workers in 1821–2, where natives' rates of mobility into the bourgeoisie were somewhat above immigrants': 7 percent for natives as against 4 percent for non-Italian immigrants. But the rates for native sons of unskilled workers fell to only 5 percent in 1846–51 and remained at the same low level in 1869. Meanwhile, the comparable rates for non-Italian immigrants rose to 14 percent in 1846–51 and 22 percent in 1869. Native sons of unskilled workers, like native sons of agriculturalists, failed to take advantage of the expanding opportunities in Marseille's bourgeoisie, whereas immigrant sons of unskilled workers, like immigrant sons of peasants, found their way into the bourgeoisie in ever-growing numbers.

The non-Italian immigrants also held the edge among sons of artisans, although in this case upward mobility into the bourgeoisie rose over time for natives and immigrants alike. Non-Italian immigrants from artisan backgrounds entered the bourgeoisie in 15 percent of the cases in 1821–2. By 1846–51 their rate of upward mobility had climbed to 20 percent, and by 1869 it had reached 29 percent. In 1821–2, natives from artisan backgrounds had found positions in the bourgeoisie in only 6 percent of the cases, slightly *below* the percentages for native sons of unskilled laborers or agriculturalists. But by 1846–51 their rate of upward mobility rose to 10 percent, and by 1869 it had reached 20 percent – a very respectable rate, but still substantially below that of the non-Italian immigrants.

If all workers' sons – sons of artisans, unskilled workers, service workers, and maritime workers alike – are combined, some of the unevenness in the figures disappears, and the sustained advantage of non-Italian immigrants over natives is clear (see Table 9.12). How can this advantage, which parallels the even clearer advantage of non-Italian immigrants among peasants' sons, be explained?

One possible explanation would be that the immigrants' advantage in mobility rates derived from superior qualifications. Non-Italian immigrants, as was seen in Chapter 7, had somewhat higher literacy rates than natives; this, in turn, should have resulted in higher levels of upward mobility. Only in 1821–2, however, was the literacy gap between natives and non-Italian migrants really significant. This can be seen in Table 9.13. In 1821–2, non-Italian immigrants were literate in 77 percent of the cases, as against 62 percent for natives and 54 percent for Italians. In 1846–51, natives, with a literacy rate of 81 percent, had nearly caught up with the non-Italian immi-

Table 9.12. *Percentage of workers' sons upwardly mobile into bourgeoisie, by migration*

	1821–2	1846–51	1869
Natives	6	7	13
Non-Italian immigrants	10	17	23
Italian immigrants	5[a]	3	6
Total	7	10	17

[a]Based on only 22 cases.

grants (83 percent) and had left the Italian immigrants (56 percent) far behind. By 1869, the native and non-Italian immigrant rates were equal at the high level of 91 percent, and the Italian rate had risen to 70. To judge from the aggregate figures, only in 1821–2 could the difference between native and immigrant literacy rates have been enough to affect patterns of mobility. Figures comparing natives and immigrants from specific occupational backgrounds do not change this conclusion significantly. Only among agriculturalists' sons did non-Italian immigrants have a substantial advantage in 1846–51, and by 1869 even this had nearly vanished.

A comparison of the mobility rates of literate natives and immigrants with those of all natives and immigrants shows that the lead of non-Italian immigrants from working-class and agricultural backgrounds held independently of literacy (see Table 9.14). It is true that in 1821–2 the lead of the non-Italian immigrants from artisan and peasant backgrounds was less among literate grooms than among all grooms, but it remained substantial. Moreover, this was partially compensated for by a decline in the lead of native unskilled workers' sons over non-Italian immigrant unskilled workers' sons (compare Tables 9.11 and 9.14). In 1846–51 and 1869, the non-Italian immigrants' lead over natives was just as great among literates as for all grooms. In short, controlling for literacy does not significantly reduce the gap in rates of upward mobility that separated non-Italian immigrants from natives.

Literacy differences also fail to explain much of the disadvantage of Italian immigrants. Italian immigrants had consistently lower aggregate literacy rates than either natives or non-Italian immigrants (see Table 9.13). Much of this difference, however, stemmed from the fact that so many of the Italians came from low-status backgrounds. As was seen in Chapter 7, some three-fifths of Italian immigrants were sons of peasants, unskilled workers, or maritime workers (see Tables 7.3, 7.12, and 7.13). When Italians are compared to men from similar occupational backgrounds, the literacy differences are substantially reduced. In 1821–2, in fact, Italian immigrants actually had rates of literacy equal to or higher than those of native-born men from comparable

Table 9.13. *Percentage of sons literate, by migration and father's occupation*

	Father's occupation										
	Business and professional	Rentier	Sales and clerical	Small business	Artisan	Service	Unskilled	Maritime	Agriculture	Miscellaneous	Total
1821–2											
Natives	100	100	87	92	59	73	50	34	26	47	62
Non-Italian immigrants	100	92	94	97	76	25[a]	36	50	60	71	77
Italians	—	100[a]	100[a]	—	62[a]	—	50[a]	33[a]	50[a]	—	54
Total	100	96	90	94	64	60	45	36	42	56	66
1846–51											
Natives	100	99	97	95	84	71	68	56	62	64	81
Non-Italian immigrants	99	97	93	92	88	79	70	52	71	83	83
Italians	93	75[a]	91	90	63	50[a]	50	28	50	11[a]	56
Total	99	97	95	94	84	72	64	51	66	71	79
1869											
Natives	100	100	97	95	95	80[a]	83	73	82	83	91
Non-Italian immigrants	98	100	95	95	94	100	85	53	86	88	91
Italians	100[a]	100[a]	100[a]	71[a]	86	—	61	63	68	50[a]	70
Total	99	100	96	94	94	96	78	72	83	85	89

[a] Based on fewer than 10 cases.

Table 9.14. *Percentage of literate sons with bourgeois occupations, by father's occupation and migration*

Father's occupation	1821–2			1846–51			1869		
	Natives	Non-Italian immigrants	Italian immigrants	Natives	Non-Italian immigrants	Italian immigrants	Natives	Non-Italian immigrants	Italian immigrants
Business and professional	82	80	—	90	85	71[b]	95	82	0[a]
Rentier	85	72	100[a]	77	59	68[a]	84	73	57[a]
Sales and clerical	40	62[b]	0[a]	53	51	40[b]	57	56	43[a]
Small business	63	43	—	72	47	11[a]	66	62	20[a]
Artisan	10	20	0[a]	11	22	8	22	30	17
Service	38[a]	0[a]	—	25[b]	40[b]	0[a]	0[a]	17[b]	—
Unskilled	13	12[a]	0[a]	8	19	3	6	26	3
Maritime	12	0[a]	50[a]	10	42[b]	0[a]	17	13[b]	0[a]
Agriculture	13[b]	24	0[a]	8	29	13	7[b]	39	10
Miscellaneous	10[b]	40[b]	—	22	35	0[a]	47[b]	35	0[a]
Total	34	42	22[b]	32	37	18	38	42	14

[a] Based on fewer than 10 cases.   [b] Based on 10 to 19 cases.

backgrounds. (See Table 9.13. It should be noted, however, that the 1821–2 figures are based on a very small number of cases.) In subsequent years, native Marseillais had consistently higher literacy rates than Italians even when educational background is taken into account, but the differences are generally much less than the aggregate difference. Italians, in short, were not so underqualified as the aggregate figures might suggest.

Yet literacy did not do Italian immigrants much good in the labor market. Even literate Italian immigrants had very high rates of downward mobility and very low rates of upward mobility; they did only marginally better than all Italians. (Compare Tables 9.11 and 9.14.) That they were unable to match the rates of natives or French-born immigrants is perhaps understandable, for they were presumably literate in Italian rather than in French. But literacy skills are easily transferred to another language once the language itself is mastered, and the education that stands behind literacy – presumably including some arithmetic and some knowledge of the larger world that is made accessible by the printed word – transcends the language barrier. The fact that even literate Italians fared so badly in the labor market demonstrates the depth of prejudice and job discrimination faced by Italian immigrants in Marseille.

Differential levels of qualification, as measured by literacy, explain very little of the variation in mobility rates of natives, Italian immigrants, and non-Italian immigrants. How, then, are the mobility differences to be explained? The unfavorable Italian rates present little mystery; they were above all the product of open prejudice and discrimination. But the high rates of upward mobility achieved by non-Italian immigrants from working-class and peasant backgrounds have no such obvious explanation. To judge from literary sources, prejudice against outsiders was not limited exclusively to Italians;[12] even non-Italian immigrants probably had to surmount some prejudice to obtain good jobs in Marseille. Their success in doing so is therefore all the more remarkable.

If the advantage of non-Italian immigrants over natives cannot be explained either by their qualifications or by the prejudices and preferences of employers, it must have resulted from differences in their values, attitudes, and behavior. The non-Italian immigrants must have been more ambitious and competitive, pursuing bourgeois occupations with greater ardor and skill than their native-born fellows. There are two respects in which the non-Italian immigrants might have differed from the natives. First, migration was selective. The native Marseillais competing for jobs in the labor market represented more or less the entire population of young men who had been born in Marseille, whereas the immigrants who were seeking jobs in Marseille were only a very small selection of the young men born in their native towns or villages. The immigrants, one might reasonably argue, were likely to be the most ambitious and adventurous of their native cohorts. We have seen that their literacy rates were equal to or better than those of Marseillais of similar occupational origins, even though most of them came from rural villages or small towns with much poorer opportunities for schooling. Their literacy rates must have been far above those of the villagers they left behind; in fact, the literacy rates of immigrants to Marseille from even the most lowly origins were well above the national averages for the male population as a whole. It has been shown, of course, that their high rates of literacy do not by themselves explain their mobility advantage. But given the circumstances in which the literacy was acquired, the immigrants' literacy rates are probably a sign of unusual ambition, of a solid determination to get ahead in the world that drove them to make the sacrifices necessary to acquire an education and drew them out of their native villages to the more promising opportunities of the big city. It was, in short, probably a self-selected elite of ambitious young small-town and village men who were competing against run-of-the-mill native sons in Marseille's labor market. If so, it is not surprising that they pursued bourgeois jobs with more ardor or that they captured a disproportionate share.

The difference between natives and immigrants that derived from the selectivity of migration was probably compounded by the effects of migration itself. Although it has been argued in Chapter 7 that migration was by no means a debilitating experience for most immigrants, it did involve some degree of uprooting. In moving to Marseille, a young man was loosening or breaking his ties with many of the social institutions that bound him to his childhood values – his family, peers, parish church, and native community. Simultaneously, he was faced with a new and usually much more heterogeneous society that offered him many choices – in both the occupational sphere and others – that had not been available to him previously. He was, in this sense, both set free from some of the social constraints that might have limited his choices in his native community and forced to confront new possibilities for which his earlier experience and values gave him only limited guidance. He might, of course, react to this challenge by retreating into the familiar – seeking out the company of home folks and finding a job in the same trade practiced by his father. But especially if his move to Marseille was motivated by ambition in the first place, he would be likely to consider the whole range of possibilities that presented themselves and to explore the occupational alternatives with an open and inquisitive spirit, seeking out those that promised the best pay, prestige, and possibilities for advancement. The openness of this occupational search would naturally be greatest for immigrant peasants' sons, who by definition could not practice their fathers' occupations in Marseille. But the discontinuity introduced into their lives by the experience of migration meant that even immigrant sons of manual workers were far more likely to entertain the whole range of occupational opportunities than were native-born workers' sons, whose dense working-class social and family relations tended to limit their search for jobs to the familiar working-class world. Immigrant peasants' sons, hence, had the highest rates of mobility into bourgeois occupations, but immigrant sons of workers also had upward mobility rates well above those of the native working class.

The meaning of mobility

The social-mobility patterns of Marseille's men provide an emphatic confirmation of the interpretation of migration set forth in Chapter 7. The argument there against the dismal view of migration was based primarily on evidence about immigrants' premigration experiences – their birthplaces, prior experiences of urban life, family backgrounds, educational preparation, etc. The data analyzed in this chapter fortify this argument by documenting the immigrants' success in the urban labor market.

It was noted in Chapter 7 that the rapid growth of Marseille's population resulted in vastly increased migration of men from low-status backgrounds and that such low-status immigrants tended to come to Marseille from ever greater distances. Such men, who lacked family wealth and were far from their native communities, ought to have been prime candidates for Louis Chevalier's "dangerous classes." But figures on social mobility show that low-status non-Italian immigrants – at least those who stayed in Marseille long enough to get married – were remarkably successful in the urban labor market. By 1869, 22 percent of non-Italian immigrants from unskilled backgrounds achieved upward mobility into the bourgeoisie, which is a rate over four times as high as that of natives from unskilled backgrounds and even slightly higher than that achieved by native-born artisans' sons. Non-Italian immigrants from peasant backgrounds did even better. They entered bourgeois positions in over a third of the cases – the highest rate of mobility into the bourgeoisie achieved by any category of men from subbourgeois origins. To judge from the social-mobility figures, the mass of plebian immigrants who were drawn to Marseille from elsewhere in France were an extraordinary lot – competitive, ambitious, able, and flexible; not the scum, but the salt, of the earth.

The only group of immigrants that seems to fit Chevalier's gloomy picture was the Italians. Less qualified than the native-born or the non-Italian immigrant population, they also had uniquely unfavorable mobility experiences: very low rates of upward mobility and very high rates of downward mobility. As a consequence of their unfavorable mobility experiences, they also had a high crime rate: Because they were heavily concentrated in low-status, high-crime occupations, their overall rate of criminality was higher than that of French-born immigrants. Yet the case of Italians can hardly be used to support a globally pessimistic view of migration. Their unfavorable mobility experience, and consequently their high crime rates, were the result of two factors: their relatively poor qualifications and the fierce discrimination to which they were subjected in Marseille's labor market. Even those Italians who came from bourgeois backgrounds or arrived in Marseille with the ability to read and write were faced with such prejudice that they found it very difficult to obtain jobs in Marseille's bourgeoisie. In short, Italians were the exception that proved the rule. It was only when an immigrant group was particularly underqualified and subjected to systematic discrimination that its mobility experience was unfavorable.

The analysis of Marseille's male social-mobility patterns also suggests some broader reflections. For the past two decades, American historians have been greatly concerned with social mobility, which they have seen as a key to the stability of the American social and political system. Relatively high rates of mobility from the working class to the bourgeoisie have been interpreted as demonstrating either that the American ideal of equality of opportunity has worked in practice, and therefore that the American system is basically just, or that American capitalism has succeeded in justifying its exploitation in the eyes of its victims by providing mobility opportunities for lucky, talented, or diligent workers. A great deal of moral and political passion has been invested in the question of social mobility.

The history of social mobility in nineteenth-century Marseille suggests that this passion has been somewhat misplaced; that social-mobility patterns are governed as much by structural constraints arising from demographic conditions and patterns of economic growth as by a society's intrinsic degree of openness. The impressive rise in upward mobility into Marseille's bourgeoisie resulted mainly from three important structural changes. The first of these, which occurred above all between 1820 and 1850, was a rise in the proportion of men from subbourgeois backgrounds who could meet the minimum standards of literacy required by bourgeois occupations. The second, which occurred above all between 1850 and 1870, was the rise of large-scale bureaucratized firms in Marseille's commercial sector and a consequent expansion of demand for clerical employees. The third was an increase in population (and therefore in demand for all categories of labor) so rapid that it could only be met by increased immigration of low-status people from rural and small-town France. This resulted in a growing gap between the occupational backgrounds of the population and the distribution of occupations available to them, thereby necessitating rising levels of upward mobility. Between 1821–2 and 1869, there was nearly a tripling of rates of upward mobility from peasant and working-class backgrounds into Marseille's bourgeoisie. This spectacular rise can be accounted for almost entirely by these three structural changes.

Moreover, there is certainly no evidence that the working class of Marseille interpreted these rising rates of mobility as a sign of the increasing justice of the social system. In the 1820s, Marseille's working class was politically quiescent. Indeed, to the extent that workers had strong political sentiments, they seem to have been predominantly royalists. By 1848, when upward mobility had risen well above its 1820s level, Marseille's workers participated actively in the revolution, and some of them even took arms against the government at the time of the Parisian June Days. By the late sixties, when opportunities for upward mobility had risen higher still, Marseille's working class was in the vanguard of the radical opposition to the Second Empire. Marseille's workers participated widely in the great strike wave of 1868, and their votes helped opposition candidates sweep the legislative elections of 1869.[13] After the fall of the Second Empire, a revolutionary commune was declared in Marseille even before the establishment of the Paris Commune of 1871.[14] Whatever the relationship between social mobility and workers' consciousness may have been, rising opportunities for mobility certainly did not immunize Marseille's working class against socialism and revolution.[15]

This is not to say that social mobility is devoid of moral and political significance. But it does suggest that the significance of high or low or rising or falling mobility is not immediately apparent, that it may vary according to historical or cultural setting. For example, high or rising rates of upward mobility may have had a greater political impact on workers in the United States, where capitalists have relied heavily on an ideology of equal opportunity to justify their hegemony, than in France, where they did not. The significance of social-mobility patterns must be discovered, not assumed. Social mobility must be seen as one aspect of broad, complex, interlocking social processes, not as an automatic key to the stability of the social system.

Finally, historical studies of social mobility have been radically incomplete. They have analyzed the mobility experience of only half the population: that of men. Have women's and men's mobility patterns been similar or divergent? Do the same structural mechanisms that explain changes in men's social mobility over time also explain changes in women's mobility? Can reasonable generalizations about the openness or justice of social systems be made solely on the basis of men's experiences? Chapter 10 attempts to explore, for one nineteenth-century city, the heretofore uncharted territory of women's social mobility.

10 Social mobility: women

The extensive historical literature on social mobility that has appeared in the last two decades has dealt almost exclusively with the mobility experience of men.[1] The reasons for the neglect of women's social mobility are at once ideological, technical, and conceptual. The ideological reasons are the most obvious. Until the revival of the feminist movement in the late 1960s, and the subsequent burgeoning of research in women's history, the question of women's mobility simply did not occur to most social historians. In order to remove any sense of moral smugness from my own efforts, I will cite myself as an example. In the late 1960s, when I began my research on social mobility in nineteenth-century Marseille, I had no thought of studying women. That I am able to do so now results from the lucky accident that the documents I used to measure men's mobility also happened to contain equally good information on women. Only belatedly, in the late 1970s, did I realize that the data on women's social mobility were potentially of great historical interest.

But why, one might reasonably ask, has someone else not recognized the potential interest of women's social mobility long ago and undertaken studies on the subject? This leads to the technical reason: The data used for most social-mobility studies cannot easily be made to yield information on the social mobility of women. Most studies have used techniques of nominal record linkage to establish intragenerational changes in men's occupations. This technique is based on tracing individuals from census to census (or city directory to city directory) and observing changes in occupational title (or, occasionally, in wealth or property ownership). The technique suffers from a major difficulty for the study of women's mobility. Because women usually changed their names when they got married, it is often impossible to trace them from one document to the next. It is therefore hardly surprising that historians using nominal-linkage techniques have not attempted to measure women's mobility. French marriage registers, however, are not subject to these same technical problems. At least from the 1840s on, they recorded the occupation and father's occupation for both spouses. They therefore can be used to establish the intergenerational mobility patterns of women as well as those of men.

Even with ideological and technical problems overcome, the analysis of women's social mobility continues to pose important conceptual problems. Social mobility implies movement or change in social status. In studies of

270

men's social mobility, status has usually been measured by occupation. Because occupation is a major determinant of a man's income, prestige, and social and economic power, tracing changes in men's occupations, either through their careers or across generations, is a reasonable measure of social mobility. But occupations have had a very different significance for women than for men. Historically, and to some extent right down to the present, women's place in society typically has been determined more by family roles as daughters, wives, or mothers than by occupational roles. Women usually have borne primary responsibility for child care, even in those cases where both husband and wife have worked. Women also have tended to move in and out of the labor force during the course of their lives, rather than remaining continuously employed and pursuing "careers" as men have done. An important concomitant of this less complete commitment to and identification with occupational roles has been low remuneration. Women have typically received between half and two-thirds as much pay as men for the same work. Finally, women normally have been restricted to a relatively narrow range of low-paying, low-status occupations conventionally defined as "women's work" – traditionally domestic service, textiles, and the needle trades, to which teaching, nursing, social work, secretarial work, and retail sales have subsequently been added.[2] Thus, although it makes sense to assess the social standing of men by their occupations, a woman's social standing historically has been determined more by the occupation of the male head of her household (her father or husband) than by her own occupation.

During the past fifteen or twenty years, women have begun to compete more successfully in the traditionally male occupational world. This means that studies of social mobility – or "status attainment," to use the current sociological term – can now treat women's social mobility in more or less the same way as men's.[3] One can now reasonably expect that the father's occupational attainment will have a major effect on the daughter's occupational attainment: A lawyer's or doctor's daughter is probably far more likely to become a doctor or lawyer than is the son of a farmer or automobile mechanic. But even as recently as fifteen years ago, the major advantage a doctor's or lawyer's daughter could expect to gain from her family background was to marry well rather than to have a successful career. Or to put the point more generally: Some women in the last decade or so, and men for centuries, have experienced intergenerational social mobility or social stability chiefly through the labor market. But until very recently, women's social mobility was governed above all by the *marriage market*.

The analysis in this chapter will be based on the premise that a woman's status was defined above all by the occupation of the head of her household. Hence the main question to be asked is how her husband's occupation compared with her father's. The woman's own occupation is of course not irrelevant to the question of social mobility. Although most occupations available to women in nineteenth-century Marseille were relatively uniform (and low) in status, there were some, for instance, unskilled labor, that might be regarded as particularly demeaning, and others, for example, teaching or nursing, that carried a certain prestige. But, as has been demonstrated in Chapter 3, many women gave up remunerated work after marriage anyway, so the premarriage occupations indicated on the marriage registers give little information about the social standing the bride was to attain in her married life. Far more important for her future was her husband's occupation. This does not mean that women's occupations can simply be ignored. In the first place, the effect of family background on the woman's occupational choice is itself an important – and little studied – historical issue. Moreover, a woman's choice of occupation may also have had an important influence on the kind of men she met and consequently on whom she married. If nothing else, it must be seen as a potentially important intervening variable in her social-mobility experience. This chapter will begin with a consideration of mobility as determined in the marriage market and subsequently examine the influence of women's occupations on their social-mobility experience.

The marriage market

Marseille's marriage market, like the market for male labor, was profoundly influenced by the changing demographic and economic structure. The crucial question for the marriage market is how the occupational backgrounds of women compared with the occupational distribution of marriageable men. This can be seen in Table 10.1. In 1821–2, the fit between brides' backgrounds and grooms' occupations was reasonably close. The biggest gaps were, familiarly, in the artisan category, where women from artisanal backgrounds were in short supply, and in the agricultural category, where women were overabundant. By 1846–51 the fit between brides' backgrounds and grooms' occupations was significantly worse than in 1821–2, and in 1869 it was worse again. The index of dissimilarity rose from 17.4 in 1821–2 to 27.8 in 1846–51 and 32.2 in 1869. The main reason was the burgeoning migration of peasants' daughters in these years. Furthermore, the widening gap between women's occupational backgrounds and men's employment patterns in Marseille also tended to increase the possibilities for upward mobility to the bourgeoisie among women of peasant or working-class parentage. In 1821–2 there were a few more grooms with bourgeois occupations than brides from bourgeois backgrounds (26.1 percent as against 24.5 percent); the figures were essentially unchanged in 1846–51 (26.4 percent as against 24.2 percent). But by 1869 a sizable gap had opened: 34.2 percent of the grooms were bourgeois, but only 21.8 percent of the brides were from bourgeois backgrounds. In each of these years, some net upward mobility into the bourgeoisie was inevitable, and by 1869 the necessary amount of net upward mobility

Table 10.1. *Profile of marriage market (in percent)*

Occupational category	Women married in 1821-2			Women married in 1846-51			Women married in 1869		
	1. Groom's occupation	2. Wife's father's occupation	3. "Excess" grooms (1 − 2)	4. Groom's occupation	5. Wife's father's occupation	6. "Excess" grooms (1 − 2)	7. Groom's occupation	8. Wife's father's occupation	9. "Excess" grooms (1 − 2)
1. Business and professional	6.2	7.7	−1.5	5.6	5.7	−.1	6.5	4.9	1.6
2. Rentier	1.9	4.1	−2.2	2.6	5.5	−2.9	1.9	4.3	−2.4
3. Sales and clerical	10.3	3.6	6.7	10.6	4.7	5.9	17.3	5.9	11.4
4. Small business	7.7	9.1	−1.4	7.6	8.3	−.7	8.5	6.7	1.8
5. Artisan	52.5	43.1	9.4	47.4	31.4	16.0	39.1	29.0	10.1
6. Service	1.3	1.9	−0.6	2.9	1.4	1.5	5.9	1.0	4.9
7. Unskilled	7.9	6.5	1.4	14.1	9.7	4.4	12.6	13.0	−0.4
8. Maritime	8.0	8.7	−0.7	5.3	5.3	0.0	5.6	3.1	2.5
9. Agriculture	3.0	12.2	−9.2	2.3	20.9	−18.6	2.0	25.2	−23.2
10. Miscellaneous	1.3	3.1	−1.8	1.5	7.1	−5.6	0.6	6.7	−6.1
All bourgeois	26.1	24.5	1.6	26.4	24.2	2.2	34.2	21.8	12.4
Index of dissimilarity			17.4			27.8			32.2
Number of cases	1,116	1,116	1,116	2,573	2,573	2,573	1,769	1,769	1,769

was substantial. In every year, in fact, the balance was more favorable to women's upward mobility than to men's. The demographic situation imparted a stronger upward bias to women's mobility patterns than to men's.

Women were considerably less likely than men to remain socially stationary. As a comparison of Tables 9.4 and 10.2 demonstrates, the proportion of women who married men in the same occupation as their father was far below the percentage of men who followed their father's occupation. Only among women from business and professional, unskilled, or maritime backgrounds did more than one woman in six marry a man with the same occupation as her father. Even in these groups, rates of occupational endogamy were below the men's rates of occupational inheritance. The most striking difference between men's and women's patterns was in the artisan category, which had the highest rates of men's occupational inheritance in 1821–2 and 1846–51, and the highest but one in 1869. By contrast, fewer than 10 percent of women from the artisan category married a man practicing her father's trade. Women were also less likely than men to remain within their father's broader occupational category, although the differences between the sexes were much less in this case. The proportion of women in the diagonal cells of Tables 10.4, 10.5, and 10.6 is consistently below that of men in the diagonal cells of Tables 9.5, 9.6, and 9.7. This difference is summarized in Table 10.3, which compares the proportion of men and of women who remained in their fathers' occupational category. This proportion dropped steadily for both sexes, but was always appreciably higher for men than for women. According to both measures, men were more likely than women to remain socially stable. The men's labor market, in other words, was more tightly constrained by parental occupational status than was the marriage market.

Tables 10.4, 10.5, and 10.6 give the details of women's marriage-based social mobility. These tables reveal that downward mobility from the bourgeoisie was appreciable for all bourgeois categories in all time periods. Women from elite backgrounds had rates of downward mobility into the working class that were very similar to those of men. (Compare Tables 10.4, 10.5, and 10.6 with Tables 9.5, 9.6, and 9.7.) The main difference between men's and women's mobility in the elite category is that women were more likely than men to be downwardly mobile from the elite to the petite bourgeoisie. The only exception was daughters of rentiers in 1821–2, who remained in the elite category in 45 percent of the cases, well above the proportion for rentiers' sons in the same year and equal to the proportion for daughters of businessmen and professionals. Women from petit bourgeois backgrounds had rates of downward mobility into the working class that were consistently higher than those of men from comparable backgrounds. Women of petit bourgeois origins generally remained in the bourgeoisie in somewhat less than half the cases; men from comparable backgrounds generally did so in somewhat more than half the cases. This difference was at least partly compensated

Table 10.2. *Percentage of brides with grooms in same occupation as bride's father*

| | Father's occupation | | | | | | | | | | |
	Business and professional	Rentier	Sales and clerical	Small business	Artisan	Service	Unskilled	Maritime	Agriculture	Miscellaneous	Total
1821–2	19	15	5	5	12	0	10	30	10	3	12
1846–51	18	5	6	4	9	0	21	16	4	1	8
1869	21	5	10	5	6	6	18	22	3	2	8

Table 10.3. *Percentage socially stationary brides and grooms*

	1821–2	1846–51	1869
Percent grooms in same occupational category as father	52	41	33
Percent brides with husbands in same occupational category as bride's father	42	31	26

for by petit bourgeois women's consistently higher rates of upward mobility into the elite, which averaged well above 10 percent. The mobility patterns of bourgeois women demonstrate once again that women tended to experience more mobility than men – apparently in both downward and upward directions.

For women from all bourgeois backgrounds combined, the proportion who failed to find bourgeois husbands was 37 percent in 1821–2, 43 percent in 1846–51, and 37 percent again in 1869. In each period, these rates of downward mobility were higher than the comparable rates for men: 34, 37, and 32 percent. But as was the case for men, there was no tendency for women's downward mobility rates to fall over time, in spite of changes in the marriage market that increased the availability of potential bourgeois husbands. Women from bourgeois backgrounds, like men from comparable backgrounds, did not manage to benefit from the increasingly favorable market situation. More and more of the available bourgeois men were claimed by upwardly mobile women from working-class or peasant backgrounds.

The tendency for women to be more mobile than men in both directions also held for those from working-class backgrounds. Although upward mobility into the bourgeoisie was only a negligible 1 percent for daughters of unskilled workers in 1821–2, it was 10 percent for daughters of service workers, 15 percent for daughters of artisans, and 16 percent for maritime workers' daughters. Overall, the rate of upward mobility for women from working-class backgrounds was 14 percent, twice the rate of men from working-class backgrounds at the same time. By 1846–51, rates had risen for women from all working-class categories except maritime workers' daughters. Daughters of unskilled workers now married bourgeois men in 8 percent of the cases, and the rate was 20 percent for artisans' daughters. Overall, 16 percent of workers' daughters had achieved mobility into the bourgeoisie, still well above the 10 percent rate achieved by workers' sons. In 1869, all categories of workers' daughters had risen to new highs. The service workers'

Table 10.4. *Bride's father's occupation by groom's occupation, 1821–2 (in percent)*

Groom's occupation	Bride's father's occupation										
	Business and professional	Rentier	Sales and clerical	Small business	Artisan	Service	Unskilled	Maritime	Agriculture	Miscellaneous	Total
1. Business and professional	38	28	5	8	1	0	1	3	2	9	6
2. Rentier	7	17	2	5	0	0	0	0	0	3	2
3. Sales and clerical	30	15	15	16	8	10	0	5	10	9	10
4. Small business	8	13	12	24	7	0	0	8	2	3	8
5. Artisan	15	22	58	41	65	76	62	38	51	57	52
6. Service	0	0	2	0	2	0	3	1	2	3	1
7. Unskilled	1	0	2	5	8	14	26	7	10	3	8
8. Maritime	0	2	2	1	7	0	8	37	5	6	8
9. Agriculture	0	0	0	1	2	0	0	0	18	3	3
10. Miscellaneous	0	2	0	0	2	0	0	0	1	6	1
All bourgeois (1 + 2 + 3 + 4)	84	74	35	52	15	10	1	16	13	23	26
Number of cases	86	46	40	101	481	21	73	97	136	35	1,116

Table 10.5. *Bride's father's occupation by groom's occupation, 1846–51 (in percent)*

Groom's occupation	Bride's father's occupation										
	Business and professional	Rentier	Sales and clerical	Small business	Artisan	Service	Unskilled	Maritime	Agriculture	Miscellaneous	Total
1. Business and professional	44	17	9	7	2	8	0	1	1	3	6
2. Rentier	11	11	3	3	1	0	1	0	1	3	3
3. Sales and clerical	23	20	21	16	8	3	4	4	8	13	11
4. Small business	6	13	12	16	8	14	3	2	5	8	8
5. Artisan	13	28	46	43	60	53	45	50	46	49	47
6. Service	1	5	2	2	2	8	36	1	5	2	3
7. Unskilled	1	4	4	4	11	6	5	12	22	15	14
8. Maritime	0	2	1	5	6	3	2	27	3	6	5
9. Agriculture	0	1	0	1	1	3	1	3	7	2	2
10. Miscellaneous	2	1	2	3	1	3	1	1	2	1	2
All bourgeois (1 + 2 + 3 + 4)	84	61	45	42	19	25	8	7	15	27	28
Number of cases	146	142	120	214	807	36	249	137	539	183	2,573

278

Table 10.6. *Bride's father's occupation by groom's occupation, 1869 (in percent)*

Groom's occupation	Bride's father's occupation										
	Business and professional	Rentier	Sales and clerical	Small business	Artisan	Service	Unskilled	Maritime	Agriculture	Miscellaneous	Total
1. Business and professional	53	27	8	9	3	6	0	2	2	2	6
2. Rentier	6	9	6	3	1	0	1	0	1	0	2
3. Sales and clerical	21	32	28	18	16	22	8	11	18	16	17
4. Small business	6	14	9	17	10	11	6	6	7	3	8
5. Artisan	12	17	36	39	50	50	47	37	32	42	40
6. Service	0	1	3	3	6	11	4	0	10	4	6
7. Unskilled	2	1	10	6	8	0	25	6	18	18	13
8. Maritime	1	0	2	3	4	0	5	35	6	9	6
9. Agriculture	0	0	0	1	2	0	2	4	4	2	2
10. Miscellaneous	0	0	0	0	0	0	1	0	1	3	1
All bourgeois (1 + 2 + 3 + 4)	85	81	50	48	30	39	16	19	28	21	34
Number of cases	87	79	105	119	513	18	230	54	446	118	1,769

daughters' upward-mobility rate of 39 percent must be discounted because it is based on so few cases. But artisans' daughters married bourgeois men in 30 percent of the cases, maritime workers' daughters did so in 19 percent, and even unskilled workers' daughters did so in 16 percent. Overall, 26 percent of workers' daughters achieved mobility into the bourgeoisie, a rate considerably above the 17 percent achieved by workers' sons. In one respect, however, women's and men's upward-mobility rates showed no appreciable differences. Both women and men from working-class backgrounds had only negligible chances of rising into the elite.

Women also had considerably higher rates of upward and downward mobility *within* the working class than did men. Artisans' daughters moved downward by marrying unskilled or maritime workers in 15 percent of the cases in 1821–2, 17 percent in 1846–51, and 12 percent in 1869. Sons of artisans experienced such downward mobility in only 10 percent of the cases in 1821–2 and 1846–51 and 9 percent in 1869. On the other hand, daughters of unskilled and maritime workers experienced high rates of upward mobility into the artisan category. Sixty-two percent of unskilled workers' daughters and 38 percent of maritime workers' daughters married artisans in 1821–2; 45 and 50 percent did so in 1846–51; and 47 and 37 percent did so in 1869. The comparable rates of mobility into the artisan category for men were considerably lower: 42 and 30 percent in 1821–2, 39 and 33 percent in 1846–51, and 42 and 33 percent in 1869. These higher levels of both upward and downward mobility are, of course, in a sense simply the obverse of women's lower rates of social stability. If women did not marry within their fathers' occupational category, many of them were bound either to marry up or marry down.

The one category of women that did not have higher rates of mobility than the comparable category of men was peasants' daughters. By contrast with workers' children, the peasants' daughters' rates of upward mobility into the bourgeoisie were no higher than the sons': 13, 15, and 28 percent for daughters in 1821–2, 1846–51, and 1869, and 11, 18, and 30 percent for sons. This unaccustomed similarity between sons' and daughters' patterns probably resulted from the fact that peasants' sons, unlike workers' sons, could not practice their fathers' occupations in Marseille. The tendency to remain in the fathers' category, which restricted both upward and downward mobility among sons of bourgeois and workers alike, could not be present among sons of peasants. Consequently, peasants' sons were as free in their search for occupations as peasants' daughters were in their search for marriage partners. One result, for both sons and daughters, was relatively high and rising rates of upward mobility into the petite bourgeoisie. Peasants' daughters were also similar to peasants' sons in their responsiveness to opportunities at all levels of the urban social hierarchy. By 1869, the occupational profile of the husbands of peasants' daughters was very close to that of the male population as a whole – except that very few peasants' daughters managed to marry into the elite. Like peasants' sons, they also responded disproportionately to the growing opportunities in the clerical and service sectors.

Overall, the similarities between men's and women's social-mobility patterns were striking. Women's mobility was certainly governed by the same hierarchical ordering of occupational categories that governed men's mobility. Most mobility, whether downward or upward, took only one step up or down the hierarchy. And the main change in the hierarchy over time – both in the marriage market and in the men's labor market – was a striking decline in the steepness of the step dividing the working class from the petite bourgeoisie. The most important difference between men's and women's social mobility was that women tended to be more mobile than men in all directions. Men were more likely to stay within the bounds of the parental occupational world than were women and therefore less likely to move either up or down.

There are a number of factors that might account for this difference. First, in an essentially patriarchal society, parents, and especially fathers, may have had a greater investment in their sons' futures than in their daughters'. Sons, consequently, may have been raised with a very strong sense that they should follow the father's trade, whereas daughters were allowed to follow their own inclinations in preparing their futures. This would have had the ironic effect of producing more upward mobility among daughters than among sons. Second, to the extent that sons learned specific occupationally relevant skills and attitudes from their fathers, the father's occupation may have had a more direct effect in channeling the son's occupational choice than it could have had on the daughter's marriage choice – whether or not the parents took as much interest in placing their daughter as in placing their son. Finally, at least in a large and complex city like Marseille, where many social contacts were bound to take place outside family control, courtship may have depended largely on the likes and dislikes of the young women and men concerned. Personal inclination may have been more likely to outweigh parental pressure in choosing a spouse than in choosing a trade. In other words, the greater independence from parents in marriage choice than in occupational choice may have been partly due to the notorious unruliness of romantic love.

Literacy and mobility

Because bourgeois occupations were essentially closed to men who could not read and write, literacy had a very powerful effect on men's social-mobility patterns. Literacy was less important as a qualification for bourgeois status among women: Illiteracy barred a man from keeping books, writing memoranda, drawing up letters of exchange, or practicing law, but it did not necessarily bar a woman from being a bookkeeper's or lawyer's wife. Nevertheless, it certainly enhanced a woman's chances of doing so.

Table 10.7. *Percentage of daughters literate, by father's occupation*

Father's occupation	1821–2	1846–51	1869
1. Business and professional	88	95	95
2. Rentier	87	72	92
3. Sales and clerical	67	74	88
4. Small business	70	79	88
5. Artisan	31	46	75
6. Service	38	62	78
7. Unskilled	14	21	50
8. Maritime	16	16	62
9. Agriculture	10	16	49
10. Miscellaneous	43	30	53
Total	38	43	67
Number of cases	1,115	2,561	1,767

As was indicated in Chapter 7, overall women's literacy rates were far below men's. Only 38 percent of brides could sign their marriage registers in 1821–2 (as against 67 percent of grooms), and only 43 percent could do so in 1846–51 (as against the grooms' rate of 79 percent). Women's rates rose more substantially over the next two decades, but were only 67 percent in 1869, still far below the men's rate of 89 percent. Provisions for women's education in Marseille and in the region that sent Marseille its immigrants clearly were utterly inadequate before the middle of the nineteenth century and were still poor in the 1860s.

Women's literacy levels varied sharply by occupational background. In each of the years covered by this study, women's literacy rates fell into four distinct occupational groups (see Table 10.7). In 1821–2, daughters of businessmen, professionals, and rentiers were literate in nearly 90 percent of the cases. Rates were considerably lower among women from petit bourgeois backgrounds, where only about two-thirds could sign their names. Among daughters of artisans and service workers only about a third could do so, and among unskilled workers, maritime workers, and peasants, rates were truly appalling: Between five-sixths and nine-tenths were illiterate. In 1846–51, the same grouping by occupations was still present – except that daughters of rentiers had slipped to the level of daughters of petits bourgeois. Some progress had been made: Nineteen of twenty daughters of businessmen and professionals now could sign their names, the rates of daughters of petits bourgeois had risen to about three-quarters literate, artisans' and service workers' daughters' rates had risen to about one-half, and even daughters in the bottom group had rates approaching one-fifth. By 1869, women from both rentier and business and professional backgrounds had literacy rates above

90 percent, and women from petit bourgeois backgrounds were approaching 90 percent. Women from artisan and service backgrounds now were literate in about three-quarters of the cases, and half were literate even among daughters of unskilled workers, maritime workers, and peasants. Women's literacy rates were slowly and belatedly leveling up.

Table 10.8 shows the effect of literacy on the likelihood that women from these various backgrounds would marry men with bourgeois occupations. Although the effects of literacy on mobility were not so stark as among men, it is clear that bourgeois men did prefer literate brides. Only 22 percent of the brides of bourgeois were illiterate in 1821–2, 25 percent in 1846–51, and 18 percent in 1869. Among rentiers, businessmen, and professionals, the proportion of illiterate brides was lower yet: 8, 8, and 2 percent. Literate women from bourgeois backgrounds had much lower rates of downward mobility than did illiterates of comparable backgrounds, and literate women from nonbourgeois origins had much higher rates of upward mobility than illiterates from similar origins. Literacy clearly constituted an important advantage in the marriage market.

There were, however, several differences between the effects of literacy on mobility among women and among men. First, illiterate women from bourgeois backgrounds had substantially better chances of avoiding downward mobility than did illiterate men from comparable backgrounds. Second, although illiterate women from working-class and peasant backgrounds had low upward-mobility rates, their rates were far above those of illiterate men from comparable backgrounds. Third, and quite surprisingly, illiterate upward-mobility rates tended to rise significantly over time. One might have expected that as literacy became more common among the female population it would have become harder for illiterate women to marry bourgeois men. But instead the rate of upward mobility among illiterate women of working-class backgrounds rose from 8 percent in 1821–2 to 10 percent in 1846–51 and 14 percent in 1869; and the upward-mobility rates of illiterate daughters of peasants rose from 11 percent, to 12 percent, to the remarkable rate of 23 percent in 1869. The reasons for this increase remain obscure, but it certainly was an important phenomenon. It indicates clearly that literacy and education had a less direct influence in the marriage market, which determined women's mobility experiences, than in the labor market, which determined men's.

Migration and mobility

Among men, immigrants had very different mobility patterns than natives. Except for Italians, who had a very unfavorable experience, male immigrants generally did quite well. Their rates of downward mobility from the bourgeoisie were above those of natives, but so were their rates of upward mobility from the working class and peasantry. On the whole, female immigrants seem

Table 10.8. *Percentage of daughters with bourgeois husbands, by father's occupation and literacy*

Father's occupation	1821–2			1846–51			1869		
	Literate	Illiterate	Total	Literate	Illiterate	Total	Literate	Illiterate	Total
1. Business and professional	93	10	84	85	71[a]	84	86	75[a]	85
2. Rentier	78	50[a]	74	73	28	61	84	33[a]	81
3. Sales and clerical	48	8	35	56	13	45	50	46	50
4. Small business	65	23	52	49	16	42	51	21	48
5. Artisan	29	9	15	27	12	19	34	18[a]	30
6. Service	25[a]	0	10	35	0	25	43	25	39
7. Unskilled	10	0	1	21	5	8	22	10	16
8. Maritime	38	10	16	16	4	7	24	10	19
9. Agriculture	29	11	13	30	12	15	33	23	28
10. Miscellaneous	46	5	23	52	16	27	33	7	21
All bourgeois (1 + 2 + 3 + 4)	75	20	63	65	22	57	66	38	63
All workers (5 + 6 + 7 + 8)	30	8	14	28	10	16	31	14	26
Total	53	9	26	46	15	28	42	18	34
Number of cases	426	689	1,115	1,113	1,449	2,562	1,184	584	1,768

[a] Based on fewer than 10 cases.

to have done neither better nor worse than their male counterparts. This can be seen by comparing Table 10.9 with Table 9.11. Italian immigrant women had a mobility experience similar to that of their male compatriots, but perhaps a little less dismal. Except in 1821–2, when the number of cases was so small as to make figures unreliable, their downward-mobility rates were above those of either natives or non-Italian immigrants. The differential, however, was less than among men. Their rates of upward mobility from peasant and working-class backgrounds started at zero in 1821–2, but had increased to higher levels than those of their male counterparts by 1869. But in spite of their slightly better performance than Italian men, Italian women suffered from the same combination of poor qualifications and powerful anti-Italian prejudice. They could not escape the general fate of Italians in nineteenth-century Marseille.

Non-Italian female immigrants, like their male counterparts, generally had higher rates of downward mobility from the bourgeoisie than natives, but higher rates of upward mobility from the working class and peasantry. In 1821–2, female non-Italian immigrants from all bourgeois backgrounds combined actually had lower rates of downward mobility than natives, but this was largely because many more of them than of the natives were daughters of rentiers, businessmen, or professionals, whose rates of downward mobility were considerably lower than those of women from petit bourgeois backgrounds. By 1846–51, when the weight of elite backgrounds among immigrants had declined, their overall rate of downward mobility from the bourgeoisie had passed the native rate, and by 1869 the gap had widened further. Female non-Italian immigrants from working-class backgrounds, however, were considerably more likely to marry bourgeois men than were native working-class women. There were a few exceptions to this generalization. In 1821–2 not one non-Italian immigrant unskilled worker's daughter married into the bourgeoisie – but then only 2 percent of their native counterparts did so. And, in 1869, native maritime workers' daughters had the same rate of upward mobility as non-Italian immigrant maritime workers' daughters, that is, 19 percent. But overall, the non-Italian immigrants had a consistent edge. This was also true among daughters of peasants, where non-Italian immigrants' daughters married into the bourgeoisie in 18 percent of the cases in both 1821–2 and 1846–51, and in 30 percent of the cases in 1869. These compared to native rates of 8, 8, and 10 percent. The non-Italian immigrant peasants' daughters' advantage was less than that of the non-Italian immigrant peasants' sons', but it certainly was substantial and consistent.

In one respect, it is surprising that the mobility experience of non-Italian immigrant women was as favorable as that of non-Italian immigrant men. After all, among the French-born, who made up a large majority of all the non-Italian immigrants, female immigration tended to be much less educationally selective than male immigration. As was demonstrated in Chapter 7,

Table 10.9. *Percentage of daughters with bourgeois husbands, by father's occupation and migration*

Father's occupation	1821–2			1846–51			1869		
	Natives	Non-Italian immigrants	Italian immigrants	Natives	Non-Italian immigrants	Italian immigrants	Natives	Non-Italian immigrants	Italian immigrants
1. Business and professional	85	83	75[a]	87	83	40[a]	84	85	100[a]
2. Rentier	79	67[b]	—	72	53	50[a]	88	73	0[a]
3. Sales and clerical	30	50[a]	50[a]	53	38	29[a]	38	49	—
4. Small business	52	56[b]	50[a]	40	48	36[b]	78	41	40[a]
5. Artisan	15	19	0[a]	17	25	9	27	31	16[b]
6. Service	0[b]	20[b]	—	23[b]	26	—	20[a]	41[b]	100[a]
7. Unskilled	2	0	0[a]	6	12	2	16	20	5
8. Maritime	13	33[b]	0[a]	6	13[b]	9	19	19[b]	14[a]
9. Agriculture	8	18	0[a]	8	18	8	10[b]	30	11
10. Miscellaneous	16	38[a]	0[a]	20	30	30[b]	29	21	0[a]
All bourgeois (1 + 2 + 3 + 4)	62	68	67[b]	60	54	38	69	59	56[a]
All workers (5 + 6 + 7 + 8)	13	18	0	14	23	6	23	30	11
Total	25	30	22	28	28	11	37	35	14
Number of cases	784	295	36	1,126	1,200	224	591	1,066	111

[a]Based on fewer than 10 cases.   [b]Based on 10 to 19 cases.

French-born male immigrants had literacy rates at least as high as those of
natives and considerably higher than those of the men they left behind in their
towns and villages. But French-born female immigrants had very low literacy
rates – below both the native rates and the overall French rates. This, it was
argued in Chapter 7, might well indicate that women's migration typically
was less motivated by ambition than was male migration, and more by a
desire, or a willingness, simply to rid the parental household of an extra
mouth. But because female immigrants were just as successful in Marseille's
marriage market as male immigrants were in the labor market, it may well
be that this argument is false, that they were no less ambitious and restless
than their male counterparts, even if they did not prepare for success in the
city by obtaining an education. In any case, the success of female immigrants
in finding bourgeois husbands suggests that the relationships among migration,
literacy, and social mobility need further examination.

Tables 10.10 and 10.11 outline the effects of migration on social mobility
separately for literate and illiterate women. They demonstrate that the effects
of migration were, on the whole, the same among literate and illiterate women.
Among literate women, non-Italian immigrant daughters of workers generally
had higher rates of upward mobility than native daughters of workers, and
Italian daughters of workers had the lowest rates. Among literate daughters
of peasants, non-Italian immigrants had far higher upward-mobility rates than
natives, and Italians were too few to yield meaningful figures at all. Downward-mobility rates had a less consistent pattern. Literate non-Italian immigrants actually had a lower rate of downward mobility from the bourgeoisie
than natives in 1821–2 and a rate only slightly higher in 1846–51. By 1869,
however, the advantage of native-born women was substantial. Although there
were too few of them in any year to make the figures reliable, literate Italian
women from bourgeois backgrounds actually had the lowest downward-mobility rates in 1821–2 and tied for the lowest in 1869. Only in 1845–51 were
their rates above those of other categories. Among literates, in short, there
were no clear and consistent differences between native and immigrant downward-mobility patterns. But upward-mobility patterns had the familiar ranking: Non-Italian immigrants did best, Italian immigrants did worst, and natives
were in between.

The effects of migration on mobility were roughly similar among illiterate
women. The downward-mobility rates of natives, Italians, and non-Italian
immigrants showed no consistent pattern. Upward-mobility rates, however,
were consistently highest for non-Italian immigrants. For all illiterate non-
Italian immigrant daughters of workers, the upward-mobility rate was already
an impressive 14 percent in 1821–2, and it climbed to 15 percent in 1846–
51 and 20 percent in 1869. Among non-Italian immigrant daughters of artisans
the rates were even higher, reaching the astonishing level of 27 percent in
1869. The rates for all illiterate native daughters of workers were much lower:

Table 10.10. *Percentage of literate daughters with bourgeois husbands, by father's occupation*

	1821–2			1846–51			1869		
Father's occupation	Natives	Non-Italian immigrants	Italian immigrants	Natives	Non-Italian immigrants	Italian immigrants	Natives	Non-Italian immigrants	Italian immigrants
1. Business and professional	85	90	86[a]	88	83	50[a]	84	86	100[a]
2. Rentier	75	69[b]	—	76	71	50[a]	87	81	—
3. Sales and clerical	30	67[a]	100[a]	65	49	40[a]	46	53	—
4. Small business	33	69[b]	100[a]	47	55	50[a]	61	44	50[a]
5. Artisan	29	29	0[a]	26	34	17[a]	32	37	22[a]
6. Service	0[a]	40[a]	—	33[a]	35[b]	—	33[a]	40[b]	100[a]
7. Unskilled	12[a]	0[a]	—	17	26	0[a]	20	25	11[a]
8. Maritime	38[b]	100[a]	—	11[b]	50	0[a]	21	33[a]	0[a]
9. Agriculture	0[a]	57[a]	—	0[a]	31	38[a]	10[b]	35	11[a]
10. Miscellaneous	44[a]	50[a]	—	46	54	100[a]	53[b]	29	0[a]
All bourgeois (1 + 2 + 3 + 4)	74	77	78[a]	67	64	47[b]	71	61	71[a]
All workers (5 + 6 + 7 + 8)	28	35	0[a]	21	34	10[b]	29	35	20
Total	50	61	70[b]	46	46	38	45	41	26
Number of cases	316	100	10	595	476	39	460	685	39

[a]Based on fewer than 10 cases. [b]Based on 10 to 19 cases.

Table 10.11. *Percentage of illiterate daughters with bourgeois husbands, by father's occupation*

Father's occupation	1821–2			1846–51			1869		
	Natives	Non-Italian immigrants	Italian immigrants	Natives	Non-Italian immigrants	Italian immigrants	Natives	Non-Italian immigrants	Italian immigrants
1. Business and professional	0[a]	33[a]	0[a]	50[a]	80[a]	—	100[a]	67[a]	—
2. Rentier	50[a]	50[a]	—	25[a]	27	50[a]	100[b]	25[a]	0[a]
3. Sales and clerical	10[b]	0[a]	0[a]	19[b]	8[b]	0[a]	20[a]	62[a]	—
4. Small business	25	20[a]	0[a]	5	28[b]	20[a]	25[a]	22[a]	0[a]
5. Artisan	7	16	—	7	18	8	7	27	11[a]
6. Service	0[a]	0[a]	0[a]	0[a]	0[a]	—	0[a]	50[a]	—
7. Unskilled	0	0[b]	0[a]	3	18	2	11	12	3
8. Maritime	9	22[a]	0[a]	4	0[b]	10	14	0[a]	17[a]
9. Agriculture	7	14	0[a]	9	15	5	0[a]	25	11[b]
10. Miscellaneous	0[b]	0[a]	0[a]	7	22	4[a]	0[b]	11	0[a]
All bourgeois (1 + 2 + 3 + 4)	20	33[a]	0[a]	14	27	22[a]	55[b]	42	0[a]
All workers (5 + 6 + 7 + 8)	6	14	0	6	15	6	9	20	7
Total	7	14	0	7	17	6	10	23	7
Number of cases	467	195	26	525	722	202	131	381	71

[a]Based on fewer than 10 cases.　[b]Based on 10 to 19 cases.

6 percent in both 1821–2 and 1846–51 and 9 percent in 1869. Except in 1821–2, these rates were not significantly above those of illiterate Italian daughters of workers, which were 0, 6, and 7 percent. Finally, illiterate non-Italian immigrant daughters of peasants had upward-mobility rates comparable to those of illiterate daughters of workers from similar geographical origins: 14 percent in 1821–2, 15 percent in 1846–51, and a remarkable 25 percent in 1869.

Two overall conclusions can be drawn from Tables 10.10 and 10.11. First, non-Italian immigrant daughters of workers and peasants were consistently more able to find bourgeois husbands than were their native-born counterparts, and this advantage held among illiterates as well as literates. Second, it was surprisingly common for illiterate daughters of workers and peasants who had migrated to Marseille from elsewhere in France or from foreign countries other than Italy to marry into the bourgeoisie in the city. Already accomplished by a seventh of such women in 1821–2, such upward mobility was accomplished by between a fifth and a fourth of them in 1869. Among non-Italian immigrants from lowly backgrounds, illiteracy constituted a much smaller handicap than might have been expected.

How did these non-Italian immigrant women, and especially the illiterate among them, achieve such high upward-mobility rates? One possibility is that they were especially likely to marry successful immigrant men, whereas natives generally married the less successful native men. These possibilities are assessed in Tables 10.12 through 10.17. Table 10.12 sets forth the pattern of intermarriage between natives and immigrants. It is clear that in each of the periods covered in this study, women from each birthplace category tended to prefer men from the same category. In 1821–2, for example, 67 percent of native women married native men, although only 59 percent of all men were natives. Even more strikingly, 54 percent of all non-Italian immigrant women married non-Italian immigrant men, although only 36 percent of all available men were non-Italian immigrants. Finally, 20 percent of Italian-born women married Italian-born men, even though only 5 percent of the available men were Italians. Similar preferences for husbands from like origins persisted, and were even intensified, in 1846–51 and 1869. In 1821–2, 20 percent more women married men from like origins than would have been the case if women from all categories of birthplace had married men without regard to origin. This percentage rose to 38 in 1846–51 and fell only slightly to 33 in 1869.[4] It is therefore plausible that the relatively high upward-mobility rates of non-Italian immigrant women resulted from their propensity to marry non-Italian immigrant men. However, it should be noted that the tendency toward marriage within the group, although substantial, was not terribly strong. Marriage between different birthplace groups also remained quite common.

The effect of husbands' geographical origins on women's chances for social mobility is examined in Tables 10.13, 10.14, and 10.15. These tables show

Table 10.12. *Percentage of women marrying men from different birthplaces, by bride's birthplace*

Birthplace of brides	Birthplace of grooms				
	Natives	Non-Italian immigrants	Italian immigrants	Total	No. cases
1821–2					
Natives	67	29	4	100	784
Non-Italian immigrants	43	54	4	101	295
Italian immigrants	34	46	20	100	35
Total	59	36	5	100	114
1846–51					
Natives	59	37	5	101	1,126
Non-Italian immigrants	27	66	8	101	1,198
Italian immigrants	18	20	62	100	224
Total	40	49	12	101	2,568
1869					
Natives	49	44	6	99	591
Non-Italian immigrants	21	71	7	99	1,066
Italian immigrants	21	30	49	100	111
Total	31	60	10	101	1,768

what percentage of women from different occupational backgrounds married into the bourgeoisie for every category of brides' and grooms' birthplaces. The women's occupational backgrounds are divided into only four categories – bourgeois, worker, agriculture, and miscellaneous – so as to maintain large enough totals in the table's cells to allow meaningful generalization. The advantage that came from marrying non-Italian immigrants was particularly great for women born in Marseille (see the first three rows of Table 10.13). Whatever their class background, bourgeois, worker, or peasant, natives were far more likely to attain bourgeois status if they married non-Italian immigrants than if they married natives. Their chances were worst, not surprisingly, if they married Italians. Among non-Italian immigrant women, those who married fellow non-Italian immigrants had a very slight advantage, if any, over those who married natives. In fact, the mobility patterns of native women who married non-Italian immigrants and of non-Italian immigrant women who married either non-Italian immigrants or natives were essentially the same and were very favorable. The patterns of natives who married natives, and of women in all marriages that involved Italians, were much less favorable.

Table 10.13. *Percentage of brides with bourgeois grooms, by bride's birthplace, groom's birthplace, and bride's father's occupation, 1821–2*

Groom's birthplace	Bride's father's occupation					
	Bourgeois	Worker	Agriculture	Miscellaneous	Total	No. cases
Native brides						
Natives	57	11	5	24	20	523
Non-Italian immigrants	70	18	18[b]	0[a]	36	226
Italian immigrants	38[a]	8	0[a]	0[a]	14	35
Non-Italian immigrant brides						
Natives	67	19	14	33[a]	29	126
Non-Italian immigrants	69	17	23	40[a]	32	158
Italian immigrants	50[a]	25[a]	0[a]	—	18[b]	11
Italian immigrant brides						
Natives	75[a]	0[a]	0[a]	—	25[b]	12
Non-Italian immigrants	62[a]	0[a]	0[a]	0[a]	31	16
Italian immigrants	—	0[a]	0[a]	—	0[a]	7
All brides						
Natives	60	12	9	25	22	661
Non-Italian immigrants	69	17	21	15[b]	34	400
Italian immigrants	49[b]	9	0[a]	50[a]	15	54

[a] Based on fewer than 10 cases.   [b] Based on between 10 and 19 cases.

The implications of these patterns are clear and important. First, they underline the disadvantages of Italians. Although the number of Italian brides and grooms was so small that none of the particular figures can be trusted, there can be no mistake about the overall pattern. In 1821–2 not a single Italian woman from a subbourgeois background managed to marry into the bourgeoisie, and the Italian men who married non-Italian women were almost never bourgeois. Second, Table 10.13 makes it clear that the high upward-mobility rates achieved by non-Italian immigrant women can by no means be accounted for by their propensity to marry fellow non-Italian immigrants. These women also managed to marry a disproportionate share of successful native-born men. In fact, they did just as well when they married natives as when they married fellow non-Italian immigrants. Finally, native women, having lost a disproportionate share of the successful native men to their non-Italian immigrant competitors, could only keep up if they managed to return the favor and marry non-Italian immigrant men. Those who married fellow natives had mediocre mobility rates.

The patterns in 1846–51 and 1869 differed in some details but were similar in their broad outlines and overall implications. In 1846–51, native women from bourgeois backgrounds had somewhat lower rates of downward mobility than non-Italian immigrant women from bourgeois backgrounds (see Table 10.14). Moreover, downward-mobility rates were no higher for native bourgeois who married natives than for those who married non-Italian immigrants. But among native women from working-class and peasant backgrounds, those who married non-Italian immigrants continued to have a substantial advantage. Among non-Italian immigrant women, the advantage of those who married non-Italian immigrants over those who married natives was clearer in 1846–51 than in 1821–2. It remained true, however, that the patterns of natives who married non-Italian immigrants and of non-Italian immigrants who married either natives or fellow non-Italian immigrants were very much alike and distinctly superior to the patterns of natives who married natives and of all women in marriages involving Italians. The only Italians who fared reasonably well in 1846–51 were Italian-born women who married non-Italian immigrant men.

In 1869, the same three categories – native women who married non-Italian immigrants and non-Italian immigrant women who married either natives or non-Italian immigrants – remained distinctly superior to all others (see Table 10.15). Native daughters of bourgeois who married non-Italian immigrants had exceptionally low rates of downward mobility in 1869, and native women from peasant backgrounds became so rare as to be negligible. As in 1846–51, Italian women who married non-Italian immigrants did substantially better than other Italians. But all in all, the conclusions reached on the basis of the 1821–2 data are valid for 1846–51 and 1869 as well. In none of these years was non-Italian immigrant women's ability to gain upward mobility dependent

Table 10.14. *Percentage of brides with bourgeois grooms, by bride's birthplace, groom's birthplace, and bride's father's occupation, 1846–51*

Groom's birthplace	Bride's father's occupation				Total	No. cases
	Bourgeois	Worker	Agriculture	Miscellaneous		
Native brides						
Natives	61	10	7	14	25	661
Non-Italian immigrants	61	19	12	27	34	413
Italian immigrants	25[a]	12	0[a]	0[a]	12	52
Non-Italian immigrant brides						
Natives	51	21	15	28	27	318
Non-Italian immigrants	57	25	19	32	30	786
Italian immigrants	38[b]	10	17	14	17	94
Italian immigrant brides						
Natives	30[b]	4	0[a]	0[a]	9	43
Non-Italian immigrants	44[a]	15	29[b]	75[a]	30	50
Italian immigrants	40[b]	4	3	0[a]	6	151
All brides						
Natives	57	13	12	19	25	1,023
Non-Italian immigrants	58	22	20	32	31	1,251
Italian immigrants	35	7	8	7	10	297

[a]Based on fewer than 10 cases.   [b]Based on between 10 and 19 cases.

Table 10.15. *Percentage of brides with bourgeois grooms, by bride's birthplace, groom's birthplace, and bride's father's occupation, 1869*

Groom's birthplace	Bride's father's occupation					
	Bourgeois	Worker	Agriculture	Miscellaneous	Total	No. cases
Native brides						
Natives	63	19	25[a]	20[b]	33	291
Non-Italian immigrants	78	31	0[a]	38[b]	47	292
Italian immigrants	29[a]	4	0[a]	0[a]	8	38
Non-Italian immigrant brides						
Natives	60	28	31	14	37	228
Non-Italian immigrants	62	32	32	23	36	761
Italian immigrants	27[b]	12	6	20[a]	13	77
Italian immigrant brides						
Natives	14[a]	17[b]	0[a]	0[a]	13	23
Non-Italian immigrants	60[a]	13[b]	18[b]	0[a]	21	33
Italian immigrants	40[a]	6	7[b]	0[a]	9	55
All brides						
Natives	61	22	27	15	34	542
Non-Italian immigrants	68	31	31	26	38	1,057
Italian immigrants	32	7	6	9	11	170

[a]Based on fewer than 10 cases. [b]Based on between 10 and 19 cases.

on their ability to marry fellow non-Italian immigrants. Their success was not a mere artifact of the success of non-Italian immigrant men. It was an achievement of their own.

Among illiterate women, however, the pattern was somewhat different, as can be seen in Table 10.16. This table includes only native and non-Italian immigrant women who married either natives or non-Italian immigrants; women whose marriages involved Italians were removed because their numbers were too few to reveal meaningful patterns. In 1821–2, the mobility rates of illiterates were less favorable than those of all women, but they followed the familiar pattern. Native women who married non-Italian immigrants and non-Italian immigrant women who married either natives or fellow non-Italian immigrants had substantially equal rates of bourgeois marriages, and substantially higher rates than did natives who married natives. In both 1846–51 and 1869, natives who married natives continued to be the least successful of the illiterate women. But in these years, non-Italian immigrant women who married fellow non-Italian immigrants did considerably better than either non-Italian immigrants who married natives or natives who married non-Italian immigrants. The record of the illiterate non-Italian immigrant women who married non-Italian immigrant men in 1869 is particularly impressive. Of those whose fathers were peasants or workers, no fewer than one in four found bourgeois husbands; and of those whose fathers were bourgeois, nearly two-thirds married bourgeois men. Astonishingly, these rates were essentially equal to the rates achieved in the same year by *literate* native women who married fellow natives (see Table 10.17).

In summary, analysis of the effect of immigration on women's mobility leads to four major conclusions. First, Italian immigrant women were notably unsuccessful – whether they were literate or illiterate, and whether they married natives, fellow Italians, or non-Italian immigrants. The unfavorable conditions facing Italians affected even non-Italian women who married Italian men; their mobility patterns were essentially the same as those of Italian women. Second, except in the case of downward mobility, where differences were inconsistent, non-Italian immigrant women had more favorable mobility experiences than native women. This advantage was particularly striking among illiterates. Third, the overall advantage of non-Italian immigrants cannot be accounted for by their tendency to marry fellow non-Italian immigrants. In fact, they did nearly as well when they married natives as when they married non-Italian immigrants. Fourth, and finally, the surprisingly good showing of *illiterate* non-Italian women was to some extent a consequence of their tendency to marry fellow non-Italian immigrants. But only to some extent: Even those who married natives did considerably better than native-born illiterate women who married natives. No matter how closely the data are inspected, the overall conclusion about the non-Italian immigrants remains the same: Even those who had not gained enough education to be able to sign

Table 10.16. *Percentage of illiterate brides with bourgeois grooms, by father's occupation, bride's birthplace, and groom's birthplace*

Groom's birthplace	Bride's father's occupation					No. cases
	Bourgeois	Worker	Agriculture	Miscellaneous	Total	
1821–2						
Native brides:						
Natives	17	5	6	0[a]	5	333
Non-Italian immigrants	29[b]	11	20[b]	0[a]	15	109
Non-Italian immigrant brides:						
Natives	25[a]	13	15	0[a]	14	84
Non-Italian immigrants	25[a]	13	15	0[a]	15	102
1846–51						
Native brides:						
Natives	16	2	7	4	4	323
Non-Italian immigrants	13[b]	10	15	10	11	165
Non-Italian immigrant brides:						
Natives	15	10	11	17[b]	11	185
Non-Italian immigrants	30	19	17	25	20	473
1869						
Native brides:						
Natives	25[a]	8	0[a]	0[a]	7	68
Non-Italian immigrants	60[a]	15	0[a]	0[a]	17	46
Non-Italian immigrant brides:						
Natives	38[a]	15	26	0[b]	20	80
Non-Italian immigrants	64[b]	24	27	17	27	274

[a]Based on fewer than 10 cases.   [b]Based on between 10 and 19 cases.

Table 10.17. *Percentage of literate brides with bourgeois grooms, by father's occupation, bride's birthplace, and groom's birthplace*

Groom's birthplace	Bride's father's occupation					No. cases
	Bourgeois	Worker	Agriculture	Miscellaneous	Total	
1821–2						
Native brides:						
Natives	69	30	0[a]	50[a]	47	190
Non-Italian immigrants	81	26	75[a]	0[a]	56	117
Non-Italian immigrant brides:						
Natives	74	53	0[a]	50[a]	57	42
Non-Italian immigrants	81	31	80[a]	50[a]	64	56
1846–51						
Native brides:						
Natives	68	22	0[a]	33[b]	44	335
Non-Italian immigrants	66	29	0[a]	58[b]	49	125
Non-Italian immigrant brides:						
Natives	63	38	33[b]	50[a]	49	132
Non-Italian immigrants	68	33	30	55	46	313
1869						
Native brides:						
Natives	65	24	67[a]	50[a]	40	223
Non-Italian immigrants	82	36	0[a]	55[b]	53	216
Non-Italian immigrant brides:						
Natives	63	35	37	30[b]	46	148
Non-Italian immigrants	62	36	37	28	42	487

[a]Based on fewer than 10 cases.   [b]Based on between 10 and 19 cases.

Table 10.18. *Brides' occupational distribution (in percent)*

	1846–51	1869
Not employed	25.5	23.4
Rentière	2.1	0.6
Business and professional	0.7	0.8
Small business	6.5	6.5
Craft	43.2	41.1
Domestic service	11.0	22.0
Unskilled	9.8	5.1
Miscellaneous	1.1	0.9
Number of cases	2,573	1,769

their names showed remarkable resourcefulness and persistent ambition. Like their male counterparts, non-Italian immigrant women had what it took to get ahead in the city.

Women's occupations and mobility

Although the occupation of a woman's husband or father was the chief determinant of her status in nineteenth-century Marseille, her own occupation also played a contributing role. This role might be of two different kinds. First, the woman's work was a significant source of income and of social prestige or social dishonor in its own right. Second, a woman's occupation had an influence on her chances in the marriage market, either by bringing her into contact with particular categories of men or by making her more or less financially attractive as a partner in the crucial economic venture of starting a family. Women's occupations are not given on the marriage registers of 1821 and 1822, but the women's occupational data on the marriage registers of 1846–51 and 1869 can be used to determine the role of women's occupations in their mobility experience in these later periods.

As can be seen in Table 10.18, women's employment was concentrated overwhelmingly in manual occupations. Only 19 brides in 1846–51 and 15 in 1869, fewer than 1 percent in either year, were employed in business or professional occupations. Most of these were schoolteachers, piano teachers, actresses, nurses, or midwives, and a few were *négociantes* – merchants. Another 2.1 percent in 1846–51 and .6 percent in 1869 were *rentières*. Holders of these "elite" positions composed fewer than 3 percent of the brides in 1846–51 and fewer than 2 percent in 1869. Another 6.5 percent in both 1846–51 and 1869 were small businesswomen – generally shopkeepers or keepers of market stalls. The majority of employed women were in skilled crafts. By

Table 10.19. *Percentage literate by bride's occupation*

	1846–51	1869
Not employed	75	92
Rentière	91	90
Business and professional	95	93
Small business	36	57
Craft	39	68
Domestic service	16	49
Unskilled	7	27
Miscellaneous	18	44
Total	43	67

far the largest number of these were either needle workers or laundresses.[5] Craft workers composed 46.1 percent of all brides in 1846–51 and 44.2 percent in 1869. The other important categories of workers were domestic servants, who accounted for 11 percent in 1846–51 but rose to 22 percent in 1869, and unskilled workers, who accounted for 9.8 percent in 1846–51 but sank to 5.1 percent in 1869. Finally, about a quarter of the brides did not engage in paid employment at all: 25.5 percent in 1846–51 and 23.4 percent in 1869.

One rough estimate of the relative status of these different women's occupations is the proportion of their practitioners who were literate (see Table 10.19). This measurement makes it clear that, with rare exceptions, it was low status for a woman to be employed at all. In 1846–51, only the rentière and business and professional categories, which were over 90 percent literate, had literacy rates over one-half. The small businesswomen, with 36 percent literate, and craft workers, with 39 percent, were both slightly below the citywide average of 43 percent. Even lower were domestic servants, with 16 percent literate, and unskilled workers, with only 7 percent. The nonemployed women, on the other hand, signed their marriage registers in three-fourths of the cases. In 1869, the literacy rates of all categories except *rentière* and business and professional had risen sharply. The overall rate of two-thirds literate was matched by craft workers, but only 57 percent of small businesswomen could sign their marriage registers. About half the domestic servants were now literate, as were about a quarter of unskilled workers. But once again the nonemployed women had a very high literacy rate of 92 percent.

A similar ranking of women's occupations also emerges from an examination of the occupational backgrounds from which their members were recruited (see Table 10.20). In 1846–51, no category of employed women drew as much as half its members from bourgeois occupational backgrounds. The highest proportion was among businesswomen and professionals, of whom 42 percent were daughters of bourgeois. The proportion from bourgeois back-

Table 10.20. *Recruitment into women's occupations (in percent)*

Bride's father's occupation	Bride's occupation								
	Not employed	Rentière	Business and professional	Small business	Craft	Domestic service	Un-skilled	Miscel-laneous	Total
1846–51									
Bourgeois	50	64	42	21	16	7	4	0	25
Worker	36	27	42	51	61	24	51	22	47
Agriculture	9	5	0	19	16	58	35	68	21
Miscellaneous	4	4	16	8	7	10	9	11	7
Total	99	100	100	99	100	99	99	101	99
Number of cases	657	55	19	168	1,111	252	83	28	2,573
1869									
Bourgeois	57	50	53	16	14	5	4	0	22
Worker	30	30	20	57	61	32	57	11	46
Agriculture	10	20	13	20	20	51	22	89	25
Miscellaneous	3	0	13	7	5	11	17	0	7
Total	100	100	99	100	100	99	100	100	100
Number of cases	414	10	15	115	727	389	90	9	1,769

grounds then sank sharply to 21 percent among small businesswomen, 16 percent among craft workers, 7 percent among domestic servants, and 4 percent among unskilled workers. In all categories, except businesswomen and professionals, the majority came from working-class and agricultural backgrounds. Craft workers were recruited especially from working-class families and domestic servants especially from peasant families. A majority of the women who did not work, whether designated as *rentières* or as not employed, came from bourgeois backgrounds. But even among them, a substantial proportion (36 percent of the not employed and 27 percent of the rentières) came from working-class backgrounds as well. The same patterns continued, most of them accentuated, in 1869. In fact, the percentage drawn from bourgeois backgrounds declined or remained unchanged for all categories of employed women except businesswomen and professionals. The crafts continued to be dominated by women from working-class backgrounds, but the backgrounds of domestic servants were now less dominated by agriculture. If working women had become more plebian in background in 1869 than in 1846–51, nonworking women had become more bourgeois: Fifty-seven percent were now from bourgeois backgrounds, and only 30 percent had origins in the working class.

The five main categories of women's occupations, then, had a fairly clear status ordering. Businesswomen and professionals were at the top, far above all other categories of employed women. The second rank was shared by small businesswomen and craft workers, with the former slightly more likely to be from bourgeois backgrounds and the latter slightly more likely to be literate. Domestic servants were next, and unskilled workers brought up the rear. The top category was tiny and not very exalted; it recruited many of its members from nonbourgeois backgrounds, and, by comparison with males, female professionals were despised and ill paid. Nevertheless, the few women who held such occupations at least had a presumptive claim to bourgeois status in their own right. The same could hardly be said for the small businesswomen. Unlike males in the small-business category, small businesswomen were indistinguishable in status from manual workers. Most were from working-class backgrounds, and many were illiterate; most probably had no shops, and they either sold fruits and vegetables from market stalls or hawked their wares in the streets. The overwhelming majority of employed women were in craft occupations, where they were generally paid only half to two-thirds the wages earned by comparably skilled men, or in domestic service, where they lived as dependents in the homes of the wealthy. The bottom of the hierarchy was made up of unskilled workers, but this category had shrunk considerably by the end of the 1860s. By comparison with men's work, women's work had only a truncated status hierarchy. The highest status for a woman was to be outside the paid labor force entirely, managing a household, commanding the servants, and perhaps engaging in some volunteer charitable activities.[6] As an avenue of social mobility, women's work was extremely limited.

Tables 10.21 and 10.22 show the distributions of women's occupations among brides from different occupational backgrounds in 1846–51 and 1869. The tables contain few surprises. At both times, about nine-tenths of the daughters of businessmen and professionals were without paid occupations, that is, were either "without employment" or *rentières*. Among rentiers' daughters, the proportion who did not work was about three-fifths in 1846–51, and it rose to about four-fifths in 1869. About half the daughters of clerical employees and small businessmen were employed in both years, most of them in crafts. About three-quarters of artisans' daughters engaged in paid labor, as did some nine-tenths of the daughters of unskilled workers, maritime workers, and peasants. Crafts were the largest category of employment for brides from all categories of working-class and peasant backgrounds. In both 1846–51 and 1869, small business was the destination of between 5 and 10 percent of women from all subbourgeois backgrounds, except daughters of maritime workers in 1846–51, whose rate of entry was a little higher. A comparable proportion of small businessmen's daughters also entered small business in both periods. Unskilled work was quite common among daughters of unskilled workers, somewhat less common among peasants' and maritime workers' daughters, and rare among artisans' daughters. Peasants' daughters were far more likely to become domestic servants than were women from any other background.

In the long run, a woman's occupation probably had its most important impact on her status through its effect on her chances in the marriage market. Some of these effects can be seen in Table 10.23. Because the cell totals would otherwise get so small as to produce unreliable figures, the bride's father's occupations in these tables are broken down into only four categories – bourgeois, worker, peasant, and miscellaneous. This table makes it clear that women who were not gainfully employed, together with the handful of businesswomen and professionals, were consistently able to make the most advantageous marriages. In both 1846–51 and 1869, and within each of the categories of occupational backgrounds, these women were more likely to marry bourgeois husbands than any others. Moreover, their advantage increased considerably between 1846–51 and 1869. Among women who did work, only the businesswomen and professionals had rates more or less equal to unemployed women. In both 1846–51 and 1869, small businesswomen from bourgeois and working-class backgrounds had a somewhat higher rate of bourgeois marriages than craft workers. Among daughters of peasants, however, the small-business and craft rates were virtually identical. Far more surprising than the relatively strong showing of small businesswomen were the successes of domestic servants. Domestic servants, it will be remembered, had literacy rates considerably below those of craft workers and small busi-

Table 10.21. *Bride's occupation by father's occupation, 1846–51 (in percent)*

Bride's occupation	Father's occupation										
	Business and professional	Rentier	Sales and clerical	Small business	Artisan	Service	Unskilled	Maritime	Agriculture	Miscellaneous	Total
Not employed	78	47	36	50	24	36	9	10	11	16	26
Rentière	10	11	0	3	2	0	0	0	1	1	2
Business and professional	0	1	2	1	1	6	0	0	0	2	1
Small business	1	4	8	9	6	8	6	13	6	8	7
Craft	11	29	49	31	57	34	53	58	32	42	43
Domestic service	0	6	2	4	5	11	8	3	31	16	11
Unskilled	1	2	2	2	6	0	24	15	16	12	10
Miscellaneous	0	0	0	0	0	0	0	1	4	2	1
Number of cases	146	142	120	214	807	36	249	137	539	183	2,573

Table 10.22. *Bride's occupation by father's occupation, 1869 (in percent)*

	Father's occupation										
Bride's occupation	Business and professional	Rentier	Sales and clerical	Small business	Artisan	Service	Unskilled	Maritime	Agriculture	Miscellaneous	Total
Not employed	90	75	43	44	20	22	4	11	9	12	23
Rentière	0	4	0	2	1	0	0	0	0	0	1
Business and professional	2	4	1	2	1	0	0	0	0	2	1
Small business	1	8	4	6	8	6	8	9	5	7	6
Craft	5	8	45	35	54	55	51	65	31	31	41
Domestic service	1	3	7	9	13	11	23	9	45	36	22
Unskilled	1	0	1	2	3	0	14	6	4	13	5
Miscellaneous	0	0	0	0	0	6	0	0	2	0	1
Number of cases	87	79	105	119	513	18	230	54	446	118	1,769

Table 10.23. *Percentage of brides marrying bourgeois grooms, by bride's occupation and father's occupation*

Bride's occupation	1846–51, father's occupation					1869, father's occupation				
	Bourgeois	Worker	Peasant	Miscellaneous	Total	Bourgeois	Worker	Peasant	Miscellaneous	Total
Not employed	73	35	32	55	55	84	60	62	57	74
Rentière	89	80[b]	33[a]	100[a]	84	40[a]	67[a]	50[a]	—	50[b]
Business and professional	62[a]	38[a]	—	67[a]	53[b]	75[a]	60[a]	—	50[a]	67[b]
Small business	39	16	14	14[a]	22	33[b]	26	22	0[a]	25
Craft	29	11	13	19	15	29	19	23	14	21
Domestic service	23	17	18	24	19	29	17	27	26	24
Unskilled	18[b]	2[a]	7	5	4	25[a]	8	5	0[b]	7
Miscellaneous	—	0[a]	0	0[a]	0	—	0	25	—	11
Number of cases	622	1,229	539	183	2,573	390	815	446	118	1,769

[a] Based on fewer than 10 cases.   [b] Based on between 10 and 19 cases.

306

nesswomen. Yet in 1846–51, workers' daughters and peasants' daughters who were employed in domestic service had rates of mobility into the bourgeoisie of 17 and 18 percent, considerably higher than the 11 and 13 percent rates of women from similar backgrounds who had gone into craft occupations, and even above the 16 and 14 percent rates of workers' and peasants' daughters in small business. In 1869, the domestic servants no longer had any consistent advantage. Among peasants' daughters, they still had the highest rates: 27 percent, as against 22 percent for small business-women and 23 percent for craft workers. Among workers' daughters, small businesswomen did best, marrying bourgeois husbands in 26 percent of the cases. Craft workers from working-class backgrounds had a rate of 19 percent, and domestic servants a rate of 17 percent. Still, even these essentially equal rates were an impressive showing for a group with a considerably lower literacy rate than the craft workers or small businesswomen. Clearly, domestic service gave workers' and peasants' daughters some kind of edge in Marseille's marriage market.

Why should this have been so? One possibility is that the surprisingly high rates achieved by domestic servants were due to the fact that virtually all of them were immigrants, whereas many of the craft workers were natives of the city. Because non-Italian immigrant women had consistently higher upward-mobility rates than natives, this factor could conceivably explain the domestic servants' advantage. The occupational distributions of immigrant and native women are given in Table 10.24. Domestic servants accounted for 21.1 percent of non-Italian immigrant brides in 1846–51 and 29.5 percent in 1869. Among natives, domestic servants were only a paltry .9 percent in 1846–51. Although domestic service was a much more important form of employment for native women in 1869, it still accounted for only 7.4 percent of the brides, about a quarter of the proportion among non-Italian immigrants. Among Italian immigrants, only 10.7 percent were domestics in 1846–51, but their 1869 rate of 26.1 percent was only a little below that of the non-Italian immigrants. These were not the only significant differences between women of different birthplaces. Nonemployed women were about twice as common among natives as among non-Italian immigrants and about twice as common among non-Italian immigrants as among Italians. Business and professional positions were considerably more common among non-Italian immigrants than among others, and unskilled laborers, not surprisingly, were particularly common among Italians.

Table 10.25 demonstrates that the good overall showing of domestic servants was partly a consequence of the domination of domestic service by non-Italian immigrants. In 1846–51, none of the native-born or Italian domestic servants married a bourgeois, but 21 percent of non-Italian immigrant domestic servants did so. In 1869, no Italian-born domestic married a bourgeois, and only 14 percent of native-born domestics did so; by contrast, the rate of non-

Table 10.24. *Brides' occupational distribution, by birthplace (in percent)*

Bride's occupation	1846–51			1869		
	Natives	Non-Italian immigrants	Italian immigrants	Natives	Non-Italian immigrants	Italian immigrants
Not employed	35.3	19.2	11.1	36.4	17.8	8.1
Rentière	2.2	2.4	0.0	0.3	0.6	1.8
Business and professional	0.6	0.9	0.4	0.5	1.1	0.0
Small business	8.2	5.7	3.3	8.6	5.0	9.9
Craft	46.1	42.5	33.6	42.4	40.7	37.8
Domestic service	0.9	20.1	10.7	7.4	29.5	26.1
Unskilled	5.5	8.2	37.3	3.9	4.6	16.2
Miscellaneous	1.2	0.5	3.6	0.3	0.6	0.0
Number of cases	1,126	1,200	244	591	1,066	111

Table 10.25. *Percentage of small businesswomen, craft workers, and domestic servants with bourgeois grooms, by father's occupation and bride's birthplace*

Bride's occupation	Father's occupation				
	Bourgeois	Worker	Peasant	Miscellaneous	Total
1846–51					
Native brides:					
Small business	53[b]	11	0[a]	17[a]	18
Craft	29	7	12	14	11
Domestic service	—	0[a]	25[a]	0[a]	10[b]
Non-Italian immi-					
grant brides:					
Small business	28[b]	32[b]	23	50[a]	29
Craft	27	17	13	19	18
Domestic service	25	20	20	28	21
Italian immigrant					
brides:					
Small business	0[a]	0[a]	0[a]	—	0[a]
Craft	44[b]	11	15[b]	50[a]	18
Domestic service	0[a]	0[a]	0[b]	—	0
1869					
Native brides:					
Small business	57[a]	30	0[a]	0[a]	31
Craft	19	15	0[b]	33[a]	16
Domestic service	67[a]	6	—	33[a]	14
Non-Italian immi-					
grant brides:					
Small business	18[b]	32[b]	22[b]	0[a]	23
Craft	35	22	26	11	25
Domestic service	22[b]	26	29	27	28
Italian immigrant					
brides:					
Small business	—	0[a]	33[a]	0[a]	9[b]
Craft	50[a]	11	33[a]	0[a]	17
Domestic service	—	0[b]	0[b]	0[a]	0

[a] Based on fewer than 10 cases.   [b] Based on between 10 and 19 cases.

Italian immigrant domestics was 29 percent. Non-Italian immigrant women, in short, were almost totally responsible for the overall success of domestic servants. But Table 10.25 also demonstrates that the case of non-Italian immigrant domestic servants was quite extraordinary. In 1846–51, their rates of bourgeois marriage were not only superior to those of other domestic servants: They were at least as good as those of non-Italian immigrant craft workers and not much inferior to those of non-Italian immigrant small businesswomen. Moreover, they were substantially better than the rates achieved by native-born craft workers and no worse than those of native-born small businesswomen. This was an impressive achievement at a time when only 17 percent of non-Italian immigrant domestic servants were literate, as against 42 percent of craft workers and 43 percent of small businesswomen from non-Italian immigrant origins, and as against 36 percent of craft workers and 34 percent of small businesswomen among natives. In 1869, non-Italian immigrant domestic servants surpassed not only other domestic servants but also both native and non-Italian immigrant craft workers and non-Italian immigrant small businesswomen. Only native small businesswomen had a better record. The literacy rate of non-Italian immigrant domestics had risen to 50 percent in 1869, but it was still below the rates of other groups: 53 percent for non-Italian immigrant small businesswomen, 67 percent for native small businesswomen, 68 percent for non-Italian immigrant craft workers, and 71 percent for native craft workers.

No other group of women in Marseille did so much with so little as the non-Italian immigrant domestic servants. Mostly illiterate, from humble backgrounds, they nevertheless married into the bourgeoisie with astonishing frequency. How and why they did so is far from certain, but three lines of explanation suggest themselves. First, it is probable that domestic service gave women a better opportunity to save money and accumulate a dowry than did working in craft occupations. Although domestic servants' wages may have been lower than the wages of craft workers, their expenses were very much lower. Whereas craft workers had to pay for food and lodging, domestic servants were provided with room and board. If they were frugal, they could save nearly the whole of their earnings. Second, employment in the households of bourgeois families, usually in neighborhoods where a high proportion of the inhabitants were bourgeois, may have given domestic servants more opportunities to meet men from bourgeois backgrounds than was true of their sisters who worked in craft occupations and usually lived in working-class neighborhoods. Third, domestic service did much to teach a rural or working-class girl bourgeois notions of respectability and the practical means of managing a bourgeois household. Petit bourgeois men may have preferred even illiterate women who had learned the workings of a bourgeois household in intimate detail to literate working women who had not acquired the necessary domestic refinements.[7] Determining which of these posited explanations is true, or if the real explanation lies in some other factor or factors, would require further research of a different kind than that on which this study is based. But whatever the explanation, the fact stands: The best way for a poor peasant's or worker's daughter to improve her chances of making a bourgeois marriage was to take a position in domestic service.

Women's and men's mobility

What were the major features of the mobility patterns of Marseille's women? And how did women's patterns differ from men's? The most important difference was that the women's labor market afforded few opportunities for social mobility. In sharp contrast to the men's labor market, where there were relatively abundant opportunities to enter occupations over the whole range of the occupational hierarchy – from bankers to bootblacks – the women's occupational hierarchy was severely truncated. Women's occupations were concentrated in relatively low-paying and low-prestige manual work. Fewer than one bride in twenty was employed in a bourgeois occupation, and even these rare female shopkeepers or professionals were often underpaid or illiterate – hardly secure in their possession of bourgeois status. Given the truncated character of the women's occupational hierarchy, women's status, and therefore women's social mobility, was determined above all in the marriage market rather than in the labor market. It was her husband's occupation, not her own, that was the chief determinant of a woman's life chances and of her standing in society.

Women's opportunities in the marriage market were shaped by the same broad economic and demographic forces that shaped men's opportunities in the labor market. The fact that a rising proportion of the population was recruited from the peasantry meant that there was a growing gap between the number of bourgeois positions available and the number of men and women from bourgeois backgrounds who were available to fill them. Partly as a result of this growing imbalance, rates of upward mobility from peasant and working-class backgrounds into the bourgeoisie increased markedly between 1821–2 and 1869, reaching quite impressive levels by the latter year. As was true for men's mobility, much of the rise in women's upward-mobility rates over time was the result of fundamental, long-term changes in economic and demographic structures.

Although men's and women's mobility were subject to the same overall economic and demographic forces and responded in broadly similar ways, there were also two important differences between men's and women's patterns. First, women's mobility rates were consistently higher than men's, both upward and downward and both between and within bourgeois and working-class categories. Although the reasons for this difference are not entirely clear, family background consistently placed tighter constraints on a man looking for an occupation than on a woman looking for a husband. Second, literacy, although a very important determinant of mobility patterns for both sexes, had a much more powerful effect among men than among women. For men, literacy was a fundamental qualification for bourgeois status. To practice a male bourgeois occupation virtually required the ability to read and write. For women, literacy was an advantage but not a requirement: To be a wife and mother in a bourgeois family did not necessitate reading and writing. It was actually possible for the upward-mobility rates of illiterate women to increase during the course of the century. Among women, the link between literacy and social mobility was contingent, not absolute.

Migration, finally, was as powerful a determinant of women's social-mobility patterns as it was of men's. Immigrants took much greater advantage of opportunities for social mobility than did natives of Marseille. Both male and female Italian-born immigrants, it is true, had dismal mobility experiences. Their poor qualifications, together with the open prejudice they faced in Marseille, meant that their downward-mobility rates were high and their upward-mobility rates low. But the much more numerous non-Italian immigrants, especially those from working-class and peasant backgrounds, were remarkably successful. Among men, this success was largely a consequence of the selective character of migration. The young men who came from the countryside to work in Marseille had managed to obtain at least a rudimentary education in small towns and villages where it was not easy to do so – and where the compatriots they left behind very often had not. There is every reason to believe that they were a particularly ambitious and able lot. Arriving in the city, less constrained by parental wishes and community expectations than the native Marseillais, they recognized and seized the opportunities that the city had to offer.

On the surface, female immigration seems to have been less selective. The young women who came to Marseille were very often illiterate and would appear to have been no better educated than the women they left behind in their natal villages. Yet they seem to have been at least as ambitious and capable as their male counterparts. The mobility rates of non-Italian immigrant women were consistently more favorable than those of native women. No less than male immigrants, female immigrants identified and seized the opportunities available to them in the city. Even the illiterates among them had a remarkable knack for finding bourgeois husbands. Partly by taking advantage of the possibilities offered by domestic service and partly by marrying successful fellow immigrants, illiterate immigrant women from the small towns and villages of rural France achieved remarkable successes in the city. They, even more than the upwardly mobile peasants' sons whom they frequently married, epitomize the indomitable determination and enterprising spirit of Marseille's nineteenth-century immigrants.

11 Conclusion: Transformation from without

This study has attempted to document several important transformations in the social life of Marseille during the half-century from 1820 to 1870 – in economy, in occupational structure, in the size, composition, and location of the population, in migration patterns, and in social mobility. The exposition has centered on changes taking place in Marseille itself and has said little about how local changes were related to larger changes in French or European society. But any attempt to explain the overall pattern of change makes clear the fundamental importance of Marseille's relations to extra-Marseillais society. Most of the changes that took place in Marseille were not internally generated; they arose from the city's complex relations to a national state and society, and to regional, national, and international markets. Marseille was an important city and was a major beneficiary of the French and international capitalist development of the mid–nineteenth century. But it was not a prime mover in the events of the era. The major innovations came from without, not from within.

This was clear in the case of economic development. Entrepreneurs from Marseille certainly participated actively in the great capitalist boom of the nineteenth century. The merchant community was ready to take advantage of rising international trade and of shifting French demand for foreign goods, particularly industrial raw materials. Moreover, most of Marseille's industrial development was based on local capital. Up to 1850, the commanding heights of the local economy were still occupied by Marseillais – a large number of wealthy merchants, some of whom doubled as bankers, and a growing number of industrialists. The center of their activities was the city's venerable chamber of commerce, which was consulted assiduously by government officials on all matters touching the local economy. But during the 1850s and 1860s, the local capitalist elite was eclipsed by a whole series of joint-stock companies centered in Paris. These companies launched the great ventures that transformed the city's economic life during the Second Empire: the railroad, the steamship companies, the joint-stock banks, the new port facilities, the rue Impériale, and the construction of commercial quarters near the new port. The merchant community still controlled the chamber of commerce, but the most important economic and financial decisions were now made in Paris, effectively beyond the chamber's reach. Until the middle of the nineteenth century, Marseille was a more or less autonomous center of economic initi-

313

ative. By 1870 it was becoming a satellite in an increasingly unified national economy dominated by Parisian capital.

Political changes also came chiefly from Paris. In this case the domination of Paris over the provinces had been firmly established since the French Revolution. Between 1815 and 1871, Marseille endured five changes of political regime, with varying mixtures of enthusiasm, resistance, and resignation. Except for the Restoration of the Bourbons in 1815, which resulted from Napoleon's defeat at Waterloo, all the regime changes were imposed by events in Paris. Their effects in Marseille were sometimes powerful. The Restoration led to local episodes of "White Terror," which did much to consolidate the hold of royalism in Marseille. The July Revolution of 1830 was greeted with little enthusiasm but little resistance; life went on more or less as before. The February Revolution of 1848 had a much greater impact. Before 1848 Marseille's working class was generally politically quiescent and had a reputation for royalism. But the Revolution provoked an immense political mobilization and a massive swing to the left. The Napoleonic coup d'etat of 1851 repressed working-class agitation but could not reverse the direction of Marseille's political evolution. Marseille was a major center of republicanism during the last years of the Second Empire, and there was an uprising in concert with the Paris Commune in 1871. As in other cities of France, the rhythm of political life in Marseille was determined by national, above all Parisian, events.[1]

The increasing subordination of French political and economic life to national and Parisian affairs is well known. What is less understood is how local societies responded to changes imposed or inaugurated from without. In Marseille, and probably in most provincial cities, some people and groups resisted change, clinging to provincial or traditional values and attitudes, whereas others embraced change wholeheartedly. In Marseille, the response to change seems to have been systematically different among natives of the city than among immigrants. Natives, in general, resisted change, whereas immigrants, on the whole, accepted, explored, and exploited the opportunities that change offered. This is quite clear in the case of social mobility, where immigrants were more responsive to opportunities for upward mobility. Natives usually confined their search to familiar jobs and social categories, remaining within the same social world as their parents. Immigrants explored the entire horizon and took special advantage of expanding opportunities in clerical occupations.

This difference between natives and immigrants was not confined to occupational mobility. When the Revolution of 1848 opened up a new world of radical democratic politics, it was the immigrants, once again, who responded most enthusiastically. Analysis of police records of participation in the radical movements shows that French-born immigrants were three times as likely to get involved in revolutionary politics as men born in Marseille.[2]

Natives either were unresponsive to the democrats' calls or clung to the traditional royalism of Marseille's popular classes; immigrants embraced the revolution. This same propensity to embrace radical ideology can also be seen in religious behavior, where immigrants were quicker than natives to abandon devout religious practice during the "dechristianization" that set in during the decades following the Revolution of 1848.[3]

How can these differences between Marseille's natives and immigrants be explained? Two complementary explanations suggest themselves. First, natives of the city grew up as part of a local culture, with distinct values, traditions, beliefs, and social practices. They were part of dense and extended networks of kin and friends who shared their assumptions and outlook and whose patterns of sociability, if we are to believe contemporary observers, kept strangers at arm's length.[4] Among the popular classes – workers, artisans, sailors, even shopkeepers – this exclusive and inward-looking pattern of social life was reinforced by a fierce religiosity, especially among women, and by the predominance of the local dialect. Marseille's dialect was quite different from other dialects of Provençal and was utterly incomprehensible to native French speakers, or to speakers of non-Provençal dialects. Until the 1840s or 1850s, when it was gradually displaced by French, this dialect was the common speech of the native population, helping to seal it off both from the French-language national culture and from French-speaking immigrants who settled in Marseille.[5]

Although many immigrants to Marseille eventually assimilated themselves to the local culture by marrying into Marseillais families and mastering the local dialect, their situation inclined them to a more national or cosmopolitan culture. Although many of them had grown up speaking dialects as obscure as that of Marseille, they usually had few compatriots in Marseille to speak with. For them, the primary language of public intercourse was French – the one language they had in common with virtually everyone in the city. Shut out of the inward-looking social life of the native Marseillais, they were far more likely to pick up the values and the outlook of the wider national society that was growing up around them in Marseille and all over France. Their less constricted social networks and their linguistic orientation made them more responsive than natives to changes in the world around them.

At the same time, the discontinuity of experience that resulted from migration may have had an effect on the psychic makeup of immigrants. By displacing people from one community to another, migration made them aware that notions they had accepted as indubitable and practices they had considered essential were in fact merely local prejudices or customs. Migration introduced a certain sense of detachment both from the sending community and from the receiving community. Their values and personalities were less fixed than those of natives; their physical mobility induced a sort of psychic or mental mobility as well. This made them more willing to accept innovative views of politics, religion, and society – and also, it would appear, to make them more susceptible to the temptations of crime. This view of the effect of migration has a precedent in the writings of Robert E. Park, the American sociologist whose work did so much to popularize the "uprooting" view of migration. In his seminal essay on "Human Migration and the Marginal Man," Park emphasized not just the demoralizing potential of migration, but also the role of immigrants in social and intellectual innovations of all sorts. The effect of migration, he said,

is to emancipate the individual man. Energies that were formerly controlled by custom and tradition are released.... The emancipated individual invariably becomes, in a certain sense, a cosmopolitan. He learns to look upon the world in which he was born and bred with something of the detachment of a stranger. He acquires, in short, an intellectual bias.[6]

Park's observations are placed in the context of a notion of the "Grand Progress of Civilization" that makes them unpalatable to the modern reader. But the essential insight about the psychic and intellectual mobility of immigrants certainly fits with the experience of nineteenth-century Marseille.

If there were important psychic and social differences between natives and immigrants, then changes in the character of Marseille's social life, and perhaps that of other nineteenth-century cities, were imposed from without in a sense quite different from the familiar story of state centralization and capitalist market expansion. New values, new modes of behavior, new political movements, declining local particularism – all these urban social changes were enhanced by the great influx of migration that fueled population growth. Nineteenth-century Marseille became a modern city with a strong orientation to national affairs largely as a result of an influx of more modern and more nationally recruited men and women. Population mobility did more than simply increase the number and diversify the geographical origins of the people who lived in Marseille. It also changed the character of Marseille's social life.

Appendix A: Marriage registers and *listes nominatives* as sources of data on the occupational structure

The marriage registers

Registers of *actes de marriage* are preserved as part of the civil registry (*état civil*) in the departmental archives of the Bouches-du-Rhône and are essentially complete. These documents recorded the occupations of all the men who married in Marseille, and, after the 1820s, also recorded the occupations of their brides. They can therefore be used to describe the city's occupational structure. The main problem with the marriage registers is that they provide information on only a select portion of the population, albeit a relatively large and representative one: the men and women who got married in any given year. This portion of the population differed in certain important respects from the population at large, with the consequence that occupational distributions obtained from marriage registers will be imperfect reflections of the actual distribution. Most of the differences between the persons marrying in a given year and the population at large are rather obvious:

1. Persons who never married escaped from the marriage registers altogether. Because rates of celibacy differed from one group of the population to another, this will introduce biases, but biases that are generally rather small. The extreme example is the Catholic clergy, which, being celibate by definition, does not appear at all in the marriage registers.

2. The marriage registers provide information chiefly on young adults, not on all age grades of the population. The age at first marriage varied from 28.8 years in 1821–2 to 30.2 years in 1869 for grooms and was virtually constant at about 26 years for brides. In addition to previously unmarried persons, there was also a sizable number of widows and widowers embarking on second marriages, who were generally older. When these are taken into account, mean ages at marriage were between 30.9 and 32.1 for grooms and between 26.7 and 27.5 for brides (see Table A.1). The range of ages represented is in fact very broad, stretching from 15 to over 80 for women and from 18 to over 80 for men in each of the years analyzed. But the heavy concentration of ages was between 17 and about 35 for brides and between 21 and about 40 for grooms. The marriage registers, in short, give a portrait primarily of the young-adult population.

3. Persons who lived in Marseille but married elsewhere were also missed

Table A.1. *Mean age at marriage*

	1821–2		1851		1869	
	No. of cases	Mean age	No. of cases	Mean age	No. of cases	Mean age
First marriage						
Grooms	1,460	28.8	1,416	29.6	1,851	30.2
Brides	1,641	26.0	1,551	26.1	2,013	26.0
Subsequent marriages						
Grooms	217	45.5	236	42.6	307	43.8
Brides	114	42.2	158	37.9	216	41.0
All marriages						
Grooms	1,677	30.9	1,652	31.4	2,158	32.1
Brides	1,775	26.7	1,709	27.2	2,229	27.5

by Marseille's marriage registers. These would include several distinct types of cases. (a) It was customary for weddings to be celebrated in the bride's place of residence, so men who lived in Marseille but married women from elsewhere are missing from the marriage registers. Of the weddings performed in Marseille, some 5 percent in 1821–2 and 1869, and 4 percent in 1846–51, united men residing outside the Commune with women from the city.[1] It seems likely that a roughly similar proportion of men from Marseille married women from outside the city and were thereby missed by the marriage registers. (b) Some men and women who migrated to Marseille and settled there must have married before migrating. Although married persons are generally less prone to migrate than unmarried persons, a certain number of immigrants to Marseille will nevertheless be missed for this reason. (c) Persons who lived and worked in Marseille for varying periods of time but married elsewhere will also be missed. Most of these, one expects, were young men and women who passed through Marseille to work for several months or a few years before either returning to their natal towns or villages or moving on to work and perhaps eventually to marry and settle down in another city. (d) A certain number of persons who married and settled elsewhere, in this case usually men from the countryside of southeastern France, migrated to Marseille to work for a few months a year to supplement inadequate agricultural earnings. They might be peasants from the Alpine region forced to seek employment in the temperate lowlands by the long and harsh mountain winters[2] or agricultural laborers from the valleys and lowlands lured to Marseille by high wages during periods of particularly intense demand for unskilled labor in the building or transportation industries. These seasonal migrations probably brought a large number of men to the city for some portion of the year, and all of them were missed by the marriage registers.

In short, the marriage registers certainly overrepresent young adults, and they miss a sizable proportion of immigrants of various types. However, they constitute a good sample[3] of a broad and highly significant portion of the community: the settled young-adult population. Data drawn from the marriage registers should therefore be adequate to indicate changes in the occupational structure over time: with considerable precision for the settled young-adult population, but less precisely for the adult population at large.

The *listes nominatives*

These *listes nominatives* are census registers, compiled street by street and household by household, with an entry for each individual counted by the census takers. In principle, these documents are the most comprehensive and accurate sources of information on the population as a whole and should therefore be the prime data source for a study of changing occupational structure. In practice, however, Marseille's *listes nominatives* are of rather doubtful value. To begin with, French censuses taken before 1851 included no systematic information on the respondent's occupation and are therefore worthless for a study of occupational structure. For the period following 1851, the problem is incompleteness of the registers. The *listes* of 1851 have been substantially preserved, although with certain significant omissions. However, the *listes* from the censuses of 1866 and 1872, which might have been used to obtain a comparable occupational distribution for the end of the period covered by this study, have survived only in part, rendering them useless for present purposes. The municipal archives of Marseille do have summary occupational tables that were compiled from the *listes* of the census of 1866, but these tables unfortunately contain several evident and important errors and can therefore be used only with a great deal of circumspection. In the end, therefore, only the *listes* of the census of 1851 proved to be really useful for establishing Marseille's occupational distribution.

Because the census of 1851 is a massive survey, with information on nearly 200,000 individuals, the work of recording and coding was reduced to manageable proportions by taking a systematic 10 percent sample of the households appearing on the *listes nominatives*. All the information given on the census forms – name, address, sex, age, marital status, occupation, and nationality – was recorded for each individual in every tenth household in the city. This information was then coded, put into machine-readable form, and analyzed by computer.

The 1851 census figures are more comprehensive than figures drawn from the marriage registers, for the census included not only settled adults of a particular age grade but all persons living in the city at the time the survey was taken. They therefore yield valuable information about children, older adults, and unmarried persons who are missing from the marriage-register data. However, the *listes nominatives* themselves were not entirely accurate. Recent work on nineteenth-century French censuses, most notably that of Etienne Van de Walle, indicates that census compilations were often seriously inaccurate. His deft and ingenious tests in *The Female Population of France in the Nineteenth Century* show numerous errors in reporting and tabulation of age, marital status, and total population of the various departments of France, and there is no reason to assume that Marseille's census was immune to similar errors.[4]

Van de Walle's methods of checking census figures, which rest on comparisons between adjacent censuses, cannot be applied to figures taken from a single year. But there are a few rudimentary tests that might help to discern glaring inaccuracies. The first concerns the total number of persons counted, and it is not reassuring. The official count of Marseille's total population in 1851 was 198,945. A systematic sample of one-tenth of the households in the *listes nominatives* should yield a count very close to one-tenth the official total, assuming that both are based on the same complete listing of the population. In fact, the total in the *listes* sample is 17,788, the number that should have resulted from a total population of 177,880. The difference between these figures is sizable: 21,105, or a shortfall of over 10 percent. Obviously, something is in error: Either there has been some mistake in sampling, recording, or computing; or the official count itself was incorrectly tabulated; or the registers of *listes* in the municipal archives of Marseille are incomplete.

A careful review of sampling, recording, and computing procedures has revealed nothing that could account for so large a shortfall, but there are some indications that the archives' collection of the *listes* may be incomplete. Before the 1851 data were recorded, the streets for which registers existed were systematically checked against the listings of streets in the Marseille city directory for 1851.[5] This checking revealed few and insignificant omissions – a few streets under construction in the suburbs that may in fact have had no resident population at the time the census was compiled and an occasional *impasse* or *cul-de-sac* in the old quarters of the city, whose few inhabitants may plausibly be assumed to have been listed with the population of adjoining streets. If the *listes* were seriously incomplete, it was not because the registers for entire streets were either not compiled or lost.

Other tests of accuracy of the data, however, were much less encouraging. The published results of the census of 1851 include tables giving breakdowns by sex and marital status of the population of Marseille and other French cities.[6] Assuming for the moment the essential accuracy of these tables, we can compare the sizes of these various categories in the official totals for Marseille with the comparable categories from the 10 percent *listes* sample, to determine more precisely where the sample's shortfalls are concentrated.

The most striking shortfall occurs in the category of unmarried males (see Table A.2), where the sample of the *listes* shows only 4,765 cases. Because the sample is 10 percent of the total number of cases on the *listes*, a figure of 4,765 implies that there were about 47,650 unmarried males on the *listes*. (This figure of 47,650 is called the "sample estimate" in the table.) The official census count of unmarried males was much higher – 61,145. Thus the shortfall of the sample estimate is very large, amounting to 13,495 individuals. The sample estimate for unmarried men amounted to only 77.9 percent of the official total. The figures for all other sex and marital-status groups are much more satisfactory, with much smaller shortfalls and sample estimates running at 90 to 95 percent of official totals. The shortfalls for groups other than unmarried males could conceivably have resulted from the destruction or loss of occasional random pages from the registers or from occasional inadvertent skipping of pages in the course of recording information for coding – or from systematic overcounting by census officials when the summary tables were compiled. But the shortfall of unmarried males can hardly be explained by such factors.

How, then, can the large discrepancy between the official total and the sample estimate of unmarried males be explained? The first alternative to examine is the possibility of a major error of tabulation on the part of census officials. Official census tabulations in nineteenth-century France were frequently in error; perhaps the discrepancy found in the Marseille figures is only a particularly gross error of this kind. One way of checking this possibility is to see whether the number of unmarried males reported in Marseille's summary tables is consistent with the proportions of unmarried males reported for other French cities in 1851.[7] In the thirteen French cities with populations over 50,000 in 1851, the mean proportion of unmarried males was 32.6 percent of the total population. The lowest proportion was in Amiens, where unmarried males made up only 25.8 percent of the population; the highest was in the naval port of Brest, where a large number of sailors brought the proportion up to 47.4 percent. The median proportion – the proportion in the city that had the same number of cities with higher proportions as with lower – was 30.4 percent. The proportion reported in the official statistics for Marseille was 30.7 percent, slightly below the mean and almost exactly at the median. If the reported figures are accepted as accurate, Marseille was very close to the average for all French cities. By contrast, the proportion of unmarried males derived from the *listes nominatives* sample (26.7 percent) would place Marseille below every large French city but Amiens. It is possible, of course, that this is where Marseille belonged. But it is certainly more prudent to assume that the published figures are essentially accurate and that the figures derived from the *listes* in fact underreport unmarried males.

Table A.2. *Sex and marital status, census of 1851; official totals and sample estimates*

	Male				Female			
	Unmarried	Married	Widowed	Total	Unmarried	Married	Widowed	Total
Official totals	61,145	35,688	4,076	100,909	52,480	35,438	10,118	98,036
Sample estimate	47,650	33,860	3,650	85,160	49,850	33,610	9,260	92,720
Shortfall of sample estimate	13,495	1,820	426	15,749	2,630	1,828	858	5,316
Sample estimate as per-centage of official total	77.9	94.9	89.5	84.4	95.0	94.8	91.5	94.6

Table A.3. *Sex by age, census of 1851*

	1. Males	2. Females	3. Sex ratio
0–7	1,288	1,339	96
8–12	664	705	94
13–17	561	704	80
18–22	705	913	77
23–7	816	952	86
28–32	909	972	94
33–7	714	684	104
38–42	701	697	101
43–7	533	490	109
48–52	554	549	101
53–7	318	338	94
58–62	231	343	67
63–7	207	206	100
68–72	155	164	95
73–7	79	95	83
Over 78	61	90	68

In what age groups is this underreporting of males concentrated? This can be discerned by examining figures on the sex distributions of different age groups in the *listes* sample (see Table A.3). The figures show females outnumbering males from birth to the early 30s, males and females roughly in balance from the late 20s to the early 50s, and females outnumbering males thereafter.[8] It is normal for females to outnumber males slightly in the 0-to-12 age group, although the inequalities are usually less pronounced than in Marseille's figures. Probably some portion of the difference between males and females in this young age group can be attributed to the common practice of sending boys to school in Aix-en-Provence, the scholarly capital of Marseille's region, where they would not be counted with their parents' families. There is also nothing unusual in the close balance between males and females in the middle-age group or in the surplus of women in the older population. What is unusual about these figures is the very large and extremely implausible surplus of females in the 13-to-27 category. It seems almost certain that the bulk of the males missing from the *listes* sample must be from this age group.

How might this gross underrepresentation of young males be accounted for? There are several likely explanations:

1. As in the younger age group, a significant number of Marseille's males in the 13-to-17 category were probably counted in Aix-en-Provence, where they attended schools. At most, however, this could account for only a few hundred cases.

2. A sizable number of young men in the 18-to-27 category were in the

military service. Young Marseillais who enlisted or were conscripted would, of course, not be counted with their families. On the other hand, there was a sizable military garrison in Marseille. Very few of the garrison troops, however, were included in the *listes nominatives*. Only twelve enlisted men appeared in the sample, and all of these were living in ordinary civilian dwellings. The enlisted men living in barracks were not enumerated in the *listes*. Unfortunately, it has not proved possible to determine the size of Marseille's garrison. The official census results do not include figures for Marseille's garrison in 1851, but they do include figures for the Bouches-du-Rhône, Marseille's department, which had 9,654. The problem is to determine how many of these lived in Marseille. Here, figures from 1872 and 1876 are helpful. In 1872, the garrison of Marseille was 7,065, and in 1876 it was 7,101. In these same years the departmental garrison was 10,263 and 9,876. Assuming that the proportion of the departmental garrison stationed in Marseille was constant, Marseille's military population must have been about 7,000 in 1851. These figures for 1851 might seem rather large, given that Marseille and the Bouches-du Rhône were officially in a state of siege following the suppression of Marseille's commune in 1871. One would expect this to have swelled the garrison considerably. However, although there was no state of siege at the time the 1851 census was taken, Marseille was a revolutionary hotspot. There had been an insurrection in 1848, and lesser confrontations between revolutionaries and the authorities were commonplace right up to the coup d'etat in December 1851. Given these circumstances, a large garrison to contain the ever-present threat of disorder is quite plausible. And because the military population was composed almost exclusively of young men in their 20s, their absence from the *listes* surely accounts for a sizable proportion of the missing young unmarried males.

3. The rest of the missing unmarried males were probably young immigrants living in hotels and rooming houses. In nearly all populations demographers have studied, adolescents and young adults are by far the most mobile group in the population.[9] Before the mid-teens, young people in nearly all societies live with their parents; after 30, most are married, have children, and settle down more or less permanently. Thus, the very age group from which most of the sample's unmarried males were missing contained an unusually high proportion of itinerant or unsettled persons. This proportion was bound to be especially high in a city like nineteenth-century Marseille, whose rapidly growing economy and population attracted a very large volume of immigration. Not all the immigrants were males, of course; in some cities female immigrants outnumbered male immigrants. But male and female immigration differed in important respects. When young women migrated to the city, they usually did so in relatively protected circumstances. Many of them secured positions as domestic servants, lodging with the family they served and living under the supervision and protection of the master and mistress of

the house. Others lodged with relatives or friends. Relatively few lived alone in hotels or rooming houses where their well-being and virtue would be far more vulnerable. Young males, however, generally migrated in a much less protective environment, commonly taking up lodging in rooming houses or hotels filled with fellow itinerants. If a significant portion of the volatile population of Marseille's rooming houses was somehow left out of the *listes* on which computations were based, this could presumably account for the remaining missing young unmarried adult males.

It seems quite likely that this may have happened. The rooming-house population, the *"population des garnis"* in the jargon of the census, was handled inconsistently in the *listes*. In some districts of the city the *garnis* were included on separate registers; in others they were included on the general registers along with other inhabitants of their streets. If a significant proportion of the special registers of *garnis* have somehow been lost, this could account for a sizable underreporting of young unmarried males of precisely the sort that seems to have happened in the *listes* sample. This hypothesis also fits with the observation that virtually no registers of entire streets were missing from the archives' collection; if the *garnis* of a given quarter were listed on separate registers, registers of all streets would still be extant even if large numbers of the inhabitants of *garnis* were missing.

It remains to estimate what proportion of the missing unmarried males can be assumed to have resulted from these different sources. The calculations that follow are of course rough and speculative, and the estimates that they establish are highly uncertain. But it seems better to provide even uncertain estimates than to grope forward with none at all. The official census results show 61,145 unmarried males in Marseille. The estimate from our sample of the *listes* is 47,650, leaving a gap of 13,495. It is the source of these missing cases that must be estimated. All sex and marital-status groups in the population were underestimated by the *listes* sample. More precisely, females and married or widowed males were underestimated by 5.5 percent. Although this error is hardly insubstantial, it is small enough to be plausibly attributed either to occasional missing or skipped pages in the registries, to inadvertent overcounting by the nineteenth-century census takers, or to both. For present purposes, in any case, it can be considered an acceptably small margin of error. Therefore, it seems just to attribute 5.5 percent of the 61,145 officially counted unmarried males – or 3,353 – to the same unknown but acceptable errors that led to underestimation of other categories of the population. This leaves 10,142 unmarried males (13,495 minus 3,443) unaccounted for. For purposes of simplicity, this figure may be rounded to 10,000.

Some male children and adolescents were probably missed by the census because they were attending school in Aix-en-Provence. These, however, will have been missed in both the *listes* and the official totals and therefore are not of concern here. It seems reasonable to assume that the military garrison of Marseille in 1851 must have had about 7,000 men. If so, then the remaining 3,000 unmarried males were probably young immigrants living in rooming houses and hotels. For purposes of describing the occupational structure of Marseille, the garrison may be ignored without serious loss. Thus the crucial missing men are the 3,000 rooming-house dwellers.

Where possible, the occupational makeup of these elusive men will be estimated by more or less plausible calculations. But their absence places real limitations on the value of any occupational figures derived from the *listes nominatives*. Neither the census nor the marriage registers, in short, can be made to yield truly reliable figures on the occupational structure of Marseille. But with appropriate care in handling them, some useful calculations can be made.

Appendix B: Occupations practiced in Marseille

I. Male occupations
1. Business and professional
Merchants/*négociants*
merchant: *négociant*

Ship captains/*capitaines marins*
ship captain: *capitaine marin, capitaine au long cours, capitaine au cabotage, maître au cabotage*

Other business/*négoce divers*
shipowner: *armateur*
insurance agent: *agent d'assurance, assureur*
businessman: *agent d'affaires, homme d'affaires*
broker: *courtier, courtier maritime, courtier de commerce, courtier d'immeubles, entrepositaire*
banker: *banquier, agent de change*
industrialist: *fabricant (grande industrie)*

Military officers/*officiers militaires*
army officer: *maréchal de camp, général, colonel, capitaine, lieutenant*
navy officer: *officier de marine*

State officials/*hauts fonctionnaires*
inspector: *inspecteur*
district attorney: *procureur*
counsellor at the prefecture: *conseilleur au préfécture*
chief of police: *chef de la police de sureté*
miscellaneous state officials: *hauts fonctionnaires divers*

Medical professions/*professions médicales*
doctor: *médecin, docteur en médecine*
surgeon: *chiurgien*
dentist: *dentiste*
pharmacist: *pharmacien*

Legal professions/*professions légales*
barrister: *avocat*
solicitor: *avoué*
notary: *notaire*
judge: *juge au tribunal, juge de paix*
jurist: *jurisconsulte*
miscellaneous legal: *bâtonnier, hommes de loi divers*

Miscellaneous professions/*professions liberales diverses*
professor: *professeur, professeur au lycée, professeur de latin, professeur de langues*
engineer: *ingénieur*

327

architect: *architecte*
writer: *écrivain, homme de lettres*
miscellaneous professional: *chimiste, cartographe, géometre, professions divers*

Artistic professions/*professions artistiques*
musician: *musicien, pianiste, professeur de musique*
singer: *artiste lyrique, chante au grande théatre*
dramatist: *artiste dramatique*
artist: *artiste, artiste peintre*
dance teacher: *professeur de danse*

Ecclesiastics/*ecclésiastiques*
priest: *prêtre*
pastor: *pasteur d'église reformée*
canon: *chanoine*
miscellaneous ecclesiastic: *recteur, séminariste, père d'école chrétienne, frère d'école chrétienne, ecclésiastique*

2. Rentier
Rentiers/*rentiers*
rentier: *rentier, bourgeois*
Proprietors/*propriétaires*
proprietor: *propriétaire*

3. Sales and clerical
State employees/*employés de l'état*
customs official: *brigadier des douanes, sous-brigadier des douanes, officiers divers des douanes.*
octroi official: *brigadier de l'octroi, sous-brigadier de l'octroi, officiers divers de l'octroi*
health officer: *capitaine à la santé, officier à la santé*
accountant: *comptable*
bailiff: *huissier*
clerk of court: *greffier*
police officer: *commissaire de police*
teacher: *institeur, instituteur communal*
tax official: *employé aux contributions directes, employé aux contributions indirectes*
policeman: *agent de police, gendarme*
postman: *courier de poste, facteur à la poste*
public weigher: *peseur publique, mesureur publique*
fireman: *sapeur-pompier*
night crier: *crieur de nuit*
miscellaneous minor state officials: *employé à la préfécture, employé à la mairie, commis principal de la marine, employé au bureau de la marine, sergent du port, visiteur des navires, employé au comptabilité, employé à la charité, employé au canal, employé aux eaux, employé au gaz, employé au Lycée, employé à la poste, employé au bureau de police*

Customs clerks/*douaniers*
customs clerk: *douanier, préposé des douanes, commis à la douane, employé à la douane, matelot à la douane, emballeur à la douane*

Octroi clerks/*employés de l'octroi*
octroi clerk: *préposé de l'octroi, employé de l'octroi*

Clerks/*commis*
  clerk: *commis*

Employees/*employés*
  bank clerk: *employé de banque, caissier de banque, employé à la caisse d'épargne*
  law clerk: *clerc d'avoué, clerc de notaire*
  traveling salesman: *voyageur de commerce, commis voyageur*
  salesman: *revendeur, commis épicier, commis mercier, facteur de tabac, facteur*
  employee: *employé, agent, commissionaire, garçon de recette, clerc*

Small business
Shopkeepers/*marchands*
  grocer: *épicier*
  cloth seller: *marchand drapier, marchand de toiles, marchand d'indiennes*
  mercer: *mercier*
  bookseller: *libraire, marchand de librairie, teneur de livres*
  hardware seller: *marchand de quincaillerie*
  grain seller: *marchand de grains*
  tobacconist: *débitant de tabacs*
  shopkeeper: *marchand, commerçant*
  miscellaneous shopkeeper: *marchand de comestibles, marchand de fromage, marchand de gibier, marchand de glaces, marchand d'huile, marchand de salaisons, marchand de sucre, marchand de volailles, tripier, marchand de rubans, fripier, marchand de chiffons, marchand d'estampes, marchand de papier, marchand de fer, marchand de plâtre, marchand de pierre, marchand de meubles, marchand de porcelaine, marchand de parapluies, marchand de nouveautés, droguiste, marchand de bois, marchand de charbon, marchand de cribles, marchand de cuirs, marchand d'oiseaux, marchand de paille, marchand de fourrage, marchand d'engrais, tenant lavoir, loueur de voitures, maquignon, herboriste, copiste, jaugeur, peseur*

Wine shop keepers/*marchands de vin*
  wine shop keeper: *marchand de vin, débitant de vin*

Café keepers/*cafetiers*
  restaurant keeper: *restauranteur, traiteur, gargotier*
  café keeper: *cafetier, tenant café, tenant débit de liqueurs, débitant de liqueurs, limonadier, cabaretier*

Innkeepers/*aubergistes*
  innkeeper: *aubergiste*
  hotel keeper: *tenant d'hôtel, maître de pension*
  rooming-house keeper: *logetier, logeur, logeur en garnis, tenant maison garnis, tenant maison meublée*

Barbers/*coiffeurs*
  barber: *coiffeur, barbier*
  wigmaker: *perruquier*

Small manufacturers/*fabricants en petite industrie*
  contractor: *entrepreneur, entrepreneur maçon, entrepreneur en bâtiment*
  shoemaker: *fabricant de chaussures, marchand de chaussures, maître cordonnier*
  tanner: *fabricant tanneur, fabricant corroyeur*

printer: *maître imprimeur*
baker: *maître boulanger*
hatter: *maître chapelier*
tailor: *maître tailleur, marchand tailleur*
cooper: *maître tonnelier*
joiner: *maître menuisier*
locksmith: *maître serrurier*
miscellaneous small manufacturers: *fabricants divers*

5. Artisan

Machinists/*mécaniciens*
machinist: *mécanicien, adjusteur mécanicien*
metal turner: *tourneur mécanicien, tourneur en cuivre*
founder: *fondeur, fondeur en cuivre*
coppersmith: *chaudronnier*
moulder: *mouleur, mouleur en fonte*
steam-engine operator: *chauffeur, chauffeur de machine à vapeur, chauffeur mécanicien*
metallurgist: *métallurgiste, affineur de métaux*

Forge workers/*forgerons*
forge worker: *forgeron, forgeur*

Light-metal workers/*petits métallurgistes*
blacksmith: *maréchal-ferrant*
plumber: *plombier, ferblantier*
tool maker: *taillandier, outilleur, tailleur de limes*
metal engraver: *graveur sur métaux, traceur sur métaux*
small-wares maker: *quincaillier*
nailer: *cloutier*
cutler: *coutelier*
pewterer: *étameur*
miscellaneous light-metal workers: *aiguisseur, arquebussier, armurier, balancier, fontannier, grillageur, poulier, malletier, soudeur, riveur*

Locksmiths/*serruriers*
locksmith: *serrurier*

Stonemasons/*maçons*
stonemason: *maçon*

Stonecutters/*tailleurs de pierres*
stonecutter: *tailleur de pierres*

Housepainters/*peintres en bâtiment*
housepainter: *peintre en bâtiment, peintre, peintre décorateur*

Joiners/*menuisiers*
joiner: *menuisier*

Miscellaneous building workers/*divers ouvriers en bâtiment*
sawyer: *scieur de long*
glazier: *vitrier*
plasterer: *plâtrier*
paper hanger: *colleur de papiers peints*
tiler: *carreleur*
sculptor: *sculpteur, sculpteur en marbre*
marble cutter: *marbrier*

Cabinetmakers/*ébénistes*
 cabinetmaker: *ébéniste*

Coopers/*tonneliers*
 cooper: *tonnelier*

Woodworkers/*ouvriers en bois*
 wood turner: *tourneur, tourneur de bois, tourneur de chaises, ouvrier en chaises*
 varnisher: *vernisseur, vernisseur de chaises*
 gilder: *doreur, doreur et argenteur*
 wheelwright: *charron*
 packing-case maker: *layetier, caissier*
 carriage maker: *carrossier*
 miscellaneous woodworkers: *ouvrier en cadres, cadreur, boiselier, cartonnier*

Tailors/*tailleurs d'habits*
 tailor: *tailleur d'habits*

Shoemakers/*cordonniers*
 shoemaker: *cordonnier*
 booter: *bottier*
 sabot maker: *sabottier*
 cobbler: *savetier*

Hatters/*chapeliers*
 hatter: *chapelier*

Bakers/*boulangers*
 baker: *boulanger*
 pastry maker: *patissier*

Confectioners/*confisseurs*
 confectioner: *confisseur, chocolatier*

Butchers/*bouchers*
 butcher: *boucher*

Jewelers and watchmakers/*bijoutiers et horlogers*
 jeweler: *bijoutier, jaôlier*
 goldsmith: *orfèvre*
 watchmaker: *horloger*

Printers/*imprimeurs*
 printer: *imprimeur, compositeur en imprimerie*
 typographer: *typographe*
 lithographer: *lithographe*
 character founder: *fondeur en caractères*

Tanners/*tanneurs*
 tanner: *tanneur, maroquinier, mégisseur*
 currier: *corroyeur*

Basket weavers/*vanniers*
 basket weaver: *vannier*

Tapestry weavers/*tapissiers*
 tapestry weaver: *tapissier*

Longshoremen/*portefaix*
 longshoreman: *portefaix*

Packers/*emballeurs*
packer: *emballeur*

Rope and sail makers/*cordiers et voiliers*
rope maker: *cordier*
sail maker: *voilier*
fishing-net maker: *auffier, ouvrier en sparteries*

Carpenters/*charpentiers*
carpenter: *charpentier*
ship carpenter: *charpentier de marine, perceur*
mast maker: *mâtier*

Ship caulkers/*calfats*
ship caulker: *calfat, goudronnier*

6. Service
Cooks and waiters/*cuisiniers et garçons*
cook: *cuisinier*
waiter: *garçon, garçon de café, garçon cafetier, garçon cabaretier, garçon
limonadier, garçon restauranteur, garçon de table, garçon de salle, garçon
de cercle, garçon d'hôtel*

Coachmen/*cochers*
coachman: *cocher, postillon, palefrenier, conducteur d'omnibus, conducteur
de diligences*
stableboy: *garçon d'écurie, tondeur, tondeur de chevaux*

Miscellaneous service workers/*services divers*
domestic servant: *domestique*
valet: *valet de chambre, valet à gage, home de confiance*
concierge: *concierge*
rural guard: *garde champêtre*
night watchman: *garde de nuit*
private guard: *garde particulier*
miscellaneous guard: *garde, garde de chemin de fer, garde de canal, gardien
de navires, garde municipal, garde de santé*
bootblack: *décrotteur*
miscellaneous service: *dégraisseur, garçon de bains, service divers*

7. Unskilled
Day laborers/*journaliers*
day laborer: *journalier*

Miners/*mineurs*
miner: *mineur*

Carters/*charretiers*
carter: *charretier, charretonnier*

Wagon drivers/*voituriers*
wagon driver: *voiturier, conducteur, voiturier-conducteur, conducteur de chevaux, roulier, camioneur*
Loaders/*chargeurs*
loader: *chargeur, chargeur de charettes, chargeur de farines*

Soap makers/*savonniers*
soap maker: *savonnier*

Sugar refiners/*raffineurs de sucre*
  sugar refiner: *raffineur, raffineur de sucre, ouvrier raffineur, ouvrier raffineur de sucre*

Tile makers/*tuiliers*
  tile maker: *tuilier, ouvrier tuilier*
  brick maker: *briquetier*

Flour millers/*minotiers*
  flour miller: *minotier*

8. Maritime
Fishermen/*pêcheurs*
  fisherman: *pêcheur, patron pêcheur*

Seamen/*marins*
  seaman: *marin, marin au commerce, marin novice, matelot*
  cabin boy: *mousse*

Miscellaneous maritime workers/*ouvriers maritimes divers*
  pilot: *pilote, pilote majeur*
  boatsman: *bâtelier, acconier, arrimeur, gabarier, avironnier, ramurier*
  maritime mechanic: *mécanicien de voyage, mécanicien sur les paquebots, chauffeur maritime*
  maritime service worker: *maître d'hôtel maritime, garçon de table à bord bateau, cuisinier marin*

9. Agriculture
Gardeners/*jardiniers*
  gardener: *jardinier, jardinier potager, jardinier fermier, jardinier fleuriste, horticulteur*

Shepherds/*bergers*
  shepherd: *berger*

Cultivators/*cultivateurs*
  cultivator: *cultivateur, cultivateur fermier, fermier-cultivateur, agriculteur*
  vinegrower: *vigneron*
  woodcutter: *bûcheron*

Farm proprietors/*propriétaires-cultivateurs*
  farm proprietor: *cultivateur-propriétaire, ménager, méger, fermier-méger, cultivateur-méger, laboureur*

10. Miscellaneous
Peddlers/*colporteurs*
  peddler: *colporteur, marchand colporteur, marchand ambulant*
  rag seller: *chiffonier, fripier ambulant*
  street performer: *chanteur, chanteur ambulant*

Soldiers/*militaires*
  soldier: *militaire, soldat*

Students/*élèves*
  student: *élève, élève externe*

Miscellaneous/*divers*
  no information: *non indiqué*
  illegible: *illégible*
  retired: *retraité, vétéran*
  refugee: *refugié*

miscellaneous: *divers*

Father unknown/*père inconnu*
  father unknown: *père inconnu*

No occupation/*sans profession*
  no occupation: *sans profession*

II. Women's occupations
1. Not employed
    Not employed/*sans profession*
      not employed: *sans profession*

2. Rentière
    Rentières/*rentières*
      rentière: *rentière*
      proprietor: *propriétaire*

3. Business and professional
    Merchants/*négociantes*
      merchant: *négociante*

    Employees/*employées*
      employee: *employée*
      clerk: *commis*

    Midwives/*sages femmes*
      midwife: *sage femme, accoucheuse*

    Nurses/*infirmières*
      nurse: *infirmière*

    Teachers/*institutrices*
      teacher: *institutrice, maîtresse*

    Actresses/*artistes dramatiques*
      actress: *artiste dramatique*

    Musician/*muscienne*
      pianist: *pianiste*
      piano teacher: *maîtresse de piano*

4. Small business
    Shopkeepers/*marchandes*
      mercer: *mercière, marchande mercière*
      cloth seller: *marchande d'étoffes, marchande d'indiennes, marchande de lingeries, marchande de broderies*
      bookseller: *libraire*
      flower seller: *fleuriste, bouquetière*
      tobacconist: *débitante de tabac*
      shopkeeper: *marchande, comerçante, marchande d'allumettes, marchande de charbon, marchande d'engrais, marchande de poteries, marchande de ferailles*

    Food sellers/*marchandes de comestibles*
      grocer: *épicière, marchande épicière*
      dairy seller: *laitière, marchande de fromage*
      butcher: *bouchère, tripière, marchande de volailles, marchande de veaux, charcutière*

fish seller: *poissionière, marchande de morue*
fruit seller: *marchande de fruits, marchande d'oranges*
food seller: *marchande de comestibles, marchande au marché, marchande de grains, marchande d'oeufs, marchande de salaisons*

Saleswomen/*revendeuses*
saleswoman: *revendeuse, revendeuse de comestibles*

Innkeepers/*aubergistes*
innkeeper: *aubergiste*
rooming-house keeper: *logeuse, logeuse en garnis, tenant chambres garnis, maîtresse de pension*
hotel keeper: *maîtresse d'hôtel*

Café keepers/*cafetières*
café keeper: *cafetière, tenant café, cabaretière*
wine seller: *marchande de vin, liquoriste, débitante de liqueurs*

Hairdressers/*coiffeuses*
hairdresser: *coiffeuse*

Small manufacturers/*fabricantes*
manufacturer: *fabricante, marchande tailleuse*

Peddlers/*colporteuses*
peddler: *colporteuse, marchande colporteur, marchande ambulente, partisanne*
rag seller: *chiffonière, marchande de chiffons*
old-clothes seller: *fripière*

5. Needle trades
Seamstresses/*couturières*
seamstress: *couturière, giletière*
tailor: *tailleuse, tailleuse en robes, tailleuse d'hommes*

Milliners/*modistes*
milliner: *modiste*

Embroiderers/*brodeuses*
embroiderer: *brodeuse, bordeuse, brodeuse de dentelles, bordeuse de souliers, piqueuse, piqueuse de brodequins*

Lingerie makers/*lingères*
lingerie maker: *lingère*

6. Other crafts
Straw plaiters/*rempailleuses*
straw plaiter: *rempailleuse, empailleuse, rempaillleuse de chaises*

Sail makers/*voilières*
sail maker: *voilière*

Rope makers/*cordières*
rope maker: *cordière*

Fishing-net makers/*auffières*
fishing-net maker: *auffière, ouvrière en sparteries*

Cigar makers/*cigareuses*
cigar maker: *cigareuse, ouvrière en tabac*

Bakers/*boulangères*
baker: *boulangère*

pastry maker: *patissière*

Textile workers/*ouvrières en textiles*
cotton spinner: *filateur de coton, cotonnière, dévideuse*
wool washer: *laveuse de laine, laveuse*

Stockingers/*bonnetières*
stockinger: *bonnetière*

Tapestry weavers/*tapissières*
tapestry weaver: *tapissière*

Shoe workers/*cordonnières*
shoe worker: *bordeuse de souliers, ouvrière en sabots*

Hatters/*chapelières*
hatter: *chapelière*

Other crafts/*métiers divers*
other crafts: *parfumière, ouvrière en pipes, matelassière, lisineuse, grenelière, colleuse, cartonnière, polisseuse, étireuse, gantière, casquetière, corsetière, vinaigrière, garniseuse, métiers divers*

7. Laundresses
Laundresses/*blanchisseuses*
laundress: *blanchisseuse*

Dyers/*teinturières*
dyer: *teinturière*

Pressers/*repasseuses*
presser: *repasseuse*

8. Domestic service
Cooks/*cuisinières*
cook: *cuisinière*

Domestic servants/*domestiques*
domestic servant: *domestique*
maid: *bonne, bonne d'enfants*
Miscellaneous domestic service: *femme de chambre, femme de confiance*

Wet-nurses/*nourrices*
wet-nurse: *nourrice*

Concierges/*concierges*
concierge: *concierge*

Housekeepers/*femmes de ménage*
housekeeper: *femme de ménage, ménagère, fait des ménages*

9. Unskilled
Day laborers/*journalières*
day laborer: *journalière, femme de peine, ouvrière*

Porters/*porteuses*
porter: *porteuse*

10. Agriculture
Cultivators/*cultivatrices*
cultivator: *cultivatrice, paysanne, travaillant dans la campagne, mégère*

Gardeners/*jardinières*

gardener: *jardinière, jardinière potagère, horticultrice*

Shepherds/*bergères*
    shepherd: *bergère*

11. Miscellaneous
    Nuns/*religieuses*
        nun: *religieuse*

    Prostitutes/*filles publiques*
        prostitute: *fille publique, fille soumise*

    Miscellaneous/*divers*
        street singer: *chanteuse*
        fortune teller: *tireuse de cartes*
        bootblack: *cireuse*
        miscellaneous: *divers*

Appendix C: Estimating artisan employers

At several points in this book, it has been necessary to estimate the number of men who were incorrectly categorized as artisans rather than as small businessmen because their occupational titles, as recorded on the *listes nominatives* of the census and on the marriage registers, did not distinguish them from their employees. The first place this occurs is in Chapter 3, where the relative sizes of Marseille's various occupational categories are estimated. There, adjustments in the number of artisans and of small businessmen are carried out on figures from the census of 1851 and the marriage registers of 1821–2, 1846–51, and 1869. The estimation procedure consists in moving an appropriate number of cases from the artisan category to the small-business category, and the main problem is determining how many cases should be moved.

During the period covered by this study, there were several surveys of Marseille's industries that gave estimates of the number of employers and employees in the handicraft trades of the city. Three of these estimates have been used in the following calculations. The earliest estimate of sufficient reliability dates from 1829–30, some eight years after the 1821–2 marriage-register data set. It was made by Jules Julliany in the third volume of his massive *Essai sur le commerce de Marseille*.[1] There Julliany gives estimates of the numbers of firms and workers in 49 different handicraft trades. When these are summed, the overall ratio of workers to masters comes out at 5.4 to 1. The second estimate comes from the manuscript report on Marseille in the "Enquête sur le travail industriel et agricole," a national survey of labor conditions undertaken by the National Assembly in 1848.[2] In most of the large cities of France, this survey was never completed, but in Marseille it was carried out in meticulous detail, and it provides a wealth of information on many aspects of labor and laboring conditions in the mid–nineteenth century. The committee compiling the report was made up of three justices of the peace and was aided by officers of the municipal government, the chamber of commerce, and representatives of workers in Marseille's various trades. Among the data presented are figures for the numbers of workers and firms in nearly all the city's industries. Once again the figures are only estimates, but they deserve to be taken seriously as the best guesses of extremely well-informed observers. On the basis of these industry-by-industry figures, one can calculate the ratio of workers to masters in the 68 handicraft trades included

338

in the survey. When this is done the ratio comes out at 5.2 workers per master, very close to the 1829–30 ratio derived from Julliany. The third estimate dates from 1866 and is based on summary occupational tables from the census of that year.[3] Again, there are figures for the number of proprietors and workers in each of Marseille's industries. When these are summed across the handicraft trades for which figures are reported, the resulting ratio is precisely the same as in 1848, 5.2 to 1.

The estimated ratios of workers to employers can then be applied to the marriage-register and *listes nominatives* data to determine how many cases should be transferred from the artisan category to the small-business category. How this has been done can be demonstrated with the 1821–2 marriage-register data. There were 755 men with artisan occupational titles in the marriage registers of 1821–2. Of these, 139 were in trades whose titles un-ambiguously designated employee status (tanners, longshoremen, packers, and ship caulkers). This leaves 636 who could have been either employers or employees. To these must be added another 17 men who identified them-selves as handicraft proprietors. The total number of grooms employed in the handicraft trades was therefore 653. If, as Julliany's figures suggest, 1 in every 6.4 of these were in fact proprietors, then there should have been 101 proprietors in the sample. Thus, 84 men (the 101 expected proprietors minus the 17 self-identified proprietors) should be shifted from the artisan to the small-business category. Consequently, the adjusted figures show 671 artisans and 189 small businessmen, as against the unadjusted figures of 755 and 105. Precisely the same procedure has been employed in calculating adjusted totals of artisans and small businessmen in the figures from the 1846–51 and 1869 marriage registers and the 1851 *listes nominatives*, which are reported in Tables 3.1, 3.3, and 3.4. Table C.1 summarizes these calculations.

The estimation procedure is slightly more complicated in the case of col-umns 3, 4, and 5 of Table 3.1. Here the figures being reported undergo a double adjustment: first, addition of cases to make up for the transients pre-sumed to be missing from the *listes nominatives*, and, second, the familiar shifting of cases from the artisan to the small-business category. In carrying out these calculations, it has been assumed that the same proportion of cases should be shifted from the artisan to the small-business category among the missing transients as in the orginal, unaugmented census data. Because 230 of the original 2,170 artisans were shifted to the small-business category, a like proportion (23) of the estimated 213 artisans among the missing cases has also been shifted to the small-business category. Hence, in the augmented figures, the number of artisans was decreased and the number of small busi-nessmen increased by 253 cases.

To generate a corrected table for intergenerational occupational mobility (see Chapter 9), a more complicated estimation procedure had to be devised. In this case it must be assumed that some small proprietors are falsely included

Table C.1. *Estimation of misclassified small businessmen*

	Marriage registers			Census of 1851
	1821–2	1846–51	1869	
1. Artisan category, raw total	775	1,361	841	2,170
2. Artisans engaged in large-scale industry	139	265	224	386
3. Artisans, small-scale industry (1 − 2)	636	1,096	617	1,784
4. Self-designated employers in small-scale industry	17	30	19	68
5. Total, small-scale industry (3 + 4)	653	1,126	636	1,852
6. Estimated proportion of employers	.154	.161	.161	.161
7. Expected number of employers (5 × 6)	101	181	102	298
8. Number of cases to be shifted (7 − 4)	84	150	83	230

both among the fathers who list their occupations as artisans and the sons who list their occupations as artisans. In generating a "corrected" table, the following three assumptions were made: (1) The proportion of proprietors in the handicraft trades was the same among fathers as among sons and was equal to 15.4 percent in 1821–2 and 16.1 percent in 1846–51 and 1869 (the same figures used in previous calculations). (2) The distribution of sons' occupations among the unidentified artisan-employer fathers was the same as among the identified artisan-employer fathers. (3) The distribution of fathers' occupations among the unidentified artisan-employer sons was the same as among the identified artisan-employer sons. Using these assumptions it is possible to construct an intergenerational occupational-mobility table that corrects simultaneously for misidentification of both artisan-employer fathers and artisan-employer sons.

This procedure can best be explained by following through the calculations for one data set. In the marriage registers of 1846–51, there were 978 grooms living in the urban neighborhoods of Marseille who designated themselves as artisans in small-scale industry. (Residents of Marseille's rural neighborhoods, it will be recalled, were eliminated from the occupational-mobility analysis.) Another 30 grooms designated themselves as employers in small-scale industry. This makes a total of 1,008 engaged in small-scale industry. Of these, 163 (.161 × 1,008) should have been employers. Hence, 133 (163 − 30) of the grooms who identified themselves as artisans were probably actually employers. The problem is to estimate the distribution of fathers' occupations among these 133 misidentified artisan employers. This is done by assuming that the occupational distribution of their fathers was the same as that of the fathers of self-identified artisan employers. The percentage distribution of fathers' occupations for the 33 known artisan employers is given in row 1 of Table C.2. The estimated occupational distribution of the fathers of misidentified artisan employers is given in row 2 of Table C.2. These are the cases that must be shifted from the artisan-grooms to the small-business-grooms category. For example, because 3.3 percent of the self-identified artisan-employer grooms were sons of clerical employees, it follows that 4 of the misclassified artisan employers (133 × .033) were also sons of clerical employees. They must therefore be shifted from the clerical-father/artisan-son cell of the 1846–51 mobility table to the clerical-father/small-business-son cell. (Consequently, they will no longer be counted as downwardly mobile.) An analogous shift must be carried out for each of the artisan-son and small-business-son cells of the mobility table.

After this operation has been completed, it is still necessary to correct for the misclassification of artisan-proprietor fathers. The method is precisely analogous to the correction for sons. Again the procedure will be described for 1846–51. There were 690 grooms' fathers who were designated as artisans in small-scale industry and another 36 who were designated as artisan employers, for a total of 726 engaged in small-scale industry altogether. Of these, 117 (726 × .161) should have been employers. The number of misclassified employers, therefore, is estimated at 81 (117 − 36). The distribution of sons' occupations for these misclassified fathers was estimated from the occupational distribution of the sons of declared artisan employers. (See rows 3 and 4 of Table C.2.) Once again, the original mobility table must be modified, this time by shifting an appropriately distributed set of cases from the artisan-father to the small-business-father category. For instance, 11 of the 81 misclassified artisan employers' sons (13.9 percent) are estimated to have been clerical workers. They are, therefore, shifted from the artisan-father/clerical-son cell to the small-business-father/clerical-son cell of the table. (Consequently, they will no longer be counted as upwardly mobile.)

When both these estimating operations have been carried out for all three data sets, the result is a set of "corrected" mobility tables, Tables C.3, C.4, and C.5. They should be compared with Tables 9.5, 9.6, and 9.7 in the text. In each year, the main difference between the "corrected" and "uncorrected" figures is a decline in the measured rate of downward mobility from small-business to various working-class occupations.

Table C.2. *Estimated occupational mobility, misclassified artisan employers*

	Business and professional	Rentier	Sales and clerical	Small business	Artisan	Unskilled	Service	Maritime	Agriculture	Miscellaneous	No. cases
1. Father's occupational distribution, self-identified artisan employer grooms, in percent	6.7	13.3	3.3	36.7	30.0	—	3.3	3.3	3.3	—	30
2. Estimated distribution of fathers' occupations, misclassified artisan employer grooms	9	18	4	50	40	0	4	4	4	0	133
3. Son's occupational distribution, fathers identified as artisan employers, in percent	8.3	5.6	13.9	50.0	13.9	—	—	5.6	2.8	—	36
4. Estimated distribution of sons' occupations, misclassified artisan employer fathers	7	5	11	40	11	0	0	5	2	0	81

Table C.3. *Father's occupation by son's occupation, 1821–2 (in percent) (corrected)*

Son's occupation	Father's occupation Business and professional	Rentier	Sales and clerical	Small business	Artisan	Unskilled	Service	Maritime	Agriculture	Miscellaneous	Total
1. Business and professional	44	17	5	6	1	0	0	0	0	3	6
2. Rentier	6	18	0	1	0	0	0	0	0	0	2
3. Sales and clerical	23	29	37	14	3	3	20	2	4	8	10
4. Small business	9	18	5	54	3	2	0	2	15	3	12
5. Artisan	12	12	44	17	82	42	53	30	40	42	49
6. Service	0	2	0	2	1	5	7	0	2	0	1
7. Unskilled	0	3	7	0	6	45	0	18	17	14	9
8. Maritime	5	2	2	5	3	2	13	47	2	11	7
9. Agriculture	0	0	0	0	0	0	0	0	17	8	2
10. Miscellaneous	1	0	0	2	0	2	7	0	3	11	1
All bourgeois (1 + 2 + 3 + 4)	82	82	46	74	7	5	20	4	19	14	30
Number of cases	93	66	41	132	339	60	15	89	105	36	1,036

343

Table C.4. *Father's occupation by son's occupation, 1846–51 (in percent) (corrected)*

| | Father's occupation | | | | | | | | | | |
Son's occupation	Business and professional	Rentier	Sales and clerical	Small business	Artisan	Unskilled	Service	Maritime	Agriculture	Miscel- laneous	Total
1. Business and professional	47	19	9	6	0	0	0	2	0	4	6
2. Rentier	10	11	2	4	1	1	0	2	1	0	3
3. Sales and clerical	22	21	31	14	4	3	15	3	11	11	11
4. Small business	10	22	9	50	9	3	7	5	7	7	13
5. Artisan	5	18	38	14	72	39	48	30	38	43	42
6. Service	0	3	3	2	2	2	7	1	5	8	3
7. Unskilled	1	2	3	3	8	46	17	9	26	14	14
8. Maritime	2	2	5	5	2	3	3	49	3	6	5
9. Agriculture	0	0	0	1	0	0	0	0	7	2	2
10. Miscellaneous	3	1	1	0	1	2	3	0	2	5	2
All bourgeois (1 + 2 + 3 + 4)	89	73	51	74	15	7	22	11	19	22	32
Number of cases	156	205	132	250	766	242	40	132	513	123	2,559

Table C.5. *Father's occupation by son's occupation, 1869 (in percent) (corrected)*

Son's occupation	Father's occupation										
	Business and professional	Rentier	Sales and clerical	Small business	Artisan	Unskilled	Service	Maritime	Agriculture	Miscel- laneous	Total
1. Business and professional	55	28	4	13	1	1	0	3	1	1	7
2. Rentier	6	10	0	3	1	0	0	0	1	2	2
3. Sales and clerical	21	24	40	15	13	6	9	5	21	20	17
4. Small business	5	17	12	39	10	6	4	7	10	10	12
5. Artisan	10	13	33	20	61	40	52	29	27	35	36
6. Service	2	5	4	3	4	4	22	1	11	3	6
7. Unskilled	1	2	0	3	6	36	9	7	21	16	13
8. Maritime	0	1	5	3	3	5	4	49	4	10	6
9. Agriculture	0	0	0	1	0	1	0	0	3	1	1
10. Miscellaneous	0	0	1	2	0	1	0	0	1	0	1
All bourgeois (1 + 2 + 3 + 4)	86	79	56	69	25	14	13	14	33	34	38
Number of cases	87	144	94	158	453	219	23	76	445	86	1,785

Notes

Preface

1 The preliminary work on social mobility, literacy, and the social and geographical origins of immigrants formed part of my doctoral dissertation. William H. Sewell, Jr., "The Structure of the Working Class of Marseille in the Middle of the Nineteenth Century" (Ph.D. dissertation, University of California, Berkeley, 1971). Work on the recruitment patterns of different trades can be found both in my doctoral dissertation and in "La Classe ouvrière de Marseille sous la Seconde République: Structure sociale et comportement politique," *Le Mouvement social* 76 (1971):27–65, and "Social Change and the Rise of Working-Class Politics in Nineteenth-Cenury Marseille," *Past and Present* 65 (1974):75–109. The former article has also been published in English as "The Working Class of Marseille Under the Second Republic: Social Structure and Political Behavior," in Peter N. Stearns and Daniel J. Walkowitz, eds., *Workers in the Industrial Revolution: Recent Studies of Labor in the United States and Europe* (New Brunswick, N.J., 1974), pp. 75–116.

1. Introduction: Marseille and urban history

1 Brian R. Mitchell, *European Historical Statistics, 1750–1975*, 2d ed. (London, 1981), pp. 86–9.
2 On French cities, see Louis Chevalier, *La Formation de la population parisienne au XIXe siècle* (Paris, 1950); Pierre Guillaume, *La Population de Bordeaux au XIXe siècle: Essai d'histoire sociale* (Paris, 1972); Maurice Agulhon, *Une Ville ouvrière au temps du socialisme utopique: Toulon de 1815 à 1851* (Paris and The Hague, 1970); Robert J. Bezucha, *The Lyon Uprising of 1834: Social and Political Conflict in a Nineteenth-Century City* (Cambridge, Mass., 1974); Joan W. Scott, *The Glassworkers of Carmaux: French Craftsmen and Political Action in a Nineteenth-Century City* (Cambridge, Mass., 1974); Adeline Daumard, *La Bourgeoisie parisienne de 1815 à 1848* (Paris, 1963); Adeline Daumard, with the collaboration of Felix Codaccioni, Georges Dupeux, Jacqueline Herpin, Jacques Godechot, and Jean Sentou, *Les Fortunes françaises au XIXe siècle* (Paris, 1973); Yves Lequin, *Les Ouvriers de la région lyonnaise (1848–1914)*, 2 vols. (Lyon, 1977); Ronald Aminzade, *Class, Politics, and Early Industrial Capitalism: A Study of Mid-Nineteenth-Century Toulouse, France* (Albany, N.Y., 1981); Leslie Page Moch, *Paths to the City: Regional Migration in Nineteenth-Century France* (Beverly Hills, Calif., 1983). On English cities, see Alan Armstrong, *Stability and Change in an English Country Town: A Social Study of York 1801–51* (London, 1974); Michael Anderson, *Family Structure in Nineteenth-Century Lancashire* (Cambridge, 1971); H. J. Dyos, ed., *The Study of Urban History* (New York, 1968); Lynn Lees, *Exiles of Erin: Irish Migrants in Victorian London*

(Ithaca, N.Y., 1979); and John Foster, *Class Struggle and the Industrial Revolution: Early Industrial Capitalism in Three English Towns* (London, 1974). On German cities, see David F. Crew, *Town in the Ruhr: A Social History of Bochum, 1860–1914* (New York, 1979); H. Zwahr, *Zur Konstitutierung des Proletariats als Klasse: Strukturuntersuchung über das Leipziger Proletariat während der industriellen Revolution* (Berlin, 1978); Allan N. Sharlin, "Social Structure and Politics: A Social History of Frankfurt am Main, 1815–1864" (Ph.D. dissertation, University of Wisconsin-Madison, 1976); and James H. Jackson, Jr., "Migration and Urbanization in the Ruhr Valley, 1850–1900" (Ph.D. dissertation, University of Minnesota, 1980). On North American cities, see Stephan Thernstrom, *Poverty and Progress: Social Mobility in a Nineteenth Century City* (Cambridge, Mass., 1964) and *The Other Bostonians: Poverty and Progress in the American Metropolis, 1880–1970* (Cambridge, Mass., 1973); Sam B. Warner, Jr., *Streetcar Suburbs: The Process of Growth in Boston, 1870–1900* (Cambridge, Mass., 1962); Natalie Rogoff, *Recent Trends in Occupational Mobility* (Glencoe, Ill., 1953); Sidney Goldstein, *Patterns of Mobility, 1910–1950. The Norristown Study. A Method for Measuring Migration and Occupational Mobility in the Community* (Philadelphia, 1958); Howard P. Chudakoff, *Mobile Americans: Residential and Social Mobility in Omaha, 1880–1920* (New York, 1972); Peter R. Knights, *The Plain People of Boston, 1830–1860: A Study in City Growth* (New York, 1971); Michael B. Katz, *The People of Hamilton, Canada West: Family and Class in a Mid-Nineteeenth-Century City* (Cambridge, Mass., 1975); Clyde Griffen and Sally Griffen, *Natives and Newcomers: The Ordering of Opportunity in Mid-Nineteenth-Century Poughkeepsie* (Cambridge, Mass., 1978); Harvey J. Graff, *The Literacy Myth: Literacy and Social Structure in the Nineteenth-Century City* (New York, 1979); Josef J. Barton, *Peasants and Strangers: Italians, Rumanians, and Slovaks in an American City, 1890–1950* (Cambridge, Mass., 1975); Stuart M. Blumin, *The Urban Threshold: Growth and Change in a Nineteenth-Century American Community* (Chicago, 1976); Kathleen Neils Conzen, *Immigrant Milwaukee, 1836–1860: Accommodation and Community in a Frontier City* (Cambridge, Mass., 1976).

3   Classic studies utilizing fiscal records include Georges Lefebvre, *Les Paysans du Nord pendant la Révolution française* (Bari, 1959; orig. pub. Lille, 1924) and *Etudes orléanaises*, vol. 1, *Contribution à l'étude des structures sociales à la fin du XVIIIᵉ siècle* (Paris, 1962); Pierre Goubert, *Beauvais et la Beauvaisis de 1600 à 1730, contribution à l'histoire social de la France du XVIIᵉ siècle* (Paris, 1960); Pierre Deyon, *Amiens, capitale provinciale. Etude sur la société urbaine au XVIIᵉ siècle* (Paris and The Hague, 1967); and Emmanuel Le Roi Ladurie, *Les Paysans de Languedoc* (Paris, 1966).

4   For a detailed methodological discussion of census documents, see E. A. Wrigley, ed., *Nineteenth-Century Society: Essays in the Use of Quantitative Methods for the Study of Social Data* (Cambridge, 1972).

5   For an excellent collection of studies of household structure, see Peter Laslett, ed., *Household and Family in Past Time* (Cambridge, 1972). Other examples include Anderson, *Family Structure*; Katz, *People of Hamilton*; and David Levine, *Family Formation in an Age of Nascent Capitalism* (New York, 1977).

6   On persistence rates and occupational mobility, see Stephan Thernstrom and Peter Knights, "Men in Motion: Some Data and Speculation about Urban Population Mobility in Nineteenth-Century America," *Journal of Interdisciplinary History* 1 (1970):7–36; Thernstrom, *Poverty and Progress* and *Other Bostonians*; Knights, *Plain People of Boston*; Sharlin, "Social Structure and Politics"; Chudakoff,

Mobile Americans; Griffen and Griffen, *Natives and Newcomers*; Katz, *People of Hamilton*; Crew, *Town in the Ruhr*; Rogoff, *Recent Trends*; Goldstein, *Patterns of Mobility*; Graff, *Literacy Myth*; and Barton, *Peasants and Strangers*.

7   *Poverty and Progress.*

8   Louis Henry, *Anciennes familles genevoises* (Paris, 1956). On the methodology of family reconstitution, see Louis Henry, *Manuel de démographie historique* (Geneva and Paris, 1967), and E. A. Wrigley, ed., *An Introduction to English Historical Demography from the Sixteenth to the Nineteenth Century* (New York, 1966). The most comprehensive reconstitution study to date is E. A. Wrigley and R.S. Schofield, *The Population History of England, 1541–1871: A Reconstruction* (Cambridge, Mass., 1982).

9   Studies using French marriage registers include William H. Sewell, Jr., "Social Mobility in a Nineteenth-Century European City: Some Findings and Implications," *Journal of Interdisciplinary History* 7 (1976):217–33; "La Classe ouvrière de Marseille"; and "Social Change"; Serge Chassagne, "La Formation de la population d'une agglomeration industrielle: Corbeil-Essones (1750–1850)," *Le Mouvement social* 97 (1976); Pierre Caspard, "La Fabrique au village," *Le Mouvement social* 97 (1976); and Lequin, *Les Ouvriers de la région lyonnaise.*

10   Louis Chevalier, *Classes laborieuses et classes dangereuses à Paris pendant la première moitié du XIXe siècle* (Paris, 1958). An English translation is *Laboring Classes and Dangerous Classes in Paris during the First Half of the Nineteenth Century*, trans. Frank Jellinek (New York, 1973).

11   The most influential statement of this thesis was by Werner Sombart in 1906. An English translation is *Why Is There No Socialism in the United States?* trans. Patricia M. Hocking and C. T. Husbands (London, 1976). A good commentary is Jerome Karabel, "Review of *Why Is There No Socialism in the United States?*" *New York Review of Books* 26 (January 1979):22–7.

12   See, for example, Ronald Aminzade and Randy Hodson, "Social Mobility in a Mid-Nineteenth Century French City," *American Sociological Review* 47 (1982):441–57.

13   See Aminzade, *Class, Politics, and Early Industrial Capitalism*; Sewell, "Social Change" and *Work and Revolution in France: The Language of Labor from the Old Regime to 1848* (Cambridge, 1980).

2.   The economic structure

1   Gaston Rambert, *Marseille, la formation d'une grande cité moderne: Etude de géographie urbaine* (Marseille, 1934), p. 165; Louis Girard, "La Politique des grands travaux à Marseille sous le Second Empire," in Chambre de Commerce de Marseille, *Marseille sous le Second Empire: Exposition, conferences, colloque organisés à l'occasion du centenaire du Palais de la Bourse, 10–26 novembre 1960* (Paris, 1961), p. 78.

2   Paul Masson, gen. ed., *Les Bouches-du-Rhône: Encyclopédie départementale*, vol. 9, *Le Mouvement économique: Le Commerce* (Marseille, 1926), p. 2.

3   Charles Carrière, *Négociants marseillais au XVIIIe siècle: Contribution à l'étude des économies maritimes*, 2 vols. (Marseille, 1973), 1:59.

4   Ibid., 65.

5   With the exception of the figure for 1660, these figures are from Michel Terrisse, "La Population de Marseille et de son terroir de 1694 à 1830" (doctoral thesis, University of Aix-Marseille, 1971), as reported in a review by Jean-Pierre Bardet, *Annales de démographie historique* (1973), 357. The figure for 1660 is from

Rambert, *Marseille*, pp. 215–16. On the plague, see Jean-Noel Biraben, "Certain Demographic Characteristics of the Plague Epidemic in France, 1720–22," *Daedalus* 97 (1968):536–45.

6   Rambert, *Marseille*, 246.
7   Bardet, Review, 366.
8   Masson, *Les Bouches-du-Rhône*, 9:83–4.
9   According to one estimate, the soap industry accounted for over half the total product of Marseille's industries in 1789. Masson, *Les Bouches-du-Rhône*, vol. 8, *Le Mouvement économique: L'Industrie* (Marseille, 1926), p. 2.
10 Ibid., 58.
11 Ibid., 72.
12 F. L. Charpin, *Pratique religieuse et formation d'une grand ville: Le Geste du baptême et sa signification en sociologie religieuse* (Paris, 1964), p. 269.
13 Masson, *Les Bouches-du-Rhône*, 9:58.
14 These figures are derived from Jules Julliany, *Essai sur le commerce de Marseille*, 2d ed., 3 vols. (Marseille, 1842), 1:145, 162, and 3:462; Casimir Bousquet and Tony Sapet, *Etude sur la navigation, le commerce et l'industrie de Marseille, pendant la période quinquennale de 1850 à 1854* (Marseille, 1857), pp. 23–9; Octave Teissier, *Histoire du commerce de Marseille pendant vingt ans (1855–74)* (Paris, 1878); and *Travaux de la Société de Statistique de Marseille*, 36 vols. (Marseille, 1837–73), 1:70, 11:48–9, and 19:92.
15 For the economic crisis of 1848–51, see Pierre Guiral, "Le cas d'un grand port de commerce: Marseille," in Ernest Labrousse, ed., *Aspects de la crise et de la dépression de l'économie française au milieu du XIXe siècle, 1846–1851*, vol. 19 of *Bibliothèque de la Révolution de 1848* (La Roche-sur-Yon, 1956), pp. 200–25.
16 Masson, *Les Bouches-du-Rhône*, 9:36, 54, 72.
17 See note 14.
18 Masson, *Les Bouches-du-Rhône*, 9:56, 75.
19 Ibid., 73.
20 Julliany, *Essai sur le commerce*, 3:397.
21 Unless otherwise noted, figures for the number of firms and number of workers in Marseille's industries are all taken from Table 2.4.
22 Armand Audiganne, *Les Populations ouvrières et les industries de la France*, 2d ed., 2 vols. (Paris, 1860), 2:247.
23 Thirty-two million francs in 1848, or 20 percent of Marseille's total industrial product. Archives Nationales (hereafter cited as AN), C947.
24 Masson, *Les Bouches-du-Rhône*, 8:72.
25 Ibid., 93–4; Julliany, *Essai sur le commerce*, 3:304.
26 AN: C947.
27 Ibid.
28 Rambert, *Marseille*, 246.
29 Julliany, *Essai sur le commerce*, 3:218.
30 Ibid.
31 Ibid., 383–4.
32 Masson, *Les Bouches-du-Rhône*, 8:160–2.
33 Joseph Mathieu, *Marseille: Statistique et histoire* (Marseille, 1879), pp. 297–8.
34 Yvonne Bocognano, "Le Commerce des blés à Marseille de 1840 à 1870," (diplôme d'études supérieures, University of Aix-en-Provence, 1958), pp. 183–4.
35 The figures for 1851 are based on my analysis of a 10 percent sample of the

census of 1851 (Archives de la Ville de Marseille; hereafter cited as AVM: 2 F 131–6, 161); the figures for 1866 are from the summary tables of the census of 1866 (AVM: 2 F 162c). I have not included female workers in these figures because the reporting of women's occupations in 1851 was very incomplete and the totals are therefore not comparable to the more complete figures from 1866.

36   The classic account is J. L. Hammond and Barbara Hammond, *The Skilled Labourer, 1760–1832* (London, 1919). Recent accounts are E. P. Thompson, *The Making of the English Working Class* (London, 1963), pp. 269–313, and Duncan Bythell, *The Handloom Weavers: A Study in the English Cotton Industry during the Industrial Revolution* (London, 1969).

37   The 1829 figures are from Julliany, *Essai sur le commerce*, 3:391–2. The 1848 figures are from the parliamentary inquiry entitled "Enquête sur le travail industriel et agricole," 1848–9, AN: C947. The 1866 figures are from the summary tables of the census of 1866, AVM: 2 F 162c.

38   Information on the size of the candy-making and crate- and barrel-making trades can be found in Christophe de Villeneuve-Bargemont, *Statistique du département des Bouches-du-Rhône*, 4 vols. (Marseille, 1821–34), 4:666, 742–4, and in the summary tables of the census of 1866, AVM: 2 F 162c.

39   Thompson, *Making of the English Working Class*, ch. 8; Christopher H. Johnson, "Economic Change and Artisan Discontent: The Tailors' History 1800–48," in *Revolution and Reaction: 1848 and the Second French Republic*, ed. Roger Price (London, 1975); Bernard H. Moss, *The Origins of the French Labor Movement: The Socialism of Skilled Workers* (Berkeley and Los Angeles, 1976), esp. ch. 1; and Aminzade, *Class, Politics, and Early Industrial Capitalism*.

40   Archives Départementale des Bouches-du-Rhône; hereafter cited as ADBdR, 403 U 53, "Jugement du tribunal correctional," 19 December 1845.

41   AN: C 947, "Enquête sur le travail industriel et agricole," 1848–9.

42   Ibid.

43   See Sewell, "La class ouvrière de Marseille," and "Social Change."

44   Julliany, *Essai sur le commerce*, 1:420.

45   Rambert, *Marseille*, 268.

46   Masson, *Les Bouches-du-Rhône*, 9:811–4.

47   Bertrand Gille, *Recherches sur la formation de la grande enterprise capitaliste (1815–1848)* (Paris, 1959), pp. 96–113.

48   Masson, *Les Bouches-du-Rhône*, 9:737.

49   Ibid., 61.

50   Ibid., 431–3.

51   Ibid., 446.

52   Ibid., 447.

53   Ibid., 67; Victor Nguyen, "Crise et vie des portefaix marseillais, 1814–1914" (diplôme d'études supérieures, University of Aix-en-Provence, 1961), pp. 79, 83.

54   Masson, *Les Bouches-du-Rhône*, 9:450–2; Nguyen, "Crise et vie," 79; Girard, "Grands travaux," 81–2.

55   Girard, "Grands travaux," 84.

56   Ibid., 85; Rambert, *Marseille*, 397.

57   Rambert, *Marseille*, 396.

58   Ibid., 86.

59   Nguyen, "Crise et vie," 13–16.

60   See Carrière, *Négociants marseillais*, 2:875–984, for a detailed description of Marseille's mercantile capitalism in the eighteenth century.

61 Nguyen, "Crise et vie," 14–15.
62 Ibid., 80–1.
63 Ibid., 79–107. See also Victor Nguyen, "Les Portefaix marseillais. Crise et déclin, survivances," *Provence historique* 12 (1962):363–97.
64 Masson, *Les Bouches-du-Rhône*, 9:369.
65 Ibid., 367–72.
66 Ibid., 372–6.
67 Julliany, *Essai sur le commerce*, 1:372.
68 Bertrand Gille, "La Banque de Marseille," *Actes du quatre-vingt-troisième congrès national de sociétés savantes*, held at Aix-Marseille, 1958, Section d'histoire moderne et contemporaine (Paris, 1959), p. 329.
69 Ibid., 333–40.
70 Masson, *Les Bouches-du-Rhône*, 9:924–9.
71 Pierre Guiral, "Quelque notes sur la politique des milieux d'affaires Marseillais de 1815 à 1870," *Provence historique* 7 (1957), p. 174, quoting A. Clapier, *Précis historique sur le commerce de Marseille* (Paris, 1863).

3. The occupational structure

1 See Michael B. Katz, "Occupational Classification in History," *Journal of Interdisciplinary History* (1976):63–88.
2 From the memoirs of Victor Gelu, *Marseille aux XIXe siècle*, ed. and ann. Lucien Gaillard and Jorgi Reboul, introduction by Pierre Guiral (Paris, 1971), pp. 141–2. Gelu was a poet and songwriter and a particularly qualified observer of the rift between bourgeois and artisan life styles. He was born in the old quarters of Marseille the son of a baker, and he grew up in Marseille's traditional artisan community. As an adult, he retained his acquaintances with workers and spent much of his time drinking and singing his songs in working-class cafés and wine shops in the old city. At the same time, he had studied with sons of the local bourgeoisie in the seminary of Marseille and the college at Aix-en-Provence and long earned his own living as a *clerc d'avoué* (law clerk).
3 The research of Adeline Daumard demonstrates this very clearly for Paris, where small businessmen tended to be wealthier than clerical employees but lived more simply. Their living quarters were more cramped, and their expenditures on such luxuries as books, fancy furnishings, and table-wear were distinctly lower. *Les Bourgeois de Paris aux XIXe siècle* (Paris, 1970), pp. 68–76.
4 Emile Littré, *Dictionnaire de la langue française* (Paris, 1863–72).
5 On the corporate tradition and its fate in the nineteenth century, see Sewell, *Work and Revolution*.
6 For a fuller discussion of the artisan trades of Marseille, see Sewell, "Structure of the Working Class," 157–222.
7 The best survey of women's work in the nineteenth century is Louise A. Tilly and Joan W. Scott, *Women, Work, and Family* (New York, 1978).
8 AN: C947, Enquête sur le travail industriel et agricole, 1848–9.
9 Tilly and Scott, *Women, Work, and Family*, p. 75.
10 On domestic servants, see Theresa McBride, *The Domestic Revolution: The Modernization of Household Service in England and France, 1820–1920* (New York, 1976).
11 In both the census and the marriage registers, the recording officials seem to have relied on self-reporting in listing occupations – simply writing down the occupational title given by the respondent, rather than forcing the respondent to

place him- or herself in some predetermined occupational category. Consequently, both census and marriage-register data give figures on occupations as they were conceived by the people of Marseille, not as they were defined by officials. This is fortunate, for it means that figures derived from different documents can be aggregated and compared without worrying about shifting official definitions of occupations.

12   AN: C947.

13   This seems to have been roughly similar to the proportion of bourgeois in the populations of Paris and Toulouse in the nineteenth century. Daumard, *Les Bourgeois de Paris*, pp. 20–2; Aminzade, *Class, Politics, and Early Industrial Capitalism*, p. 23 (Aminzade's figures have to be recategorized to make them comparable to the figures for Marseille).

14   These figures are adjusted as described in Appendix C and therefore include a number of men in the handicraft trades who did not indicate that they were proprietors.

15   Skilled workers in all trades that either were factory trades in 1821–2 or subsequently became factory trades are included here as factory artisans. This includes forge workers, machinists, tanners, glass workers, and ship caulkers. Because the proportion of the workers in each of these trades who actually worked in factories increased over this period, these figures actually understate considerably the extent of the rise of factory artisan trades.

16   These include masons, stonecutters, painters, joiners, and the various trades in the miscellaneous-building category (see Appendix B).

17   Once again, these figures are adjusted to remove some miscategorized small employers. This adjustment was carried out by assuming that the ratio of workers to masters was the same in the building trades as in small-scale industry as a whole.

18   These figures include the usual adjustment.

19   This figure includes soap makers, sugar refiners, and wool combers. Other unskilled factory workers seem to have called themselves *journaliers*.

20   It is my impression that omissions were particularly serious for married women.

21   For these purposes, rentières are considered as not employed.

22   Even among those domestics who married in Marseille in 1846 and 1851, only 4.3 percent had been born in Marseille.

23   See Abel Chatelain, "Migrations et domesticité féminine urbaine en France, XVIIIᵉ siècle–XXᵉ siècle," *Revue d'histoire économique et sociale*, 47.

4. Occupational status

1   The sociological literature on occupational rankings is vast. A classic monograph on the subject is Albert J. Reiss, Jr., *Occupations and Social Status* (New York, 1961). See especially Otis Dudley Duncan, "A Socioeconomic Index for All Occupations," in *ibid.*, 109–38. Other representative contributions are J. H. Goldthorpe and K. Hope, *The Social Grading of Occupations: A New Approach and Scale* (Oxford, 1974); Robert W. Hodge, Paul M. Siegel, and Peter H. Rossi, "Occupational Prestige in the United States, 1925–63," *American Journal of Sociology* 70 (1964):286–302; Edward O. Lauman, *Prestige and Association in an Urban Community: An Analysis of an Urban Stratification System* (Indianapolis, 1966); Edward O. Lauman and Richard Senter, "Subjective Social Distance, Occupational Stratification, and Forms of Status and Class Consciousness: A Cross-National Replication and Extension," *American Journal of Sociology*

81 (1976):1304–38. On the question of group differences in rankings of occupations, see Morgan C. Brown, "The Status of Jobs and Occupations as Evaluated by an Urban Negro Sample," *American Sociological Review*, 20 (1955):561–6; Michael J. Armer, "Intersociety and Intrasociety Correlations of Occupational Prestige," *American Journal of Sociology* 74 (1968):28–36; and Paul M. Siegel, "Occupational Prestige in the Negro Subculture," in Edward O. Lauman, ed., *Social Stratification: Research and Theory for the 1970s* (Indianapolis, 1970), pp. 156–71.

2   See especially Donald J. Treiman, *Occupational Prestige in Comparative Perspective* (New York, 1976).

3   See, for example, Adeline Daumard and Francois Furet, *Structures et relations sociales à Paris au milieu du XVIIIe siècle* (Paris, 1961); Daumard, et al., *Les Fortunes françaises*; Marcel Couturier, *Recherches sur les structures sociales de Chateaudun, 1525–1789* (Paris, 1969); Stuart M. Blumin, "Mobility and Change in Ante-bellum Philadelphia," in Stephan Thernstrom and Richard Sennett, eds., *Nineteenth Century Cities* (New Haven, Conn., 1969); Jackson Turner Main, *The Social Structure of Revolutionary America* (Princeton, N.J., 1961); and Katz, "Occupational Classification."

4   The precise meaning of being able to sign one's name is, of course, not altogether clear. Some people may have learned to sign their names without knowing how to write or perhaps even to read; others may have known how to read but could not sign their names. But surely most signers could both read and write, and most nonsigners could do neither. Even if some individual cases are ambiguous, these few cases should have very little influence on the overall outcome of this measure.

5   Emile Ripert, *La Renaissance provençale, 1800–1860* (Paris, 1917).

6   The best account of the nineteenth-century French bourgeois women's life style is Bonnie G. Smith, *Ladies of the Leisure Class: The Bourgeoises of Northern France in the Nineteenth Century* (Princeton, N.J., 1981).

7   The only exceptions to this are the "legal professions" and "other professions" categories in 1821–2, each of which is represented by only 5 cases.

8   In carrying out these calculations, the percentage scores of each occupation were weighted by the number of cases on which the score was based. Hence, large occupations were counted more heavily than small occupations, with the result that the mean is exactly equal to the population mean.

9   The formula for this latter conversion is $S = 10 D + 50$, where S equals the numerical score and D equals the standard-deviation score. For example, an occupation with an 86 percent literacy rate in 1869 would have a standard-deviation score of 0 and would therefore have a numerical score of 50. An occupation with a literacy rate of 72 percent would have a standard-deviation score of -1 and a numerical score of 40 ($-10 + 50$).

10   These correlation coefficients, and all others comparing scores across years, are based only on those occupations that were large enough to have assigned scores in both years in question. There were 58 such occupations for the correlation between 1821–2 and 1846–51, 65 for the correlation between 1846–51 and 1869, and 53 for the correlation between 1821–2 and 1869. For those unfamiliar with correlation techniques, a coefficient of 1.00 indicates a perfect correspondence between two variables, -1.00 indicates a perfect negative correspondence, and .00 indicates no relationship whatsoever. Coefficients on the order of .9, thus, indicate an extremely close correspondence.

11   Take the example of the legal professions in 1869. For some reason, one lawyer

was recorded as being illiterate. Because an illiterate lawyer is a contradiction in terms, we must assume that this was an error on the part of the official who drew up the marriage act. Lawyers were, however, credited with a 92 percent literacy rate and a corresponding literacy score of .54. This ranked them 35th among the 65 occupations scored. This is obviously a grossly inaccurate ranking, for lawyers were first or tied for first in every other ranking for every year. The inaccuracy is canceled out in the summary score, however, where the legal professions once again ranked first, thanks to their very high score on the witness scale.

12   In fact, the correlation between summary scales composed of these two measures and scales composed of all three are higher than .99 in both 1846–51 and 1869. In other words, the scales constructed by these two different methods are essentially identical.

13   In 1821–2 artistic professions were combined with other professions, owing to insufficient numbers.

14   In fact, the continuity probably stretched over a far longer span than a mere fifty years. Correlation of the Marseille summary scale with Donald J. Treiman's "Standard International Occupational Prestige Scale" – which he claims is valid in contemporary societies all over the world – yields coefficients of .59 in 1821–2, .72 in 1846–51, and .77 in 1869. In other words, Marseille's occupational-status hierarchy was strikingly similar to those of present-day societies. See Treiman, *Occupational Prestige* and "A Standard Occupational Prestige Scale for Use with Historical Data," *Journal of Interdisciplinary History* 7 (1976):283–304.

5.   The urban framework

1   Audiganne, *Les Populations ouvrières*, 2:235.
2   Ibid.
3   Rambert, *Marseille*, 148.
4   Ibid., 192.
5   Ibid., 205–6.
6   Ibid., 216.
7   Ibid.
8   Ibid., pp. 271–2. Both the open spaces within the seventeenth-century perimeter and the remains of the walls themselves can be seen in Figure 5.2.
9   Ibid., 261–2.
10   Ibid., 289; ADBdR: M4/44 (list of factories subject to the laws on child labor, 1843); ADBdR: 12 U 8 (list of factories employing twenty or more workers in 1850 and 1851).
11   Yves Janvier, "L'Industrie du bâtiment à Marseille de 1815 à 1851" (diplôme d'études supérieues, Faculté des lettres, Aix-en-Provence, 1964), p. 33.
12   As explained in Appendix A, the actual sex ratio in Marseille was over 100; the ratio derived from the *listes nominatives* is low only because a significant number of males are missing from the *listes*. However, differences that show up between districts in the *listes nominatives* data are probably real ones. The sex ratio is the number of men divided by the number of women, multiplied by 100.
13   Rambert, *Marseille*, 282.
14   Gelu, *Marseille au XIXe siècle*, 336–7.
15   Ibid., 383.

6. The demography of urban growth

1 Mathieu, *Marseille: statistique et histoire*, 6; Charpin, *Pratique religieuse*, 269; and Pouthas, *La Population française*, 98.

2 Mathieu, *Marseille: Statistique et histoire*, 34–5. These figures are taken from the official *actes de naissance* and *actes de décès* of these years.

3 The formula for the birth rate in a given census interval is as follows: Let B = the total number of births in a given census interval, let P_1 and P_2 = the population of Marseille at the beginning and end of the census interval. The average annual birth rate for the census interval is equal to $B \bigg/ \left[\dfrac{5}{2}\left(P_1 + P_2 \right) \right]$. The formula for death, natural increase, and migration rates are analogous.

4 Thernstrom and Knights, "Men in Motion," 7–36, and Thernstrom, *Other Bostonians*, 16.

5 Sharlin, "Social Structure and Politics," 41–3.

6 Chudacoff, *Mobile Americans*; Griffen and Griffen, *Natives and Newcomers*; Knights, *Plain People of Boston*; Katz, *People of Hamilton*; and Crew, *Town in the Ruhr*.

7 Charpin, *Pratique religieuse*, 269.

8 Ibid., 273.

9 Ibid., 277.

7. Migration

1 See Robert E. Park, "Human Migration and the Marginal Man," *American Journal of Sociology*, 33 (May 1928), 881–93, and Robert E. Park and Ernest W. Burgess, *The City* (Chicago, 1925).

2 See, for example, Oscar Handlin, *The Uprooted: The Epic Story of the Great Migrations that Made the American People* (Boston, 1951).

3 *Classes laborieuses et classes dangereuses.*

4 For an excellent critique and evaluation of Chevalier's argument, see the review by Robert J. Bezucha, *Journal of Social History* 8 (1974):119–24.

5 See, for example, *Annales de démographie historique*, 1970 and 1971, special numbers on migration.

6 The most important exception is, in fact, Louis Chevalier. He was trained as a demographer, and his earlier work *La Formation de la population parisienne* was an admirable example of restrained empirical description.

7 An exception to this approach, among the demographers, is Barbara A. Anderson, *Internal Migration during Modernization in Late Nineteenth-Century Russia* (Princeton, N.J., 1980). Historians who have considered the broader social ramifications of migration include Maurice Garden, *Lyon et les lyonnais au XVIIIe siècle* (Paris, 1971); Robert Eugene Johnson, *Peasant and Proletarian: The Working Class of Moscow in the Late Nineteenth Century* (New Brunswick, N.J., 1979); and Jackson, "Migration and Urbanization."

8 See, for example, John S. MacDonald and Leatrice D. MacDonald, "Chain Migration, Ethnic Neighborhood Formation, and Social Networks," *Millbank Memorial Fund Quarterly* 42 (1964):82–97; Peter C. W. Gutkind, "African Urbanism, Mobility, and the Social Network," *International Journal of Comparative Sociology* 6 (1965):48–60; B. H. Herrick, *Urban Migration and Economic Development in Chile* (Cambridge, Mass., 1965); Charles Tilly and C. Howard Brown, "On Uprooting, Kinship, and the Auspices of Migration,"

International Journal of Comparative Sociology 7 (1967):139–64; Harley L. Browning and Waltraut Feindt, "Selectivity of Migrants to a Metropolis in a Developing Country: A Mexican Case Study," *Demography* 6 (1969):347–57; Douglas S. Butterworth, "A Study of the Urbanization Process among Mixtec Migrants from Tilantongo in Mexico City," in William Mangin, ed., *Peasants in Cities: Readings in the Anthropology of Urbanization* (Boston, 1970); Harvey M. Choldin, "Kinship Networks in the Migration Process," *International Migration Review* 7 (1973):163–75; L. H. Long, "Migration Differentials by Education and Occupation: Trends and Variations," *Demography* (1973), 243–58; A. Speare, "Urbanization and Migration in Taiwan," *Economic Development and Cultural Change* 22 (1974):302–19.

9   Examples are Thernstrom, *Poverty and Progress*, on the Irish in Newburyport, Massachusetts; Barton, *Peasants and Strangers*, on the Italians, Slovaks, and Rumanians in Cleveland; Conzen, *Immigrant Milwaukee*, on the Germans in Milwaukee; and Lees, *Exiles of Erin*, on the Irish in London.

10 Perhaps the most systematic efforts to date are Moch, *Paths to the City*, and James H. Jackson, Jr., "The Occupational and Familial Context of Migration in Duisberg, 1867–1890," *Journal of Urban History* 8 (1982):235–70, and "Migration and Urbanization." Other research pointing toward the same conclusions includes Allen R. Newmann, "The Influence of Family and Friends on German Internal Migration, 1880–85," *Journal of Social History* 13 (1979):277–88; Walter D. Kemphoefner, "The Social Consequences of Rural–Urban Migration in Imperial Germany: The 'Floating Proletariat' Thesis Reconsidered," Social Science Working Paper 414, California Institute of Technology, January 1982; Anderson, *Family Structure*, which has evidence on family ties among migrants; Barton, *Peasants and Strangers*, which has evidence on both family ties and links with the place of origin; and Graf, *Literacy Myth*, 65–9, which finds that the European migrants to North America were more likely to be literate than the compatriots left behind.

11 One indication that this may have been true is that for grooms who were born in Marseille, the parents' residence is unknown in only 8 percent of the cases, as against 24 percent for immigrant grooms.

12 Maurice Agulhon, "La Fin des petites villes dans la Var intérieure au XIXe siècle," in *Villes de l'Europe occidentale du Moyen Age au XIXe siècle*, Actes du colloque de Nice (27–8 March 1969), nos. 9–10 of *Annales de la Faculté des Lettres et Sciences Humaines de Nice* (Monaco, 1969), pp. 323–6. See also his "La Notion de village en Basse-Provence vers la fin de l'Ancien Régime," *Actes du 90e Congrès national des Sociétés Savantes (Nice, 1965)*, Section d'histoire moderne et contemporaine, vol. 1 (Paris, 1966), pp. 277–301, and *La Vie sociale en Provence intérieure au lendemain de la Révolution* (Paris, 1970), pp. 59–61. James R. Lehning, in *The Peasants of Marlhes: Economic Development and Family Organization in Nineteenth-Century France* (Chapel Hill, 1980), finds that from 1851 to 1856 the highest rates of out-migration from the village of Marlhes, in the mountains just south of Saint-Etienne, were among liberal professions and artisans.

13 The number of cases in some of these categories is very small, so the percentages given in Tables 7.5 and 7.6 must be regarded as very rough estimates.

14 This difference between long- and short-distance migration may not have been limited to Marseille. John Modell has found that long-distance immigrants into Reading, Pennsylvania, had distinctly better jobs than those who came from nearby. This could, of course, indicate a difference in postmigration occupational

mobility rather than in premigration occupational origins, but in either case it would seem to argue that long-range migration was more highly selective. "The Peopling of a Working-Class Ward: Reading, Pennsylvania, 1850," *Journal of Social History* 5 (1971):71–95.

15 See Abel Chatelain, "Migrations et domesticité," 506–628; and Theresa M. McBride, *Domestic Revolution.*

16 A study of illegitimate pregnancy in eighteenth-century Marseille shows that domestic servants were particularly likely to bear illegitimate children. However, it also shows that most seducers were either artisans or fellow domestic servants, not masters. Ollivier, "Grossesses illégitimes à Marseille" (Mémoire de Maîtrise, Université de Provence, Aix-en-Provence, n.d.), plates 16 and 28. (This mémoire is available at the ADBdR.) In mid-nineteenth-century Amiens, domestic servants were more likely to become unwed mothers than any other occupational group except unskilled workers. R. Burr Litchfield and David Gordon, "Closing the 'Tour': A Close Look at the Marriage Market, Unwed Mothers, and Abandoned Children in Mid-Nineteenth-Century Amiens," *Journal of Social History* 13 (1980):464–6.

17 My thinking on these questions has been influenced by Joan W. Scott and Louise A. Tilly, "Women's Work and the Family in Nineteenth Century Europe," *Comparative Studies in Society and History* 17 (1975):36–64, and Tilly and Scott, *Women, Work and Family.*

18 Figures on kinship ties must be based on 1851 alone, for I did not record parents' residence from the marriage acts of 1846.

19 This change in the character of migration, with elite migration being increasingly replaced by mass migration of rural and low-status people fits the theories put forward by William Peterson, "A General Typology of Migration," *American Sociological Review* 23 (1958):256–66, and Wilbur Zelinsky, "The Hypothesis of the Mobility Transition," *Geographical Review* 61 (1971):219–49.

20 Because I did not record parents' residence on the 1846 marriage registers, figures on brides' and grooms' premigration occupational backgrounds are based on 1851, rather than on both 1846 and 1851.

21 E. Levasseur, *La Population Française* (Paris, 1891), vol. 2, p. 491.

22 The figure is actually for the period 1816–20. Ibid., 478.

23 The national average for brides was 35 percent in 1816–20, 53 in 1854, and 63 in 1869. Ibid., 478, 491.

8.   Dangerous classes?

1 See Marshal B. Clinard, *Anomie and Deviant Behavior: A Discussion and Critique* (New York, 1964).

2 The records of the *tribunal correctionnel* are in series 403U in the ADBdR in Marseille. The records of the *cour d'assises* are in series 163U in the Aix-en-Provence branch of the ADBdR.

3 Edwin H. Sutherland and Donald R. Cressy, *Criminology*, 8th ed. (Philadelphia, 1970), pp. 121–6.

4 For an explanation of the use of these age categories, see note 8 in Appendix A.

5 Sutherland and Cressy, *Criminology*, 217.

6 The petty thieves were the only category of criminals sufficiently numerous to make such a cross-tabulation meaningful. It was to accumulate enough cases to allow for this kind of multivariate analysis that thefts from 1844 to 1847 were recorded and added to the cases already recorded for 1848 to 1850. The number

of thefts tried in the *tribunal correctionnel* from 1848 to 1850 was 596. By including the entire 1844–50 period, the number of cases was increased to 1,218. Some of the men accused of theft were acquitted, leaving 1,086 convicted petty thieves.

7   The following discussion is based only on data from the *tribunal correctionnel*. The records of the *cour d'assises* do not give the street addresses of criminals.

8   The proportions of the adult males over 17 who lived alone in districts 1, 3, and 4 were 17, 21, and 23 percent. The only other quarter with a proportion this high, district 11, with 17 percent, was not really a hotel and rooming-house district. Its "solitary" men were nearly all lodged in barracks maintained by chemical factories located in this district, far from the city proper.

9   Chevalier, *Classes laborieuses et classes dangereuses*. The best known of the nineteenth-century observers was Honoré Antoine Frégier, *Des classes dangereuses dans la population des grandes villes et des moyens de les rendre meilleures*, 2 vols. (Paris, 1840).

9.   Social mobility: men

1   The best known historical studies of occupational mobility in America are those of Thernstrom, *Poverty and Progress* and *Other Bostonians*. See also Rogoff, *Recent Trends in Occupational Mobility*; Goldstein, *Patterns of Mobility*; Blumin, "Mobility and Change"; Chudakoff, *Mobile Americans*; Katz, *People of Hamilton*; Griffen and Griffen, *Natives and Newcomers*; and Barton, *Peasants and Strangers*.

2   For a survey of international research on social mobility, see S. M. Miller, "Comparative Social Mobility: A Trend Report and Bibliography," *Current Sociology* 9 (1960). A survey of historical research on social mobility in Europe is Hartmut Kaelble, *Historical Research on Social Mobility: Western Europe and the USA in the Nineteenth and Twentieth Centuries* (New York, 1981). The same author has edited a collection of historical mobility studies, *Geschichte der sozialen Mobilität seit der industriellen Revolution* (Königstein, 1978). See also Crew, *Town in the Ruhr*; and Allan N. Sharlin, "From the Study of Social Mobility to the Study of Society," *American Journal of Sociology* 85 (1979):338–60.

3   See, for example, Elbridge Sibley, "Some Demographic Clues to Stratification," *American Sociological Review* 7 (1942):322–30, and Leo F. Schnore, "Social Mobility in Demographic Perspective," *American Sociological Review*, 26 (1961):407–23.

4   The index of dissimilarity between two distributions is calculated by summing the absolute values of the differences between the percentages in the two distributions and dividing this sum by two.

5   See, e.g., Otis Dudley Duncan and Robert W. Hodge, "Education and Occupational Mobility, A Regression Analysis," *American Journal of Sociology* 68 (1963):629–44; Peter M. Blau and Otis Dudley Duncan, *The American Occupational Structure* (New York, 1967); Otis Dudley Duncan, *Socioeconomic Background and Achievement* (New York, 1972); Robert M. Hauser, "Schools and the Stratification Process," *American Journal of Sociology* 74 (1969):587–611; William H. Sewell and Robert M. Hauser, *Education, Occupation, and Earnings: Achievement in the Early Career* (New York, 1975); William H. Sewell, Robert M. Hauser, and David L. Featherman, eds., *Schooling and Achievement in American Society* (New York, 1976). For nineteenth-century France, see Patrick J. Harrigan, *Mobility, Elites, and Education in French Society of the Second Empire* (Waterloo, Ontario, 1980). See also Graff, *Literacy Myth*, 72–81.

6   The non-Italian foreign born were too few to constitute a separate category. They
    have been added to the French-born immigrants rather than to the Italians because
    their patterns of mobility were much closer to those of the French born.
7   François Mazuy, *Essai historique sur les moeurs et coutumes des Marseillais au
    XIXe siècle* (Marseille, 1853), p. 179.
8   AN: C947, Enquête sur le travail industriel et agricole.
9   On 30 May 1851, Marseille's top judicial officer, the Procureur de la République,
    outlined the procedures that the police had just taken to ensure better surveillance
    of Italians. He justified surveillance on the grounds that "most of them, always
    ready to throw themselves into insurrections, commit the greatest excesses in
    moments of disorder." In fact, Italians were vastly underrepresented in the in-
    surrectionary events of the era. See Sewell, "La Classe ouvrière" and "Social
    Change."
10 M. Sauze, *De la mendicité dans le département des Bouches-du-Rhône* (Marseille,
    1846).
11 See the reports in the newspaper *Le Progrès social*, 11–14 March 1848; ADBdR:
    M6/11, police report dated 16 March 1848, and M6/25, letter from Jacques
    Bernabo to the Commissaire de la République, dated 9 April 1848; and AVM:
    1 D 73, sessions of the municipal commission of 9 March and 25 March 1848.
12 Mazuy, *Essai historique*, 181; Gelu, *Marseille au XIXe siècle*, 92.
13 Antoine Olivési, "Marseille," in *Les Elections législatives de mai 1869*, ed.
    Louis Girard, *Bibliothèque de la Révolution de 1848*, vol. 21 (Paris, 1960), pp.
    77–123.
14 Antoine Olivési, *La Commune de 1871 à Marseille et ses origines* (Paris: Marcel
    Rivière, 1950).
15 For some thoughts on connections between social mobility and workers' con-
    sciousness, see Sewell, "Social Mobility." For an interpretation of the history
    of working-class radicalism in Marseille, see Sewell, "Social Change."

10. Social mobility: women

1   See note 1, Chapter 9.
2   On women's work in France, see Tilly and Scott, *Women, Work and Family*.
3   The literature on this subject has expanded vastly since the early 1970s. See,
    e.g., Donald J. Treiman and Kermit Terrell, "The Process of Status Attainment
    in the United States and Great Britain," *American Journal of Sociology* 81
    (1975):563–83; McKee McClendon, "The Occupational Status Attainment Pro-
    cesses of Males and Females," *American Sociological Review* 41 (1976):52–64;
    David L. Featherman and Robert M. Hauser, "Sexual Inequalities and Socio-
    economic Achievement in the United States 1962–73," *American Sociological
    Review* 41 (1976):462–83; Joe L. Spaeth, "Differences in the Occupational
    Achievement Process Between Male and Female College Graduates," *Sociology
    of Education* 50 (1977):206–17; Neil D. Fligstein and Wendy C. Wolf, "Sex
    Similarities in Occupational Status Attainment: Are the Results due to the Re-
    striction of the Sample to Employed Women?" *Social Science Research* 7
    (1978):197–212; J. Treas and A. Tyree, "Prestige versus Socioeconomic Status
    in the Attainment Process of American Men and Women," *Social Science Re-
    search* 8 (1979):201–21; William H. Sewell, Robert M. Hauser, and Wendy C.
    Wolf, "Sex, Schooling, and Occupational Status," *American Journal of Soci-
    ology* 86 (1980):551–83; and Therese L. Baker, "Class, Family, Education, and
    the Process of Status Attainment: a Comparison of American and British Women
    College Graduates," *Sociological Quarterly* 23 (1982):17–31.

4   The way these percentages have been calculated can be clarified by the example of 1821–2. In 1821–2, 59 percent of all grooms were natives, 36 percent were non-Italian immigrants, and 5 percent were Italian immigrants. If native women had married without regard to men's birthplaces, 59 percent of their grooms, or 463 (i.e., 784 × .59) would have been natives. In fact, 661 were natives. Analogous calculations indicate that had there been no preference for spouses from the same birthplace category, 106 of the grooms of non-Italian immigrant women would have been non-Italian immigrants (as against an actual figure of 158), and 2 of the grooms of Italian immigrant women would have been Italian immigrants (as against an actual figure of 7). Hence, 117 more brides married grooms from their own birthplace categories than would have had there been no preference for such grooms. (The number 117 is equal to the sum of 523 − 463, 158 − 106, and 7 − 2.) The number 117 is 20 percent of 571, the total number of marriages between same-category brides and grooms that would have obtained in the absence of preference (571 = 463 + 106 + 2). The percentages in other years were calculated analogously.

5   The craft workers include the needle-trade workers, laundresses, and other craft categories discussed in Chapter 3.

6   See Smith, *Ladies of the Leisure Class.*

7   Theresa McBride has also argued that domestic servants often had favorable social-mobility experiences. She notes both the good real wages of domestics and the importance of training in bourgeois household management. See her *Domestic Revolution.* David M. Katzman has found that the real wages of American domestic servants were superior to those of women who worked in other manual trades. See his *Seven Days a Week: Women and Domestic Service in Industrializing America* (New York, 1978), pp. 303–14.

11.   Conclusion: Transformation from without

1   On Marseille's political history, see Masson, ed., *Les Bouches-du-Rhône,* vol. 5, *La Vie politique et administrative* (Paris and Marseille, 1929), and vol. 10, *Le Mouvement social* (Paris and Marseille, 1923).

2   Sewell, "Working Class of Marseille."

3   Charpin, *Pratique religieuse,* 124.

4   Mazuy, *Essai historique*; Agricol Perdiguier, *Mémoires d'un compagnon* (Moulins, 1914; Paris, 1964), p. 91.

5   On linguistic patterns and popular culture in Marseille, see Gelu, *Marseille*; Mazuy, *Essai historique*; and Sewell, "Social Change," 90–5.

6   Park, "Human Migration," 887–8.

Appendix A

1   These non-Marseillais are, of course, excluded from the calculations made in this study.

2   For discussion of seasonal migration of the French Alpine population, see Raoul Blanchard, *Les Alpes occidentales,* vol. 7, *Essai d'une synthèse* (Paris and Grenoble, 1956), pp. 547–57.

3   In a purely statistical sense, the persons getting married in a given year are not a sample at all, but a universe – because all members of that class of phenomena are included. But, in a broader sense, the persons marrying in a given year can be considered a sample of the settled young-adult population as a whole. When

"marriage-register samples" are spoken of hereafter, the term is to be understood in this latter, broader sense.

4 Etienne Van de Walle, *The Female Population in the Nineteenth Century: A Reconstruction of 82 Departments of France* (Princeton, N.J., 1974).

5 The city directory, *L'Indicateur Marseillais* for 1851, is part of the collection of the municipal archives.

6 France, *Statistique de la France*, 2d ser., *Territoire et population* (Paris, 1855).

7 Ibid.

8 Here and elsewhere in this book, ages are categorized so as to center on ages ending in zero or five (i.e., 18–22, 23–27, and so on). This is contrary to the common practice of setting categories that begin with ages ending in zero or five (i.e., 15–19, 20–4, and so on). This is done because the ages transcribed in all the documents used for this study are self-reported, and many persons reported ages rounded to the nearest five years. Age categories beginning with numbers ending in zero or five would therefore tend to miscategorize the presumably sizable number of persons who rounded their ages upward. Centering the age categories on ages ending in zero and five minimizes such miscategorizations.

9 William Peterson, *Population*, 3d ed. (New York, 1975), p. 288.

Appendix C

1 Pp. 391–2. Julliany was a merchant from Marseille, a founding member of his city's Société de Statistique, a municipal councillor and an officer of the Chambre de Commerce during the July Monarchy, and the author of several books on economic questions. He knew more about the economy of Marseille than any other man of his era, and his estimates are therefore worthy of some confidence.

2 AN: C947.

3 AVM: 2F 162C.

Bibliography

Agulhon, Maurice. "La Fin des petites villes dans la Var intérieure au XIXᵉ siècle." In *Villes de l'Europe Occidentale du Moyen Age au XIXᵉ siècle*. Actes du colloque de Nice (27–8 March 1969). *Annales de la Faculté des Lettres et Sciences Humaines de Nice*, 9–10. Monaco, 1969.

————. "La Notion de village en Basse-Provence vers la fin de l'Ancien Régime." *Actes du 90ᵉ Congrès National des Sociétés Savantes (Nice, 1965). Section d'histoire moderne et contemporaine*, vol. 1. Paris, 1966.

————. *La Vie sociale en Provence intérieure au lendemain de la Révolution*. Paris, 1970.

————. *Une Ville ouvrière au temps du socialisme utopique: Toulon de 1815 à 1851*. Paris and The Hague, 1970.

Aminzade, Ronald. *Class, Politics, and Early Industrial Capitalism: A Study of Mid-Nineteenth-Century Toulouse, France*. Albany, N.Y., 1981.

Aminzade, Ronald and Hodson, Randy. "Social Mobility in a Mid-Nineteenth Century City." *American Sociological Review* 47 (1982):441–57.

Anderson, Barbara A. *Internal Migration during Modernization in Late Nineteenth-Century Russia*. Princeton, N.J., 1980.

Anderson, Michael. *Family Structure in Nineteenth-Century Lancashire*. Cambridge, 1971.

Armer, Michael J. "Intersociety and Intrasociety Correlations of Occupational Prestige." *American Journal of Sociology* 74 (1968):28–36.

Armstrong, Alan. *Stability and Change in an English Country Town: A Social Study of York 1801–51*. London, 1974.

Audiganne, Armand. *Les Populations ouvrières et les industries de la France*. 2d ed. 2 vols. Paris, 1860.

Baker, Therese L. "Class, Family, Education, and the Process of Status Attainment: A Comparison of American and British Women College Graduates." *Sociological Quarterly* 23 (1982):17–31.

Bardet, Jean-Pierre. Review of Michel Terrisse, "La Population de Marseille et de son terroir de 1694 à 1830." *Annales de démographie historique* (1973).

Barton, Josef J. *Peasants and Strangers: Italians, Rumanians, and Slovaks in an American City, 1890–1950*. Cambridge, Mass., 1975.

Bezucha, Robert J. *The Lyon Uprising of 1834: Social and Political Conflict in a Nineteenth-Century City*. Cambridge, Mass., 1974.

Biraben, Jean-Noel. "Certain Demographic Characteristics of the Plague Epidemic in France, 1720–22." *Daedalus* 97 (1968):536–45.

Blanchard, Raoul. *Les Alpes occidentales*. 7 vols. Vol. 7. *Essai d'une synthèse*. Paris and Grenoble, 1956.

Blau, Peter M., and Duncan, Otis Dudley. *The American Occupational Structure*. New York, 1967.

Blumin, Stuart. "Mobility and Change in Ante-Bellum Philadelphia." In *Nineteenth Century Cities: Essays in the New Urban History*, ed. Stephan Thernstrom and Richard Sennett, pp. 165–208. New Haven, Conn., 1969.

362

The Urban Threshold: Growth and Change in a Nineteenth-Century American Community. Chicago, 1976.

Bocognano, Yvonne. "Le Commerce des blés à Marseille de 1840 à 1870." Diplôme d'études supérieures, University of Aix-en-Provence, 1958.

Bousquet, Casimir, and Sapet, Tony. *Etude sur la navigation, le commerce et l'industrie de Marseille, pendant la période quinquennale de 1850 à 1854.* Marseille, 1857.

Brown, Morgan C. "The Status of Jobs and Occupations as Evaluated by an Urban Negro Sample." *American Sociological Review* 20 (1955):561–6.

Browning, Harley L., and Feindt, Waltraut. "Selectivity of Migrants to a Metropolis in a Developing Country: A Mexican Case Study." *Demography* 6 (1969):347–57.

Butterworth, Douglas S. "A Study of the Urbanization Process among Mixtec Migrants from Tilantongo in Mexico City." In *Peasants in Cities: Readings in the Anthropology of Urbanization,* ed. William Mangin. Boston, 1970.

Bythell, Duncan. *The Handloom Weavers: A Study in the English Cotton Industry during the Industrial Revolution.* London, 1969.

Carrière, Charles. *Négociants marseillais au XVIII ᵉ siècle: Contribution à l'étude des économies maritimes.* 2 vols. Marseille, 1973.

Caspard, Pierre. "La Fabrique au village." *Le mouvement social* 97 (1976).

Charpin, F. L. *Pratique religieuse et formation d'une grand ville: Le Geste du baptême et sa signification en sociologie religieuse.* Paris, 1964.

Chassagne, Serge. "La Formation de la population d'une agglomeration industrielle: Corbeil-Essones (1750–1850)." *Le mouvement social* 97 (1976).

Chatelain, Abel. "Migrations et domesticité feminine urbaine en France, XVIIIᵉ siècle-XXᵉ siècle." *Revue d'histoire économique et sociale* 47 (1969):506–28.

Chevalier, Louis. *Classes laborieuses et classes dangereuses à Paris pendant la première moitié du XIXᵉ siècle.* Paris, 1958.

La Formation de la population parisienne au XIXᵉ siècle. Cahier no. 10 of the Institut National d'Etudes Démographiques. Paris, 1950.

Laboring Classes and Dangerous Classes in Paris during the First Half of the Nineteenth Century. Trans. Frank Jellinek. New York, 1973.

Choldin, Harvey M. "Kinship Networks in the Migration Process." *International Migration Review* 7 (1973):163–75.

Chudakoff, Howard P. *Mobile Americans: Residential and Social Mobility in Omaha, 1880–1920.* New York, 1972.

Clapier, A. *Précis historique sur le commerce de Marseille.* Paris, 1863.

Clinard, Marshal B. *Anomie and Deviant Behavior: A Discussion and Critique.* New York, 1964.

Conzen, Kathleen Neils. *Immigrant Milwaukee, 1836–1860: Accommodation and Community in a Frontier City.* Cambridge, Mass., 1976.

Couturier, Marcel. *Recherches sur les structures sociales de Chateaudun, 1525–1789.* Paris, 1969.

Crew, David F. *Town in the Ruhr: A Social History of Bochum, 1860–1914.* New York, 1979.

Daumard, Adeline. *Les Bourgeois de Paris aux XIXᵉ siècle.* Paris, 1970.

La Bourgeoisie parisienne de 1815 à 1848. Paris, 1963.

Daumard, Adeline. With the collaboration of Felix Codaccioni, Georges Dupeux, Jacqueline Herpin, Jacques Godechot, and Jean Sentou. *Les Fortunes françaises au XIXᵉ siècle.* Paris and The Hague, 1973.

Daumard, Adeline, and Furet, François. *Structures et relations sociales à Paris au milieu du XVIIIᵉ siècle.* Paris, 1961.

Deyon, Pierre. *Amiens, capitale provinciale. Etude sur la société urbaine au XVIIᵉ siècle.* Paris and The Hague, 1967.

Duncan, Otis Dudley. *Socioeconomic Background and Achievement.* New York, 1972.

"A Socioeconomic Index for All Occupations." In *Occupations and Social Status,* ed. Albert J. Reiss, Jr. New York, 1961.

Duncan, Otis Dudley, and Hodge, Robert W. "Education and Occupational Mobility, a Regression Analysis." *American Journal of Sociology* 68 (1963):629–44.

Dyos, H. J., ed. *The Study of Urban History.* New York, 1968.

Featherman, David L., and Hauser, Robert M. "Sexual Inequalities and Socioeconomic Achievement in the United States 1962–73." *American Sociological Review* 41 (1976):462–83.

Fligstein, Neil D., and Wolf, Wendy C. "Sex Similarities in Occupational Status Attainment: Are the Results due to the Restriction of the Sample to Employed Women?" *Social Science Research* 7 (1978):197–212.

Foster, John. *Class Struggle and the Industrial Revolution: Early Industrial Capitalism in Three English Towns.* London, 1974.

France. *Statistique de la France. Résultats généraux du dénombrement de 1872.* Nancy, 1874.

France. *Statistique de la France.* 2d ser. *Territoire et Population.* Paris, 1855.

Frégier, Honoré Antoine. *Des classes dangereuses dans la population des grandes villes et des moyens de les rendre meilleures,* 2 vols. Paris, 1840.

Gaillard, Jeanne. *Paris la Ville.* Paris, 1977.

Garden, Maurice. *Lyon et les lyonnais au XVIIIᵉ siècle.* Paris, 1971.

Gelu, Victor. *Marseille aux XIXᵉ siècle.* Ed. and ann. Lucien Gaillard and Jorgi Reboul; introduction by Pierre Guiral. Paris, 1971.

Gille, Bertrand. "La Banque de Marseille." *Actes du quatre-vingt-troisième congrès national de sociétés savantes,* Aix-Marseille, 1958, Section d'histoire moderne et contemporaine. Paris, 1959.

Recherches sur la formation de la grande enterprise capitaliste (1815–1848). Paris, 1959.

Girard, Louis. "La Politique des grandes travaux à Marseille sous le Second Empire." In Chambre de Commerce de Marseille, *Marseille sous le Second Empire: Exposition, conférences, colloque organisés à l'occasion du centenaire du Palais de la Bourse, 10–26 novembre 1960.* Paris, 1961.

Goldstein, Sidney. *Patterns of Mobility, 1910–1950. The Norristown Study. A Method for Measuring Migration and Occupational Mobility in the Community.* Philadelphia, 1958.

Goldthorpe, J. H., and Hope, K. *The Social Grading of Occupations: A New Approach and Scale.* Oxford, 1974.

Goubert, Pierre. *Beauvais et le Beauvaisis de 1600 à 1730, contribution à l'histoire social de la France du XVIIᵉ siècle.* Paris, 1960.

Graff, Harvey J. *The Literacy Myth: Literacy and Social Structure in the Nineteenth-Century City.* New York, 1979.

Griffen, Clyde, and Griffen, Sally. *Natives and Newcomers: The Ordering of Opportunity in Mid-Nineteenth-Century Poughkeepsie.* Cambridge, Mass., 1978.

Guillaume, Pierre. *La Population de Bordeaux au XIXᵉ siècle: Essai d'histoire sociale.* Paris, 1972.

Guiral, Pierre. "Le cas d'un grand port de commerce: Marseille." In *Aspects de la crise et de la dépression de l'économie française au milieu du XIXᵉ siècle, 1846–1851,* ed. Ernest Labrousse. Vol. 19 of *Bibliothèque de la Révolution de 1848.* La Roche-sur-Yon, 1956.

"Quelque notes sur la politique des milieux d'affaires Marseillais de 1815 à 1870."
    Provence historique 7 (1957):155–74.
Gutkind, Peter C. W. "African Urbanism, Mobility, and the Social Network." *International Journal of Comparative Sociology* 6 (1965):48–60.
Hammond, J. L., and Hammond, Barbara. *The Skilled Labourer, 1760–1832*. London, 1919.
Handlin, Oscar. *The Uprooted: The Epic Story of the Great Migrations that Made the American People*. Boston, 1951.
Harrigan, Patrick J. *Mobility, Elites, and Education in French Society of the Second Empire*. Waterloo, Ontario, 1980.
Hauser, Robert M. "Schools and the Stratification Process." *American Journal of Sociology* 74 (1969):587–611.
Henry, Louis. *Anciennes familles genevoises*. Paris, 1956.
    Manuel de démographie historique. Geneva and Paris, 1967.
Herrick, B. H. *Urban Migration and Economic Development in Chile*. Cambridge, Mass., 1965.
Hodge, Robert W., Siegel, Paul M., and Rossi, Peter H. "Occupational Prestige in the United States, 1925–63." *American Journal of Sociology* 70 (1964):286–302.
Jackson, James H., Jr. "Migration and Urbanization in the Ruhr Valley, 1850–1900." Ph.D. dissertation, University of Minnesota, 1980.
    "The Occupational and Familial Context of Migration in Duisberg, 1867–1890." *Journal of Urban History* 8 (1982):235–70.
Janvier, Yves. "L'industrie du bâtiment à Marseille de 1815 à 1851." Diplôme d'études supérieur, University of Aix-en-Provence, 1964.
Johnson, Christopher H. "Economic Change and Artisan Discontent: The Tailors' History 1800–48." In *Revolution and Reaction: 1848 and the Second French Republic*, ed. Roger Price. London, 1975.
Johnson, Robert Eugene. *Peasant and Proletarian: The Working Class of Moscow in the Late Nineteenth Century*. New Brunswick, N.J., 1979.
Julliany, Jules. *Essai sur le commerce de Marseille*. 2d ed. 3 vols. Marseille, 1842.
Kaeble, Hartmut. *Geschichte der sozialen Mobilität seit der industriellen Revolution*. Königstein, 1978.
    Historical Research on Social Mobility: Western Europe and the USA in the Nineteenth and Twentieth Centuries. New York, 1981.
Kamphoefner, Walter C. "The Social Consequences of Rural–Urban Migration in Imperial Germany: The 'Floating Proletariat' Thesis Reconsidered." Social Science Working Paper 414, California Institute of Technology, Jan. 1982.
Karabel, Jerome. "Review of *Why Is There No Socialism in America?*" *New York Review of Books* 26 (January 1979):22–7.
Katz, Michael B. "Occupational Classification in History." *Journal of Interdisciplinary History* (1976):63–88.
    The People of Hamilton, Canada West: Family and Class in a Mid-Nineteenth-Century City. Cambridge, Mass., 1975.
Katz, Michael B., Doucet, Michael J., and Stern, Mark J. *The Social Organization of Early Industrial Capitalism*. Cambridge, Mass., 1982.
Katzman, David M. *Seven Days a Week: Women and Domestic Service in Industrializing America*. New York, 1978.
Knights, Peter R. *The Plain People of Boston, 1830–1860: A Study in City Growth*. New York, 1971.
Laslett, Peter, ed. *Household and Family in Past Time*. Cambridge, 1972.

Lauman, Edward O. *Prestige and Association in an Urban Community: An Analysis of an Urban Stratification System.* Indianapolis, 1966.

Lauman, Edward O., and Senter, Richard. "Subjective Social Distance, Occupational Stratification, and Forms of Status and Class Consciousness: A Cross-National Replication and Extension." *American Journal of Sociology* 81 (1976):1304–38.

Lees, Lynn. *Exiles of Erin: Irish Migrants in Victorian London.* Ithaca, N.Y., 1979.

Lefebvre, Georges. *Etudes orléanaises.* 2 vols. Vol. 1. *Contribution à l'étude des structures sociales à la fin du XVIIIᵉ siècle.* Paris, 1962.

Les Paysans du Nord pendant la Révolution française. Bari, 1969. Orig. pub. Lille, 1924.

Lehning, James R. *The Peasants of Marlhes: Economic Development and Family Organization in Nineteenth-Century France.* Chapel Hill, 1980.

Lequin, Yves. *Les Ouvriers de la région lyonnaise (1848–1914).* 2 vols. Lyon, 1977.

Le Roi Ladurie, Emmanuel. *Les Paysans de Languedoc.* Paris, 1966.

Levasseur, E. *La population française.* 2 vols. Paris, 1891.

Levine, David. *Family Formation in an Age of Nascent Capitalism.* New York, 1977.

Litchfield, R. Burr, and Gordon, David. "Closing the 'Tour': A Close Look at the Marriage Market, Unwed Mothers, and Abandoned Children in Mid-Nineteenth-Century Amiens." *Journal of Social History* 13 (1980):458–72.

Littré, Emile. *Dictionnaire de la langue française.* Paris, 1863–72.

Long, L. H. "Migration Differentials by Education and Occupation: Trends and Variations." *Demography* (1973):243–58.

McBride, Theresa. *The Domestic Revolution: The Modernization of Household Service in England and France, 1820–1920.* New York, 1976.

McClendon, McKee. "The Occupational Status Attainment Processes of Males and Females." *American Sociological Review* 41 (1976):52–64.

MacDonald, John S., and MacDonald, Leatrice D. "Chain Migration, Ethnic Neighborhood Formation, and Social Networks." *Millbank Memorial Fund Quarterly* 42 (1964):82–97.

Main, Jackson Turner. *The Social Structure of Revolutionary America.* Princeton, N.J., 1961.

Masson, Paul. Gen. ed. *Les Bouches-du-Rhône: Encyclopédie départementale.* Vol. 5. *La Vie politique et administrative.* Paris and Marseille, 1929. Vol. 8. *Le Mouvement économique: L'Industrie.* Marseille, 1926. Vol. 9. *Le Mouvement économique: Le Commerce.* Paris and Marseille, 1926. Vol. 10. *Le Mouvement social.* Paris and Marseille, 1923.

Mathieu, Joseph. *Marseille: Statistique et histoire.* Marseille, 1879.

Mazuy, François. *Essai historique sur les moeurs et coutumes des Marseillais au XIXᵉ siècle.* Marseille, 1853.

Miller, S. M. "Comparative Social Mobility: A Trend Report and Bibliography." *Current Sociology* 9 (1960).

Mireur, Hyppolyte. *Le Mouvement comparé de la population à Marseille, en France et dans les états de l'Europe.* Paris, 1889.

Mitchell, Brian R. *European Historical Statistics, 1750–1975.* 2d ed. London, 1981.

Moch, Leslie Page. *Paths to the City.* Beverly Hills, Calif., 1983.

Modell, John. "The Peopling of a Working-Class Ward: Reading, Pennsylvania, 1850." *Journal of Social History* 5 (1971):71–95.

Moss, Bernard H. *The Origins of the French Labor Movement: The Socialism of Skilled Workers.* Berkeley and Los Angeles, 1976.

Newmann, Allen R. "The Influence of Family and Friends on German Internal Migration, 1880–85." *Journal of Social History* 13 (1979):277–88.

Nguyen, Victor. "Crise et vie des portefaix marseillais, 1814–1914." Diplôme d'études supérieures, University of Aix-en-Provence, 1961.

"Les Portefaix marseillais. Crise et déclin, survivances." *Provence historique* 12 (1962):363–97.

Olivési, Antoine. *La Commune de 1871 à Marseille et ses origines.* Paris, 1950.

"Marseille." In *Les Elections législatives de mai 1869,* ed. Louis Girard, vol. 21, pp. 77–123. *Bibliothèque de la Revolution de 1848.* Paris, 1968.

Ollivier. "Grossesses illégitimes à Marseille." Mémoire de Maîtrise, University of Aix-en-Provence, n.d.

Park, Robert E. "Human Migration and the Marginal Man." *American Journal of Sociology* 33 (1928):881–93.

Park, Robert E., and Burgess, Ernest W. *The City.* Chicago, 1925.

Perdiguier, Agricol. *Mémoires d'un compagnon.* Moulins, 1914; Paris, 1964.

Peterson, William. "A General Typology of Migration." *American Sociological Review* 23 (1958):256–66.

Population. 3d ed. New York, 1975.

Pouthas, Charles H. *La Population française pendant la première moitié du XIXᵉ siècle.* Paris, 1956.

Rambert, Gaston. *Marseille, la formation d'une grande cité moderne: Etude de géographie urbaine.* Marseille, 1934.

Reiss, Albert J., Jr. *Occupations and Social Status.* New York, 1961.

Ripert, Emile. *La Renaissance provençale, 1800–1860.* Paris, 1917.

Rogoff, Natalie. *Recent Trends in Occupational Mobility.* Glencoe, Ill., 1953.

Sauze, M. *De la mendicité dans le département des Bouches-du-Rhône.* Marseille, 1864.

Schnore, Leo F. "Social Mobility in Demographic Perspective." *American Sociological Review* 26 (1961):407–23.

Scott, Joan W. *The Glassworkers of Carmaux: French Craftsmen and Political Action in a Nineteenth-Century City.* Cambridge, Mass., 1974.

Scott, Joan W., and Tilly, Louise A. "Women's Work and the Family in Nineteenth Century Europe." *Comparative Studies in Society and History* 17 (1975):36–64.

Sewell, William H., and Hauser, Robert M. *Education, Occupation, and Earnings: Achievement in the Early Career.* New York, 1975.

Sewell, William H., Hauser, Robert M., and Featherman, David L., eds. *Schooling and Achievement in American Society.* New York, 1976.

Sewell, William H., Hauser, Robert M., and Wolf, Wendy C. "Sex, Schooling, and Occupational Status." *American Journal of Sociology* 86 (1980):551–83.

Sewell, William H., Jr. "La classe ouvrière de Marseille sous la Seconde République: Structure sociale et comportement politique." *Le Mouvement social* 76 (1971):27–65.

"Social Change and the Rise of Working-Class Politics in Nineteenth-Century Marseille." *Past and Present* 65 (1974):75–109.

"Social Mobility in a Nineteenth-Century European City: Some Findings and Implications." *Journal of Interdisciplinary History* 7 (1976):217–33.

"The Structure of the Working Class of Marseille in the Middle of the Nineteenth Century." Ph.D. dissertation, University of California, Berkeley, 1971.

Work and Revolution in France: The Language of Labor from the Old Regime to 1848. New York, 1980.

"The Working Class of Marseille Under the Second Republic: Social Structure and Political Behavior." In *Workers in the Industrial Revolution: Recent Studies of Labor in the United States and Europe*, ed. Peter N. Stearns and Daniel J. Walkowitz, pp. 75–116. New Brunswick, N.J., 1974.

Sharlin, Allan N. "From the Study of Social Mobility to the Study of Society." *American Journal of Sociology* 85 (1979):338–60.

――――. "Social Structure and Politics: A Social History of Frankfurt am Main, 1815–1864." Ph.D. dissertation, University of Wisconsin-Madison, 1976.

Sibley, Elbridge. "Some Demographic Clues to Stratification." *American Sociological Review* 7 (1942):322–30.

Siegel, Paul M. "Occupational Prestige in the Negro Subculture." In *Social Stratification: Research and Theory for the 1970s*, ed. Edward O. Lauman, pp. 156–71. Indianapolis, 1970.

Smith, Bonnie G. *Ladies of the Leisure Class: The Bourgeoises of Northern France in the Nineteenth Century*. Princeton, N.J., 1981.

Sombart, Werner. *Why Is There No Socialism in the United States?* Trans. Patricia M. Hocking and C. T. Husbands. London, 1976.

Spaeth, Joe L. "Differences in the Occupational Achievement Process Between Male and Female College Graduates." *Sociology of Education* 50 (1977):206–17.

Speare, A. "Urbanization and Migration in Taiwan." *Economic Development and Cultural Change* 22 (1974):302–19.

Sutherland, Edwin H., and Cressy, Donald R. *Criminology*. 8th ed. Philadelphia, 1970.

Teissier, Octave. *Histoire du commerce de Marseille pendant vingt ans (1855–1874)*. Paris, 1878.

Terrisse, Michel. "La Population de Marseille et de son terroir de 1694 à 1830." Doctoral thesis, University of Aix-Marseille, 1971.

Thernstrom, Stephan. *The Other Bostonians: Poverty and Progress in the American Metropolis, 1880–1970*. Cambridge, Mass., 1973.

――――. *Poverty and Progress: Social Mobility in a Nineteenth Century City*. Cambridge, Mass., 1964.

Thernstrom, Stephan, and Knights, Peter. "Men in Motion: Some Data and Speculation about Urban Population Mobility in Nineteenth-Century America." *Journal of Interdisciplinary History* 1 (1970):7–36.

Thompson, E. P. *The Making of the English Working Class*. London, 1963.

Tilly, Charles, and Brown, C. Howard. "On Uprooting, Kinship, and the Auspices of Migration." *International Journal of Comparative Sociology* 7 (1967):139–64.

Tilly, Louise A., and Scott, Joan W. *Women, Work and Family*. New York, 1978.

Travaux de la Société de Statistique de Marseille. 36 vols. Marseille, 1837–73.

Treas, J., and Tyree, A. "Prestige versus Socioeconomic Status in the Attainment Process of American Men and Women." *Social Science Research* 8 (1979):201–21.

Treiman, Donald J. *Occupational Prestige in Comparative Perspective*. New York, 1976.

――――. "A Standard Occupational Prestige Scale for Use with Historical Data." *Journal of Interdisciplinary History* 7 (1976):283–304.

Treiman, Donald J., and Terrell, Kermit. "The Process of Status Attainment in the United States and Great Britain." *American Journal of Sociology* 81 (1975):563–83.

Van de Walle, Etienne. *The Female Population in the Nineteenth Century: A Reconstruction of 82 Départements of France*. Princeton, N.J., 1974.

Villeneuve-Bargemont, Christophe de. *Statistique du département des Bouches-du-Rhône*. 4 vols. Marseille, 1821–34.

Warner, Sam B., Jr. *Streetcar Suburbs: The Process of Growth in Boston, 1870–1900*. Cambridge, Mass., 1962.

Wrigley, E. A., ed. *An Introduction to English Historical Demography from the Sixteenth to the Nineteenth Century*. New York, 1966.

Nineteenth-Century Society: Essays in the Use of Quantitative Methods for the Study of Social Data. Cambridge, 1972.

Wrigley, E. A., and Schofield, R. S. *The Population History of England, 1541–1871: A Reconstruction*. Cambridge, Mass., 1982.

Zelinsky, Wilbur. "The Hypothesis of the Mobility Transition." *Geographical Review* 61 (1971):219–49.

Zwahr, H. *Zur Konstitutierung des Proletariats als Klasse: Strukturuntersuchung über das Leipziger Proletariat während der industriellen Revolution*. Berlin, 1978.

Index